Religions
of
Antiquity

Religion, History, and Culture
Selections from The Encyclopedia of Religion

Mircea Eliade
EDITOR IN CHIEF

EDITORS
Charles J. Adams
Joseph M. Kitagawa
Martin E. Marty
Richard P. McBrien
Jacob Needleman
Annemarie Schimmel
Robert M. Seltzer
Victor Turner

ASSOCIATE EDITOR
Lawrence E. Sullivan

ASSISTANT EDITOR
William K. Mahony

Religions
of
Antiquity

EDITED BY
Robert M. Seltzer

Religion, History, and Culture
Selections from The Encyclopedia of Religion

Mircea Eliade
EDITOR IN CHIEF

MACMILLAN PUBLISHING COMPANY
New York
COLLIER MACMILLAN PUBLISHERS
London

Macmillan Publishing Company
866 Third Avenue, New York, N.Y. 10022

Collier Macmillan Canada, Inc.

Library of Congress Catalog Card Number: 89–12102

Printed in the United States of America

printing number
1 2 3 4 5 6 7 8 9 10

Library of Congress Cataloging-in-Publication Data

Religions of antiquity.

    (Religion, history, and culture)
    "Selections from the Encyclopedia of religion."
    Bibliography: p.
    1. Middle East—Religion.   2. Greece—Religion.
3. Rome—Religion.   4. Religions—History.   I. Seltzer,
Robert M.   II. Encyclopedia of religion.   III. Series.
BL1060.R438   1989   291'.0938   89-12102
ISBN 0-02-897373-9

CONTENTS

MAPS

PUBLISHER'S NOTE

Since publication of *The Encyclopedia of Religion* in 1987, we have been gratified by the overwhelming reception accorded it by the community of scholars. This reception has more than justified the hopes of the members of the work's editorial board, who, with their editor in chief, cherished the aim that it would contribute to the study of the varieties of religious expression worldwide. To all those who participated in the project we express again our deepest thanks.

Now, in response to the many requests of our contributors and other teachers, we take pride in making available this selection of articles from the encyclopedia for use in the classroom. It is our hope that by publishing these articles in an inexpensive, compact format, they will be read and reflected upon by an even broader audience. In our effort to select those articles most appropriate to undergraduate instruction, it has been necessary to omit entries of interest primarily to the more advanced student and/or to those who wish to pursue a particular topic in greater depth. To facilitate their research, and to encourage the reader to consult the encyclopedia itself, we have thus retained the system of cross-references that, in the original work, served to guide the reader to related articles in this and other fields. A comprehensive index may be found in volume sixteen of the encyclopedia.

Charles E. Smith
Publisher and President
Macmillan Reference Division

INTRODUCTION

How can a group of religions be brought into relationship in a manner that does justice to the uniqueness of each and yet presents them against a common background? In recent decades the academic field of religious studies has made great strides in formulating neutral yet sensitive methods and concepts for examining the varieties of religious expression, methods and concepts that avoid subordinating religions to each other or forcing them into a procrustean bed of a single evolutionary path from the "primitive" to the "advanced." We are now quite aware of how easy it is to insinuate one's own norms and attitudes into the study of other cultures. If "religion is the organization of life around the depth dimension of experience," as Winston L. King proposes in the article "Religion" in volume 12 of *The Encyclopedia of Religion,* we now realize that non-Western religions respond to that dimension in quite different ways than do Judaism, Christianity, and Islam; indeed, within the history of these theistic religions themselves are to be found divergent, sometimes sectarian tendencies that are best made accessible by quite different approaches than those usually applied to the study of dominant, mainstream forms of religious organization and expression. It was a major aim of *The Encyclopedia of Religion* to avoid the bias and slant of earlier encyclopedias of religion of this century, great works of scholarship though these were, when dealing with religion outside the Western world and with nonconformist religious tendencies within Europe and America.

There is another area where it is all too easy to impose the categories of Judaism and Christianity on material that needs to be understood in its own terms: the several families of ancient religions of Middle Eastern and Mediterranean origin that served as the matrix out of which the monotheistic religions developed. These too need to be understood according to their own structures and principles as unique expressions of that "depth dimension" of human affairs.

The present volume brings together overviews of the distinctive religious traditions of the Middle East and Europe before the emergence of classic rabbinic Judaism and early and patristic Christianity. Limitations of space made it impossible to include the religious aspects of every ancient culture of this region, or to push the chronological limits to the religions of the Neolithic era or to pre-Minoan and pre-Roman Europe. The reader must consult the encyclopedia itself for articles on those subjects and for detailed treatment of the gods, rituals, texts, and other particulars of the traditions included.

If separating the traditions treated in this book from Judaism and Christianity enables the reader to see these religions on the front of the stage rather than as part of the background, the question remains how such disparate traditions can be brought into relationship with each other. In fact, the relationship is an old one, accomplished over the almost four thousand years of ancient history that this book spans by a common historical geography. The diverse cultures, societies, economies, and languages of ancient Mesopotamia, Egypt, Iran, and the Mediterranean litoral came to be interconnected, to impinge on each other, and occasionally to fuse, sometimes giving rise to new religious forms. The first articles in this book describe the religious traditions of the Tigris and Euphrates and the Nile river valleys that took shape in the fourth millennium BCE. We then move outward from the original homeland of high civilization to the Canaanite and Hittite areas to the west of Mesopotamia and to the Iranian traditions in the highlands to the east in the second and first millennia BCE.

Within this expanded network of civilizations two religious traditions crystallized—the ancient Israelite religion as transmitted in the Hebrew scriptures and the early Zoroastrian tradition of the *Gāthās* and other texts of the Avesta. These achieved an exceptionally high degree of self-consciousness and universality as a result of their location in the great empires that dominated the region in the first millennium BCE: the Assyrian empire of the eighth and seventh centuries BCE, with its new structures of military command and political control; the Neo-Babylonian empire of Nebuchadnezzar in the sixth century; and the immense Persian empire formed by Cyrus the Great in the 530s, which stretched from Asia Minor to India and lasted until Alexander the Great's conquests two centuries later.

Part one of this book treats the religions of the ancient Near East; parts two and three depict the religions of Hellenism and hellenization, including the impact of Alexander's conquest of the Persian empire on the native traditions in that area and the equally powerful stamp left by Hellenic culture on the expanding Roman empire in the western Mediterranean and in the east as well. As background for the efflorescence of cosmopolitan, international Hellenism at its most dynamic, we move backward in time to regions on the periphery of the Middle East: the islands of the Aegean and of mainland Greece and ancient Italy. The early kingdoms and the many city-states of these regions were gradually brought together into the new sovereignties formed after the conquests of Alexander the Great: the Greco-Macedonian kingdom of the Seleucids based in Syria and Asia Minor, that of the Ptolemies based in Egypt, the Parthian empire in Persia and Mesopotamia, and the smaller states in Asia Minor, Palestine, and the Trans-Jordan of the second and first centuries BCE. The period under consideration climaxes finally in a Roman empire stretching from the Atlantic up to but not including ancient Mesopotamia, and a Sassanian dynasty that took over Mesopotamia and Persia after 226 CE. The religions of this complex ecumene of the fourth century BCE to the fourth century CE are covered in the article on Zoroastrianism, in the description of Roman religion in the imperial period, in the overview of the complex mosaic of Hellenistic religiosity, and in articles on new cults and religions that appeared within the Hellenistic, Roman, and Persian societies of late antiquity.

The recovery of all these religious traditions and, even more important, the ongoing effort to elucidate their meanings, represent a remarkable scientific achievement in a century of great scientific achievements. Few of these ancient religious traditions were understood in their own terms a century ago; some were not known at all. Our knowledge of these traditions was made possible by the work of hundreds of scholars, who painstakingly deciphered long-lost ancient languages, translated cuneiform texts from so many different sites, uncovered and edited caches of Hellenistic literary documents, clarified the original nuance of religious terms and concepts that had become overlaid with latter meanings, excavated ancient temples, tombs, and shrines, and gained a sense of the significance of the iconography and rituals associated with these sacred places. These same scholars categorized everyday and household objects for their religious significance and analyzed the mythopoetic forms, themes, and variations of the high civilizations, formulated methodologies to reconstruct the precanonical levels of later scriptural traditions and the manner in which local deities were merged into major pantheons, and much more. While all this painstaking and detailed work will continue, the next stage of the academic resurrection of these so-called dead religions certainly entails synthesis and integration of knowledge. The essays in this book, all by experts of international reputation, constitute a step toward that new totality of knowledge of humanity's response to the ultimate.

ONE

RELIGIONS OF THE ANCIENT NEAR EAST

1

MESOPOTAMIAN RELIGIONS

THORKILD JACOBSEN

Ancient Mesopotamia is the country now called Iraq. Its northern part, down to an imaginary line running east-west slightly north of modern Baghdad, constituted ancient Assyria, with the cities of Ashur (modern Qal'at Shergat), which was the old capital; Calah (Nimrud); and Nineveh (Kouyundjik), which took its place later, at the time of the Assyrian empire in the first millennium BCE. The country consists of rolling plains resting on a bed of rocks. Rainfall over most of the area is sufficient to sustain a cereal crop. The main river is the Tigris, which traverses the country from northwest to southeast. The language spoken in historical times was Assyrian, a dialect of Akkadian, a Semitic language related to Hebrew and Arabic.

The southern part of Mesopotamia, south of the imaginary line mentioned, was ancient Babylonia, with Babylon (Babil) as its capital. The country here is flat, alluvial plain, and the average rainfall is too scant to allow a cereal crop. The country thus depends on artificial irrigation for its agriculture. It was in antiquity crisscrossed by a formidable net of rivers and canals. Such rains as fall are, though, sufficient to bring up pasture of grasses and herbs in the desert for a short grazing season in the spring. The language spoken was the Babylonian dialect of Akkadian.

The designations *Assyria* and *Babylonia* are appropriate only for the second and first millennia BCE, or, more exactly, from about 1700 BCE on, when Ashur and Babylon rose to political prominence. Before that time the later Assyria was known as Subartu, while what was to become Babylonia consisted of two main parts. Dwellers of the region north of an imaginary line running east-west slightly above Nippur (Nuffar) in historical times spoke Akkadian, while those of the region south of it spoke Sumerian, a language unrelated to any other known language or language family. The northern region was known as Akkad in Akkadian and as Uri in Sumerian, while the southern one was called Sumer or, more correctly, Shumer in Akkadian, Kiengir in Sumerian.

The capital of Akkad was in early times the city of Kish (Uheimir); later on, the city Akkad (not yet located) took its place. The country was traversed by two major rivers, the Tigris flowing along the eastern border areas and the Euphrates farther to the west. The course of the Euphrates was, however, not the same then as it is today. Its main branch flowed by Nippur and east to Shuruppak (Fara), then south

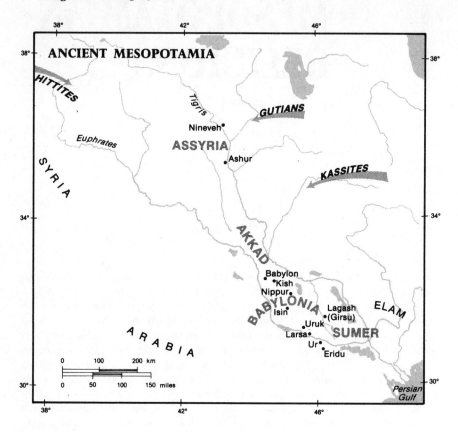

to Uruk (Warka), and on to Ararma (in Akkadian, Larsa; now Senkereh) and Ur (Muqayyir). Above Nippur an arching branch, the Arahtu, took off in a westerly direction, flowing by Babylon before rejoining the main course; another branch flowed south to Isin (Ishan Bahriyāt). In an easterly direction a major arching branch, the Iturungal, took off, flowing by Adab (Bismāya) to Zabalam (Bzeikh), Umma (Joha), and Patibira (Medina) before rejoining the main course at Ararma. At Zabalam the Iturungal sent a branch east, then south, to serve Girsu (Tello), Lagash (Tel al Hiba), and Nina (Zurghul). The main course of the Euphrates south of Uruk sent a branch south to Eridu (Abu Shahrein).

Economically, as mentioned, both Akkad and Sumer depended mainly on irrigation agriculture. There were, however, also other important economies. The region around Uruk and south along the Euphrates was, then as now, famous for its date groves; herding of sheep and oxen provided wool and dairy products as well as meat; fishing and hunting were important along the rivers and in the southern marshlands.

Capital cities in Sumer were Uruk and Ur; later on, Isin and Ararma. Of central religious and political importance was Nippur, seat of the god Enlil.

History

The earliest settlement of Mesopotamia of which we have evidence took place in the north, in the plains of the later Assyria. Here small agricultural villages, dependent essentially on rain agriculture and herding, occurred as early as the seventh millennium BCE. In the south, the later Babylonia, settlement began in the sixth millennium only, with what is known as the Ubaid period. The people who settled were most likely the forebears of the later Sumerian-speaking people of the region. Their settlement form seems originally to have been one of campsites and seminomadic small villages located along natural watercourses. They depended partly on irrigation hoe agriculture, partly on herding and fishing. Each tribe had a fixed center, a "treasury" in which it kept stores and religious objects that would have been inconvenient to take along on wanderings. Such tribal centers appear to have formed the nuclei of many of the later cities and central sanctuaries, to judge from their names.

The period of the earliest occupation, the Ubaid period, was a long one, and it saw, toward its end, the rise of the first cities. They lined the edge of the southern marshes and may well have owed their existence to a combination of the varied economies of the region: irrigation farming, herding, fishing and hunting; the key requirement for the rise of a city is the availability of economies able to sustain a massing of population on a small space.

Among these first cities were Eridu, Ur, and Uruk, and with the Uruk period, which followed in the late fifth millennium, the cities and the lifestyle they fostered had grown to a point where, as the period was coming to an end around 3500 BCE, we can speak for the first time of true civilization, characterized by magnificent sculpture, monumental architecture, and—most important of all—the invention and development of writing.

As to political forms then in vogue, the occurrence of the term for general assembly *(unkin)* in the early inscriptions is of interest. It belongs in a political pattern called "primitive democracy." Supreme power was vested in a general assembly, which served as a court, as a legislative assembly, and as the authority for electing officers, such as the religio-economic manager, the *en,* and in times of crisis, a war leader, the *lugal,* who served for the time of the emergency only. This pattern made its imprint on early myths and survived as a feature of local government down into the second millennium. In the following Jemdet Nasr and Early Dynastic periods there are suggestions that the pattern of primitive democracy was extended from a local to a national scale with the formation of a league of the city-states along the Euphrates, which met for assembly in Nippur. What specific circumstances could have induced these city-states to forget their local rivalries and join in a common effort is not known for certain, but a plausible guess would be that pressure from invading Akkadian-speaking nomads from the west, which should date to about this time, would have constituted a danger clear and present enough to impose unity, at least for a while.

Whatever unity may have been imposed by the common need to stem the Akkadian advance can have been of short duration only. The Early Dynastic period quickly became one of wars between city-states, which vied with one another for hegemony over the country. The first city to achieve such status was Kish in the north, and its rulers maintained that status long enough to make the title "king of Kish" a term for overlordship over all of Sumer and Akkad. After Kish, various other cities, prominent among them Uruk and Ur, held the hegemony for shorter periods, always precariously and open to successful challenge.

The warlike conditions of life made their mark on the kind of political leadership that had evolved, that of the *en* and the *lugal.* The *en* was basically a person who produced abundance. He or she participated as spouse of the city deity in the yearly fertility drama of the Sacred Marriage, and generally, through personal charisma, managed city affairs productively. One might speak of a "priest-king" or "priest-queen." The *lugal* was quite different. The term means "great householder," not "great man," as it is generally translated, and the *lugal* was originally the son of a major landowner, chosen in the assembly for his military prowess and for the house servants of his paternal house, who would form the core of the army and its high command. As times grew more warlike—and evidence for war appears already with the late Uruk period—the *en,* if he wished to retain his leadership, was forced to turn his abilities to military leadership also, while the *lugal,* who originally had been chosen for the term of an emergency, tended to become permanent as the threat of war became so. This imposed on him responsibility also for the religious, administrative, and economic tasks that belonged originally to the *en,* so that the functions of the two offices tended to merge. The old title of *en* was continued in Uruk. Almost everywhere else that of *lugal* was preferred. A new title of rather more restricted claim, which made its appearance in the Early Dynastic period, was that of *ensi,* "productive manager of the arable lands." It designated the official in charge of plowing, and thus of the city's draft animals, which in war would serve the chariotry of its army. The *ensi,* therefore, tended to become the political head of the community, its ruler. [*See* Kingship, *article on* Kingship in the Ancient Mediterranean World.]

At the very end of the Early Dynastic period a ruler of the city of Umma succeeded in extending his domain to include all of Sumer and Akkad. After an unsuccessful campaign in the north he was defeated and his realm taken over by Sargon of Akkad (c. 2334–2279). Sargon's successors kept a precarious hold on the south until, at the accession of Naram-Sin (c. 2254–2218), that region made itself independent. Akkad continued to flourish, however, deriving its wealth from its position on the major overland route from the Mediterranean to Iran and India, a route the Akkad rulers carefully policed. The city's wealth may have been the cause of an attack on it by a coalition of neighboring countries. Naram-Sin met their armies one by one and defeated them, thus regaining control of all of Mesopotamia. This feat so awed his fellow citizens that they deified him and chose him city god of Akkad. Under Naram-Sin's successors Akkad went into decline, and the Gutians, invaders from the eastern mountains, for a while took control. They were defeated, and the country liberated, by Utuhegal of Uruk, who in turn was succeeded by the famous third dynasty of Ur. Under that dynasty a well-integrated administrative system was developed. The formerly independent city rulers now became governors appointed by, and responsible to, the king and his corps of central officials.

The third dynasty of Ur ended in disaster. A breakthrough of Mardu tribes, nomads of the western desert, disrupted communications and isolated the former city-states from the capital, Ur, which lost control of all but the immediately adjacent territory. Eventually the city fell to an invading force from Elam and was mercilessly looted. Its fall spelled the end of Sumerian civilization even though the language, as the vehicle of culture and learning, continued to be taught in the schools.

The third dynasty of Ur was followed by two long-lived dynasties, one of Isin and one of Larsa, which divided the country between them. They in turn gave way to the short-lived rule of all of Babylonia by Hammurabi of Babylon (fl. 1792–1750), famous for his law code, and his son Samsu-iluna. Late in the latter's reign the south and middle of Babylonia again made itself independent, now under the name of the Sea Land. It covered much the same territory as had Sumer, and its kings consciously stressed their role as heirs to Sumer's ancient language and culture. The dynasty of Babylon fell to a raid by the faraway Hittites around 1600 BCE. When the Hittites had withdrawn, invaders from the mountains, the Kassites, took control and ruled Babylonia for a substantial length of time. One of these Kassite kings, Ulamburiash, conquered the Sea Land and thus unified Babylonia once more. The major rivals of the Kassite kings were the rulers of Assyria, which since the time of Hammurabi had grown in power and influence.

The Kassite dynasty fell before an attack by Shutruk-Nahunte of Elam, who controlled the country for a while. Then a move to regain independence developed in Isin, and the energetic ruler Nebuchadrezzar I (1124–1103) completely liberated the country, defeated Elam, and brought back the statue of Marduk, the city god of Babylon, which the Elamites had earlier taken as booty. From this time on begins the rise of that god to a position of supreme power in, and creator of, the cosmos. Before then the traditional view with Enlil as supreme god had held sway as the officially accepted one.

The following centuries saw a steady rivalry between Babylonia and Assyria, with the latter eventually victorious. After a gradual extension of their authority over Syria by the Assyrians, Tiglath-pileser III (745–727) conquered Babylonia, and under his successors, Sargon II, Sennacherib, Esarhaddon, and Ashurbanipal, it remained an Assyrian dependency even though at times it had its own Assyrian-appointed king and a semblance of independence. Throughout this time, however, Babylonia remained a thorn in the side of its Assyrian overlords. It even drove Sennacherib to the extreme of obliterating the city, only to have it restored by his son Esarhaddon.

Assyria fell in 609 BCE, after the capital, Nineveh, had been captured in 612 in a combined attack by the Medes and the army of Babylonia. Here an Aramean, Nabopolassar, had achieved freedom from the Assyrian yoke and founded a dynasty. After participating with the Medes in the destruction of Nineveh and Assyria, he turned to the conquest of Syria, which was accomplished by the crown prince Nebuchadrezzar, who followed his father to the throne in 605.

In 539 BCE Babylon opened its gates to the Persian king Cyrus. The last indigenous ruler, Nabonidus, had incurred the hatred of the Marduk priesthood through his championship of the moon god Sin of Harran and his attempts at religious reform. For part of his reign he left rule in Babylon to his son Belshazzar and withdrew himself to the Tema Oasis in Arabia. With him ended Babylonian independence.

Divine Forms: The Numinous

Basic to all religion, and so also to ancient Mesopotamian religion, is, I believe, a unique experience of confrontation with power not of this world. The German theologian and philosopher Rudolf Otto called it the numinous experience and characterized it as experience of a *mysterium tremendum et fascinans,* a confrontation with a "wholly other" outside of normal experience and indescribable in its terms. It is the human response to it in thought (myth and theology) and action (cult and worship) that constitutes religion.

Since what is met with in the numinous experience is not of this world, it cannot be described, for all descriptive terms necessarily reflect this-worldly experience and so fall short. At most, therefore, it will be possible to seek to recall and suggest the human response to the numinous experience as closely as possible by way of analogy and evocative metaphor. Every religion, accordingly, has evolved standardized versions of such metaphors. They form the link from firsthand to secondhand experience, become the vehicle of religious instruction, and form the body of collective belief. They will differ, naturally, with the different civilizations in which they are grounded and from which their imagery is taken. Study of any given religion must thus begin with the study of its favorite and central metaphors, taking due care not to forget that they are but metaphors and so are no end in themselves but are meant to point beyond. [*See* Iconography, *article on* Mesopotamian Iconography.]

PHYSIOMORPHISM

Turning, then, to the world of ancient Mesopotamian religion, its most striking characteristic seems to be an innate bend toward immanence. The numinous was here experienced as the inwardness of some striking feature or phenomenon of the situation in which it was encountered, as a will and power for that phenomenon to be in its particular form and manner and to thrive. It was therefore natural that it should be considered to have the form and name of the phenomenon whose inwardness it constituted. It was also natural that the early settlers should have been drawn particularly to those numinous forces that informed phenomena vital to their survival, the early economies, and that they should have wished to hold onto them and maintain them through cult and worship.

The original identity of numinous powers with the phenomena they were thought to inform is indicated by divine names such as *An* ("heaven") for the god of heaven, *Hursag* ("foothills") for the goddess of the near ranges, *Nanna* ("moon") for the moon god, *Utu* ("sun") for the sun god, *Ezen* ("grain") for the grain goddess, and so forth. Occasionally an honorific epithet, such as *en* ("productive manager, lord") or *nin* ("mistress"), was added, as in *Enlil* ("lord wind") and *Nintur* ("mistress birth-hut"). In some cases the mythopoeic imagination elaborated on a phenomenon to bring out its character more vividly, as when the numinous thundercloud Imdugud ("rain cloud") takes form as an enormous bird floating on outstretched wings and emitting its thunderous roar through a lion's head, or when Gishzida ("well-grown tree") is given form as the stock of a tree entangled in roots having the form of snakes, thus visualizing the belief of the ancients that tree roots could come alive as snakes.

The early selectivity of powers experienced in phenomena of vital economic importance to the settlers shows in the distribution of city gods, who must be considered coeval with their cities, over the various regional economies of the country. The extreme south is marshland with characteristic economies such as fishing, fowling, and hunting. Here was Eridu, the city of Enki, whose other names were *Daradim* ("wild goat fashioner") and *Enuru* ("lord reed-bundle"), signifying power in the marsh vegetation and in the reed bundles with which reed huts were constructed. Farther east, in Nina, resided Enki's daughter Nanshe, goddess of fish, the numinous force producing the teeming schools of fish that gave the fisherman his livelihood. South of Nina, in Kinirsha, was the home of Dumuzi-Abzu ("producer of healthy young ones of the marsh"), the mysterious numinous will and power for the young of marsh fauna to be born healthy and unimpaired. Through the marshlands along the Euphrates runs also the country of the ox herdsman and the orchardman. To the ox herdsman's pantheon belonged the bull god Ningublaga and his consort Nineiagara ("lady of the creamery"). In Ur resided Nanna, the moon god envisaged by the herdsman as a frisky young bull with gleaming horns—the new moon—grazing in the pasture of heaven. In Ararma, farther up river, resided the sun god Utu, whose round face was seen as the round face of a bison. At Uruk, finally, was the cow goddess Ninsuna ("mistress of the wild cows"), who was herself visualized as cow-shaped, and her bull-god husband, Lugalbanda. The ox herdsmen grazed their herds on the young shoots of reed and rushes in the marshes along the Euphrates. Closer to the river itself was the country of the orchardmen, who depended on the river for the irrigation of their plantations. To them belonged Ninazu of Enegir, seemingly a god of waters, and his son Ningishzida ("master of the good tree") of Gishbanda, a deity of tree roots and serpents. His wife was Ninazimua ("mistress of the well-grown branch"). Damu, city god of Girsu on the Euphrates, was a vegetation god, especially, it would seem, the power for the sap to rise in plants and trees in the spring. Farther up still, at Uruk—in antiquity as today a center of date culture—there was Amaushumgalana, the power for animal growth and new life of the date palm, and his consort Inanna, earlier Ninana ("mistress of the date clusters"), a personification of the date storehouse.

At Uruk the country of the orchardmen and the oxherds joins that of the shepherds; called the *edin,* it is a wide, grassy steppe in the heart of Sumer, ringed around by the Euphrates and the Iturungal. Here on the western edge is Uruk with Inanna of the shepherds, goddess of the rains that call up verdure and grazing in the desert, and her young husband, Dumuzi ("producer of healthy young ones"). This pair was also worshiped in Patibira on the southern edge, and in Umma and Zabalam on the eastern edge. On the southern edge lies also Ararma with the sun god Utu and his son Shakan, god of all four-legged beasts of the desert, and to the north is the domain of Ishkur, god of the thundershowers that turn the desert green like a garden in the spring.

North and east of the *edin,* finally, lay the plowlands with cities dedicated to cereal and chthonic deities, or deities of the chief agricultural implements, the hoe and plow. Shuruppak on the Euphrates was the home of Ansud, goddess of the ear of grain and daughter of Ninshebargunu ("mistress mottled barley"). Farther up the river was Nippur with Ansud's divine husband, Enlil; and since Enlil's winds were the moist winds of spring that made the soil workable, he also was god of the oldest and most versatile agricultural implement, the hoe. Nippur—the city rather than its sacred quarter around Enlil's temple, Ekur—was also the home of Enlil's son Ninurta ("master plow"), god of the younger implement, the plow, and charged in Nippur with the office of plowman *(ensi)* on his father's estate. Identified by the ancients with Ninurta were the gods Pabilsag ("first new shoot"), who in Isin was husband of the city goddess Nininsina ("mistress of Isin"); and Ningirsu ("master of [the city] Girsu"), who in Girsu, southeast of the *edin,* was essentially a god of the thundershowers and the floods of spring. Farther north, in Cutha, resided the netherworld gods Meslamtaea ("the one issuing from the luxuriant *mesu* tree")—presumably originally a tree deity—and Nergal. In Kish resided Sabbaba ("ever spreading the wings"), a god of war and originally, perhaps, of the thundercloud. In Babylon Merodakh, or Marduk ("calf of the storm"), was the city god. He was a god of the thunderstorm envisaged as a roaring young bull.

ANTHROPOMORPHISM

It seems reasonable to consider the physiomorphic forms the original and oldest forms under which the gods were envisaged, yet one should probably not altogether exclude the possibility that the human form may be almost equally early. The two forms were not mutually exclusive, and a deity might well choose to appear now under one, now under another. Seal impressions from the late Uruk period show the ritual scene of the sacred marriage with the goddess Inanna in her physiomorphic form of storehouse gateposts on some, in her human form on others. A later example is a statement about Gudea, ruler of Lagash (fl. c. 2144–c. 2124 BCE), who lived shortly before the third dynasty of Ur and whose goddess mother was the cow goddess Ninsuna. He is said to have been "born of a good cow in its woman aspect." As late as the early first millennium, a hymn to the moon god revels in attributing to the god physiomorphic and anthropomorphic forms alike: he is a prince, a young bull, a fruit self-grown, a womb giving birth to all, and a merciful, forgiving father.

Although human and nonhuman forms thus could coexist peacefully, there are indications that they were not always equally favored. The human form was clearly seen as more dignified and appropriate than the nonhuman one and tended to eclipse it. [*See* Anthropomorphism.]

One outcome of this attitude was representations in which the two different kinds of form were blended but with the human features dominant. In Girsu, for instance, at the end of the Third Early Dynastic period a mace head dedicated to Ningirsu, god of thundershowers and floods, shows the donor in a pose of adoration before the god in his old form of a thunderbird. Somewhat later, when Gudea saw the god in his dream, Ningirsu was essentially human in form although he retained the thunderbird wings and merged the lower part of his body with a flood. From the time of Gudea stems also a vase dedicated to Ningishzida that shows the god in his cella with the door open and flanked by two gatekeepers in dragon form. The god appears in his original form of the stock of a tree entwined by serpent-shaped roots. To this same period belongs a relief that shows Ningishzida introducing Gudea to Ningirsu. Here he is in completely human form except for two heads of serpents peeping out from his body at the shoulders. In much similar fashion, vegetation deities on seals are shown with branches and greens protruding from their bodies as if—in the words of the archaeologist Henri Frankfort—their inner being was seeking to burst asunder the imposed human form.

Composite forms such as the above still recognize the relevance of the nonhuman forms and preserve their essential characteristics even if the human form clearly dominates; but more radical trends away from the physiomorphic representation deliberately separated the deity from the phenomenon which he or she informed. The deity became a power in human shape; the phenomenon subsided into a mere thing owned or managed by the deity, and the form derived from it into a mere emblem.

Thus, for instance, the goddess Hursag ("foothills") ceased being the deified foothills themselves and became instead Ninhursaga ("mistress of the foothills"). Similarly, the deified wild cow became Ninsuna ("mistress of wild cows"). Gishzida ("good tree") turned into Ningishzida ("master of the good tree"). Ningirsu's form of thunderbird was referred to by Gudea as his emblem, and it adorns—and perhaps protects—Ninurta's war chariot on the famous Stela of the Vultures. Inanna, as goddess of the morning and evening star, had the physiomorphic form of the small, round disk which that star looks like in the Near East. That too became an emblem carried as a standard by the contingent from her clan when Gudea called it up for work on the temple he was building.

As so often with religious beliefs, so also here: no change is ever a clean break. Although demoted to emblems, the old forms did not altogether lose their potency. It is in these forms, as standards, that the gods followed the army in war and gave victory, and it is in these forms that the gods sanctioned oaths. Oaths were taken by touching them.

At times the aversion felt for the older, nonhuman forms must have been intense enough to engender open enmity. This seems to have been the case with the thunderbird, which from being Ningirsu's early shape became first a mere emblem of his and then was listed by editors of the myth about him, called *Angim,* among the god's captured enemies pulling his triumphal chariot. In still later time the bird—often shown as a winged lion rather than as a lion-headed bird—even became the god's chief antagonist. Thus in the Akkadian myth of Anzu (the Akkadian name of the bird) the god victoriously routs and subdues his own former self. A pictorial representation of the battle graced his temple in Nimrud. In these later materials Ningirsu is called by the name of Ninurta, the god of Nippur with whom he was early identified.

SOCIOMORPHISM

Man is a social being: he exists in a context of family and society generally, so in attributing to the gods human form the ancients almost unavoidably attributed to them also social role and status. One such basic context implied in the human form was that of family and household. In the case of major deities the household could be sizable, resembling that of a manorial lord.

The factors that determined the grouping of deities into a given divine family are not always obvious and may have been of various kinds—similarity of nature, complementarity, spatial proximity, and so forth. Similar character probably dictated the grouping of seven minor cloud goddesses as daughters of the god of thundershowers, Ningirsu. The nature of their mother, Ningirsu's wife, Baba, is less clear; she may have been a goddess of pasture. Ningirsu's son Igalima ("door leaf of the honored one") appears to be a deification of the door to Ningirsu's court of justice. Since clouds were seen to rise as mist from the marshes, the positing of the rain-cloud god Asalluhe as son of the god of the marshes, Enki, seems understandable. So too does the marriage of Amaushumgalana, the power producing the date harvest, to Inanna, the goddess of the storehouse. A logical connection seems observable also between the aspect of Enlil in which he is god of the older agricultural implement, the hoe, and that of his son Ninurta, god of the younger implement, the plow; but only too often no explanation readily suggests itself.

Our most complete picture of a major divine household is given by Gudea in the hymn known as Cylinder B. It lists the minor gods who served as functionaries in Ningirsu's house, that is, his temple, lending divine guidance to the human staff. Thus Ningirsu's oldest son Shulshagana served as majordomo, the traditional role of the eldest son. His brother Igalima functioned as chief gendarme responsible for the maintenance of law and order on the estate. Ningirsu's septuplet daughters served as his handmaidens and also presented petitions to him. He had two harpists—one for hymns, one for elegies—and a chambermaid, who bathed him at night and saw to it that his bed was provided with fresh straw. For the task of administering his estate and sitting in judgment in disputes that might arise, the god had a divine counselor and a secretary *(sukal)*. There were two generals, and an assherd to look after the draft animals. Goats and deer on the estate were cared for by a divine herder of deer; a divine farmer looked after the extensive agricultural holdings; a tax gatherer supervised the fisheries; and a ranger protected the wildlife of the estate against poachers. A high constable and a night watchman kept the estate safe.

In addition to their local functions of looking after their estates, most of the major deities had also wider, national responsibilities as officers of the divine polity into which the sociomorphic view was gradually transforming the cosmos. Highest authority in this divine state was a general assembly of the gods, which met in Nippur in a corner of the forecourt of Enlil's temple, Ekur, called Ubshuukkinna. An and Enlil presided; the gods took an oath to abide by the decision of the assembly, and voted by saying "Heam" ("May it be!"). The assembly served as a court—it once even banned Enlil himself—and it elected cities and their rulers to hold sway over all of Sumer and Akkad. The election was for a term only, and when the assembly decided a term was ended, it voted to overthrow the reigning city and transfer its kingship to another city and ruler.

Besides the office of king, the divine state knew also more permanent offices. For the most part these offices, which were called *me* ("office, function"), were reinterpretations of functions already innate in the gods in question, the phenomena and processes of which they were the indwelling will and power; they were now envisaged as the official duties of members of a divine bureaucracy. A comprehensive statement of this view of the cosmos is found in the myth *Enki and the World Order,* which tells how Enki, acting on behalf of Enlil, institutes the proper course of natural phenomena and the manner of engaging in human industries, appointing in each case a divine official to be responsible for them. The regime of the Tigris and the Euphrates thus comes under the administration of the "inspector of canals," the god Enbilulu. Other officials are appointed for the marshes and the sea; the storm god Ishkur is made the official in charge of the yearly rains. For agriculture the farmer god Enkimdu and the grain goddess Ezinu are appointed; for the wildlife, the god of beasts, Shakan; for the flocks, Dumuzi, the shepherd; for just boundaries, the god of justice, Utu; for weaving, the spider goddess, Uttu; and so forth.

The Pantheon

A pantheon seeking to interrelate and to rank the innumerable deities the ancient Mesopotamians worshiped, or merely recognized, in cities and villages throughout the land evolved gradually through the diligent work of scribes, who produced lists of divine names as part of their general lexical endeavors. The resulting scheme as it is known to us from old Babylonian copies was based primarily on the prominence in the cosmos of the cosmic feature with which the deity in question was associated, secondarily on his or her family and household ties. It is thus anthropomorphic and sociomorphic in character. First came the deities of heaven, the winds, the eastern foothills, and the underground fresh waters, each with his or her family and household. Then followed deities of smaller entities such as the moon, the sun, and the morning and evening star. A following section dealing with deities of the Lagash region was probably not part of the original list, since that region was considered enemy territory down to the time of the third dynasty of Ur. Last came the deities of the netherworld. In its main lines, and necessarily highly selectively, the pantheon may be presented as follows (Akkadian names, when different from the Sumerian ones, are given in parentheses).

AN

An (Anum) was god of the sky and father of the gods. The main center of An's cult seems to have been in Uruk. An was given form mythopoeically as a mighty bull whose bellowing was heard in the thunder. The rain was seen as his semen impregnating the earth *(ki)* and producing vegetation. As the cloudy skies vanished with the spring, An as Gugalanna ("great bull of heaven") was thought to have been killed and gone to the netherworld. A different tradition saw An (Anum) as the sky in its male aspect married to An (Antum), the sky in its female aspect. She, like her husband, was given bovine form and seen as a cow, whose udders, the clouds, produced the rain. An important aspect of An was his relation to the calendar, the months having their characteristic constellations that announced them. To this aspect belonged monthly and yearly festival rites dedicated to An. [*See also* An.]

ENLIL

God of wind and storms, Enlil was the most prominent member of the divine assembly and executor of its decrees. The city of Enlil was Nippur (Nuffar), with his temple, Ekur. He was married to the goddess Ninlil ("lady wind"), who was also known as Ansud ("long ear of grain"). Her mother was Ninshebargunu, the barley goddess, and her father, Haya, was keeper of the seal with which the doors of Enlil's granaries were secured. Originally in keeping with the agricultural ambience of his wife, Enlil would seem to have been the power in and for the moist winds of spring that soften the hard crust on the soil and make it tillable. Thus he was also god of the oldest tool of tillage, the hoe. With the hoe, after he had invented it, he broke—according to one myth—the hard crust on the earth at Uzumua ("flesh-grower"), in Nippur, so that mankind could shoot up like plants from the earth. [*See also* Enlil.]

Two quite different myths deal with the wooing of Ninlil or Ansud by Enlil. In one he follows successfully established procedures for winning her. In the other, more primitive one, Ninlil, disregarding her mother's instructions, deliberately tempts Enlil to take her by force by bathing in the canal of the town. Enlil is then banished from the city by the assembly of gods for his misdeed and leaves for the netherworld. Ninlil, pregnant with the moon god Suen (Sin), follows him. On the road Enlil, posing successively as gatekeeper of Nippur, man of the river of the netherworld, and ferryman, persuades her to lie with him that she may conceive a further child, who may take Suen's place in the netherworld. Thus Suen's nether-world brothers, Meslamtaea, Ninazu, and Ennugi, are engendered. The myth ends—oddly to a modern reader—with a paean to Enlil as a source of fertility: "A lord of great consequence, a lord of the storehouse are you! A lord making the barley grow up, lord making the vines grow up are you! Lord of heaven, lord of abundance, lord of earth are you!"

The aspect of Enlil in which he was the benevolent provider of abundance is clearly an old one, and it was never lost sight of. With time, however, his character took on also more grim features. As leader of the divine assembly and executor of its decrees, he became the power for destruction of temples and cities, the all-obliterating storm with which the assembly overthrew dynasties and their capitals as it shaped history. This later aspect of Enlil is prominent in laments, where more and more the will of the assembly becomes subsumed in his will, and it is for him alone to relent and to restore what he had destroyed. In the first millennium, as Marduk of Babylon rose to preeminence, Enlil, as representative of the often-rebellious south, even came to be treated as enemy and evil in northern Babylonia, as is clear from his role in ritual texts; or he was totally ignored, as in the late creation epic *Enuma elish,* which celebrates Marduk as the creator and ruler of the cosmos.

Besides the tradition which had Ninlil or Ansud as consort of Enlil, there existed a variant one in which he was paired with the goddess Ninhursaga, the older Hursag ("foothills"). Here probably also belongs an aspect of Enlil in which he was seen as a mountain deity, his name in that capacity being Kurgal ("great mountain") and that of his main temple, Ekur ("mountain house"). The connection between this moun-tain aspect and his aspect as god of the wind appears to correlate with the fact that the ancients believed the home of the winds to be in the mountains. Enlil would thus originally have been specifically the east wind, *imkura* ("wind of the moun-tains").

On Ninhursaga, Enlil begat the seasons of the year, Winter and Summer, and he also fathered the god of the yearly flood of the Tigris, Ningirsu. In the form the myth of the latter takes in Gudea's references to it, Ningirsu is the semen of Enlil red-dened in the deflowering. This may be taken to refer to the waters of the melting snow in the high mountains in Iran (Enlil as Kurgal) in the spring. The waters make their way through the foothills *(hursag),* where the clay they absorb gives them a reddish hue, to pour into the Tigris, swelling it to flood, Ningirsu.

NINURTA

In Nippur, the town itself—as distinct from the sacred area around Ekur—had as city god a son of Enlil called Ninurta, whose wife was the goddess Nin-Nibru ("queen of Nippur"). Ninurta's name may be interpreted as containing a cultural loanword, *urta* ("plow"), thus identifying him as god of that implement, much as his father, Enlil, in one aspect was god of the older agricultural tool, the hoe. Ninurta held in Nippur the office of plowman *(ensi)* for Ekur, and at his yearly festival the king opened the plowing season behind a ceremonial plow. Ninurta was early iden-tified with Ningirsu of Girsu, and myths pertaining to the latter were freely attributed to him, so that it often is difficult to determine which traits are original to whom.

A clear case is that of the myth *Lugale,* which can be shown to belong originally to Ningirsu. It depicts the god as a young warrior king who learns that a rival has arisen in the mountains and plots to kill him. He sets out with his army for a preemptive strike, attacks impetuously, and faces disaster, but is saved by advice from his father to send out a heavy rain, which lays the dust that his adversary, one Azag, had raised against him, nearly suffocating him. He then succeeds in killing Azag and goes on to organize the regime of the Tigris, bringing its waters down for irrigation. Before that they had flowed into the mountains, where they froze. To hold the waters on their new course, Ningirsu constructs a barrier of stone, the foothills *(hursag)*, and when his mother comes to visit he presents it to her as a gift, renaming her Ninhursaga ("mistress of the foothills"). Last he sits in judgment over Azag's warriors, various kinds of stones that he had captured, and imposes rewards or punishment according to their conduct in the war. His judgments determine the nature and the distinguishing traits of the stones in question for all time. He finally returns victoriously home.

To Ningirsu probably also belongs the myth *Angim* (mentioned above), which describes the god's victorious return from war and how he has to tone down his boisterous behavior lest he upset his father, Enlil. The basis for the tale would seem to be a spell for averting thunderstorms—Ningirsu was god of the thunderstorm— from Nippur. Conceivably a hymn praising Ninurta in his relation to various stones could be in origin Ningirsu material.

So perhaps also is a myth telling how the thunderbird stole the tablets of destiny from Enki in Eridu, how Ninurta set out to recover them, intending to keep them for himself, and how, when his weapon stunned the bird, it let go its hold of the tablets, and they of themselves returned to Enki. Frustrated in his ambition, Ninurta then raised a flood against Eridu, but Enki craftily had a turtle dig a pit, and he lured Ninurta into it. Underlying the myth is apparently a concept of the rain cloud rising as mist from the swamps, Enki's underground waters *(apsu)*, and, moving in over the mountains, the flight of the thunderbird. The return of the waters in the flood is seen as the god's jealous attack on Enki, and his imprisonment in the turtle's pit must stand for the eventual dwindling of the flood to a trickle between towering banks, the pit. [*See also* Ninurta.]

NUSKU

To Enlil's houshold belonged Nusku, in origin a god of lamps. He served as Enlil's trusted vizier and confidant.

NINHURSAGA

Ninhursaga ("mistress of the foothills"), earlier simply Hursag ("foothills"), was the power in the fertile near slopes of the eastern mountains, the favorite grazing grounds in the spring. Her cities were Kesh, not yet identified, and Adab, the modern mound Bismaya. In addition to the name *Ninhursaga,* the goddess was also known as *Ninmah* ("august mistress"), *Dingirmah* ("august deity"), and *Nintur* ("mistress birth-hut"), her name as goddess of birth. Her Akkadian name was *Beletili* ("mistress of the gods"). She, An, and Enlil formed in the third millennium the ruling triad of cosmic powers. [*See also* Ninhursaga.]

ENKI

Enki (Ea) was god of the underground fresh waters that come to the surface in rivers, pools, and marshes. The Sumerians imagined them as a vast subterranean freshwater sea, which they called Abzu or Engur. Enki's city was Eridu (Abu Shahrein), where he resided in the temple called Eengura ("house of the deep"). A myth tells how he built it and celebrated its completion with a feast for his father, Enlil, in Nippur. Enki's mother was the goddess Namma, whom the scribes listed as Enlil's housekeeper. Other evidence suggests that she was the deified riverbed that gave birth to the god of the river, Enki. Her name seems to mean "mistress vulva," and it may be that the mythopoeic imagination of the ancients saw the chasm of the empty riverbed as the vulva of the earth. Enki's spouse was called Damgalnunna ("great spouse of the prince"), a name that tells us little about her. Enki's vizier was a Janus-faced god, Sha (Usmu).

The name *Enki* means "productive manager [lord] of the soil," which must seem highly appropriate for the god of river waters in a society dependent on irrigation agriculture. In a hymn he describes himself in this aspect, saying: "When I draw near unto heaven, the rains of abundance rain down; when I draw near unto the earth, the early flood at its height comes into being; when I draw near unto the yellowing fields, grain piles are heaped at my command." Water not only slakes the thirst of men, animals, and plants, it also serves to cleanse. In that aspect, as power to cleanse, Enki appears in rituals of purification from all that defiles, including evil spirits attacking man, causing disease and uncleanness. One such elaborate ritual, meant to purify the king of possible evil caused by an eclipse, has the form of a trial before the sun god in which Enki sends a messenger, the exorcist, to speak for the claimant, the polluted king, and undertakes to enforce the verdict. This he does by washing all evil away with his water. The ritual is called Bitrimki ("bathhouse"). In other rituals Enki provided the effective incantation and prescribed the needed cleaning and healing acts, and it is not too much to say that he occupied a central position in all white magic for combating demons of illness. [*See also* Enki.]

Since Enki always knew what to do to drive away demons, he generally rated as the most resourceful and ingenious of the gods. He was skilled in every craft, and under different names he served as patron deity for most of them. His practical ingenuity also made him a born organizer. He was the one who organized the cosmos for Enlil in the myth *Enki and the World Order,* discussed above. Enki in the myths told about him never uses force; instead he gains his point by cunning deftly exercised. An example is the story of Adapa, the steward of Enki, or rather of Ea, for the text uses his Akkadian name. When Adapa once was summoned to appear before Anu in heaven for having broken the wing of the south wind, Ea told him how to gain the goodwill of the two gods who guarded the gate so that they would intercede for him. Ea also warned him not to eat and not to drink, for he would be offered the bread of death and the water of death. All went as planned, and Anu was appeased by the intercession of the doormen. When Adapa refused food and drink, however, Anu was surprised and asked why. Adapa told him, and Anu burst into laughter. The food and drink would actually have made Adapa immortal, which Ea knew and did not want to happen.

A rather more momentous occasion on which Enki showed his cunning was when he saved the human race from destruction at the hand of Enlil. We are told about it in the Sumerian story of the flood, which forms part of the myth called the *Eridu Genesis.* Mankind, having been created and provided with leadership—in the form of kings—by the gods, prospered and proliferated, to the extent that the noise they made became so irksome to Enlil that he persuaded the assembly of the gods to

e out man with a universal flood. Enki, who was present, was able to warn the
pious King Ziusudra to build an ark. Ziusudra followed the advice and was eventually accepted among the gods and granted eternal life as reward for saving all living
things.

A far more detailed—and conceivably more original—version of this story is
found in the Akkadian tale of Atrahasis ("the surpassingly wise"), who here takes the
place of Ziusudra. The story falls into two halves, each clearly originally a separate
tale. The first half tells how in the beginning the gods themselves had to work for
their food, digging the needed irrigation canals. They eventually rebelled, and Ea
thought of the solution, creating man to do the hard work. To that end a god was
killed and his blood mixed into the clay from which man was to take form. The
mother goddess gave birth to him, and there was general rejoicing. The second half
tells how mankind proliferated on earth and with their noise kept Enlil from going
to sleep. Enlil therefore tried to cut down on man's numbers by a succession of
diseases and famines, but each time Ea found ways of stopping the evils before it
was too late, and soon man again proliferated as before. Finally Enlil decided on a
desperate means: wiping out mankind with a flood. Again Ea frustrated the plan, by
having Atrahasis build an ark in which he survived with his family and the animals.
As he emerged from the ark he offered a sacrifice, and the gods were delighted, for
all through the flood, with no humans to offer sacrifice, they had suffered severely
from hunger. Only Enlil was wroth, but him Ea appeased by instituting plans for
population control: barrenness, child disease, and so forth. Thus harmony in the
universe was reestablished. As given in the tale of Atrahasis, the story of the flood is
the most detailed we have. A shorter version—shorn of any motivation for the
flood—was added to the *Epic of Gilgamesh* by the later editor Sinliqiunnini. In the
story of Adapa, Enki used his ingenuity against Anu; in the flood story, against Enlil.
[*See also* Atrahasis.]

A third myth, *Enki and Ninmah,* pits Enki against the third in the triad of highest
deities, Ninhursaga, whom the myth calls Ninmah. Like the Atrahasis story, this composition consists of two separate myths only very loosely connected. The first of
these is a Sumerian counterpart to the first part of the Atrahasis story, where the
refusal of the gods to work had Enki propose the creation of man. Here he is fathered by "the engendering clay of Abzu," which once also fathered Enki, and he is
given form and is borne by Enki's mother, Namma. The second myth begins with a
party given by Enki to celebrate the birth of man. As he and Ninmah, who had
assisted Namma as birth helper, drink deeply, Ninmah begins to boast that she controls men's fortunes, determining whether they will be good or bad. (That makes
little sense if she was, as here, a mere midwife. Apparently, in the original myth
underlying this part of the composition she was, as in the Atrahasis story, the one
who gave shape to the embryo of man and bore it as an infant.) Enki accepts her
challenge, waging that he can counter anything she can think up. She then creates a
series of misshapen or otherwise defective human beings, but for each one Enki is
able to think of a place in society where it can function and support itself. When
Ninmah finally gives up, Enki proposes that he try his hand and that she find a place
for his creature. He then fashions an embryo and has it given premature birth by a
woman provided by Ninmah. There is nothing Ninmah can do for it, and she breaks
out in lament. Enki, however, calms her with a conciliatory speech, pointing out that
it is precisely her contribution, the maturing of the embryo in the womb, that it

lacked. The man's contribution to the engendering of a child is not enough by itself; the woman's is needed too. And so he praises her powers.

The question thus raised, of the respective share of the male and the female partner in procreation, seems to have been variously answered at different times. The first part of *Enki and Ninmah* gives the woman all the credit. Man was engendered from clay, formed, and given birth—as it specifically states—without a male being involved. Somewhat similarly, the tale of Atrahasis has man created from clay and divine blood and formed and given birth by Nintur, that is, by Ninmah. Enki's contribution in both cases was chiefly the idea of making man. In the second part of *Enki and Ninmah,* however, this changes. Enki's power to create an embryo, although not to mature it and give it birth, is stressed; and finally, in the account of the creation of man in *Enuma elish* at the turn of the first millennium, the birth goddess has vanished, and Enki does the creation all by himself.

One final odd composition with Enki as its hero remains to be mentioned, *Enki and Ninhursaga.* It be gins with praise of the island of Dilmun (modern Bahrain) and its pristine purity at the beginning of time. It then tells how Enki provided it with fresh water and made it a port and an emporium. Next we hear how Enki attempts to seduce Ninhursaga but is rejected until he proposes marriage, making her his wife. She gives birth to a daughter, whom Enki seduces as soon as she becomes nubile, fathering a second daughter, whom in turn he seduces and makes pregnant. Her daughter, Enki's granddaughter, is Uttu, the spider goddess, and Ninhursaga warns her against Enki. Uttu therefore refuses to let him into the house unless he brings wedding gifts of fruits. He does so, and when Uttu lets him in, he takes her by force. Uttu's screams bring Ninhursaga, who removes Enki's semen and sows it. From it eight plants grow up. Later, passing by, Enki notes the plants, and as his vizier gives them names, Enki eats them. Ninhursaga, discovering what has happened, vows never to look upon him with her life-giving eye. The plants, Enki's semen, which he swallowed, then begin to develop as embryos in his body. Being male, he is unable to give birth to them, and so falls critically ill. The gods are greatly distressed, but the Fox offers to bring Ninhursaga. It does so; she is released from her vow, places Enki in her vulva, and successfully gives birth to eight deities, who are named and given status, their names serving as grotesque puns on the words for the part of Enki's body from which they come. The last is the goddess of Dilmun.

The stress on Dilmun, and on Enki's amorous success with his daughter, granddaughter, and, in one version, great-granddaughter, the "comely spider goddess Uttu," is hardly meant to be taken seriously. Presumably, the earthy humor of the composition was intended to amuse visiting sailors from Dilmun when they were entertained at the court of Ur.

ASALLUHE

Asalluhe ("man-drenching Asar"), city god of Kuar, near Eridu, and god of rain clouds, was Enki's son. He appears predominantly in incantations against all kinds of evil doings. Floating as a cloud above the earth, he was in a position to observe what was going on below and duly reported it to his father, Enki, who was not in a similar, favorable position to observe. On hearing Asalluhe's account, however, out of his profound knowledge he was able in each case to tell how the evil was to be countered. Identified with Asalluhe in later times was Marduk.

MARDUK

Marduk, or preferably Merodakh, city god of Babylon, was an old Sumerian deity who, like Ninazu in Eshnunna (discussed below) and Meslamtaea in Cutha, was taken over by the Akkadian invaders. His name, abbreviated from *(A)marudak* ("calf of the storm"), characterizes him as a god of thunderstorms visualized as a bellowing young bull. The thundershowers of spring mark the appearance of verdure in the desert and of plowing and sowing; thus Marduk's chief festival, the Akiti (Akitu), or "time of the earth reviving," was further described as "of the seed plowing." His city was Kadingira ("gate of the god"), translated into Akkadian as Babilim. The name indicates a settlement grown up at the entrance to a sanctuary, presumably Marduk's temple Esagila ("house with head held high"). Throughout the third and second millennia, it would seem, Marduk's status was little more than that of a local city god. With the advent of the first millennium, however, began his rise to supreme god of the universe and his rivalry for that honor with Ashur of Assyria. [*See also* Marduk.]

Marduk's claim to supremacy was celebrated in the creation epic *Enuma elish,* in which he is presented as savior of the gods and creator and organizer of the cosmos. The myth begins by tracing world origins from a watery chaos of fresh waters, Apsu, and salt waters, Tiamat, the sea. From them stemmed various generations of gods: Lahmu and Lahamu; Anshar and Kishar, the horizon; Anu, heaven; and Nudimmud or Ea. The younger gods, getting together to dance, proved disturbing to the older generations, who prized peace and quiet. Tiamat, as a long-suffering mother, bore with it, but Apsu decided to get rid of the troublemakers. However, before he could carry out his evil design he was overcome and slain by Ea, who then built for himself a house on top of Apsu's body. There Ea engendered his son Marduk. Anu, inordinately fond of his grandchild, fashioned the four winds for little Marduk to play with. The winds disturbed the still surface of the sea, creating billows. This greatly vexed the older gods, and they were able to rouse Tiamat to action. An army was assembled to destroy the younger gods and was placed under the command of Tiamat's paramour Kingu. The threat to the gods was serious and caused consternation among them. Both Ea and Anu, who were sent to cope with the crisis one after the other, failed and turned back. Finally, since the gods were in deepest despair, Ea suggested to the leader of the gods, Anshar, that Marduk be summoned to champion the gods. Marduk came and was willing to undertake the task, but he demanded full authority. The gods agreed, gave him the power for his word to come true, and made sure by a test that his word now had that effect. Marduk then rode to battle on his storm chariot. The sight of him overwhelmed the enemy; only Tiamat dared face him, but after an angry exchange of words, as she opened her maw to swallow him, he drove in the winds and then killed her with an arrow. Her army he took captive, enclosing it in a net held by the four winds. Out of the carcass of Tiamat Marduk then created the extant universe. He split her in two, and made out of one part heaven; out of the other, earth. To prevent her waters from escaping he provided bolts and guards. In heaven, directly opposite Ea's Apsu, he built his own house, Esharra, which the text says was the sky. He then fashioned the constellations, organized the calendar, fixed the polestar, and gave the moon and sun orders about their motion.

When Marduk returned home, he was hailed by the gods, who reaffirmed their allegiance to him. His first demand of them, then, was that they build him a city, to be called Babylon. He then pardoned the captive gods, who gratefully hailed him as king and savior and promised to build his city for him. Their willingness moved Marduk to think of a means of lightening their labors, and he decided to create man. An assembly was called. Kingu was denounced as the instigator of the rebellion and was slain, and out of his body Ea fashioned man. Marduk then divided the gods into two groups, one celestial and one terrestrial. The gods for the last time took spade in hand and built the city Marduk wanted, Babylon. At a great housewarming party to celebrate the completion of Babylon, Marduk was appointed permanent king of the gods. The myth ends with the gods naming Marduk's fifty names, each of which expressed a power that he held. Marduk's consort was the goddess Sarpanitum; his son, the god of Borsippa near Babylon, was Nabu, god of the scribal art. [See also Nabu.]

NANNA

Nanna (also Suen or Sin) was the god of the moon. His city was Ur (Muqayyir); his temple there, Egishnugal. His wife was Ningal. His own name, *Nanna,* would seem to designate him as the full moon, while *Suen* would be the name of the sickle moon. He was regularly envisioned in a bull shape, an image that the hornlike shape of the sickle moon may have encouraged. He was also visualized as a herder driving his herd—the stars—across the pastures of heaven, or as riding in the heavens in a boat, the sickle moon. A late myth—actually an incantation to ward off the evils of an eclipse of the moon—tells how he was attacked by storm demons after they had lured the storm god, Ishkur, and Inanna, who aspired to queenship of heaven, to their side. The attack was noted, however, by Enlil, who alerted Enki and had him send Marduk to the rescue. [See also Nanna.]

UTU

The god of the sun and of justice and fair dealings was Utu (Shamash). His cities were Ararma (Larsa) in the south and Sippar in the north. His temple in both cities was called Ebabbar; his wife was Ninkurra (Aya). As judge, Utu presided each day in various temples at specific places called "the place of Utu." He was greeted in the morning as he rose on the horizon, heard cases all day, and was sped on his way in the evening, at sundown. During the night he sat in judgment in the netherworld. The cases he heard, whether by day or by night, were apparently normally such as were brought by the living against ghosts and demons that plagued them. [See also Utu.]

ISHKUR

Ishkur (Adad) was the god of rains and thunderstorms. A text, basically a spell to avert a threatening thunderstorm from Nippur, tells him to go away so as not to disturb his father, Enlil, with his clamor. His original form seems to have been that of a bull. In many ways he resembles Ningirsu, but he seems to be more specifically a herder's god, the power in the spring rains that bring up pasture in the desert. [See also Adad.]

INANNA

Inanna (Ishtar) was earlier called *Ninana*, which can be understood as either "mistress of the date clusters" or "mistress of heaven." The center of her worship was, in the south, at Uruk, in the temple called Eana, and in the north at Hursagkalamma, near Kish. Characteristic of her is her great complexity and many-sidedness. It is apparent that a variety of originally different deities were syncretized in her and also that the ancients had been able to blend these differences into a fascinating, many-faceted, and convincing character. Normally she was envisioned as a rather willful, high-handed, young aristocratic girl of marriageable age or else as a young bride. Her lover or husband is a form of the god Dumuzi (Tammuz). In the complex image the goddess presents it seems possible to distinguish the following aspects, presumably once independent figures.

1. As goddess of the storehouse of dates, Inanna was at home in Uruk, situated in a famous date-growing region. Her name *Ninana* here stands for "mistress of the date clusters"; the name of her temple, *Eana*, for "house of the date clusters." Here, at the gate of the storeroom *(egida)*, she received her bridegroom, Amaushumgalana ("the one great source of the date clusters"), that is, the one great bud that the date palm sprouts annually. He was the power that made the date palm produce; their wedding and his entering Inanna's house constitute a mythopoeic view of the bringing in of the date harvest. As the rite of this marriage was performed later, the ruling king not only took the role of, but actually became, Amaushumgalana, while the goddess would have been incarnate in the queen, Ninegala ("mistress of the palace"). In the literature relating to Inanna's wedding she is therefore often called by that epithet, and in love songs written for that occasion it is often difficult to tell whether they celebrate Inanna's love for Amaushumgalana or perhaps rather that of the human queen for her husband. The cult of Inanna in her aspect of goddess of the date storehouse was a happy one. There was no sense of loss, no "death" of the god. The dates, eminently storable, were always with the community, and so was the power they represented.

2. Rather different was another aspect, also at home in Uruk, but in the Uruk of sheepfolds rather than of date groves. In this aspect Inanna was the power of the thundershowers of spring, on which the shepherds depended for pasturage in the desert. In this aspect she was paired with Dumuzi, the shepherd. Her early form was apparently that of the lion-headed thunderbird, which remained with her as an attribute. Besides it, and more or less replacing it, was also the form of the lion alone.

3. Closely related to Inanna's aspect as goddess of the thunderstorm was her aspect as goddess of war. The thunderous rumble of the primitive war chariot made it easy to see and hear thunder as the chariot's counterpart in the sky. The ferocious nature of other forms such as lions and bulls fitted easily into the image. As goddess of war, Inanna led the Dance of Inanna, the moving of the battle lines toward each other as if they were lines of dancers. In the myths about her she subdues the insubmissive Ebeh mountain range in southern Assyria.

4. An astral aspect of both Inanna and the Akkadian Ishtar is that of goddess of the morning and evening star, with which she forms a triad with her father, the moon god, and her brother, the sun god. Her precise function in this role is not clear except insofar as her appearance marked the beginning and the end of the working day. As goddess of the morning and evening star her name was understood to mean

"mistress of heaven," and her celestial affinities conceivably also encouraged an interpretation of the name of her temple, *Eana,* as "house of heaven" and a belief that it had originally descended from heaven. There is even evidence that in later times she managed to supplant the goddess of heaven, An (Antum), as spouse of the god of heaven, An (Anum), and became queen of heaven. In the *Eclipse Myth* she unsuccessfully conspires with the storm demons to obtain that position, but in a later myth, the *Elevation of Inanna,* the august assembly of the gods itself petitions An to marry her, and she is invested with supreme powers among the gods.

5. Finally, as protector of harlots, Inanna was herself envisaged as a harlot. Her original form in this aspect was that of the owl, which, like the harlot, comes out at dusk. Correspondingly her name as harlot was *Ninnina* ("mistress owl"). In Akkadian her name was *Kilili.* [*See* also Hierodouleia.]

In the myths dealing with Inanna a frequently occurring motif is her insatiable desire for power. In the *Eclipse Myth,* as noted, it leads her to conspire with the evil storm demons; in *Enki and the World Order* she complains bitterly that all other goddesses have offices and only she has none, so Enki tries to assuage her. In the myth *Inanna and the Parse,* that is, Inanna and the divine offices called in Sumerian *me,* we are told how she visited Enki in Eridu, how he drank deeply at the party welcoming her, and how in an expansive mood he conferred upon her one office after another. Wisely, she decided to leave immediately for home with her newly won offices, so that when Enki woke up sober and wanted the offices back it was too late. The myth lists the offices one by one; they constitute a formidable list. Owing, probably, in large part to the syncretistic background of the image of Inanna, the offices attributed to her show little unity or coherent pattern; rather, they form a motley collection of variorums. That did not trouble the ancients though; instead, they gloried in Inanna's versatility, and a major hymn to her even makes a point of praising her as goddess of opposites, of insult and veneration, downheartedness and good cheer, and so on. [*See also* Inanna.]

Inanna's lust for power is also an important motif in the best known of the myths about her, *Inanna's Descent to the Netherworld.* It prompts her to descend to the realm of death to wrest queenship over it from its rightful queen, Ereshkigal. The attempt fails, and Inanna is killed and turned into a cut of meat gone bad and hung on a peg. When she fails to return, her loyal handmaiden Ninshubura seeks help, first from Enlil in Nippur, then from Nanna in Ur, and finally from Enki in Eridu. Only Enki can think of a means to help. He creates two creatures from the dirt under his fingernails and sends them to the netherworld with instructions to condole with Ereshkigal, who, as is her custom, laments children who have died before their time. Then, when moved by the creatures' concern she grants them a wish, they are to ask for the tainted meat hanging on a peg and to throw on it the grass and water of life which Enki has given them. They follow the instructions, and Inanna rises alive. As she is about to leave the netherworld, however, its ruling gods stop her and decree that she must provide a substitute to take her place. So she is accompanied by a detachment of netherworld police to ensure that she will designate a substitute to go back with them.

On the journey back to Uruk she is met by one loyal servant after another, all clad in mourning for her, and she refuses to hand any of them over to the demons. When they reach Uruk, however, they come upon her young husband, Dumuzi, sitting in fine clothes and enjoying himself listening to the music of reed pipes. This flagrant lack of concern infuriates Inanna, and in a flash of jealous rage she hands him over to the demons, who carry him off. In his distress he calls upon his brother-in-law, Utu, god of justice and fairness, and asks Utu to change him into a gazelle— in another version into a snake—so that he can escape his captors. Utu does so, and Dumuzi escapes, only to be again caught; again he escapes, until finally he is caught for good in his sheepfold. The story ends with Dumuzi's sister Geshtinanna, the goddess of the grapevine, seeking him. Eventually, advised by the Fly, she finds him and joins him in the netherworld. In distress at the undeserved misfortune of both Dumuzi and his sister, Inanna decrees that they may share the obligation to serve in the netherworld as her substitute: Dumuzi will serve half a year below; then he will return to the world above while his sister takes over. She in turn will return after half a year as he goes below.

This ends the tale, and a closer look at it will suggest that *tale* rather than *myth* is the proper designation, for it is most easily understood as a composite of dead myths put together for dramatic effect by the storyteller and haphazardly embellished. The myth of Inanna's death and transformation into a cut of spoiled meat is best understood as an original myth in which she represents the underground storehouse for meat; she becomes like a grave when the meat rots in summer, but she is revived—as the storehouse is restocked with fresh meat from the flocks fed on the grass and water of life, the pastures of spring. The myth has nothing to do with Inanna's aspect as the morning star, in which the storyteller has her present herself when she seeks entry into the netherworld. The second part of the tale was originally a separate myth dealing with Dumuzi rather than with Inanna, and it has also come down, in slightly variant forms, as a separate, self-contained myth.

DUMUZI

Like Inanna, and perhaps even more so, does her lover and bridegroom, Dumuzi (Tammuz), present a highly complex, syncretized image, one in which it is not always easy to sort out cleanly the various strands woven into it. [*See also* Dumuzi.] Some fairly distinct aspects do, however, stand out and may reasonably be assumed to represent originally separate, independent deities. They are the following.

1. *Dumuzi as Amaushumgalana,* the power for productivity in the date palm. His marriage to Inanna as numen of the storehouse celebrates the bringing in of the date harvest. His cult was based in Uruk.

2. *Dumuzi the shepherd,* the power causing ewes to produce normal, well-shaped lambs. His bride was Inanna as goddess of the spring rain showers that call up verdure for pasture in the desert. The vanishing of the power he represented when the lambing season came to an end was seen as the death of the god, to be observed with wailing and lament.

3. *Dumuzi of the beer.* No separate distinctive name sets apart this aspect of the god. The texts dealing with it sometimes use the name *Dumuzi,* sometimes *Damu.* They involve the search for him after his death by his sister and mother.

4. *Damu the child,* the power for the sap to rise in plants and trees in the spring. Considered lost during the dry summer, he was sought by his mother and found coming down the river, presumably with the beginning of the early flood in spring. His cult was based in Uruk.

5. *Damu the conscript,* an aspect of the god under which he was seen as a young boy liable for military service. He has been taken forcibly from his mother by brutal recruiters, and she seeks him, gradually realizing that he is dead. What precise power he represented is not clear; most likely it was one connected with the welfare of cattle herds. His cult was based in Girsu (Tello) on the Euphrates.

The myths about these various aspects of Dumuzi naturally fall into two groups, those dealing with wooing and wedding and those dealing with his death and the search for him. To the first group belongs a dialogue between Inanna and Dumuzi in which he has found a house for them near her parents. She does not know that they have chosen him as her future husband, and he teases her, stating that his family is like her family, as it were. Eventually he enlightens her, and she is well pleased. The Inanna of this tale seems very young. Slightly older, she appears in a tale in which Dumuzi's sister Geshtinanna tells him that Inanna invited her in and told her how she, Inanna, suffered from love for her brother. Dumuzi is quick to ask leave to go, and is off to ease the damsel's suffering. At about the same age, Inanna appears in a different story, awaiting Dumuzi toward evening. They had met and fallen in love the day before, and when Dumuzi appears he impetuously propositions her. She promptly turns him down and apparently—the text is broken here—makes him propose properly. When the text resumes they are on their way to her mother's house to announce the engagement.

Another story tells how Inanna's brother Utu has arranged a marriage for her but is unsure about how she will receive the news. He therefore speaks obliquely, proposing to bring her fresh flax for a linen sheet. He does not say that it is to be her bridal sheet, but she immediately understands. Afraid to hear her brother's choice in case it turns out to be a wrong one, she postpones the crucial question, pretending that she has nobody to ret the flax, spin it, double the thread, weave it, dye it, and bleach it, but each time Utu offers to bring the flax already prepared. So at last she has to come to the point: who is to lie down with her on it? When Utu tells her it is Amaushumgalana, she is overjoyed. The wedding itself is recounted in a tale which begins with Inanna sending for her bridegroom and attendants, specifying what gifts they are to bring. They appear before the house, but Inanna is in no hurry. She bathes and dresses in all her finery and listens to instructions from her mother about the obedience due to her parents-in-law. Eventually she opens the door to Dumuzi—the formal act that concludes a Sumerian marriage—and presumably (the text is broken here) leads him to the bridal chamber for the consummation of the marriage. A wedding feast probably follows the next morning. When the text resumes, Dumuzi is leading his young bride to his house and wants first to take her to his personal god that he may bless the marriage. But Inanna is thoroughly frightened, so Dumuzi tries to hearten her by telling her what an honored position she will occupy in the household and how no domestic work whatever will be demanded of her.

The other group of myths, centering on the death of the young god, is perhaps best represented by the myth called the *Dream of Dumuzi.* In it, Dumuzi has an ominous dream that Geshtinanna interprets as boding death for them both. Dumuzi sends her up on a mound as lookout, and she reports the arrival of a boat with evil recruiters. Dumuzi decides to hide in the desert, but first he tells his sister and colleague where he will be. When the recruiters land and offer bribes for information, Geshtinanna is steadfast; however, the colleague betrays his friend. Dumuzi is captured but appeals to Utu to help him escape by turning him into a gazelle. Utu does so, and Dumuzi does escape, only to be again caught. This repeats itself until he flees to his fold. The pursuers break in, wrecking everything on their way, and Dumuzi is killed. A similar myth, the *Most Bitter Cry,* also describes the attack on the fold and the rude awakening of Dumuzi, naked and a prisoner. He manages to escape and flees toward Uruk. As he tries to cross the Euphrates, however, he is swept off by the flood and drowns before the eyes of his horrified mother, Duttur, and wife, Inanna.

LUGALBANDA AND NINSUNA

Lugalbanda ("fierce king") and Ninsuna ("mistress of the wild cows") were apparently city god and goddess of Kullab, a city that was early absorbed into Uruk. Both were deities of cattle, but with the absorption of his city Lugalbanda seems to have lost definition, and even his divine status. He appears in historical times predominantly as an ancient king of the first dynasty of Ur, and his achievement in the extant epic about him, that of a supernaturally gifted messenger, was probably tacked on precisely because nothing else was known about him. Ninsuna for her part managed to keep her divine status. She was the tutelary goddess of Gudea of Lagash and, curiously enough, in that role was the consort of Ningishzida, not of Lugalbanda.

NINGIRSU

Ningirsu ("master of Girsu") was the city god of Girsu, with the temple Eninnu. His wife was the goddess Baba. Ningirsu was god of the thunderstorms in spring and of the spring flood of the Tigris. His early form was that of the thunderbird, an enormous eagle or vulture with a lion's head out of which thunder roared. Ningirsu was early identified with Ninurta of Nippur, and a great deal of his mythology was therefore transferred to the latter (it has been discussed above). *Ninurta* was also the name under which the god was borrowed by the Assyrians when he became prominent as god of war.

GATUMDUG

Gatumdug was goddess of the city of Lagash (Al Hiba), south of Girsu. The meaning of her name is not clear, but other evidence suggests that she was also a goddess of birth giving.

NANSHE

The goddess of fowl and fish was Nanshe. She was city goddess of Nina (Zurghul), with the temple Siratr. She was, according to Gudea, the interpreter of dreams for the gods.

NINMAR

City goddess of Guabba and seemingly a goddess of birds was Ninmar.

DUMUZI-ABZU

Dumuzi-Abzu was city goddess of Kinirsha, and the power for fertility and healthy new life in the marshes.

NININSINA

Nininsina ("mistress of Isin") was city goddess of Isin (Ishan Bahriyat), south of Nippur, which served as capital of Sumer for most of the time after the third dynasty of Ur until the advent of the Old Babylonian period. She seems to have been envisaged in the shape of a dog and was presumably the goddess of dogs. Her special powers were those of the physician. Her daughter Damu—different from the boy of Girsu on the Euphrates—followed in her mother's footsteps as goddess of healing.

ERESHKIGAL

The name of the goddess Ereshkigal (Allatum) meant "queen [of the] greater earth." The ancients believed that there was a "larger heaven" above the visible sky that connected with a "larger earth" below the observable earth. In the larger earth was the realm of the dead, of which Ereshkigal was queen, although a variant—and conflicting—belief located the realm of the dead in the eastern mountains. The ancients imagined it as a walled city. As with cities on earth, the wall served not only to keep out enemies but also to keep in people—as, for instance, the slaves—who were not free to leave the city. It had its own police and a court where the sun god presided during the night. Existence there was dreary. If one had no son to make funerary offerings, one lived like a beggar, but with many sons one could enjoy a degree of comfort. Reasonably well off were also young men killed in battle—they had their parents take care of them—and small children, who played with golden toys. In the second and first millennia ideas about existence below seem to have become even darker: dust was said to cover all; the dead were clad in feathers like birds; and when an Assyrian prince visited the netherworld in a vision, he found it full of horrifying monsters. Ereshkigal herself was cast in the image of a mourning woman, pulling her hair and raking her body with her nails for grief as she lamented the children dead before their time. In the late myth of Nergal and Ereshkigal she plaintively tells of her joyless life: even when young she never played as other young girls did. Ereshkigal's husband seems to have been originally Gugalanna ("great bull of heaven"). A variant, perhaps later, tradition has Ninazu as her spouse, and finally Nergal became king of the netherworld with Ereshkigal as his queen.

NINAZU

The meaning of the name *Ninazu* is not clear, but it apparently has to do with water. Most likely, since he was a netherworld god, his name refers to the waters underground. His wife was Ningirda ("mistress [well-]rope"), a daughter of Enki. In the north, in Eshnunna (Tel Asmar) in the Diyala region, where his Akkadian name was *Tishpak* ("outpouring"), he was a god of rain storms. His city in the south was Enegir on the lower Euphrates.

NINGISHZIDA

Ningishzida ("master of the well-grown tree") was the god of trees, especially the powers in the root that nourish and sustain the tree. As god of tree roots he was naturally seen as an underground, netherworld power. His office there was that of throne bearer, an old title for the head of the constabulary. Ningishzida's wife was Azimua ("well-grown branch"). His city was Gishbanda on the lower Euphrates. The ancients thought that there was a common identity between tree roots and snakes, the latter being roots moving freely. Accordingly, Ningishzida was also the god of serpents, and his older form, as noted above, was that of the stock of a tree around which serpent roots wind, the whole resembling the Greek caduceus.

NERGAL

The other names of Nergal ("lord great city"), originally probably designating different gods, were *Meslamtaea* ("the one issuing from the luxuriant *mesu* tree") and *Irra*. *Meslam* or *Emeslam* ("house Meslam") was the name of Nergal's temple at Cutha, in Akkad. [*See also* Nergal.]

A myth preserved in a copy found at Tell al-'Amarna in Egypt and dating from the thirteenth century BCE tells how Nergal came to be king of the netherworld. Once when the gods were feasting they sent a message down to Ereshkigal inviting her to send up her vizier, Namtar, to fetch her a portion of the delicacies. She did so, and when he arrived all the gods rose respectfully except one, Nergal, who rudely remained seated. When Namtar reported this, Ereshkigal furiously demanded that the offending god be delivered up to her so that she could kill him. But when Namtar came for Nergal, Ea had changed his appearance so that Namtar did not recognize him. Later, however, Ea told Nergal to take a throne down to Ereshkigal to placate her. Nergal was understandably reluctant, but Ea insisted and gave him demons to hold open the gates of the netherworld so that he could get out fast if needed. However, he met with no resistance, pulled Ereshkigal down from her throne by the hair, and threatened to kill her. When she pleaded for her life, offering marriage and rule over the netherworld, Nergal accepted, kissed her, and wiped away her tears, saying wonderingly, "It was but love you wanted of me from months long ago to now." A later version greatly enlarges on the tale. It has Nergal visit the netherworld twice, the first time to bed Ereshkigal against Ea's advice and to escape, the second time to stay after Ereshkigal has passionately pleaded with the gods for his return.

Another myth, the *Irra Epic,* celebrates Nergal under the name *Irra* (an Akkadian name meaning "scorched earth"), which most likely originally designated a separate god. The epic tells how Irra was roused to action by his weapon, Sibittu (the name means "heptad"), and how he persuaded Marduk to leave him in charge of the world while Marduk went to have his jewels cleaned. Irra's first act was to foment rebellion in Babylon and have it ruthlessly put down by the commandant of the Assyrian garrison in that city. Next Irra had riots, rebellions, and wars spread all over the country, and might have destroyed it completely had not his vizier, Ishum, reasoned with him and persuaded him to leave a remnant. The epic ends with self-praise by Irra, who nowise regrets his deeds of violence—rather, he suggests that he may cut loose again at any time.

ASHUR

Ashur was city god of Ashur (Qal'at Shergat) and chief god of Assyria. No recognizable features characterize him other than those that belong to his role as embodiment of the political aspirations of his city and nation. Even his wife and the name of his temple are not truly his own; they were borrowed from Enlil as part of Ashur's aspiration to the universal dominion for which Enlil stood. Basically, thus, he may in origin simply have been a *numen loci*—a spirit inhabiting a place and imbuing it with its character—named from the place where his presence was sensed. [*See also* Ashur.]

The Temple

The earliest Mesopotamian temples may have been in origin storehouses in which nomadic or seminomadic tribes kept their sacred objects and provisions, which were too cumbersome to carry along on their wanderings. Very soon, though, these structures would have been considered, as always later, dwellings of the gods to whom they belonged. The earliest recognizable form was that of a dwelling house with a large, rectangular middle room from which two smaller rooms projected at the end, creating a T-shaped effect. With time the projecting rooms disappeared and left a rectangular room that was entered from a door in one of the sidewalls near its end. At the short end-wall farthest from the door was a dais that kept the seat of the owner, in this case the god, out of the floor-level draft. In later times a niche in this end-wall steadied a baldachin, or tentlike aedicula, further protecting the god. Before the dais a curtain shielded him from profane eyes. On low benches along the side-walls stood statues of worshipers to remind the god of the people they represented and their needs. The god himself was, to judge by depictions dating from as early as the late Uruk period, represented by a statue in physiomorphic or anthropomorphic form. Facing it—conceivably inside the hanging—stood a large vase with greenery of various kinds, sometimes placed over a drain, into which petitioners received in audience by the god would pour libations before presenting their petitions.

Temples were by preference built on existing high ground; in addition, frequent rebuildings, during which stumps of the old walls were left while their upper parts were dumped in the space between them as fill to make a new building site, tended to create a small mound under the new rebuilding. In fact, this development, by which a temple came to stand on the walls of earlier ones, became in later time so much a part of the concept of a temple that builders created underground artificially filled-in walls for the actual walls to rest on. Such a filling was known as a temple terrace *(temen)*. At the time of the third dynasty of Ur, possibly already in the time of the dynasty of Akkad, these mounds were built high, with stairs leading up to the temple on top, and were squared off to form a stage tower, the so-called ziggurat. [*See* Pyramids, *overview article.*] With larger temples it became customary in early dynastic times to surround them with a protective oval wall, called an *ibgal*. The pattern for this may conceivably have been the long curved pile of camel-thorn gathered for fuel with which bedouins—then as now—ringed their camps in the desert. It served the double purpose of protection and a handy fuel supply. Inside the oval, along its sides, were the various storerooms, kitchens, and workshops for the temple personnel, while the house on top of the terraced tower constituted the god's living quarters: bedroom, bath, and so on. Often a few side rooms were added to the central structure.

In time—as can be seen by comparisons of temple plans from Khafaje with those for the later one at Ishchali—a tendency toward squaring off the oval and greatly enlarging the plan of the temple on the high terrace led to a new concept of the older design. The central room was enlarged so that its lower parts with the door became the size of a court. At its end the hanging or hangings were replaced with walls having doors in the middle, thus creating a rectangular cella with the niche and dais at the middle of the far side-wall, a so-called broad-room cella, which became standard for Sumero-Akkadian and Babylonian temples from the third dynasty of Ur on. The remainder of the original central room developed into a court with surrounding rooms. A gate and covered landing midway up the stairs leading to the temple above often served as court of justice in which the god sat in judgment. In Assyria the development from the bent-axis approach took a different course. There the door was relocated around the corner nearest to it to the middle of the end-wall facing the wall with the niche and dais, thus creating the long-room type of temple. [*See also* Temple, *article on* Ancient Near Eastern and Mediterranean Temples.]

The temple, rising over the houses of the community, was visible and tangible proof of the god's presence and, more, that he was himself a member of the community and had a stake in it, with his house, his servants, his oxen and sheep, and his fields in grain. To have the temple was a privilege. To build it or rebuild it needed divine approval, which was not always granted. The story of the *Cursing of Akkad* told of the dire consequences of King Naram-sin's willful decision to rebuild Ekur in Nippur without Enlil's permission. Even rebuilding after enemy attack and demolition needed divine cooperation. The god had to be roused from his state of shock after the catastrophe to make him able to act, so laments to soothe him and to recall past happiness were part of the ritual. Originally these laments had clear reference to a specific historical situation; later they were generalized for wider use. In later times they became obligatory for any rebuilding, since that implied demolition of the existing structure, and some even became part of the daily program of temple music and were used to awaken the temple personnel in the morning. Older than the laments for the destruction of a temple are, it would seem, hymns to temples. They celebrate the specific powers inherent in the temple to uphold the welfare of the country. The *Cursing of Akkad* tells how the peace of the country, its harvest of grain, and so on vanish when corresponding parts of Ekur are demolished. In fact, the temples shared in inordinate measure in the particular kind of holiness that characterizes the gods inhabiting them, and it is often difficult to distinguish between god and temple. The temple shares name and function with its god as if it were his embodiment.

The Cult

The communal cult of the gods was of two kinds, celebrating the appropriate festivals of the various gods at appropriate times and providing daily services such as would be required by any high human dignitary. The earlier of these are undoubtedly the festivals, most of which are best understood as communal magic rites for prosperity developed into cult dramas performed by community representatives. There is evidence for various types of such dramas: the Sacred Marriage, the Death Drama, the Journey Drama, and the Plowing Drama. Others may have existed. [*See* Drama, *article on* Ancient Near Eastern Ritual Drama.]

The Sacred Marriage is attested in Uruk as early as the late Uruk period. The ruler *(en)* "became" the god of the date palm, Amaushumgalana, and brought the harvest as wedding gift to the date storeroom of the temple. His wife—one presumes—similarly "became" the goddess of the storehouse, Inanna, and opened the door for him, thereby concluding the marriage and lasting union of the powers for producing and storing the dates. Their meeting at the gate is depicted on the famous Uruk Vase and on contemporary cylinder seals. In this early form the source of abundance clearly was the god. In later times—as shown by materials from Isin and Larsa—emphasis oddly changed, and the goddess came to be seen as the conveyor of bounty. The high point was now a blessing by the goddess of the marital couch after the king had proved his prowess as bridegroom. By Isin-Larsa times, too, focus was no longer narrowly on dates but on prosperity generally. A special form of the rite—perhaps at home among herders—saw it still quite directly as sympathetic magic for fertility. Here the rising of the king's member in the sexual congress of the rite immediately made plants and greenery shoot up. [*See* Hieros Gamos.]

The Death Drama had the function of performing for the dying god of fertility—characteristically Dumuzi—the rites of lament due to the dead. Such data as we have suggest that processions of mourners went into the desert in early summer lamenting the god in dirges sung by representatives of his mother, sister, and young widow. The rite was a magic strengthening of the emotional bonds with the god, a seeking to have him back. [*See* Dying and Rising Gods.]

In the Journey Drama, the god, perhaps represented by his image or an emblem, traveled to visit a god in some other city. There are references to a yearly visit to Eridu by Ningirsu traveling from the Lagash region, and similarly there are texts connected with such a journey by Ninurta of Nippur. Whether in so traveling these gods conferred a boon on Enki and Eridu, or conversely were themselves the beneficiaries, is not always clear. In a myth about Enmerkar, founder of Uruk, a ritual journey he made to Eridu is mentioned in terms suggesting that he was reconfirmed or enhanced in his office of lord *(en)*, that is, of provider. Most likely also the myth of Inanna and the offices she obtained from a not-too-sober Enki preserves memories of a rite in which Inanna's various offices were authenticated from Eridu. A rather full statement of a ritual journey is given in a text describing how Nanna of Ur travels up by boat to visit his father, Enlil, in Nippur, bringing first fruits from the products of the south. He is warmly received and leaves to go back to Ur with matching gifts from the agricultural lands around Nippur. The Plowing Drama of Ninurta's festival that opened the plowing season in Nippur is thus far unique. The king himself guided the plow, and a report was made to Enlil.

Last there is the Battle Drama. It seems to be at home with gods of the thunderstorms of spring, Ninurta and Marduk, and it is conceivable that it was once performed to activate these powers, to rouse the thunderstorms that were seen—as in the relevant myths—as the divine warrior attacking the mountains. There is, however, no evidence so far to indicate performance in such terms. The name of Marduk's main festival, Akitu ("time of the earth reviving"), does, as mentioned earlier, refer to an early aspect of him as the power causing natural abundance, but there is no indication of any battle drama. Such ritual evidence as we have for this type of drama all shows a later, completely politicized form behind which little if any trace of earlier implications survives. The materials for the Battle Drama are contained largely in cultic commentaries from Ashur, which, however, are clearly Babylonian in origin and reflect the bitter political rivalry between Babylon and the Sea Land to the south. Braziers and torches are lighted to signify the burning of Kingu, Anu, and

Enlil. A chariot arriving with great show of martial prowess is Nabu, who was sent against Enlil and now returns victorious. A loaf of bread is bounced by the king and a bishop, who represent Marduk and Nabu. The loaf is the heart of Anu, whom Marduk bound and whose heart he tore out.

The Babylonian epic of creation, *Enuma elish*, which tells how Marduk "vanquished Tiamat and assumed kingship," reflects the same political conflict, with Marduk representing Babylon and Tiamat representing the sea and the Sea Land. It is generally—and perhaps rightly—assumed to be a cult myth corresponding to a dramatic ritual reenactment of this primordial battle each new year. [*See* Enuma Elish.] However, our knowledge about the actual ritual of the Akitu festival in later times is scant in the extreme. We know that *Enuma elish* was read on one occasion and that Sennacherib, when he tried to transfer the festival to Assyria with Ashur as its hero, decorated the gates to his Akitu house with a relief showing the battle with Tiamat, but that is all. Otherwise such information as we have indicates that on the tenth of the month of Nisan, Marduk traveled by boat to the Akitu house, where a feast was celebrated on the eleventh, and that he then returned to Babylon. That is all. Not usable, unfortunately, for reconstructing the festival is a lengthy commentary called—not too happily—*Death and Resurrection of Marduk*. It has been shown to be an Assyrian, anti-Babylonian propaganda pamphlet, and it does not mention any death of Marduk. [*See also* Akitu.]

The trend toward sociomorphism imposed on the gods the patterns of the human family and household, and this in turn implied service such as was rendered to a human magnate in providing for his bodily comfort and assisting in the running of his estate. All of this became the daily temple cult, as described earlier. A further implication of anthropomorphism and sociomorphism was that since the god had become ruler of the community, it was essential to know what he wanted done. Thus a variety of methods of communication was developed. Some of these left the initiative to the god: he might show signs in the stars or on earth that the initiated could interpret. Others were available when man needed to know the divine will. The earliest of these methods of communication of which we have evidence are dreams sought by incubation in the temple, and inspection of the liver of a sacrificed kid for propitious or nonpropitious shape. This latter method was used by Gudea as a check on the message obtained when he was dreaming. An extensive and highly detailed literature serving as textbook for these and many other manners of prognostication developed during the second and first millennia. Originally meant as guides for rulers and war leaders, this literature soon broadened its scope to take in the fortunes of ordinary citizens. [*See* Divination.]

For conveying human wishes and needs to the gods and asking for help, a ritual of seeking audience to present petition and prayers was developed. The petitioner was led in before the deity with his greeting gift, usually a lamb or a kid. Here he libated water or wine in a huge vase with greenery that stood before the deity, and he spoke a formal greeting prayer. He then presented his petition. As the ritual for seeking an audience with the god was an occasional one, dependent on special circumstances, so the cult comprised other rituals for use in exceptional situations. I have mentioned the elaborate one called Bitrimki ("bathhouse"), which aimed at lustration of the king when he was threatened by the defiling evil of an eclipse of the moon; others were available for the rebuilding of a temple or for making or replacing a cult statue. In this last ritual great pains were taken to nullify by powerful incantations the fact that the statue was a work of human hands, and to make of it instead a god born in heaven.

The cult so far described was the communal, public cult. There was, however, a private cult as well. City life and its ever-greater differentiation between the fortunes of families and individuals and those of other families and individuals encouraged feelings that special success was due to a god's personal interest in a man and his family, while, conversely, misfortune would seem to be due to the god's abandonment of his ward for some reason or other. Thus the term for having luck became "to acquire a god." Since no achievement could be had without divine help, that of engendering a child necessarily implied such intervention. A god and goddess entered the body of the human father and mother and made the mother conceive. Thus the god and goddess who were assumed to have helped became family deities and were visualized in the image of a father and mother. As such they also took on the protective roles of parents, chief among which was to defend their wards against demons of disease and inspire successful thought and action. They had their altars and received daily offerings in the house of their wards, and prayers and petitions were addressed to them there.

The close connection between the personal god and success could not but raise problems, for experience showed that virtue was not always rewarded; rather, a virtuous man might fall ill or suffer other miseries such as should have happened to evildoers only. The obvious solution, that the virtuous man unwittingly must have offended his god, was accepted in a measure, and prayers often asked for enlightenment as to how a sufferer had sinned, so that he could do penance and mend his ways; but as a general explanation it did not carry full conviction, and the vexing problem of the righteous sufferer arose. It is dealt with in two major compositions datable to Middle Babylonian times. One is called *Ludlul* ("let me praise"), after its beginning, "Let me praise the possessor of wisdom." It tells of a pious and just man who suffers one misfortune after the other but does not lose his trust in Marduk. Eventually Marduk takes pity on him and restores him to health and prosperity. No real answer to the problem of why he had to suffer is attempted; the text merely holds out the conviction that the gods can have a change of heart and take pity. The other composition is known as the *Theodicy*. It is in the form of a dialogue between two friends about the fact that evil men appear to prosper, whereas good men fall on evil days. Here, too, there is no real answer, only a conviction that eventually retribution will come to evildoers.

The question of the innate justice—or, rather, injustice—of existence is also dealt with in a famous work known as the *Epic of Gilgamesh*. It tells how Gilgamesh, an ancient ruler of the city of Uruk endowed with exceptional vigor, drives his people too hard. They complain to the gods, who create Enkidu, a wild man who becomes a friend and brother of Gilgamesh. Together they set out to kill a famous warrior, Huwawa, who lives far away in the cedar mountains. They succeed. After their return to Uruk, Gilgamesh scornfully turns down a marriage proposal from the city goddess Ishtar. In her anger at being rejected she borrows the bull of heaven in order to kill Gilgamesh, but he and Enkidu overcome it. Then, however, things catch up with the two friends: the gods decide that Enkidu must die for having killed Huwawa. Gilgamesh is inconsolable at the loss of his friend and at the thought that he, too, must die. He therefore sets out on an arduous journey to an ancestor of his, Utanapishtim, who had gained eternal life. Eventually Gilgamesh reaches him, but Utanapishtim has no solace to offer. He invites Gilgamesh to try fighting Sleep—Death's younger brother, so to speak—but Gilgamesh fails miserably to keep awake. So Utanapishtim gives him clean clothes and sets him on his way home. There is no escape from death, however unjust it seems that man may not live forever.

It seems likely that the original epic ended here. At a later date, probably in the Middle Babylonian period, a certain Sinliqiunnini reworked the epic from a radically different point of view. Where the outlook of the earlier epic was tragic—a tale of a quest for eternal life that failed—the reworking saw Gilgamesh as a heroic traveler to romantic foreign parts who recovered hidden knowledge of the ancient times. A long story about the flood was added, as well as a further tale about a plant with the power to rejuvenate, which Gilgamesh obtained only to lose it again by carelessness. An introduction and conclusion stressed Gilgamesh's achievements, including lasting fame as builder of the city walls of Uruk. Finally, part of a Sumerian tale in which Enkidu describes conditions in the netherworld was tacked on, perhaps by some copyist. Passionate protest against existential evil thus became pleasure in romantic quest for hidden knowledge in faraway lands. [*See also* Gilgamesh.]

BIBLIOGRAPHY

Bottéro, Jean. *La religion babylonienne*. Paris, 1952.

Dhorme, Édouard. *Les religions de Babylonie et d'Assyrie*. Paris, 1945.

Dijk, V. van. "Sumerische Religion." In *Handbuch der Religionsgeschichte*, vol. 1, edited by Jes Peter Asmussen, Jørgen Laessøe, and Carsten Colpe, pp. 431–496. Göttingen, 1971.

Frankfort, Henri, et al. *Before Philosophy*. Harmondsworth, 1949. First published as *The Intellectual Adventure of Ancient Man* (Chicago, 1946).

Hooke, S. H. *Babylonian and Assyrian Religion*. New York, 1953.

Jacobsen, Thorkild. *The Treasures of Darkness: A History of Mesopotamian Religion*. New Haven, 1976.

Laessøe, Jørgen. "Babylonische und assyrische Religion." In *Handbuch der Religionsgeschichte*, vol. 1, edited by Jes Peter Asmussen, Jørgen Laessøe, and Carsten Colpe, pp. 497–525. Göttingen, 1971.

Meissner, Bruno. *Babylonien und Assyrien*, vol. 2. Heidelberg, 1925.

Pritchard, J. B., ed. *Ancient Near Eastern Texts relating to the Old Testament*. 3d ed. Princeton, 1969.

Ringgren, Helmer. *Religions of the Ancient Near East*. Translated by John Sturdy. Philadelphia, 1973.

2

EGYPTIAN
RELIGION

Leonard H. Lesko

Before beginning to survey ancient Egyptian religion, a number of limiting factors must be considered. The data upon which this survey rests come from all periods and many different sites, but these times and places are very unevenly represented. Clearly, more data survive from the later periods, from the south of the country (Upper Egypt), and from the very highest social strata. Some cult centers were totally lost long ago. Others required periodic renovation, while the increased devotion and/or increased wealth of later generations also led to large-scale rebuilding efforts. Because of this it is often impossible to survey what went on for thousands of years at the major temples of Memphis and Heliopolis, difficult to assess the cultic changes at major sites such as the Karnak and Luxor temples, and almost impossible to reconstruct the pre-Greek beliefs and cultic practices from the largely Ptolemaic remains at the sites of Edfu, Dendera, and Philae. Material from numerous cemeteries in the deserts near town sites, sometimes on the opposite side of the Nile, provides more eschatological data than anything else, but it also occasionally provides doctrinal, devotional, ethical, or cosmological information about one or another of the creeds of ancient Egypt. Monumental architecture is often not synchronous with monumental pieces of religious literature, and some of the most commonly repeated texts are often much less insightful than some unique, fragmentary pieces.

RELIGIOUS TEXTS AND HISTORICAL SETTING

Of the texts that survive from ancient Egypt, the religious literature as a whole remains the most difficult to comprehend. There are a variety of explanations for this, including the carelessness of scribes, the composite nature of the collections, efforts to keep the material esoteric or arcane, and also factors having to do with the modern editing of the texts. In examples from both temple walls and papyri, the original scribe's efforts have been mishandled by copyists and artists. Texts chosen from different sources for a new purpose were not always fully understood by the scribes, who tried to incorporate old or unfamiliar bits. For much of the religious literature we are simply not familiar enough with all the mythological allusions, the magic, the rites, and the puns, and in the case of the Ptolemaic material, efforts were made originally to encode the texts with widespread and multifold sign substitution. These

Ptolemaic hieroglyphs, which contain much of the accumulated myths and rituals at several major sites, also were not completely consistent from one site to another. One problem with modern editions of the religious literature is that the major concern has been to establish the best text by assembling parallels, with the result that the individual complete manuscripts are not understood or easily compared. The order of the texts in these editions is generally not that of any individual manuscript, and the variations that occur are completely lost in them, and in the translations made directly from them.

On the positive side, it should be noted that a large quantity of texts have been published now, and these include almost all the texts on several large temples. The temple texts furnish descriptions of the deities, their mythic significance, daily rites, and festivals, and to some extent the interaction between the human and divine worlds. Not all of the texts have been translated yet, but some important ones on rites and feasts have been, and attempts based on the texts found on the temple walls to explain the function of various parts of temples are not far off the mark. The major collections of mortuary or funerary texts from tombs are also available now, and preliminary published translations at least present the different Egyptian views concerning the afterlife and provide additional information concerning almost all aspects of Egyptian religion. There have also been numerous studies dealing with individual deities or concepts based on the phenomena encountered in all sources, and while these may not accurately reflect what the religion was for any one time or place, they do provide useful references for future synchronic studies, and again are probably not terribly far from the mark. Surveys of all of ancient Egyptian religion, also for the most part phenomenological, almost always have important observations to offer, though they do tend to be much less accurate in their generalizations and their subjectivity is often too significant an ingredient. Any details from which such generalizations are made may have applied to only an individual or a small group, when many different levels of belief and devotion were possibly current at the same time. To some extent, the survey that follows indicates trends, tendencies, and what apparently was appealing or approved at the highest levels, with the political motive often as weighty as the religious.

Already in prehistoric times, burial customs indicated a belief in life after death, which would have required that the body be preserved along with some household furnishings and food offerings. The expectation or hope was for a life after death that was not unlike human existence in this world. The locations of tombs and position of the bodies in their graves became traditional, and the traditions may have been more or less religious. Bodies were usually in a crouched position on their left sides with the head to the south and facing west, a custom that could be associated with the cult of Osiris or other gods of the dead in a western necropolis, or even with the location of the setting sun and perhaps the cult of the sun god. The exceptional site with a head to the north could also be understood in terms of an astral cult (reflected in later Pyramid Texts), with the goal of the deceased being to join the imperishable stars in the northern sky. There has been a great deal of speculation concerning the association of various cults with different localities in Egyptian prehistory, some of this based on finds but most on later evidence and claims. With the wealth of material available from historical context, it is surely best to omit speculation on undocumented origins and on the supposed interactions of the various prehistoric cult centers.

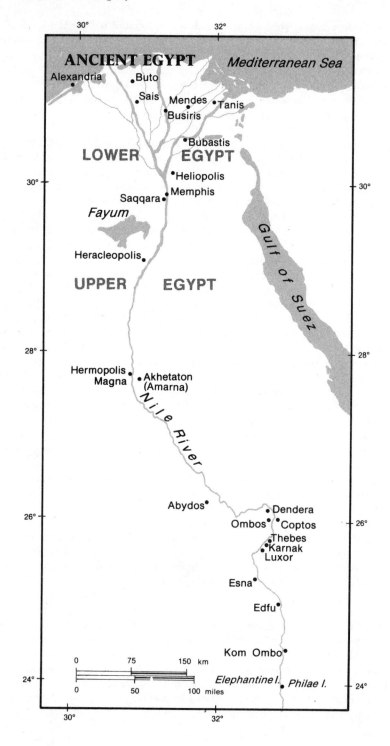

At the very beginnings of Egyptian history the slate palette of Narmer (c. 3110–3056 BCE) shows this king of Upper Egypt, who is wearing the white crown of the south, smiting a northerner, while on the reverse side of the palette Narmer is shown wearing the red crown of Lower Egypt. Whether Narmer or his son, Aha, was actually the first king (later known as Menes) of the first dynasty is still debatable, but some of the emblematic representations on the palette may have mythological significance. Both the bull and the falcon can represent aspects of the king's power, but the latter seems very likely to be associated with the identification of the king as the god Horus, a principal element in the myth of divine kingship. Since all but one king of Egypt is known to have been identified with the title "Horus," this myth is both very early and also, perhaps, one of the cornerstones of Egypt's success. There are several aspects of Horus, however, and even several Horuses, so that the full and precise meaning of this early representation could easily be overstated if it were said that all we know of the association of the king and Horus from later texts had already been formulated at this stage. Many accretions must have occurred with later explication. The divinity of the pharaoh and the notion of divine or sacred kingship have recently been challenged because of specific later references indicating that there were clear distinctions between the respect accorded the kings and the worship accorded the greatest gods. It will be seen, however, that the myth persisted, undoubtedly supported by the kings, some without doubt more vigorously than others.

Menes, besides identifying with Horus and unifying or reunifying the Two Lands, traditionally founded the capital, Memphis, and erected a temple there, presumably to the god Ptah. His civic contributions were equaled by his religious devotion, and he was thus an exemplary model for all succeeding kings. The kings of the first two dynasties probably had both tombs and cenotaphs that supported the new role of dual kingship, but their monuments at Abydos may also have had some bearing on the relationship of the living Horus to the deceased Osiris, whose cult was later at least maintained there. The fact that kings at the end of the second dynasty could take a "Seth" or a "Horus and Seth" title would indicate that the myth of the contending of Horus and Seth for the patrimony of Osiris was certainly known. But it is doubtful that this reflected a shift in religious belief; more likely a it was political move that was given a mythological framework.

For the first half of the Old Kingdom—the third and fourth dynasties—the great pyramids themselves remain, unfortunately, the principal monuments to the current beliefs. The attention given to these elaborate tombs clearly surpassed any other contemporaneous projects and would seem to show that the power of the king was reflected in the cult of his divine kingship. If the pyramids are not exclusively symbolic of royal power, they could also be symbols of divine power, either of the Horus-king or of his new father, the sun god, Re. The famous statue of Khafre with his headdress incorporating the Horus Falcon can be used to argue for the former, but the title "Son of Re," the use of *Re* in the theophoric royal names, and the true pyramid shape associated with the sun's rays and/or the Benben stone of Re point to the likelihood of either a developed or developing solar cult. In the second half of the Old Kingdom—the fifth and sixth dynasties—the central importance of the cult of Re is very well documented. The kings generally have *Re* in their name, and in addition to their smaller pyramids, they constructed substantial temples to the sun god. The story of the *Miracles That Happened in the Reign of King Khufu* (Westcar Papyrus) was probably written in the Middle Kingdom, but it reflects what was viewed as having happened earlier. The text purports to prophesy that a new dynasty will succeed Khufu's successors and that its first three new kings will be born to the wife of a priest of Re.

Much more significant for our understanding of the religion of this period and of much that had been developing and evolving before it are the Pyramid Texts, first recorded in the interior burial rooms of the pyramid of Unas, the last king of the fifth dynasty. These texts in vertical columns, lacking the illustrations and rubrics of later such mortuary or funerary literature, provided a combination of rituals, hymns, prayers, incantations, and offering lists, all designed to ensure that the king would reach his goal in the afterlife and have the information and provisions that he would need there. The texts were evidently compiled by priests connected with the temple of Re at Heliopolis. They indicate acceptance of the fact that the king is a god who ascends to the sky, joins Re on the solar bark for his voyage back and forth across the heavens, and guards Re and guides his bark past the perils, usually snakes, that threaten them. The rites, some of which may have taken place in these rooms or in the mortuary temple or valley temple to the east of the pyramid, included provision for opening the tomb, sacrificing an ox, and breaking jars for magical protection. The descriptions of the ascension in the tomb's antechamber provide alternative explanations that may have come originally from separate sources. They have the king ascending on the wings or backs of birds, on the incense wafting upward, on reed rafts, or on the outstretched arms of gods forming a ladder for him. On entering the tomb the king is still addressed as Horus; on ascension to the sky he is called Osiris. In the so-called cannibal hymn, he devours gods to acquire their attributes. He protests his guiltlessness and claims his divine perquisites. Within the burial chamber the king is presented to the great gods, and the offering-lists and spells are provided for him, while on the west gable are inscribed the serpent spells, incantations possibly intended to protect the tomb or to be used in guiding Re's bark.

Apart from the central theme of this collection, we learn much more about the religion of Egypt from these texts through the king's relationship to various deities and also through citations or mythological allusions from the texts of the other religions of the Egyptians. Here the king's genealogy is presented clearly by making him the product of the Heliopolitan Ennead. This family of nine gods represents a cosmological or cosmogonical explanation of creation by Atum (the complete one), who by himself created Shu (air) and Tefnut (moisture). From this pair, Geb (earth) and Nut (watery sky) came forth, and in the next generation they produced the two brothers Osiris and Seth and their sisters, Isis and Nephthys. Osiris, the eldest, rulled on earth in place of his father, but he was slain by his stronger brother, Seth. It fell to Osiris' son, Horus, born after his death, to avenge the slaying and assume the rule of this world.

In the form in which this genealogy survives, the significance of the Ennead is really subordinated to the son, Horus, on the one hand, and on the other to Re, who is alternately assimilated to Atum or placed before him as his creator. In the Pyramid Texts the Ennead is personified as the goddess Hathor (House of Horus), and so Re and Hathor are the parents of Horus just as surely as Osiris and Isis. Horus is also said here to be a son of Sekhmet, a statement of interest since Sekhmet was the consort of Ptah, the creator god of Memphis. According to later texts (the

Shabaka Stone), Ptah sprang forth from primeval chaos conceiving the creator, Atum, in his heart and bringing him forth on his tongue by speaking his name. The chaos from which Ptah came is also known as the Hermopolitan Ogdoad: the four pairs of deities represent the different aspects of chaos from which an egg appeared as the inundation receded at Hermopolis, thus producing the creator. The names of the four pairs are not consistent in different texts, but they generally include Amun and Amaunet (hiddenness), Kuk and Kauket (darkness), Huh and Hauhet (formlessness), and Nun and Naunet (the watery abyss). The creator god of Hermopolis might well have been Thoth, the moon god of that city, but in these Heliopolitan texts the creator remains Atum, while Thoth is included as a member of the Ennead and as a companion of Re in the sky. Since the son of Ptah and Sekhmet is Nefertem, the child appearing from the lotus, the king was associated with the scions and creator gods of all three of these important and early cult centers of Egypt.

It should be noted that the roles of both Thoth and Ptah in this connection are not spelled out, but they seem to be clearly alluded to. There were thus probably some limits on how far the Heliopolitan priests would go in assimilating the doctrines and deities of their counterparts or rivals. To some extent the priests of the other temples must have approved of some such accommodation to guarantee the continuing favor and actual support of the crown, but since the formulation had been Heliopolitan, the cult of Re became preeminent, and for the most part it remained so for most of Egyptian history.

In the fifth dynasty society in general became more open, and many of the highest offices in the land could be attained by people not related to the royal family. At least a few utterances from the Pyramid Texts indicate that they were not written originally for a king, so that the goal of a blessed hereafter was not exclusively a royal prerogative. Further decentralization of power occurs in the sixth dynasty, and local nomarchs are provided with quite respectable tombs. These tombs may have been equipped with religious texts on coffins or papyri that have not survived, but certainly in the First Intermediate Period, with the breakdown of central authority, several claimants to kingship, and actual civil war, the claimants to earthly power also made claim to divinity.

The texts on the interior of the single or nested wooden coffins of nobles from many sites in Egypt are in some cases identical to the earlier royal Pyramid Texts, and in other cases are considerably expanded. The texts from different sites vary more than the texts found at each site. The local differences are not all explained as yet, but some reasonably significant collections of spells labeled "books" on the coffins from El Bersha (the necropolis of Hermopolis) have been studied. These coffins have on their fronts (the side faced by the mummy lying on its left side) a false door to facilitate the deceased's mobility; a painted table of offerings to provide sustenance; a plan and description of the Field of Hetep, which is at least one version of the paradise these Egyptians hoped for; and a list of ship's parts, information useful for the deceased, who joins the sun god in his bark and guides it through the skies.

On the inside surface of the bottom of most of the El Bersha coffins was painted an elaborate illustrated plan or map with descriptive texts known today as the Book of Two Ways. (The Book of Two Ways is a collection within the Coffin Texts.) The plans are all roughly comparable, with a blue waterway surrounded by mounds to represent the day sky, and a black land route, surrounded by water, representing the night sky. This cosmological plan provided the earliest illustrated guidebook to the beyond and attempted to locate various uncommon demons as well as some commonly known terms for places in the afterlife. Apart from the central plan, however, the book is really two different books. The earliest version was apparently written as a guide for followers of the Osirian religion, and the goal of several of its sections was to aid these followers to pass the various gates and demon keepers leading to the mansion of Osiris. The later version has the plan and one section as a guide to the route leading to the mansion of Osiris, but it also has one whole section dealing with Thoth, another dealing with Re, and a conclusion that ties together the whole in terms of knowledge of spells about the beyond. If the deceased knows the spells to the first stage, he will become a star in the sky with the moon god, Thoth. If he knows them to the next stage he will join Osiris in his mansion, and if he knows all the spells he will join Re on his bark in the sky. These goals also appear to be put in terms of social standing, commoners being associated with Thoth, great ones with Osiris, and, obviously, royalty with Re. What this does is to democratize the hereafter by making the highest goals available to anyone who has the book. It was clearly based on an original Osirian text, and in the hands of the priests of Re it would have become a good prosyletizing text for the solar religion.

The Book of Two Ways concludes with the famous statement by the All-Lord, Re, that he "made the four winds that every man might breathe," "made the great flood that the poor as well as the great might have power," "made every man like his fellow (I did not command that they do evil. It is their hearts that disobey what I have said)," and "made their hearts to cease forgetting the West, in order to make divine offerings to the gods of the nomes." The All-Lord says, "it is with my sweat that I created the gods. Mankind is from the weeping of my eye," and a little later he adds that after the deceased has spent millions of years between Re and Osiris, "we will sit together in one place. Ruins will be cities and vice versa; house will desolate house." These remarks provide rather interesting insights into the metaphysics and ethics of the Re religion as well as a noteworthy example of early ecumenism. These particular Coffin Texts came from a necropolis of Hermopolis, in middle Egypt. Whether Re priests from Hermopolis or Heliopolis were responsible is still debatable. But another text of this same chaotic period, from Heracleopolis in middle Egypt, although it is a literary text in the "instruction" genre, is actually one of the most religious documents surviving from ancient Egypt. A compact section at the end provides in capsulized form the complete philosophy and theology of the Re religion:

One generation of men passes to another, and God, who knows characters, has hidden Himself, . . . so worship God upon his way. . . . The soul goes to the place it knows. . . . Beautify your mansion in the West, embellish your place in the necropolis with straightforwardness and just dealing; . . . more acceptable is the character of the straightforward man than the ox of the wrongdoer. Serve God, that He may do the like for you, with offerings for replenishing the altars and with carving; it is that which will show forth your name, and God is aware of whoever serves Him. Provide for men, the cattle of God, for He made heaven and earth at their desire. He suppressed the greed of the waters, he gave the breath of life to their noses, for they are likenesses of Him which issued from His flesh. He shines in the sky for the benefit of their hearts; He has made herbs, cattle, and fish to nourish

*them. He has killed His enemies and destroyed His own children, because they had
planned to make rebellion; He makes daylight for the benefit of their hearts, and
He sails around in order to see them, . . . and when they weep, He hears. . . .
He has made for them magic to be weapons to ward off what may happen.*

From this we see that Re is hidden, omniscient, provident, responsive and just.
Men, who are created in the likeness of God, and for whom heaven and earth were
created, must worship God, and provide for their fellow men. Hypocrisy is of no
avail, but God gave men magic to ward off "what may happen."

This text of the instruction of a Heracleopolitan king to his son, Merikare, anticipates the fall of the tenth dynasty (2040 BCE) to the Theban family of dynasty eleven.
Coffin Texts continue to be used in the Middle Kingdom, and this indicates that for
the most part the religion or religions of the people did not change drastically with
this change in government. The official doctrine of the state, however, had to be
supported by a great deal of political propaganda literature to account for the reunification under the new Theban king, Mentuhotep II, then the apparent usurpation
by his vizier, and finally the assassination of this vizier become king, Amenemhet I.
Amenemhet had already returned the capital to the north and constructed defenses
on Egypt's borders, but he was apparently not prepared for the threat from within
his own palace. The change from dynasty eleven to dynasty twelve was also marked
by a shift in the Theban's titular god and the formulation of a new national god.
Previously Montu, a war god, was worshiped at perhaps four separate temples in the
Theban nome, but with Amenemhet ("Amun is in front") Amun and his new cult
begin a long and steady growth in the south in spite of the fact that the kings of this
and succeeding dynasties ruled from the north. The new god is perhaps a conflation
of Montu with Min, the ithyphallic fertility god of Coptos, which had been allied with
Thebes in the war against Heracleopolis, and also, of course, with Amun, the first of
the primordial gods of Hermopolis. This latter element may have provided the
priority of the new god in the minds of the formulators, but the association with Re
as Amun-Re was probably the significant factor in guaranteeing some continuity with
the earlier dynastic gods.

The king of the twelfth dynasty was still Horus, but beginning with Senusret I
(1971–1928 BCE) important new claims to kingly divinity surface. In the *Story of
Sinuhe* Senusret I is called a god without peer, "no other came to be before him."
In order to consolidate his power, Senusret III deposed a number of powerful nomarchs and divided the country into departments that were to be administered from
the capital by his appointees. At the same time, in a cycle of songs in his honor and
in a loyalist instruction he is called the "unique divine being" and is identified as
Re himself. Remarkably, the propaganda literature of this dynasty remained popular
for at least 900 years, and the tradition of Senusret's special position among the kings
of Egypt also survived through Greek sources to the present.

The Second Intermediate Period was marked both by internal weakness eventually
giving way to division and by foreign occupation of at least the major part of the
delta. These Hyksos rulers were eventually driven out of their capital at Avaris by a
new Theban family, which reunited the land and began the period of greatest im-
perialistic expansion, the New Kingdom. The new family was devoted to the cult of
Amun-Re at Karnak, and also had a special interest in the moon god in several earlier
forms, including Iah (the moon itself), Thoth, and Khonsu, who was now the son of

Amun-Re and Mut (the mother). Thutmose I (c. 1509–1497 BCE), perhaps the first king of the eighteenth dynasty to have a palace in the north, was also responsible for leading expeditions far into Syria, perhaps to the Euphrates. His credentials as a god-king were evidently well established, but not those of his successors. His daughter by his chief wife had to become consort to his son by a lesser wife to secure that son's succession as Thutmose II. But when the latter died, handing over the throne to a son by another wife, his half sister and chief wife, Hatshepsut, took the throne for herself. There were probably very practical explanations for her success in this maneuver, but the justification she chose to propagate was her own "divine birth." She had this recorded on the walls of her mortuary temple at Deir al-Bahri, which depicted Amun-Re in the form of her father, Thutmose I, coming to her mother Ahmose, who conceived the goddess-king, the female Horus.

Hatshepsut's mythologizing goes beyond this with the commemoration of her restoration efforts since the expulsion of the Hyksos. They had "ruled without Re," and she was indeed favored by the gods of Egypt. She had extensive work done at the temple of Karnak, adding a new sanctuary, pylon gates, and very tall obelisks, monumets as much to herself as the Amun-Re, her father. Her small cult temple at Medinet Habu (ancient Djeme) probably has particular significance mythologically for the later association of the Hermopolitan Ogdoad with this sacred site. According to a Ptolemaic text in the Khonsu temple at Karnak, Amun was the father of the fathers of the Ogdoad who (as Ptah) created the egg at Hermopolis and later traveled *(khenesh)* to Thebes in his new name of Khonsu. Together with the Ogdoad, he is in the tomb chamber in the necropolis at Medinet Habu. Indeed, it seems likely that Hatshepsut and her supporters were concerned not only with her genealogy but with the genealogy of the Theban gods. Her husband's son, Thutmose III, who succeeded her and eventually tried to blot out her memory, was primarily involved with military expeditions to Syria and Palestine, and he used his additions to the Karnak temple to publicize his victories. The temple became wealthy and influential because of his generosity and devotion. His successors continued to benefit from and build upon his achievements in the international sphere; foreign alliances, foreign wives, and foreign deities were all introduced in this period, which peaked in the reign of Amenhotep III (1403–1366 BCE).

The son of Amenhotep III, who may have been his coregent for as long as ten years, changed his name from Amenhotep IV to Akhenaton by his fifth year and moved his residence to a new site, Akhetaton (modern Tell al-'Amarna). He devoted himself to one aspect of the solar cult, the sun disk (Aton) itself. He saw himself and perhaps his wife, Nefertiti, as the only representatives or intermediaries between the Aton and the rest of creation. Akhenaton's monolatry or henotheism, while apparently accepted by his chief officials, eventually did bring him into direct conflict with the powerful temple staff of Karnak. His supporters attacked the name "Amun" and the word *gods* throughout the Theban area. They were probably sent to eradicate the full name "Amun-Re, King of the Gods," but this attempt to erase (primarily from monuments) the term *gods* has been viewed by many as a monotheistic revolution. Later reaction to Akhenaton as a heretic is known, but what he intended or how far he went to not as clear. The Aton was not his creation either as an icon or as a deity. It had increased in significance in the early eighteenth dynasty. The emblems of almost all the gods of Egypt survive from Tell al-'Amarna, indicating that Akhenaton's followers either had no fear of keeping them or had greater fear of abandoning them. The fact that Akhenaton's own prenomen is Waen-Re ("the unique one of Re") is indicative of his continued acceptance of the old solar cult, or perhaps even of the Heliopolitan priests' support of the new cult. Something of Akhenaton's attitude toward the Aton in this international period can be seen in the following excerpt from his famous hymn to the Aton.

> How plentiful it is, what you have made, although they [the creatures made by Aton] are hidden from view, sole god, without another beside you; you created the earth as you wished, when you were by yourself, before mankind, all cattle and kine, all beings on land, who fare upon their feet, and all beings in tehe air, who fly with their wings.

> The lands of Khor and Kush and the land of Egypt: you have set every man in his place, you have allotted their needs, every one of them according to his diet, and his lifetime is counted out. Tongues are separate in speech, and their characters as well; their skins are different, for you have differentiated the foreigners. In the underworld you have made a Nile that you may bring it forth as you wish to feed the populace, since you made them for yourself, their utter master, growing weary on their account, lord of every land. For them the Aton of the daytime arises, great in awesomeness.

> All distant lands, you have made them live, for you have set a Nile in the sky that it may descend for them and make waves upon the mountains like the sea to irrigate the fields in their towns. How efficient are your designs, Lord of eternity: a Nile in the sky for foreigners and all creatures that go upon their feet, a Nile coming back from the underworld for Egypt.

Most aspects of this hymn can be found stated in almost identical terms in the universalist hymn to Amun-Re, so it cannot be regarded as totally original or epoch-making in itself. A claim in the hymn that there is no other who knows the Aton except his son, Akhenaton, is noteworthy, and the statement that the whole land was founded and its crops were raised by the Aton for Akhenaton and Nefertiti is ego-centric, to say the least.

Akhenaton's coregent and short-lived successor, Semenkhkare, who some now believe may have been none other than Nefertiti herself, seems to have attempted reconciliation with the priesthood of Amun-Re. But Tutankhaton (c. 1348–1339 BCE), who next assumed the throne, changed his name to Tutankhamen, had statues of himself made both as Amun and as Osiris, and decorated the Luxor temple with scenes of the restored Opet feast. (The main feature of this feast was the procession of Amun's cult image from the Karnak temple to the Luxor temple and back.) He even had a restoration stela set up at Karnak. After his death and that of his successor, Ay, the temple reliefs and stela were usurped by his former general, Horemheb, who on becoming king began attacks on his four predecessors who were involved with the movement, now regarded as heretical.

Horemheb's successor was his vizier, who came from Tanis. As Ramses I he began the nineteenth dynasty, which for various reasons is seen as most significant in the history of Egyptian religion. On the one hand, the pharaohs of this dynasty had to indicate their continuity with the past and assure their support in all the cult centers of Egypt. They built extensively at all the old temple sites and went overboard to demonstrate their polytheism. Temples now had multiple chapels and sanctuaries dedicated to various deities, but the monuments also were used as propaganda to show the power of the kings, to depict their victories, to record their legitimate succession, and to indicate their great devotion to the gods and their munificence to both the gods and their own subjects. On the other hand, the pharaohs succeeded in reinstating their own god, Seth, whom they commemorated as having been in their new capital since the time of the Hyksos. Seth was included in the royal names now and also had one of the Egyptian armies named for him.

In the early Ramessid period the tombs of nobles had much less of the biographical material and scenes of everyday life that were common earlier. Now the emphasis was on the funerary rites and any religious offices the deceased had held. There appears to be a very conservative religious reaction to what had taken place in the eighteenth dynasty. Even the literary texts have primarily mythological settings and content for stories, but interestingly, these often make the gods look foolish and cannot be considered very pietistic. Women, evern goddesses, in these texts are cast in an unflattering light, again perhaps in reaction to the powerful queens of the preceding dynasty. The long reign of Ramses II produced numerous temple constructions with colossal statues and representations of himself, but these seem to indicate that he was glorifying himself as much as any of the other gods. The group of four deities at the back of his temple at Abu Simbel shows that he was placing himself on the same level as the three earlier dynastic gods of Egypt—Ptah, Re-Harakhty, and Amun-Re.

The religious texts with which people were buried in the New Kingdom and later are now known as the *Book of Going Forth by Day* but they actually constituted at least two different collections, again emphasizing in introductions or conclusions either an Osirian or a solar afterlife, often with some elements of both in between. These papyri, illustrated with vignettes, vary greatly in length and include many interesting chapters, such as that with the servant statue or Shawabti spell (chap. 6), the heart spell (chap. 30), a spell to enable the deceased to have all requisite knowledge in one chapter (chap. 162), and the famou negative confession and judgment scene (chapt. 125). The negative confession is not confession at all but rather a protestation of innocence between fourty-two judges of the underworld. Following the psychostasia, or weighing of the deceased's heart, in relation to the feather of Maat, or Truth, the deceased inevitably escapes the devourer and is presented to Osiris, but most often goes forth past the gatekeepers and joins Re as well. The New Kingdom copies of the *Book of Going Forth by Day* are commonly called the Theban recension because so many copies come from Theban tombs. But the texts generally, even in the negative confession, indicate a northern origin, most likely Heliopolitan. Many texts outside of the negative confession are modifications or corruptions of the earlier Coffin Texts versions.

The negative confession, though less than ideal as a code of ethics, cannot be ignored, since it survived in thousands of copies spanning fifteen hundred years. A portion of the fuller list follows:

O Wide-of-Stride, who comes forth from Heliopolis,
    I have not committed evil.
O Embracer-of-Fire, who comes forth from Babylon,
    I have not stolen.
O Nosey, who comes forth from Hermopolis,
    I have not been covetous. . . .

O Dangerous-of-Face, who comes forth from Rosetau,
I have not killed men.
O Ruti, who comes forth from heaven,
I have not damaged the grain-measure. . . .
O Breaker-of-Bones, who comes forth from Heracleopolis,
I have not told lies. . . .
O White-of-Teeth, who comes forth from the Fayum,
I have not trespassed. . . .
O-Eater-of-Entrails, who comes forth from the Thirty,
I have not practised usury. . . .
O Wanderer, who comes forth from Bubastis,
I have not gossiped. . . .
O Wamemti-Serpent, who comes forth from the place of judgment,
I have not committed adultery.
O Maa-Intef, who comes forth from the Temple of Min,
I have not defiled myself. . . .
O Ser-Kheru, who comes forth from Wensi,
I have not been quarrelsome.
O Bastet, who comes forth from the sanctum,
I have not winked.
O His-Face-behind-Him, who comes forth from Tep-het-djat,
I have not been perverted; I have not had sexual relations with a boy. . . .
O Tem-sep, who comes forth from Busiris,
I have not been abusive against a king.
O Acting-with-His-Heart, who comes forth from Tjebu,
I have not waded in water.
O Flowing-One, who comes forth from Nun,
My voice has not been loud. . . .

The judges and the places from which they come are not consistently prominent or frightening and cannot logically be connected with the forty-two nomes of Egypt, but while a few of the statements have uncertain meaning, the vast majority are perfectly clear and not particularly surprising.

From the beginning of the eighteenth dynasty the principal religious text selected to decorate the walls of the royal burial chambers was the so-called book of Amduat, or *That Which Is in the Netherworld*. This book, which resembles a large-scale papyrus unrolled on the walls, treats of the voyage of the solar bark through the hours of the night sky, but it involves Sokar, the god of the Memphite necropolis (Rosetau), as chief god of the underworld. The nineteenth-dynasty kings, different as they may have been from their eighteenth-dynasty counterparts, were also buried in tombs in the Theban Valley of the Kings, but their tombs were more elaborately decorated, with relief carving and paintings of the *Book of Gates* and the journey of the sun through the body of the goddess Nut.

When Ramses II made peace with the Hittites some time after the nearly disastrous battle of Kadesh, a thousand deities on either side were called to witness, and foreign deities such as Anat, Astarte, and Reshef became even more popular in Egypt. His successor, Merneptah, was beset with attacks from Libyans and the Sea Peoples. It is from his reign that the earliest surviving reference to Israel is found, but without other corroborating documentation for the story of the Exodus aside from its reasonably accurate setting.

Ramses III of the twentieth dynasty was the last great pharaonic ruler of Egypt. His building efforts included a separate small temple at Karnak, as well as a very large mortuary temple for himself at medinet Habu. This latter, which survives in very good condition, contains descriptions of the complete festivals of Min and Sokar in addition to the usual battle scenes, and it also has an elaborate calendar of feasts and offerings. The whole was surrounded by a wall with two fortifiable gateways, which probably reflect the worsening political situation of the whole country. There were strikes by the royal tomb workers, who had to be provisioned by the temple storehouses; there were attacks by a coalition of foreigners, principally Libyan; and finally, the king was slain in a harem conspiracy. In addition to punishing those responsible, his son Ramses IV recorded in a very interesting document, the great Papyrus Harris I (c. 1150 BCE), all the benefacations that his father had made to the temples of Egypt. The Wilbour Papyrus, of slightly later date (1140 BCE), confirms that the temple of Amun-Re alone controlled an exorbitant amount of land and the population of a large area in middle Egypt hundreds of miles away.

By the end of the twentieth dynasty the High Priest of Amun, Herihor, was for all practical purposes the ruler of Upper Egypt, and the twenty-first dynasty began with one of his sons assuming the kingship at Tanis in the north while another succeeded him as high priest in the south. Several of the priestly successors also claimed royal titles in the Theban area, and eventually the two offices were combined in one. Unlike the earlier usurpations of viziers or generals, who undoubtedly had a military power base, the base for the priests seems to have been primarily economic. The process can be traced back to the nineteenth dynasty, to a priestly family that gained control not only of the temple treasury but also of the royal treasury. Throughout the Ramessid period there are indications that all was not what it was supposed to be in this period of religious fervor. Banquet songs stress a *carpe diem* attitude; a workman in the royal necropolis shows no respect for his deceased king, and eventually almost all of the Theban tombs were systematically looted. Some of the robbers were accused and tried, but evidently those chiefly responsible got away with their crimes. The priests reburied the royal mummies, but with none of their original trappings or treasure. The priests apparently did not approve of the reinstatement of Seth by the Ramessid kings, and the god's name was attacked at their capital in the north.

When a Libyan family, the twenty-second dynasty, took over in the Third Intermediate Period they ruled from the north also, but controlled the south by appointing a daughter to serve as Divine Adoratress of Amun, a new position above that of high priest. The Nubian Piye (Piankhy), a very devout follower of Amun, conquered all of Egypt to set things right there but did not remain to rule himself, although he did appoint his sister (Amenirdis I) to be the successor of the current Divine Adoratress (Shepenwepet I) when she eventually died. His good intentions were not sufficient, however, and the Nubians (twenty-fifth dynasty) did return to rule the country, losing to the Assyrians, who installed the Saite (twenty-sixth) dynasty. This period marked one of the last Egyptian revivals, with a great deal of temple and tomb construction. In many respects the Saite period harked back to the Old Kingdom; several huge Theban tombs of this time had extensive collections of the Pyramid Texts.

With the Persian conquest of Egypt by Cambyses in 525 BCE, there are indications that the conquering kings had good intentions with regard to maintaining the cultural, legal, and religious traditions of the Egyptians. Although Herodotus, who was not unbiased, accused Cyrus of sacrilege in Egypt, it is known that this king dutifully performed burial rites for an Apis bull and also had small temples erected to the Egyptian gods. The Persian satraps who actually administered the country were doubtless less highly esteemed, probably deservedly so. With several native rebellions and one last gasp of independence in the thirtieth dynasty, Egypt fell again to the Persians, and in turn welcomed Alexander the Great in 332 BCE as a savior from the Persian oppressors.

Alexander was probably convinced of his own divinity on visiting the oracle of Amun at the Siwa oasis, but this was not enough to guarantee a long life. Under his successor, Philip Arrhidaeus, the sanctuary of the Karnak temple was rebuilt. When Alexander's general, Ptolemy, became king of Egypt, much new construction was begun. Alexandria, with its library, museum, and new government offices, was founded, while other Greek cities in Egypt were enlarged or planned. Under the Ptolemys truly great temples were erected at some ancient cult sites, and countless smaller temples, gates, appendages, and inscriptions were added to other places. All the main structures at the temple of Horus at Edfu are Ptolemaic. The vast main temple and its surrounding walls are covered from top to bottom with scenes and texts dealing with Horus, his myths and rituals. The texts have undergone a complicated encoding with a sixfold increase in the number of hieroglyphic signs used, and a wide range of possible substitutions for many standard signs is also encountered. The language is classical Middle Egyptian, and presumably the texts were from earlier material chosen by Egyptian priests from their own libraries, or perhaps from several sites in Egypt. The inscriptions are quite distinctive but often difficult to translate. They seem intentionally obscure despite their accessibility, and the encoding must have been used to make these texts more esoteric or arcane to their own followers and perhaps to the Greeks as well.

The temple of Hathor at Dendera has similar encoding of texts, as well as *mamisi* (birth houses) for the goddess, secret crypts, and a combined Egyptian-Greek zodiac on the ceiling of a small room on the temple's roof. The dual temple of Haroeris and Sobek (the crocodile god) at Kom Ombo may have had a crypt for oracular pronouncements. At Esna the creator god, Khnum, who fashions on the potter's wheel, is commemorated. The temple of Isis on the island of Philae had many separate buildings with inscriptions dating well into the Roman period. The cult of Isis, incorporating much of the cult of Hathor as well, is probably better known now from the Isiac temples in the rest of the Mediterranean than it is from this, the greatest center of the worship of the Egyptian goddess of love. Now that the entire temple complex has been moved to higher ground on a neighboring island, much more work will be possible here. Following construction of the old high dam at Aswan, the temple was under water for most of the year. Another major Oriental cult in the Greco-Roman world that had at least some roots in Egypt was that of Serapis, whose name comes from Osiris and the Apis bull of Ptah of Memphis. These particular sacred bulls, chosen for their markings, had been mummified and buried in large sarcophagi at the Serapium in Saqqara throughout much of the late period in Egyptian history.

Alexandria early became one of the principal centers in the world for the study of philosophy and theology, and when Egypt converted to Christianity many of the Alexandrian church fathers became deeply embroiled in controversies. Philo, Origen, Arrius, and Clement represent a few of the different positions originating in Alexandria. Traditional Greek philosophers and pagan, Jewish, Christian, orthodox, and heterodox interpretations—all had their adherents here, living virtually side by side for some time. The Septuagint and Hexapla were produced here, and the Coptic gnostic library found in Upper Egypt at Naga Hamadi probably originated here as well. The hermetic tractates may provide some link to earlier Egyptian notions, but the apocrypha and *Gospel of Thomas* preserved in this archive most likely originated elsewhere.

Monasticism in both its eremetic and cenobitic forms originated and became very popular in Egypt, partially spread by conditions in the country under the Romans, who overtaxed the people and provided them little protection from the Blemmyes' invasions. The monasteries provided food, protection, and solace. The monastic rule of Pachomius became the standard in many Egyptian monasteries, and it was introduced to the west by John Cassian, becoming the basis of Western Benedictine monasticism.

The early Christians in Egypt suffered persecution under the Romans, but after Rome converted to Christianity, the pagans suffered as well. The Neoplatonic philosopher Hypatia was stoned to death in Alexandria in AD 415, and the last outpost of paganism in the Roman empire, at the temple of Isis at Philae, was finally overcome in the late fifth century. When the Arab general 'Amr ibn al-'Aṣ took Egypt in 641 conversion to Islam was rapid, due as much to economic advantages as to the attractions of the Qur'ān.

CONCEPTIONS OF THE UNIVERSE

The ancient Egyptians conceived of their universe in a number of different ways. One view was that the firmament *(bia)* was a huge inverted metal colander, from which pieces fell; these wonders or marvels *(biau)* included meteoric iron *(biat)*, which was used in making ceremonial implements such as the adzes for the ritual of the Opening of the Mouth. This ritual was performed to give life to statues or other representations and also to revivify the mummies of the deceased. According to another view, the sky was a giant cow whose four legs were supported by four deities, while other deities (stars) on small crescent-shaped boats sailed on her belly. This heavenly cow may be associated with Hathor, who according to the Heliopolitan cosmogony was variously seen as consort of Re and mother of Horus, but also as consort of Horus and mother of Ihy, a form of the sun god to whom she gives birth. The sun god, Re, is also frequently shown being born to the goddess Nut, whose body spans the sky from east to west. According to the Heliopolitan cosmogony she should, of course, be descended from him. Nevertheless, as regularly depicted on the ceilings of royal bed chambers, the sun appears and crosses the goddess's body during the day, but is swallowed by her at night, passing through her body from west to east to be born again.

All of these concepts view the earth as quite solid, generally flat, and practically limitless in extent. The sky (Nut) receives her support from the earth (Geb), and sometimes is shown held apart from him by the air god, Shu. All that the sun encounters in its day and its night voyage is above the earth. The locations generally translated as "netherworld" or "underworld" *(imht* and *duat)* both actually appear to have been in the sky originally. Some descriptions indicate that the Egyptians also conceived of an undersky *(nenet)* and a topsy-turvy afterlife, so that one of the terms *(duat)* seems to have been relocated later. As if this were not confusing enough, another mythological cosmology would have one form of the falcon god, Horus, represent the entire sky, with his two eyes as the sun and the moon. The moon was the eye injured in the battle with his uncle, Seth, to avenge the death of his father, Osiris, in order to assume his inheritance. This great Horus would seem to be as much greater than Re, the sun, as the Heliopolitan Re of the Pyramid Texts is above his son, the Horus-king. Such seemingly incompatible cosmologies may represent either earlier separate traditions or later attempted rationalizations.

CONCEPTIONS OF HUMAN NATURE AND DESTINY

The Egyptians' view of their own nature certainly varied in some respects from time to time, place to place, and person to person, but a few terms persisted expressing notions about their ontology that are reasonably consistent. People were created in God's image, from the weeping of his (Re's) eye, were conceived in God's heart (mind) and spoken by his tongue (Ptah), or were fashioned on the potter's wheel (Khnum). Man's body had to be preserved so that he could properly live again in the afterlife. To ensure this a replica of the body was thought to have been fashioned by the gods at birth; more were made later by sculptors and painters as stand-ins for bodies that might be lost. These *ka* figures, enlivened by the Opening of the Mouth ritual, served as second effective personalities, but they could also be protecting genii. At least by the Late Period even the great gods such as Re and Thoth have a number of these *ka*s or "attributes," including Hu (authoritative utterance), Sia (perception), Maa (sight), and Sedem (hearing).

The term most closely approximating "soul" for the Egyptians was *ba,* which was represented in hieroglyphic as a small bird and was also depicted in burial scenes departing from the body as a bird flying up to the sky. In at least one literary text, the *Dispute of a Man with His Ba,* this conscience or other self is present in life to be argued with and to help the person make up his mind after considering both sides of a question, in this case the serious question of whether to go on living. Another literary text, the *Lamentations of Khakheperreseneb,* has the scribe address his heart *(ib),* which cannot respond, rather than his *ba.* It was generally the heart that was considered the seat of both intellect and will.

Another significant aspect of man's person or personality is his *akh,* or "spirit," which is what remains apart from the body or at least is not limited by the body after death. A person wants to become an *akh aper,* an "equipped spirit" or "perfect spirit," in the afterlife, and to this end he prepares himself with the required religious spells from one or the other collections available, often including as many books and variations as possible and both full and shortened versions. The spirits in the hereafter were sometimes thought to be not content to rest in peace in a blessed state, nor were they always allowed to. Another literary text, the *Ghost Story,* tells of a long-dead spirit who appears to a priest and requests that his cracked and drafty tomb be repaired. Many letters to the dead are also found; they were left with food offerings by living relatives to urge some specific action on their behalf in the spirit world. These usually mention past favors and show confidence in the deceased's ability to effect change for righting the injustice.

GODS, CULTS, AND MAGIC

While the deceased in the necropolis were regularly called *akhs*, they were also occasionally termed *netjeru* ("gods"). A curse left on a square block at the door of a tomb threatened dire consequences to anyone who disturbed even a pebble in the tomb, and it advised finding a place that would not impinge upon the tombs of any of the gods in the necropolis. For the Egyptians the word *netjer* ("god") was used broadly to cover all levels of divinity, from the greatest gods to the justified dead (that is, those declared "true of voice" in the judgment before Osiris). Monotheism, if it ever existed in ancient Egypt, was never clearly formulated and apparently was never established as doctrine in any of the native religions. From almost all periods come texts that indicate the uniqueness of one or the other gods, usually some form of the sun god, but this monolatry or henotheism cannot be demonstrated to have the exclusivity necessary to fit the modern definition of monotheism.

There are numerous references to "god" and "the god" in Egyptian literary texts, particularly in the instructions. In some cases these may refer to a local god or to the king, but most frequently they refer to Re or Pre (the sun). He is often called the *neb-er-djer* ("lord to the limit, universal lord"), and can indeed appear practically transcendent, as in the *Instruction for Merikare,* quoted above. The only important point lacking here is a statement that no other god exists, but of course this can also be said of the Hebrew Bible and the New Testament. Tradition is the principal source for both the Jewish and the Christian monotheistic doctrine, but it is lacking for Egyptian religion. Without this tradition the multiplicity of denominations and sects, the veneration of saints, and the loose use of "divine" and "godlike" for popular heroes would all conspire to challenge the generally accepted monotheistic aspect of modern Western religions and of Western civilization. For the Atenist heresy of Akhenaton the situation is somewhat different, since the *Hymn to the Aton* states that there is no god beside (or like) Aton, there was an attack on other gods and the plural "gods," and Akhenaton was later clearly regarded as having attempted to disrupt the established religious system. Most likely the notion of monotheism was present in this period, in some minds at least, though it was harshly dispelled. By syncretizing the names and aspects of various deities into powerful new gods, the Egyptians widened the gap between the greatest god and all the rest. Re-Atum, Amun-Re, and Pre-Harakhty were unchallenged national gods each in his own time.

Probably second in importance to the great national gods was the cult of the god of the dead. This evolved very early, evidently from several separate cults. The cult of Osiris, originally from Busiris, superseded the cults of Khentyimentiu ("foremost of the westerners") and Wepwawet ("opener of the ways") from Abydos and Siut, respectively. The cults of Osiris and Re intermingle in most of the mortuary literature, and in at least one instance come close to merging. When the cult of Sokar becomes a major element in royal funerary literature and later in all the funerary literature of the New Kingdom, it leads to perhaps the ultimate syncretism in the late New Kingdom of Ptah-Sokar-Osiris-Tatenen.

The Osiris cult certainly permeated almost all aspects of Egyptian culture. Osirid statues decorated the courts of temples, and the Osiris suites are a major feature of the mortuary temples. Every owner of a book of mortuary literature is given the title "Osiris," and every deceased person named in tomb or stela has the epithet "true of voice" or "vindicated" with respect to his last judgment before this great god. The association of Osiris with death, resurrection, fertility, and the Nile touched everyone, and his cult center at Abydos, where he was supposed to have been buried, became the most important pilgrimage site in the country.

The living king is generally called the "good god," while the deceased king is the "great god." Whether death actually enhanced the king's status is debatable. As the embodiment or incarnation of the god Horus, he is already a major god on earth, and much of the doctrine of his divinity and his perquisites was widely published and accepted. Certainly the king who instructed Merikare was more aware personally of his limitations than Senusret III or Ramses II would have been. The whole concept could have been viewed in different ways at different times by different people. Based on the number of persons who had as their goal in the afterlife something approaching or equaling the goals of their kings, perhaps more would have believed in their sovereign's divinity and their own potential divinity than some modern scholars are now prepared to accept. Of course there are exceptions—the *Song of the Harper* and the story of the *Man Who Was Tired of Life* both reflect despair about the afterlife. Some kings were assassinated, and all the royal tombs were robbed. Aware of the difficulty of securing their burials, the Egyptians tried incredible masses of stone, secret hidden passages, tricks, provision of security guards, and also magic and curses. In a sense all of these would have been attempts by believers to thwart the unbelievers.

Some individuals, even nonroyal personages, attained a state of divinity far above the ordinary. The cult of deceased kings would generally not have outlived the endowment of their funerary establishment, but Amenhotep I, together with his mother, Ahmose Nefertari, continued for centuries to be venerated by the workmen of Deir al-Medineh as the great patrons or patron saints of the place. The architect of the step pyramid of Djoser at Saqqara, Imhotep, was deified, and his cult became ever more popular more than two millennia after his death. He was revered as a sage and was also identified with the Greek god Asklepios. Another architect and sage, Amenhotep Son of hapu (the epithet is traditionally part of his name), was also exceptionally revered. In sum, the Egyptians seem to have had a number of different levels of divinity, several equivalent to different levels of sainthood, with only one word, *netjer,* to cover them all.

Worship of animals does not seem to have been a significant element in any of the religions of Egypt. The use of animals to represent some attributes of gods, or the gods themselves, is frequent, and in most religious artwork their primary importance is clearly in differentiating the principals. The conventional linking of the falcon with Horus, the falcon and disk with Re, the cow with Hathor, the baboon or ibis with Thoth, the jackal with Anubis, the crocodile with Sobek, and the ram with Amun-Re was generally recognized throughout the country and in all periods following its formulation, whereas strictly anthropomorphic representations would have been confusing. It is possible that for some ritual reenactments priests would have worn the animal masks of the gods and recited the words attributed to the gods in numerous temple reliefs. The cobra Edjo of Buto and the vulture Nekhbet of Al-Kab are usually represented in their totally animal forms, but they are protective deities for the king of Upper and Lower Egypt, and were more intimidating in this form.

The often malevolent but sometimes protective deity Seth is represented as either partially or totally animal, though there was in antiquity, and there is now, little agreement as to what the animal was. Pig, hippopotamus, donkey, hound, and giraffe are all plausible in different documents or reliefs. Evil beings or demons are often composite, fanciful creations that must be armed with knives to be really threatening. The evil serpent Apophis, perhaps the greatest demon, is repulsed from attacking the sun god by means of numerous serpent spells, but it is also driven back by the spears, and bows and arrows of protecting deities such as the four sons of Horus—Imesty, Hapi, Duamutef, and Khebeksenuef—who are also the protective gods represented on the Canopic jars containing the internal organs of the mummified dead.

Although oxen and smaller cattle were among the offerings made to the gods in their temples, the Apis bull, which was emblematic of and sacred to Ptah in the New Kingdom and later, had a very special position and would have been considered by many as the embodiment of a god on earth. Burials of each successive Apis bull and its cow mother were performed with great solemnity. Later, in the Greek period, the proliferation of cemeteries for mummified cats sacred to both Bast and Paket, crocodiles sacred to Sobek, ibises sacred to Thoth and Imhotep, baboons sacred to Thoth, and falcons sacred to Horus reached all parts of Egypt, to the point that demand for some of these creatures as votive offerings began to exceed the supplies available; sometimes people who thought they had purchased jars with mummified animals actually left sealed jars of sand to be buried in the huge catacombs at sacred sites.

Magic was clearly a significant aspect of Egyptian life. Again, as noted in the *Instruction for Merikare*, magic was considered a gift of the great god, Re. There was a goddess called Weret-Hekau (Great of Magic), and several texts refer to the books containing the secret knowledge of Thoth, whom the Greeks later identified with Hermes and whose legendary knowledge is still being touted by certain groups today (e.g., the Rosicrucians). The Egyptians had magical spells believed to prolong life, to alter fate, to help in romance, and to combat any number of physical and mental afflictions. A combination of entreaty and threat is found in one type of love charm:

> Hail to you, Re-Harakhty, father of the gods!
> Hail to you, Seven Hathors, who are adorned with strings of red thread!
> Hail to you, all the gods of heaven and earth!
> Come make so-and-so [f.] born of so-and-so come after me,
> Like an ox after grass, like a nursemaid after her children, like a
>   herdsman after his herd!
> If you do not make her come after me, then I will set fire to Busiris
>   and burn Osiris.

Some magic spells survive in the funerary literature, some references occur in the literature, and much is found in the medical texts. The rubrics of chapters in the New Kingdom *Book of Going Forth by Day* frequently provide information about the very ancient origins of these spells for transformation and glorification, and they also provide instructions concerning the rites accompanying recitation of the spells. In some cases complete secrecy is required, and we frequently encounter the claim that a particular spell was tried and proved a million times. Chapter 64 of the *Book of Going Forth by Day* is "The Chapter for Knowing the Chapters of Coming Forth by Day in a Single Chapter." Its rubric adds:

> *If this chapter is known by the deceased, he will be mighty both on earth and in the otherworld, and he will perform every act of a living person. It is a great protection that has been given by God. This chapter was found in the city of Hermopolis on a block of iron of the south, which has been inlaid with real lapis lazuli, under the feet of the god during the reign of his majesty, the king of Upper and Lower Egypt, Menkaure, justified [i.e., deceased], by Prince Hordedef, justified. He found it when he was journeying to make an inspection of the temples. One Nakht was with him who was diligent in making him understand it, and he brought it to the king as a wonderful object when he saw that it was a thing of great mystery, which had never before been seen or looked upon.*
>
> *This chapter shall be recited by a man who is ritually clean and pure, who has not eaten the flesh of animals or fish, and who has not had intercourse with women. And you shall make a scarab of green stone, with a rim plated with gold, which shall be placed in the heart of a man, and it shall perform for him the opening of the mouth. And you shall anoint it with anti-unguent, and you shall recite over it these spells. . . .*

The words that follow are the heart spell of chapter 30. The discovery of the text by such a famous sage in so significant a place clearly enhanced its value.

Those Egyptian medical texts that deal with surgical procedures tend to be reasonably scientific, but for the vast majority of human ailments treated in most medical texts the Egyptians relied on magic—potions, poultices, or salves applied with written or recited spells. Headaches and stomach disorders are obvious targets, and there are lengthy series of spells for hastening birth that recall the travail of Isis in giving birth to Horus.

Magic was also used in the Execration Texts, which the Egyptians devised to overcome enemies perhaps too difficult to overcome by any other means. These bowls or figurines, inscribed with a fairly standard selection of the names of Egypt's foreign and domestic enemies plus all evil thoughts, words, and deeds, were deliberately smashed to try to destroy any and all persons and things listed thereon.

The Opening of the Mouth ritual, already referred to above, was obviously a magical rite to bring to life mummies and other representations of individuals. Sculpted portraits (called reserve heads) in Old Kingdom mastaba tombs were magical stand-ins. The eradication from statues, stelae, and tomb and temple walls of names and representations of individuals was thought to be a way of eliminating those persons magically. The texts in some tombs had the animal hieroglyphs either halved or with knives in them, to prevent them from being a danger to the deceased. The names of individuals involved in the harem conspiracy against Ramses III were often changed in the records to evil-sounding names, primarily so that the evil person's memory would not live on. In this same conspiracy, magic was also apparently involved in the making of waxen images by the conspirators. Exactly how these were to be used is unclear.

In addition to reserve heads and *ka*-statues, the deceased in his tomb frequently had a supply of servant statues. In the earlier periods they were shown doing exactly what they would have done in life, but in the New Kingdom they were represented merely as mummified figures, with chapter 6 of the *Book of Going Forth by Day* written on them. This is the magic spell that says that if the deceased is called upon to do any work in the afterlife, such as moving sand from one bank to another, the "answerer" (the figurine) will respond that he is present to do it. A different type of magic is found in the *Cannibal Hymn,* in Pyramid Text utterances 273–274. Here the deceased king goes about devouring the gods, both to demonstrate that he has gained power over them in death and in order to acquire their strength and attributes.

POPULAR RELIGION AND PERSONAL PIETY

Among the numerous amulets used by the Egyptians a few stand out and deserve attention. Probably the best-known amulet and symbol is the *ankh* sign, the hieroglyph for "life," which is most frequently shown being presented by the gods to men. Considerably more important for the Egyptians was the *Udjat-eye,* the eye of Horus, which symbolized the sacrifice endured by Horus in his struggle to avenge his father's murder. This eye was used to designate any offering or sacrifice and also to represent the sun and the moon gods and their barks. Similar falcon eyes are found on the fronts of Middle Kingdom coffins, presumably to enable the deceased to see; on the prows of boats and in mummy wrappings these might also have been chosen to ward off evil.

The scarab bettle was a symbol that had religious significance, but it was frequently used for the very practical purpose of identification, as a seal bearing the owner's name on its flat underside. Some scarabs have ornamental decoration and the vast majority have royal names, usually of Thutmose III or Ramses II. The scarab itself was a symbol of the sun god, apparently derived from the image of this beetle slowly pushing along a nutritious ball of dung. The Egyptian word for this beetle was *kheper,* a homonym for their word meaning "to come to be" or "to happen," and the word also became the name of the early-morning sun deity. Re, then, is the powerful and bright noonday sun, and Atum the old and worn-out evening sun.

Two symbolic figures often found on amulets seem to have been primarily associated with household deities and were particularly important for their connection with fertility and the successful conclusion of pregnancy. These are of the gods Bes, the grotesque human-faced baboon or monkey, and Taweret, the not very attractive female hippopotamus/crocodile who stands on her hind legs and holds another amulet, the "knot of Isis," in her hands. Amulets of the frog goddess, Heket, and the knot of Isis were probably used similarly by women. The feather of Maat (Truth or Justice) also symbolized order, and in those countless temple scenes showing the king presenting to various deities the small figure of the goddess wearing the feather and seated on a basket, the king is both claiming and promising to preserve order on earth on behalf of all the other gods. The plump hermaphrodite figures of Happy are symbolic of the fertility of the Nile in flood and are frequently shown typing together the sedge plant of Upper Egypt and the papyrus of Lower Egypt.

The numerous stelae and votive offerings left at cult centers provide adequate testimony of the personal piety of the Egyptians. Many of the stelae were inscribed with a plea to the god of the place, and some had a human earor ears carved on them as if to entreat the god to be especially attentive. Since the common people would not have had access to the god in the interior of his temple, they had their own preferred shrines, statues, or reliefs of the god (often Amun) "who hears prayers" outside the temple proper but within the sacred precincts. If they were patient they could wait to approach the god on his processions in connection with major feasts. These occasions were regularly used to make requests of the gods, and the nod of the god, perhaps aided by the shoulders of the men carrying the god, was considered a significant oracular response. The "power" or "manifestation" of a god is mentioned in several texts as punishment for an offense (e.g., being blinded for lying) or as a force compelling a person to recant earlier testimony. Some women called "knowledgeable" could use their powers for conjuring or healing. Omens were important to the Egyptians, many different dreams were interpreted as good or bad, and at least by the Late Period they had calendars of lucky and unlucky days.

One final indication of the religiosity of the Egyptians and also of their trust in magic is the very frequent occurrence, both on stelae and in graffiti, of a list of good works the writer had done, followed by his request that any passerby reading the text pronounce his name and the formula "A thousand bread, beer, oxen, and fowl," so that some day he would magically receive these stereotypical offerings. The Egyptians had a great deal of confidence in both the written and the spoken word and a proper respect for things sacred. A women from Deir al-Medineh accused of stealing a workman's tool compounded her guilt enormously when she swore a false oath and it was discovered that she stole not only the tool but also a vessel from a temple.

TEMPLES

The priests and priestesses of ancient Egypt included a very high percentage of the population. The king himself seems to have been the principal intermediary between gods and men. He is shown making offerings, pouring libations, and burning incense before almost all the gods in all the temples. How much of the ing's time was actually spent in religious ritual is not known and probably varied from dynasty to dynasty and from one king to another. The large amount of civil authority delegated to viziers would have released time for more religious activities if that were desired. Some kings, however, seem to have preferred leading military expeditions, perhaps finding these more essential or more interesting.

The actual high priests of each temple had different titles. The word used most frequently was *hem-netjer* ("servant of the god"), which the Greeks rendered as "prophet." The great temple of Amun-Re at Karnak had four ranked prophets, and the first prophet had one of the highest positions in the land. In addition to his religious duties involving the daily temple ritual and rites connected with many special feasts, he exercised temporal power over a vast amount of landholdings and over the people who worked those lands. He also served as a judge in the tribunal headed by the vizier. Some did rise to the higher priestly offices by coming up through the ranks and being recognized for their abilities, but it was also the case that they could start at the top, apparently with the king's patronage. Royal princes frequently held the post of high priest of the temple of Ptah at Memphis. At Thebes the office of high priest often was hereditary, and it became a power base from which individuals could claim and acquire the kingship of the entire land (twenty-first dynasty).

Little is known about the lesser prophets, though the office of second prophet seems in one case to have been given over to a queen, Akhmose Nefertari of the eighteenth dynasty, either to exercise the office or to award it to another. Later a famous fourth prophet of Amun, Montuemhet (twenty-sixth dynasty), was simultaneously mayor of Thebes, and his great wealth and prestige probably accrued from that position. It is not known whether any of these figureheads and administrators were also knowledgeable theologians.

Those temple scribes who were familiar with the sacred writings were called *chery-heb* ("lector priest"). It was their responsibility to interpret omens and dreams, to know the magical spells required for any eventuality, and to read the required texts for the rituals of embalmment and burial. The scribes most likely also provided the copies of funerary texts that people wanted to be buried with, and would either have served as physicians themselves or would have provided the magical medical spells that the physicians used.

In all the temples most of the lesser tasks were in the hands of the faithful. All would be called upon to do their monthly service, and since they were regularly divided into four phylae, this meant that they alternated but served three months out of the year. These common priests (*wabu,* "pure ones") shaved their hair, washed frequently in the sacred lakes near the temples, and maintained ritual purity to enable them to serve the god in his mansion. They served as porters, watchmen, and attendants, assisted with offerings and rites, and probably did their share of cleaning, polishing, painting, and moving things around.

There was of course a major distinction between the city cult temples and the mortuary temple establishments. The great mortuary temples grew out of the smaller chapels erected above shaft tombs, and these in turn developed from the small offering niches in Old Kingdom mastaba tombs. The offerings to be left at the chapels of nobles or temples of kings were provided by endowments, and the priests who administered the endowments were called *hemu-ka* ("servants of the *ka*"). If the endowment included lands, the produce would have provided offerings as well as an income for the individual "priests." They would also benefit from the unconsumed offerings that they provided each day. These endowments became an important part of the individual's property and tended to be collected and handed on to heirs.

Women in all periods shared at least some priestly responsibilities and enjoyed priestly titles. In the Old Kingdom many women were priestesses of Hathor, Neith, or Nut. In the early New Kingdom the great royal wives were also the "god's wives of Amun" and as such bore the next divine son, but they did as well participate with male priests in temple rites. Of course Hatshepsut as king (she took the masculine title, and even wore a false beard) was also priest, but remarkably, Nefertiti appeared alone or with her daughter, making offerings to her god, Aton. The wives of nobles and even the working women of Deir al-Medineh were very frequently called songstresses of Amun and were depicted in tombs bearing two symbols of this office, the sistrum and the *menit*-necklace, with which they provided musical accompaniment for rituals at both the great and the lesser temples. Women in general also served as *ka*-priests and professional mourners. In the late New Kingdom the wives of the high priests of Amun held the title of chief concubine of Amun-Re, but while it is known that they had a great deal of influence, it is not known precisely what religious responsibilities they had. Daughters of the first prophets of Amun were given the title of "God's Wife" in the twenty-first dynasty, and then, to assume greater control of the south, the Tanite kings gave this position to their own daughters. The next step in the process is the evolution of a new position, that of Divine Adoratress, from the office of God's Wife; the new position is clearly ranked above that of the high priest. Since the Divine Adoratress remains a virgin, she adopts her successor from among the daughters of the king.

The Egyptian temple was the mansion of the god, his abode on earth or, at least, the abode of his principal cult statue. The daily ritual for a god in his temple was limited to a few priests present, and consisted of their approaching the sanctuary, opening the shrine, removing the statue, undressing it, washing it, censing it, making offerings to it, clothing it in fresh garments, replacing it, sealing the shrine, and retreating, with care taken to sweep away their footprints. Although the faithful did not have the opportunity to participate in the daily ritual, they were able to see the god during special feasts, when the statue of the god would leave the temple. For the feast of Opet the statue and shrine of the god Amun-Re was taken from its sanctuary at the Karnak temple, placed on a bark held aloft by priests with carrying poles on their shoulders, and carried to its river transport for the two-mile voyage to the Luxor temple, the southern harem, for a sojourn there before the return voyage. The Beautiful Feast of the Valley involved Amun-Re's voyage across the river to western Thebes to visit the major temples there, but numerous stops were made at small temples and way stations along the route. In addition to these great feasts of Amun-Re recorded at the Luxor and Karnak temples, the mortuary temple of Ramses III at Medinet Habu contains records of the festival processions of Min and Sokar illustrated in great detail.

MYTHOLOGY

Mythology is encountered in almost everything that survives from ancient Egypt. Texts, whether religious, historical, literary, medical, or legal, or merely personal correspondence, all contain mythological allusions. Art of all kinds and on all scales, and artifacts of all types, made use of easily recognizable mythological symbols. This does not mean that everything had a ritual purpose or that the Egyptians had narrow one-track minds, but it does show how mythology and religion had permeated the culture, and also how artisans and craftsmen could capitalize on this.

It is not surprising to find that the Egyptians' mythology was not detailed and collected in any one place, but surely the various traditions were handed down by word of mouth and were generally well known. Temple libraries, known in the Late Period as "houses of life," certainly contained medico-magical texts, and also would have had many ritual, historical, and theological texts and treatises. Many of these contained mythological material, but none was entitled *Egyptian Mythology*. There may have been individual texts relating to the individual cults or sites, such as Papyrus Jumilac. The cosmogonical myths that were excerpted for use in the mortuary literature and that have been briefly summarized above were included in the Pyramid Texts to indicate the power of the king, his genealogy, or his goal, rather than to explain or justify the other gods. The temple texts of individual gods are remarkable for the little mythological information they contain and the vast amount of knowledge they presume.

Some texts, such as the *Story of the Two Brothers* and the *Blinding of Truth by Falsehood,* are in large part mythological without being mythic in purpose. The

Contendings of Horus and Seth has a totally mythological setting, but it is a burlesque of the real myth, and perhaps a sophisticated attack on the entire pantheon
as well. The *Myth of the Destruction of Mankind* is slightly more serious in intent,
showing men to be totally at the mercy of the gods if they cross them. In this myth
Hathor was sent to slay men because they had plotted in the presence of Re, but Re
decided to save them by making bloodlike red beer to deceive and distract her. The
goddess became so drunk that she could not perceive mankind, and what had begun
as a story about punishment for sin becomes an etiological explanation for drinking
to the point of drunkenness at the feast of Hathor. Another remarkable document
from the late Ptolemaic period is Papyrus Jumilac, which provides the entire religious history, largely mythological, of the otherwise little known eighteenth nome
of Upper Egypt.

SURVIVALS

Egyptian religion does not seem to have been greatly changed by any outside influences. In the New Kingdom several Asiatic deities were introduced into the Egyptian
pantheon, including Reshef, Kadesh, Anat, and Astarte. The story of *Astarte and the
Insatiable Sea* has been proposed as one example of Egyptian borrowing from the
Ugaritic *Poem of Baal,* but the counterargument for the indigenous nature of most
of the contents of this text posits that only the names of the principals were changed
to those of well-known Semitic deities. The Canaanite god Baal was regularly identified with Seth, and later many Greek gods became identified with the older Egyptian gods (e.g., Hermes-Thoth, Hephaistos-Ptah, and Min-Pan). The Isis-aretalogies
that survive in Greek have a few descriptions of the goddess that may be traced back
to Egyptian antecedents, but for the most part the composition appears to have been
primarily Greek. Many scholars have seen similarities between the Egyptian *Hymn
to the Aton* and the biblical *Psalms,* the *Instruction of Amenemope* and *Proverbs,* or
the collections of Egyptian love songs and the *Song of Songs.* If there were instances
of borrowing (and this is not universally accepted), they would in each case have
been from the slightly earlier Egyptian texts.

Among the religious survivals from ancient Egypt, the language used in the Coptic
Christian liturgy down to the present time represents the latest stage of ancient
Egyptian, but it is written in the Greek alphabet. The decoration of early Coptic
textiles used as vestments had incorporated *ankh* signs as well as *udjat*-eyes. As
noted above, the institution of monasticism in both its eremetic and cenobitic forms,
and the earliest monastic rule, can be clearly traced to Egypt. Whether the late cult
of Isis had any influence on the story of the Blessed Virgin, or whether the story of
the death and resurrection of Osiris influenced the gospel narrative of Christ, would
be hotly contested by many Christians. In doctrinal matters it has been proposed
that the Egyptian triads (such as that of Amun, Mut, and Khonsu of Thebes) influenced the concepts of the Trinity and the Holy Family, and that descriptions of the
Field of Hetep (paradise) and of places of torment in the afterlife were predecessors
for the concepts of heaven and hell. Slightly less controversial would be the question
of Egyptian influence on the doctrines of the resurrection of the body and the communion of saints. The traditional sites for the finding of the infant Moses at the
river's edge, and the places visited by the Holy Family on their sojourn in Egypt, are
indeed very old, but how accurate they are historically is questionable. Surviving

traditions in modern Egypt include the use of mourners at funerals, visits to tombs, the leaving of food offerings, and the burning of incense at services. Modern beliefs in afreets or ghosts certainly have ancient roots, and the modern Luxor processions carrying boats on the feast of the Muslim saint Abul Hagag are clearly reminiscent of ancient festivals.

CONCLUSIONS

In general the Egyptians seem to have been very religious, believed in an afterlife, and devoted much of their energy to preparing for this. Their preparations included both the physical burial equipment and the spiritual: rites, temple services, offerings, good works, and avoidance of evil deeds. They believed that they were destined from birth to a particular fate, but they were also optimistic that they could, perhaps with the help of a god, change an unfortunate fate. They desired a long life and eventually a proper Egyptian burial. To a great extent they wanted to continue living after death a life very like their life on earth. They were clearly optimistic about vindication in a last judgment and their ability to attain the highest goals in the afterlife.

Two characteristic features of Egyptian religious literature are syncretism and a multiplicity of approaches, and these perhaps show steps in the process of developing doctrine. In the case of the descriptions of the afterlife, the Egyptians could on the one hand place separate, mutually exclusive descriptions side by side without indicating that one is better or more accurate than another; on the other hand, they could combine in the same document aspects from different traditions in a new, apparently superior, composite, and theoretically logical entity. Perhaps this was one way of dealing with the problem of conservatively maintaining the old while also accepting the new.

The Egyptians did not believe in the transmigration of souls, but among the hymns, guidebooks, offering texts, and rituals with which the deceased were buried are many spells for transformations—often into the form of birds, perhaps because of a desire to achieve their apparent freedom. Presumably, an Egyptian purchased the texts he wanted well in advance of his death. Some manuscripts could have been read in advance by their owners, but many texts are quite flawed in extant copies and might not have been intelligible even if the person had bothered to read them. Scribes also had serious problems understanding some texts, and in at least one case (*Book of Going Forth by Day,* chap. 17) a tradition of various interpretations is handed down in the form of glosses incorporated into the text.

Hymns are probably a good gauge of the religiosity and sophistication of the priest-scribes and theologians, as well as of the believers, of ancient Egypt. The short hymns, perhaps excerpts, found in the earlier mortuary literature eventually developed into carefully constructed, easily read, edifying, and glowing tributes to the gods that spell out the gods' links with nature and their special concern for mankind. The *Hymn to the Nile,* the *Hymn to Amun-Re,* the *Hymn to the Aton,* hymns found in nobles' tombs to the rising and setting sun, and the hymns to Osiris and to Re in the *Book of Going Forth by Day* might not be as exciting and different as the so-called *Cannibal Hymn.* But these were very proper and popular works, indicating a considerable refinement in ancient Egypt that is not often recognized and appreciated by historians of religion.

BIBLIOGRAPHY

Allen, Thomas George. *The Book of the Dead or Going Forth by Day.* Chicago, 1974.

Anthes, Rudolf. "Egyptian Theology in the Third Millennium B.C." *Journal of Near Eastern Studies* 18 (1959): 170–212.

Assmann, Jan. *Ägyptische Hymnen und Gebete.* Zurich, 1975.

Bell, H. Idris. *Cults and Creeds of Graeco-Roman Egypt.* Liverpool, 1953.

Bonnet, Hans. *Reallexikon der ägyptischen Religionsgeschichte.* Berlin, 1952.

Breasted, James H. *The Development of Religion and Thought in Ancient Egypt.* New York, 1912.

Černý, Jaroslav. *Ancient Egyptian Religion.* London, 1952.

Englund, Gertie. *Akh: Une notion religieuse dans l'Égypte pharaonique.* Uppsala, 1978.

Erman, Adolf. *Die Religion der Ägypter: Ihr Werden und ihr Vergehen in vier Jahrtausenden.* Berlin, 1934.

Faulkner, Raymond. *The Ancient Egyptian Pyramid Texts.* Oxford, 1969.

Faulkner, Raymond. *The Ancient Egyptian Coffin Texts.* 3 vols. Oxford, 1973–1978.

Frankfort, Henri. *Kingship and the Gods.* Chicago, 1948.

Frankfort, Henri. *Before Philosophy.* Baltimore, 1954.

Frankfort, Henri. *Ancient Egyptian Religion.* New York, 1961.

Greven, Liselotte. *Der Ka in Theologie und Königskult der Ägypter des Alten Reiches.* Glückstadt, 1952.

Griffiths, J. Gwyn. *The Origins of Osiris and His Cult.* Leiden, 1980.

Hornung, Erik. *Altägyptische Höllenvorstellungen.* Leipzig, 1968.

Hornung, Erik. *Ägyptische Unterweltsbücher.* Zurich, 1972.

Hornung, Erik. *Conceptions of God in Ancient Egypt.* Ithaca, N.Y., 1982.

Junker, Hermann. *Die Götterlehre von Memphis (Schabaka-Inschrift).* Berlin, 1940.

Kees, Hermann. *Das Priestertum in ägyptischen Staat vom Neuen Reich bis zur Spätzeit.* Leiden, 1953.

Kees, Hermann. *Der Götterglaube im alten Ägypten.* 2d ed. Berlin, 1956.

Kees, Hermann. *Totenglauben und Jenseitsvorstellungen der alten Ägypter.* 2d ed. Berlin, 1956.

Lesko, Leonard H. "Some Observations on the Composition of the Book of Two Ways." *Journal of the American Oriental Society* 91 (1971): 30–43.

Lesko, Leonard H. "The Field of Hetep in Egyptian Coffin Texts." *Journal of the American Research Center in Egypt* 9 (1971–1972): 89–101.

Morenz, Siegfried. *Egyptian Religion.* Ithaca, N.Y., 1973.

Morenz, Siegfried. *Religion und Geschichte des alten Ägypten: Gesammelte Aufsätze.* Weimar, 1975.

Morenz, Siegfried, and Dieter Müller. *Untersuchungen zur Rolle des Schicksals in der ägyptischen Religion.* Berlin, 1960.

Moret, Alexandre. *Le rituel du culte divin journalier en Égypte d'après les papyrus de Berlin et les textes du temple de Séti Premier à Abydos.* Paris, 1902.

Mueller, Dieter. "An Early Egyptian Guide to the Hereafter." *Journal of Egyptian Archaeology* 58 (1972): 99–125.

Otto, Eberhard. *Das Ägyptische Mundöffnungsritual.* Wiesbaden, 1960.

Piankoff, Alexandre. *Shrines of Tut-Ankh-Amon.* Princeton, 1955.

Piankoff, Alexandre. *The Wandering of the Soul.* Princeton, 1974.

Posener, Georges. *De la divinité du Pharaon.* Paris, 1960.

Sauneron, Serge. *Les prêtres de l'ancienne Égypte.* Paris, 1957.

Sauneron, Serge. *Les fêtes religieuses d'Esna.* Cairo, 1962.

Schweitzer, Ursula. *Das Wesen des Ka im Diesseits und Jenseits der alten Ägypter.* Glückstadt, 1956.

Sethe, Kurt H. *Dramatische Texte zu den altägyptischen Mysterienspielen.* Leipzig, 1928.

Sethe, Kurt H. *Amun und die acht Urgötter von Hermopolis.* Berlin, 1929.

Sethe, Kurt H. *Urgeschichte und älteste Religion der Ägypter.* Leipzig, 1930.

Spiegel, Joachim. "Das Auferstehungsritual der Unaspyramide." *Annales du Service des Antiquités de l'Égypte* 53 (1956): 339–439.

Vandier, Jacques. *La religion égyptienne.* Paris, 1944.

Vandier, Jacques. *Le Papyrus Jumilhac.* Paris, 1961.

Westendorf, Wolfhart, ed. *Aspekte der spätägyptischen Religion.* Wiesbaden, 1979.

Wilson, John A. *The Burden of Egypt.* Chicago, 1951.

Wolf, Walther. *Das schöne Fest von Opet.* Leipzig, 1931.

Žabkar, Louis V. *A Study of the Ba Concept in Ancient Egyptian Texts.* Chicago, 1968.

Zandee, Jan. *Death as an Enemy.* Leiden, 1960.

3

GODDESS WORSHIP IN THE ANCIENT NEAR EAST

MERLIN STONE

The veneration of goddesses in the ancient Near East was a major component in these cultures that belong to the most ancient civilizations of history. From the artifacts and information gleaned primarily from archaeological excavations in the areas now known as Arabia, Cyprus, Egypt, Iran, Iraq, Israel, Jordan, Lebanon, Sinai, Syria, and Turkey, evidence of goddess worship ranges from small godess statues of the eight millennium BCE found in Jericho to the suppression and closing of goddess shrines in Arabia during the seventh century CE.

Artifacts of goddess reverence from preliterate periods, such as small statues, murals, relief plaques, and other ritual objects, as well as the remains of goddess temples, have been brought to light from many areas of the Near East. Goddess statues found at Jarmo in northern Iraq are dated to the late seventh millennium BCE. At Çatal Hüyük, southeast of Konya in Turkey, statues, murals, and remains of temples containing goddess images are dated to the mid-seventh millennium, while goddess statues found at Hacilar, northwest of Antalya in Turkey, are dated to the mid-sixth millennium. Goddess statues discovered in the area along the Tigris river near Mosul and Erbil in Iraq are dated to the Hassuna period of the mid-sixth millennium. Excavations of the Halaf period settlements that stretched across Syria and northern Iraq revealed goddess statues from the early sixth millennium. From levels of early settlement at Ur and Uruk (later Erech, now Warka), northwest of Basra near the mouth of the Euphrates in Iraq, goddess statues are dated to the early fifth millennium, a few centuries earlier than the goddess statues and artifacts found at Badarian sites of Egypt.

Although evidence of goddess worship in the preliterate periods mentioned above provides a great deal of knowledge, the most specific and clarifying information about goddess reverence in the Near East survives from the literate civilizations of the third millennium onward. This is the information that has been obtained from the discovery and deciphering of ancient writings that include inscriptions, temple documents, law codes, epic legends, prayers, and other written materials related to the worship of the goddess. These ancient writings were once pressed into tablets of damp clay, inked by reed pens on papyri, carved into brick and stone, or even inscribed on such objects as statues, vases, and doorposts. They reveal the beliefs of ancient goddess worshipers through the words of the actual devotees who wrote of them beginning with the third millennium.

From this wealth of information it is now clear that no single name, symbol, image, set of rituals and beliefs, or natural element such as the sun, moon, earth, or stars can be said to represent all goddess reverence in the Near East. The artifacts and written evidence reveal numerous customs, rituals, and legends, a wide variety of symbols and attributes, and a vast array of names, titles, and epithets associated with the goddesses in these areas. To a great extent, this variety results from the existence of goddess worship in many quite separate geographic locations and for periods of thousands of years. Beliefs and imagery often varied even from one town or small settlement to another, each having developed its own local deities and beliefs. As ancient city-states or towns conquered or merged with others over the centuries, the deities and beliefs of the peoples also merged and were oftentimes synthesized into ever more complex theological systems. To add to this complexity, a great number of titles and epithets were applied to goddess figures, many of these used to refer directly to the goddess, such as the titles of the goddess Anat of Ugarit in northern Canaan (western Syria), Balatu Darkati (lit., "lady of dominion") and Balatu Samen Ramem ("lady of the high heavens"), or the title of the goddess Asherah of Ugarit, Elat, meaning simply "goddess." The goddess Au Set of Egypt, better known as Isis, was known as "mother of one thousand names."

The wealth of evidence now available refutes several earlier assumptions about ancient goddess worship in the Near East. One of these was that goddess reverence was most often symbolically associated with the earth or the moon. We now know that several goddess figures were associated with the sun, such as Wurusemu of Anatolia (Turkey), who was most often referred to as the sun goddess of Arinna, and the goddess Shapash (Shaps), known as the sun in the texts of Ugarit. Writings concerning the goddess Inanna, whose worship was widespread in many areas of Sumer (southern Iraq), reveal that she was linked symbolically with the planet Venus, as were the Akkadian (Babylonian) goddess Ishtar, the goddess Eshtar of Ebla in northern Canaan, and the goddess Ashtoret (also known as Astarte) of Canaan and Cyprus. The symbolism of the planet Venus in the worship of Ashtoret emerges in later texts about the goddess Aphrodite of Cyprus and Greece and in the worship of the goddess known as Venus in Rome.

The goddess Au Set was associated with the star Sothis (Sirius), whereas the Egyptian goddess Nut, cited as the mother of Au Set, was depicted and described as the entire heavens, stars spread across her body as she was shown arching protectively over earth. The Sumerian goddess Nammu, who was described as the one who gave birth to heaven and earth and all other deities, was associated with the sea, as was Asherah, also known as the "mother of deities" in writings from Ugarit.

Although there were some Near Eastern goddess figures associated with the moon, such as Nikkal in Ugarit and Hekate in western Anatolia, and although the goddess Ninhursaga of Sumer may have been associated with the earth, the moon and earth were far from widespread symbolic elements linked to goddess reverence in the Near East, as is commonly believed. It is interesting to note that in Egypt the moon was represented by the male deity Khonsu, in Sumer by the male deity Nanna, and in Akkad by the male deity Sin; among the Hittites of Anatolia, who worshiped the sun goddess of Arinna, the moon was represented by the male deity Kushukh.

A second commonly held assumption is that all goddess worship of the ancient Near East can be categorized under the term "fertility cults." It is true that within the worship of certain Near Eastern goddess figures there were rituals and prayers for the greater abundance of crops and cattle. What is excluded by such a single-faceted term is a multitude of other aspects, attributes, and powers associated with ancient goddess figures.

Wurusemu, invoked as sovereign of heaven and earth, as well as Inanna, Ninlil, and Nanshe of Sumer, were each mentioned individually in the texts of various cities as the one who bestowed the divine right to rule and govern the land. Inanna was also said to hold the power of judgment and decision and the control of the law of heaven and earth. Ishtar was described in prayer as holding the fate of everything in her hand. Both Seshat (Sefchet) of Egypt and Nidaba (Nisaba) of Sumer were revered as the tutelary deities of writing and written language, whereas the goddess Sekhmet of Egypt, and Anat, Ishtar, and Ashtoret were each called upon for help in battle. In certain areas of Sumer, the goddess called Gula and Bau (Bawa) were invoked as divine physicians and the guardians of medicine and healing. The goddess Nanshe of the city of Girsu (Tello) in Sumer was described as the judge of all humankind on New Year's Day. She was also known as the guardian of ethics and morals who was concerned about compassion for the widow and the orphan, the weak and the poor. The Egyptian goddess Maat represented righteousness and truth; the hearts of those who had died were thought to be judged by being weighed on a scale against the weight of an ostrich feather that Maat wore in her headdress, good deeds keeping the heart light enough to enter the final field of peace. Both Seshat and Asherah were revered as tutelary deities of architecture and building.

The goddess Hathor of Egypt, whose worship was often brought into close alignment with Isis, gave life to people with the touch of her *ankh,* the ritual object that signified life. [*See* Cross.] Ishtar, and Nidaba, Ninsuna, and Nina of Sumer, as well as the goddess Buto (Ua Zit, Wadjet, Uatchit) of Egypt, were thought to prophesy the future through the oracular priestesses who tended their shrines. While the Sumerian goddess Nammu was credited with the creation of the universe and all other deities, her daughter Ninhursaga (Ninmah, Nintur) was described as the creator of people. The forming of humankind was attributed to the goddess as Aruru or Mama, known as "mother womb" and "creator of destiny" by the Akkadians. The goddess Cybele was invoked as "mother of deities," as was the Hurrian goddess Hepat and the Hittite Wurusemu; all three of these goddess figures are known from Anatolia. The goddess Nut, also called "mother of deities," and the goddess Ereshkigal of Sumer were described as those who watched over the dead; the goddess Ninsikil was regarded as the guardian deity of the Sumerian paradise, Dilmun. It is perhaps Isis about whom there is the most comprehensive information, derived from ancient Egyptian writings as well as from the later classics of Greece and Rome. Isis was described as the one from whom all being arose, oldest of the old, the one who makes the universe spin, the roadmaker of the paths of stars, the one who first established justice, who first gave law to the people, who had the power to make the Nile rise and irrigate the land, the inventor of agriculture, flaxen textiles, and the first sail.

Our present knowledge of the powers attributed to ancient goddess figures of the Near East now makes it clear that the earlier label of "fertility cults" falls quite short of encompassing the complex and multifaceted nature of goddess worship as it was known in ancient times. It is also vital to bear in mind that our information comprises only what has so far been discovered. Cities described in ancient texts as major religious centers of goddess worship, such as Arinna, said to be one day's journey from Hattushash (Boğazköy) in Turkey, and Per Uto (Buto), believed to be near or beneath Dessuk on the delta of Egypt, have not yet been specifically located. The relatively recent find of the city-state of Ebla in northwestern Syria, which has brought many surprises to both archaeology and religious history, revealed the name of the goddess worshiped there as Eshtar, establishing links among Ishtar of the Akkadians and Astarte of Canaan.

Once aware of the many differences in ancient goddess reverence, we may also observe certain similarities and connections that emerge from the evidence. According to one legend about Isis, as related by Plutarch, her brother-husband Osiris had been murdered in a plot engineered by their brother Seth. The coffer containing his body then floated up the Nile and out into the Mediterranean Sea, finally washing ashore at the Canaanite city of Byblos (Gebal). Through her continual efforts to find the body and give it a proper burial, the griefstricken Isis traced the body to the royal palace at Byblos. The coffer had become embedded in a tamarisk tree that had then been used for a pillar in the palace. Isis brought the body back to Egypt and hid it in the marshes of Buto, but Seth discovered the hiding place and cut the body into fourteen pieces. Isis then set out in a papyrus skiff and as she found each piece she gave it a solemn burial in the place she had found it. This legend is obviously linked to the frequently mentioned Egyptian belief that specific parts of Osiris were buried in separate locations of Egypt. Since Byblos is known to have been a trading port and possibly even a colony of Egypt from early dynastic periods, this legend also reflects the connections between goddess worship in the two areas. Lucian wrote that the rituals at Byblos, which were celebrated for the goddess Baalat and the death of her young consort Adonis, were actually much the same rituals as those for Isis and Osiris in Egypt. Several stone reliefs discovered at Byblos depict Baalat with images that are identical to those of the Egyptian Isis.

Other connections between goddess worship in separate areas may be seen in an inscribed prayer of Queen Pudu Hepa of fourteenth-century-BCE Hattushash. In this inscription Pudu Hepa stated that she regarded the goddess Hepat, whom she had worshiped when she was a Hurrian princess, as much the same goddess she then knew as a Hittite queen, the sun goddess of Arinna. Legends of Sumer and Akkad show that the goddess Ishtar was thought of as much the same deity as the Sumerian Inanna. This connection is most apparent in the legends of the *Descent of Ishtar* and the *Descent of Inanna,* both accounts describing the descent of the goddess into the underworld of the dead. Links among Egypt, Sinai, and Canaan are evident in inscriptions to Baalat discovered at Egyptian malachite mines at Serabit el Khadim on the Sinai peninsula, as well as in the multitude of small relief plaques of Astarte found in Canaan on which the image of the goddess also bears a very close resemblance to Egyptian images of Isis or Hathor. Showing the goddess standing upon a lion, holding serpents or flowers in her outstretched arms, these plaques were most often marked simply *qadesh* ("holy"). Judging from the number of them that have been discovered, they appear to have been owned by many people in the land of Canaan, even in Israelite areas and periods.

Another type of artifact that links goddess reverence in separate areas are certain stones, possibly meteorites, that were regarded as sacred to the goddess. [*See* Megalithic Religion, *article on* Prehistoric Evidence.] At the temple of Aphrodite at Paphos, Cyprus, a specific stone was anointed with oil each year on the feast day of the goddess, which was celebrated at about the time of the vernal equinox. A stone that was sacred to Baalat at Byblos was described by Sanchuniathon of Berytus (Beirut) as "containing the souls of all people." The Black Stone at Mecca is thought originally to have been sacred to the Arabian goddess al-'Uzzā, the "mighty one," whose shrine and worship existed at Mecca until the suppression of this worship upon the institution of Islam. Some of the most interesting events surround the black stone of Pessinus in Anatolia, sacred to the goddess Cybele. During the Roman battles with Carthage (Punic Wars) a sibylline oracle decreed that the Romans would win the war if the black stone of Cybele was brought to Rome. This was done in 204 BCE. The war ended shortly afterward and a temple for Cybele was built to house the stone in Rome. From that time, great processions and rituals were held for Cybele at the time of the vernal equinox. The Roman rituals included the commemoration of the death of Cybele's young lover Attis, an effigy of Attis hung upon a tree each year. It was said that three days after his death Attis rose from the dead, bringing salvation to the worshipers of Cybele.

In many areas of the ancient Near East, such as Sumer, Babylon, and Canaan, worshipers of the goddess, known as "sacred women" *(qadishtu* or *Ishtaritu),* performed sexual rituals within the temple complex. [*See* Hierodouleia.] These sexual rituals were included in a listing of cultural assets (the *mes*) that the goddess Inanna brought to Erech, as explained in the Sumerian legend, the *Transfer of the Arts of Civilization from Eridu to Erech.*

One of the similarities between goddess worship in different areas that has been of major interest to scholars is the relationship between the goddess and her less powerful young consort, sometimes described as her son. This relationship may be observed in legends and rituals concerning Inanna and Dumuzi, Ishtar and Tammuz, Astarte and Tammuz (or Eshmun or Adonis), and Cybele and Attis. The relationship of Astarte and Adonis survived in the Greek legends of Aphrodite and Adonis, most probably through the channel of the island of Cyprus, where the worship of Astarte and Aphrodite as "queen of heaven" was brought into close alignment at Citium, Amathus, and Paphos.

These consorts of the goddess appear to be the origin of ideas about kingship in the ancient Near East. The position of king was closely aligned with the idea of loving and being loved by the goddess. In several Sumerian texts the king is referred to as "the beloved of Inanna, fit for her holy lap." Sargon of Akkad wrote of his love and devotion to the goddess Ishtar and how she in turn provided him with special protection and privileges. The concept of divine right to the throne through a special connection with the goddess of the land was at times ritualized in a *hieros gamos,* a sacred marriage between the man who was to be king and the priestess who represented the goddess. [*See* Hieros Gamos.] The texts of King Shulgi of Ur in Sumer may be a record of the words spoken by the priestess and the king in the sacred marriage, for in them we read, "When he has made love to me on the bed, then I in turn shall show my love for the lord, I shall make for him a good destiny; I shall make him shepherd of the land" and "Goddess, I will perform for you the rites that constitute my royalty." These customs concerning kingship help to explain inscriptions such as the one describing Ishtar as "she who holds the reins of kings" and the one concerning the sun goddess of Arinna as "she who controls kingship in heaven and on earth." Such attitudes and rituals probably reflect earlier periods of matrilineal descent in which the right to the throne, or to leadership of the clan or tribe, was inherited through the female line.

An extremely interesting aspect of goddess worship in the ancient Near East is its repeated appearance in the Hebrew scriptures (Old Testament). We read in *Judges* 2:13 and 3:7 and in *1 Samuel* 7:3–4 that the religion of the goddess as Asherah or Astarte continually rivaled the religion of the Hebrew Yahveh. Writers of the Hebrew scriptures referred to Astarte as "Ashtoreth," a name that implied shame. Throughout *1* and *2 Kings* there are references to the installation of and reverence for the *ash-erim* (pl., also *asherot;* sg., *asherah*), which were wooden poles or trees, possibly carved, associated with the worship of the goddess Asherah.

In Judah, the southern Hebrew kingdom whose capital was in Jerusalem, kings such as Rehoboam, Jehoram, and Ahaziah were described as having erected the *asherim* or revering them. Judah's King Asa, who demolished and removed many of the sacramental objects of the Canaanite worship, deprived his own grandmother (or mother, according to a Masoretic text) Maacah of the position of queen mother because she had made an image of Asherah (*1 Kgs.* 15:13).

The kings of Israel, the northern Hebrew kingdom whose capital was in Samaria, were continually accused by the biblical writers of erecting and allowing *asherim* in the holy places of Israel. Kings Omri, Ahab, Joram, and even the sons of Jehu (the soldier king who massacred the entire house of Ahab in the name of Yahveh) were even more severely criticized for following the practices of the ancient Canaanite religion, which included the worship of Asherah. During the reign of King Ahab, his wife Jezebel kept a large number of clergy for Asherah in Samaria, cited as 400 in 1 Kings 18:19. Queen Jezebel was the daughter of the Sidonian King Ethbaal and had apparently been raised within the religion of Asherah. It seems to have been customary for Hebrew kings to allow their foreign wives to practice their own religions, for even before Ahab's time King Solomon not only allowed his Sidonian wife to worship Astarte in Jerusalem but took part in this worship himself (*1 Kgs.* 11:5, 11:33).

These references to Asherah in the biblical periods of the tenth to sixth centuries BCE in Judah and Israel were more fully understood upon the discovery of ancient Ugarit. In the Ugarit tablets there are many references to Asherah as the "mother of the deities," and to her worship not only in Ugarit but also in Tyre and Sidon.

The religious historian who studies goddess worship in the ancient Near East may spend a lifetime examining the enormous number of artifacts and writings related to the subject, arriving at various analyses and theories. But the most obvious fact may be of greatest interest to people of today—that in the lands that brought forth Judaism, Christianity, and Islam, God was once worshiped in the form of woman.

[*See also the entries on specific goddesses mentioned herein.*]

BIBLIOGRAPHY

Gordon, Cyrus H., trans. *Ugarit and Minoan Crete.* New York, 1966. Translations of poetry and prose texts from Ugarit of northern Canaan, containing many passages about Anat, Asherah, and Shapash.

Gurney, O. R. *The Hittites.* 2d ed. Harmondsworth, 1976. Overview of the Hittite civilization in central Anatolia that includes information about the sun goddess of Arinna, Hebat (Hepat), and Kubaba.

Kramer, Samuel Noah. *The Sumerians: Their History, Culture, and Character*. Chicago, 1963. Survey of this earliest of literate civilizations and its religious beliefs about goddess figures such as Nammu, Ninhursaga, Inanna, and others by the outstanding scholar who has deciphered so much of the written material from Sumer.

Langdon, Stephen. *Tammuz and Ishtar*. Oxford, 1914. Presentation of the texts and rituals concerned with the Akkadian Ishtar and the antecedents of this goddess in Sumer.

Pritchard, J. B., ed. *Ancient Near Eastern Texts relating to the Old Testament*. 3d ed. Princeton, 1969. An anthology of translations of writings from Egypt, Anatolia, Mesopotamia, and other areas of the ancient Near East. Includes long hymn to Ishtar translated by Ferris J. Stephens.

Stone, Merlin. *When God Was a Woman*. New York, 1976. A comprehensive account of goddess worship in the many cultures of the ancient Near East, providing an overview of legends, rituals, and beliefs about the deity as female. Includes a twelve-page bibliography for further study on the subject.

Stone, Merlin. *Ancient Mirrors of Womanhood: Our Goddess and Heroine Heritage*. 2 vols. New York, 1979. Includes accounts of individual goddess figures and an extensive bibliography.

4

HITTITE
RELIGION

Harry A. Hoffner, Jr.

The exact origin of the Hittites, an Indo-European people, is not known. Invading Asia Minor from the east, by the middle of the second millennium BCE they had established an empire covering the greater part of that region. Their empire declined after 1200 BCE, owing to Indo-European invasions and the growing power of Assyria.

NAMES OF GODS

Knowledge about Hittite society, culture, and religion has increased since the deciphering of their cuneiform writing, on clay tablets found early in the twentieth century AD at Bogazköy (in Turkey). Hittite society was ethnically and linguistically diverse, with Hattian, Hurrian, and even some Semitic elements, and this diversity is evident in the divine names.

The earliest identifiable stratum is the Hattian. The Hattians were resident in central Anatolia before the Indo-European Hittites arrived. They had a long tradition of settled urban life. It is understandable that a people open to influences from its neighbors, as the Hittites were, would early adopt the worship of Hattian deities. Because the Hattic language is still very poorly understood, we can only partially understand the meanings of the divine names. Some are common nouns for elements of nature: *Eshtan* ("sun, day") *Izzishtanu* ("favorable day"), *Kashku* ("moon"), *Kait* ("grain"). Others denote status: *Kattahha* ("queen"), *Wurunkatte* ("king of the land"), *Shulinkatte* ("king of the *suli*"), *Kattishhabi* ("king god"), *Teteshhawi* ("great god").

The Hurrian language is better understood than Hattic. Still, because the number of Hurrian words that we can translate is not large, it is not possible to interpret many Hurrian divine names. [See Hurrian Religion.] The influence of Sumerian and Akkadian religious vocabulary and divine epithets is obvious. Aya, Ishhara, Ellil (Enlil), Anu, and Alalu were originally Mesopotamian deities.

NATURE OF DEITY

In Hittite art the gods were depicted either by their animal totems or anthropomorphically. The texts concur in depicting them in human terms. Gods needed to eat, drink, sleep, and exercise. They needed companionship, ego-building, and love (including sexual intercourse). They made mistakes through lack of knowledge. They could be deceived. They needed to be informed by others. Each possessed a specialized skill that put him in demand by both mortals and other gods. In myths gods were born and died (i.e., were killed). But very little, if anything, indicates that they aged or became senile. That what they did was not always just or fair is clear from the prayers, in which the human petitioner chides them for mistakes and pleads for fair treatment. Although no god was omniscient, some possessed very wide knowledge and every god was superior to humans in knowledge. In instructions to priests and temple officials, mortals who thought to conceal their offenses from a god were warned of the futility of the attempt. Although every god was more powerful than any mortal, none was omnipotent, and degrees of power were quite diverse among them.

FUNCTIONS OF A DEITY

As each mortal had his rank and function in human society, so each deity had his position and role, not only among his fellow deities but in concourse with humanity and the cosmos.

General Functions. While it is not possible to completely reconstruct the hierarchy of Hittite deities, it is clear that in convocations of gods certain figures naturally assumed leadership. In the Old Hittite vanishing-god myths (see below) it is the storm god who presides. But although he presides, he is not always able to enforce his will on the other gods. He must ask advice, plead his case, and seek volunteers for missions. Occasionally he is able to command another figure.

Hierarchical organization is also seen in the New Hittite pantheon. There is a fixed sequence in the god-lists in the state treaties, and there is an order of both gods and goddesses in the processional reliefs at Yazılıkaya, near Bogazköy. In the myths *Kingship in Heaven* and *The Kingship of the God Lamma* we see how rival factions fight over the position of king of the gods. The god Lamma boasts that his exalted position allows him to control the other gods. In the prayers of Hattusilis III and of his queen, Puduhepa, lower-ranked gods are requested to present the mortals' prayers favorably to their superiors in the pantheon. To be sure, the question is not entirely one of rank. The intercessor god is usually a favorite child or grandchild of the senior god. Indeed, the hierarchy which we describe is that of a large, extended family in which the patriarch and matriarch possess considerable power to direct their descendants and the descendants of their brothers and sisters.

In their prayers the Hittites reminded the gods that they required worshipers who would bring regular food-offerings; thus it was in their own interest that they protect and bless the community of faithful worshipers. But aside from this maintenance of the cult, mortal assistance was rarely needed by the gods. In a mythological context we see examples in the two versions of the Illuyanka myth. The disabled storm god must be helped to vanquish his adversary, the great serpent Illuyanka. On the divine level he is assisted by the goddess Inara. She in turn, for no obvious reason, needs the help of the mortal Hupashiya, which she bargains for by consenting to have sexual intercourse with him. But though she subsequently lives with him as a sex partner, she dominates him completely and apparently punishes his unfaithfulness to her with death. Outside of the mythological texts, when a god needed the service of a mortal he revealed himself through omen, oracle, or dream. His request was always viewed as a command, which could not be ignored.

Gods "served" mortals by ensuring material prosperity, protecting them from enemies and natural catastrophes, hearing their prayers, making known to them their sins, and forgiving them (sometimes after a punishment). Although the Hittites apparently believed in an afterlife, at least for their kings and queens, there is no evidence that they prayed or made sacrifices in order to obtain life after death or a better quality of existence in that afterlife.

Specialized Functions. Just as there were storm gods who sent rain and winds to fertilize the crops and make them prosper, so there were deities of grain and vineyards, deities of the rivers who gave water for irrigation, deities of springs, deities of the forest, and deities of wildlife who gave success in hunting. Under the influence of Mesopotamian concepts, the sun god Ishtanu was the all-seeing dispenser of justice to humans and even to animals. There were war gods (the Zababa type) who gave victory to the Hittite armies. There was a god who could confer invisibility on the Hittite troops and enable them to attack the enemy by surprise. There were deities who sent and withdrew plagues, both upon the Hittites and their enemies. There were deities of human sexual potency. And although one might ask one's personal god for any of these boons, there were divine specialists for many tasks.

PANTHEON

The Hittites called the aggregate of gods and goddesses "the thousand gods," and there may indeed have been that many. The total number of divine names known from the tablets and inscriptions is slightly more than six hundred, a total arrived at by culling the entire written corpus. The number of deities worshiped in any one Hittite city or town would be much smaller. Lists of divine names are found in state treaties, where the gods of both contracting parties are invoked to ensure that the oaths taken will be kept. Divine names are sometimes listed together with offerings to be made to them either at a particular festival or during the course of a year. In the famous imperial sanctuary at Yazılıkaya, we see carved in low relief on the walls of the sanctuary a dual procession of gods and goddesses, the males proceeding from left to right and the females from right to left, with the chief male and female deities meeting at the architectural focus point. The total number of divine figures in the preserved parts of the two processions is seventy-one. This assemblage represents the official imperial pantheon of the last half century of the Hittite kingdom. It is a completely Hurrianized pantheon, with deities of the Hattian and Hittite-Luwian strata syncretized, where possible, with Hurrian deities. This process of syncretism made possible a considerable reduction in the total number of deities, since several could be included under one (in this case, Hurrian) name. Other divine names in the inscriptions may represent either gods without a cult (e.g. purely literary figures) or gods from cult sites away from the capital who were never admitted into the official state cult.

MYTHOLOGY

Mythological texts in the Hittite language may be subdivided into two groups: those of Anatolian origin and those of foreign origin. Myths deriving from Old Hittite originals are all Anatolian. The deities who figure in the Old Hittite Telepinu and

Illuyanka myths and the other disappearing-god myths are a mix of what Emmanuel Laroche calls Hattian and Asianic. The myth of the moon falling from heaven occurs in both a Hattic and a Hittite version. There is very little about the Hittite version that linguistically recalls Old Hittite, yet it is surely possible that a long tradition of recopying has removed almost all traces of its original Old Hittite language. Although Kamrushepa is a Hittite replacement for the original Hattic name of this goddess of magic, there is no reason to doubt that the myths in which she figures also belong to this Hattian group. All of the Anatolian myths are associated with incantations or rituals. The myths of non-Anatolian origin are all post–Old Hittite. They are generally independent of any incantation or ritual. One exception is the Ashertu myth, part of which describes a ritual to exorcize and purify Baal.

Vanishing-God Myths. These myths, the best known of which is about the god Telepinu, are paradigms for dealing with natural catastrophes such as drought, blight, and diseases affecting livestock. The god who disappears must be located, appeased, and brought back. On the mythological level this is accomplished by non-human agents. The bee searches for, finds, and stings awake the sleeping god. The goddess Kamrushepa carries out a ritual to appease him. When transferred to the real world of those who are suffering from such a catastrophe, the search for the missing god entails a determination by oracle of which god is angry. Texts recording such oracular inquiry are extremely common in the New Hittite period, but have now been identified in the Old Hittite script, showing that his procedure was probably as common in the earlier period as in the later one. The pacification and return of the god is accomplished by a magic ritual of the type called *mugawar* in Hittite. Directions for such *mugawar*s accompany the vanishing-god myths; other *mugawar*s are described in ritual texts. It is a characteristic ritual form among the Hittites.

Illuyanka Myths. Two stories on the same tablet are about the conflict between the storm god and his antagonist, the great serpent Illuyanka. *Illuyanka* is in fact not a name but a common noun, meaning "serpent" or "snake." But this particular reptile is clearly large and strong enough to have once defeated and disabled the storm god. In both stories the initially defeated storm god secures the help of a mortal who utilizes a trick to help the storm god triumph in his return match with the reptile. In the first version the goddess Inara and her mortal partner, Hupashiya, make Illuyanka and his brood drunk so that they cannot go back down into their hole in the ground. While they are helplessly drunk, Hupashiya ties them up, and when the storm god comes he is able to kill them. In the second version the storm god's own son by a mortal woman marries the daughter of Illuyanka and apparently uses his right as a son-in-law to ask a gift from Illuyanka. He receives his father's eyes and heart, which he passes on to the storm god. Renewed in his powers, the storm god defeats Illuyanka.

Like the vanishing-god myths, these two stories express natural catastrophes in the mythological terms of a disabled storm god. The disabled god is incapable of restoring himself and needs mortal cooperation, which is but a mythological counterpart of the actual mortal activity in the realm of magic rituals. The breakdown in nature is expressed mythologically as a giant serpent that must be subdued and killed. Reptiles are not a common symbol of evil in Hittite, but it is a fact that in the New Hittite myth of Hedammu a giant reptile is opposed by the goddess Ishtar.

Unlike other Hittite myths, the first version of the Illuyanka story is localized, through the mention of the land of Tarukka, in north-central Anatolia. The second version takes place near an unnamed sea.

Kumarbi Cycle. The theme of this group of stories is kingship among the gods. In *Kingship in Heaven* kingship is first held by Alalu, one of a previous generation of gods, who at the time of the Hittite storyteller are envisaged as dwelling in the netherworld and who bear the name "former gods." After a mere nine years of reign Alalu is driven from his throne by his erstwhile cupbearer, Anu, and he takes refuge in the netherworld. Alalu's own son, Kumarbi, becomes Anu's cupbearer for nine years. Then Anu and Kumarbi do battle, and Kumarbi drives his father's usurper from the throne. Since Anu (Sum., An) was the god of the sky, he tries to escape to the sky. But Kumarbi catches him, drags him down, and emasculates him by biting off and swallowing his genitals. Anu curses Kumarbi and prophesies the birth, from the swallowed genitals, of the god who will ultimately displace Kumarbi. Since Kumarbi is Alalu's son, he hopes to prevent his own removal by Anu's issue. This is the motivation for the emasculation. But fate cannot be denied. The genitals produce in Kumarbi several gods who are "born" from him, one of whom is Teshub, the storm god, who eventually deposes Kumarbi. In the *Song of Ullikummi* the deposed Kumarbi produces issue of his own, a great stone monster conceived by his intercourse with a huge rock, to depose and destroy Teshub. Another myth in this cycle, the *Kingship of Lamma,* also treats the theme of kingship among the gods. Thus the entire cycle of Kumarbi myths deals with struggle among the gods for supremacy.

Tales of Appu, the Cow and the Fisherman, and the Hunter Keshshi. These stories, of which unfortunately only a portion is preserved, were edited almost forty years ago as Hurrian tales in Hittite translation. But it is now known that only the Keshshi story has a Hurrian background. No names in the Appu story, either of gods or humans, are Hurrian, although the geographical setting appears to be somewhere to the east of Mesopotamia. Nor is there any indication of Hurrian elements in the *Cow and the Fisherman.* The fisherman's city is Urma, which is unlocalized. Keshshi marries a woman with the Hurrian name Shintalimeni, whose brother is Udubsharri. The theme of the Appu story is twofold: (1) One cannot escape the fate which marks us at birth; and (2) although evil appears to prevail for a time, the justice of the gods will ultimately triumph. Appu has two sons, to whom the names Unjust and Just are given, and they grow up to fulfill their names. Unjust takes advantage of Just until their case comes to the attention of the gods. And although the end of the story is on a part of the tablet that has broken away, the short prooemium introducing the story predicts the end: the gods always vindicate the just men and destroy the unjust.

Not enough is preserved of the *Cow and Fisherman* to discern a theme. Very little is preserved also of the *Keshshi* story, but it appears that Keshshi has angered the gods by neglecting their cult and doting on his new wife, and that he will suffer for this.

Baal, Elkunirsha, and Ashertu. This West Semitic myth about three deities, familiar to us from the Ugaritic myths and the Old Testament, was somewhat inaccurately translated into Hittite. Clues to the wording of the West Semitic original can be found in those places where *parallelismus membrorum* in the original was distorted in translation. The story itself resembles the incident of the patriarch Joseph and

Potiphar's wife. Ashertu propositions Baal, and when he refuses, she threatens to get even. He reports the incident to her husband, Elkunirsha, who gives him permission to humble her. He does so, telling her that he has killed her sons. Thereupon Ashertu laments their death and eventually becomes reconciled to Elkunirsha, even turning him against Baal. Ishtar (Astarte), Baal's sister, overhears them plotting against her brother and flies "like a bird" to meet him in the desert, where she warns him. There the tablet breaks off, leaving the narrative unfinished. An attached ritual describes the purification of Baal, which probably followed some injury to him connected with this plot.

THE HITTITE TEMPLE

Six Hittite temples have been excavated at Bogazköy. In addition to the cella, where the cult image of the deity was found, each contained a number of rooms that were used to house the permanent personnel and to store temple revenues. Each temple had a central courtyard. Worshipers crossing the courtyard from the temple entrance passed through a portico into the cella, which apparently could accommodate only priests and a small number of worshipers. Some larger temples, such as the principal temple in the lower city at Bogazköy (Temple I), may have contained two or more cellae and therefore housed the cult images of more than one god. In the terminology of the texts, therefore, going from the "house" of god A to the "house" of god B might have been possible without leaving the confines of a single multi-roomed structure.

As in other cultures, the Hittite temple—through its craftsmen personnel, its real estate farmed by sharecroppers, and its shares of booty taken by the king in battle—generated a large amount of revenue. Because we lack private economic documents, we cannot tell whether in Hatti, as in Babylonia, the temple served as a lending agency, similar to a modern bank. It is not, however, improbable that it did so.

Cult Images. Although, thanks to rock reliefs depicting Hittite gods and goddesses, we have some idea of the appearance of their cult images, these latter (being made of precious metals, which would have been carried off by the destroyers of Bogazköy) have not survived. Small images in gold or silver have indeed survived, but the full-size cult images that stood in the temple cella have not. About these we are informed in the inventory texts called statue descriptions, which give a fairly good idea of the appearance of the statues. I quote an example.

> *The Storm God of Invocation: a gold statue of a standing man with wings coming out of his shoulders. In his right hand he holds a gold ax. In his left hand a gold symbol of good. He stands on an* awiti-*animal, its teeth plated with silver, its chest plated with gold. To the left and right of the wings stand [the attendant goddesses] Ninatta and Kulitta.*
>
> *The Storm God of the Sky: a gold-plated statue of a seated man. In his right hand he holds a* hattalla-club. *In his left hand he holds a gold symbol of good. On top of two mountain gods, portrayed as standing men, silver-plated. Underneath is a silver base. Two silver rhytons. . . .*
>
> *The Storm God of the House: a silver model of a bull's head and neck, facing forward. . . .*

The Warrior God (Zababa): a silver statue of a standing man. In his right hand he holds a tukul-mace. In his left hand he holds a shield. Underneath stands a lion. Under the lion is a silver-plated base . . . one silver ashshuzeri-*vessel. He has no attendant.*

Sun God of the Sky: a silver statue of a seated man. On his head are silver fishes. Beneath him is a wooden base.

From reports of oracle inquiries we learn that the god was thought to be angered when the platings of gold and silver on his statue became worn. When an oracle indicated this, the king had to instruct goldsmiths or silversmiths to replate the image.

Temple Personnel. Periodically, the king commissioned a census of the temples of the realm. Each city, town, or village was listed with its deities and temple(s). For each deity the census listed two types of male clergy and one type of female clergy. If for any reason a sanctuary lost any of its quota of clergy, it was restaffed. A small staff of two or three clergy was necessary even for a small sanctuary; in the main temple at Bogazköy there were many more. No term corresponding to *high priest* is known in Hittite, but a presiding official for the large, urban temples must have existed.

The larger temples also maintained a staff of craftsmen. A list of the craftsmen employed in the main temple at Bogazköy enumerates goldsmiths and silversmiths, potters, leatherworkers, stonecutters, engravers, weavers, kitchen personnel, and various kinds of musicians. They lived and worked in a precinct just south of the main temple complex. Surviving texts describe the elaborate measures taken to ensure the ritual purity of these temple workers and their counterparts who served the needs of the king. Temple watchmen patrolled the precincts night and day to guard against fire and the intrusion of unwanted "unclean" animals. Visitors had to be escorted by temple guards from the main entrance to their appointments inside the temple and back to the exit once their business was done. Unauthorized persons were not allowed access to the holy precincts. In general, foreigners were not allowed in the Hittite temple; only privileged foreigners, perhaps ambassadors at the court, were allowed admittance under special circumstances.

Cultus. As stated above, the gods were treated like rich and powerful men. The description of the transporting of the images uses verbs inappropriate to the transporting of living persons, indicating that the Hittites were well aware that the image was not in fact the god but merely symbolized his presence. Still, the image was treated with the same deference that would be paid to any important personage. It was put to bed at night in the god's bedroom. In the morning it was aroused, washed and groomed, presented with food, and brought out to its cult platform for the day's round of receiving visitors (priests, dignitaries, and so on). On festival days it was put on a litter and carried through the streets to a pleasant meadow outside the city, where ceremonies, prayers, offerings, and even music, acrobatics, and games were performed to entertain the deity. The invisible divine beings symbolized by these statues were also viewed as leading a busy and active life. Ritual prayers invoking their presence in times of great need recognized that the god in question might have gone on a journey to the mountains or even to some foreign land.

No extant tablet contains the entire cultic calendar for the temples of Bogazköy. Texts describing festivals, however, make it evident that the busiest seasons of the year for festivals were fall and spring. The summer was occupied with harvesting and with the king's annual military campaigns. In the winter it was too cold for the outside activity often required at festivals, although we do know that the Festival of the Year took place toward the end of the winter. We possess elaborate descriptions of some of the major festivals and lists naming many other festivals about which we know relatively little. The personal participation of the king (and sometimes also the queen) was very important. At times of military crisis a king might even have to leave command of the armies to a subordinate in order to return to Bogazköy to celebrate a religious festival. Not to do so constituted an unforgivable affront to the gods that could prove disastrous.

The activities of worship were prayer (addressing the god either to invoke, praise, or petition him), sacrifice (presenting to the god gifts of food and drink), and entertainment (music, games, reciting myths). The musical instruments were drums, stringed and reed instruments, and horns. Singing was done in any of various languages, depending upon the deity's ethnolinguistic background: Hattic, Luwian, Hittite, Palaic, Hurrian, or Babylonian. In the cult of the Hattian gods a lead singer and a chorus sang antiphonally. Hattian deities were addressed in worship under two names: the name used among mortals and that among the gods.

The premise underlying all Hittite prayer is that gods thought like mortals and could be influenced by pleasant words and gifts. The paradigm for the divine-human relationship was a master-slave one. A human could expect from his divine lord or lady just what a slave could from his master.

More than one Hittite noun was used to designate what we call "prayer." *Mugawar (mugeshshar)* referred to the invocation of the god's presence through words and ritual acts. Praise, adulation, and adoration were called *walliyatar;* petition was *wekuwar*. Reply to accusations of sin (i.e., self-justification or protestation of innocence) was *arkuwar*. A single Hittite prayer often contained several of these types of expression.

Sacrifices were made of domestic animals, principally bulls, cows, sheep, and goats. For certain Hurrian rituals, birds were sacrificed. The cult never prescribed the sacrifice of a wild animal. The animal was killed and its meat prepared to serve as the god's food; no expiatory use was ever made of the blood of the sacrifice.

Animals given to the god were to be healthy specimens. Persons who knowingly substituted scrawny or unhealthy animals for healthy ones were guilty of a serious offense. In some rituals alternate, less expensive victims were accepted from poor worshipers. All sacrifices were to be presented promptly at the prescribed time, and delayed sacrifices or rituals were not accepted. Priests were warned in instructive texts not to tolerate excuses from worshipers who wished to postpone required rites of sacrifice. Especially appropriate at the time of their first harvesting were vegetable and grain offerings; they too had to be brought promptly.

REVELATION

The gods communicated their will to mortals in several ways. A surviving oracle text in Old Hittite script proves that oracular inquiry already existed at that time. In the Old Hittite *Telepinu Proclamation,* warnings from the gods about serious offenses came through the words of the "men of the gods," who a number of scholars have taken to be prophets of some type. A third method—dreams—is not attested earlier than the New Kingdom. Communication of a god's will to a king, queen, or prince is first mentioned in the prayers of Mursilis II and first attested in the childhood of Hattusilis III, the son of Mursilis II. At a certain point in a ritual for a man suffering from sexual impotence, the sufferer is instructed to sleep in a holy place and report his dreams.

SIN, DEATH, AND THE AFTERLIFE

Several Hittite words are translated as "sin," "offense," or "crime." Those occurring in prayers are *washtai-*, *washtul*, and *shallakardatar*. The first two refer to a deed with evil or unpleasant consequences and in most cases they must be translated as "sin." But either "sin" or "offense" can be expressed by the word *haratar*. A particularly serious offense of a special sexual nature is *hurkel*, which in most instances coincides with what we would call incest. *Shallakardatar* is a deliberate and high-handed offense against a deity.

From the Hittite point of view, sins against the gods could be deliberate or accidental. In either case they had to be identified, confessed, and (in most cases) corrected. Identification of sins committed unwittingly was possible only through consulting the god by oracle. The process was an involved one. By posing questions requiring only a "yes" or "no" answer one gradually narrowed the field of possibilities until a specific offense was determined. Then the question was posed: "Is the god angry for this reason only, and not for any additional reason?" If the answer to this was "yes," the inquiry was terminated. If "no," the inquiry continued until the final cause was identified.

Confession necessitated a promise to make amends. If the offense was the neglect of some religious duty such as a sacrifice, the offender promised to make up the sacrifice, sometimes with a greater outlay of offerings. Two Hittite words denoted gifts to make amends for these sins of neglect: *sharnikzel* and *mashkan*. The former also referred to compensation for injury or breach of contract in civil law, while the latter in profane usage meant a gift or bribe. If the gods punished a person for committing a sin, this did not absolve him from the obligations of confession and compensation. Animal sacrifices were not used to expiate sin, nor did the compensatory gifts mentioned above constitute an expiation. Rather, a man's offense against a god was viewed as completely analogous to his offense against another man, and the terminology (e.g., *sharnikzel*) was identical.

Relatively little is said in the surviving Hittite texts about the fate of man after death. The Old Hittite Kantuzzili prayer rather philosophically observes that if one were to go on living under the present circumstances eternally, that might turn out to be a night- mare, for the ills of this life would become eternal. This would turn out to be a grievance *(kattawatar)*, that is, a ground for complaint against the gods. In the description of the lengthy ritual for cremation and interring of the ashes of a dead king we learn that certain farming implements were burned in order to accompany the deceased king to the next life, so that he might cultivate the soil there. In the Hittite laws, a clause dealing with a wife's predeceasing her husband decrees that before her dowry can be released to her widowed husband, he must burn certain of her personal possessions. This burning doubtless served the same purpose as the burning of the farming implements for the dead king. In many cultures, items of personal value to the deceased are placed in the grave with the dead body, a practice strongly suggesting use of the articles in an afterlife. In the case of the Hittite king our texts explicitly confirm this interpretation. Descendants of the dead man continued to make offerings to his spirit. This practice is also attested in Hittite texts. In one instance, King Muwatallis, when he moved the royal residence from Bogazköy to Tarhuntassa, transferred to the new residence the statues of the gods and the "dead [ancestors]."

A Hittite religious belief maintained that the spirit of a dead person with a grievance against a living person might continue to haunt the latter until the grievance was resolved. The precise nature of the grievance was determined in the same way as sins against a god: by oracular investigation. When the grievance had been resolved and the spirit had been pacified, he was "set on the road," that is, he was sent on his way to the abode of the dead.

Hittite texts never reveal where that abode was. The Hittite cosmology allowed for a heaven above, where most of the gods dwelled, and the netherworld beneath, where the remainder lived. But we do not know if the dead resided in either of these places. In a ritual intended to remove certain evils and safely dispose of them forever where they could not harm mankind, the dead were magically put into large copper vessels and covered with lids of lead. According to one version of the incantation, these vessels were at the bottom of the sea; according to the other version, in the netherworld. This, of course, does not prove that the spirits of the dead were confined in the netherworld. It only suggests that unwelcome things were kept there.

BIBLIOGRAPHY

Bittel, Kurt. *Hattusha: The Capital of the Hittites.* New York, 1970. See pages 91–112.

Bittel, Kurt. "The Great Temple of Hattusha-Boğazköy." *American Journal of Archaeology* 80 (1976): 66–73.

Gurney, O. R. *Some Aspects of Hittite Religion.* London, 1977.

Güterbock, Hans G. "Hittite Religion." in *Forgotten Religions,* edited by Vergilius Ferm, pp. 83–109. New York, 1950.

Güterbock, Hans G. "The Song of UlliKummi." *Journal of Cuneiform Studies* 5 (1951): 135–161 and 6 (1952): 8–42.

Güterbock, Hans G. "Religion und Kultus der Hethiter." In *Neuere Hethiterforschung,* edited by Gerold Walser, pp. 54–73. Wiesbaden, 1964.

Güterbock, Hans G. *Les hieroglyphes de Yazilikaya: À propos d'un travail récent.* Paris, 1982.

Hoffner, Harry A., Jr. "Hittite Mythological Texts: A Survey." In *Unity and Diversity,* edited by Hans Goedicke and J. J. M. Roberts, pp. 136–145. Baltimore, 1975.

Hoffner, Harry A., Jr. "A Prayer of Muršili II about His Stepmother." *Journal of the American Oriental Society* 103 (1983): 187–192.

Kammenhuber, Annelies. "Hethitische Rituale." In *Kindlers Literatur-Lexikon,* edited by Gert Woerner et al., vol. 3. Zurich, 1965–1967.

Masson, Emilia. *Le panthéon de Yazilikaya: Nouvelles lectures.* Paris, 1981.

Moyer, James C. "The Concept of Ritual Purity among the Hittites." Ph.D. diss., Brandeis University, 1969.

Otten, Heinrich. *Hethitische Totenrituale.* Berlin, 1958.

Otten, Heinrich. "The Religion of the Hittites." in *Historia Religionum,* edited by C. Jouco Bleeker and Geo Widengren, vol. 1, *Religions of the Past,* pp. 318–322. Leiden, 1969.

Sturtevant, Edgar H., and George Bechtel. *A Hittite Chrestomathy.* Philadelphia, 1935.

Sürenhagen, Dietrich. "Zwei Gebete Ḫattušilis und der Puduḥepa." *Altorientalische Forschungen* 8 (1981): 83–168.

Ten Cate Houwink, Ph. H. J. "Hittite Royal Prayers." *Numen* 16 (1969): 81–98.

5

CANAANITE
RELIGION

Alan M. Cooper

The term *Canaanite* is variously used in both ancient and modern sources. Most popularly, it refers to the indigenous population of the southwestern Levant, which, according to biblical traditions, was displaced by Israelite conquerors late in the second millennium before the common era. This popular usage is, however, both too narrow geographically and fraught with sociohistorical difficulties. In this article, the term *Canaanite religion* will refer mainly to the one Northwest Semitic religion of the second millennium that is presently well attested, the Ugaritic. It should be borne in mind, however, that ancient sources do not necessarily support the often-asserted equation of "Ugaritic" with "Canaanite," if the terms of the equation are linguistic, ethnic, or political. And in any case, the undoubtedly idiosyncratic Ugaritic data do not facilitate a generally applicable description of "Canaanite" (or, more accurately, "Northwest Semitic") religion.

Before the late nineteenth century, there were only two sources for the study of the Canaanite religion. The first, the Hebrew scriptures, contains numerous references to the Canaanites and their practices, which are generally condemned as abominable (e.g., *Lv.* 18:3, 27–28). As early as the first century BCE, the biblical commentator Philo of Alexandria recognized that Canaan was the biblical symbol of "vice," which the Israelites were naturally bidden to despise (*De cong.* 83–85). It is generally agreed that the biblical witness to Canaanite religion is highly polemical and, therefore, unreliable; biblical evidence must at the least be used with extreme caution, and in conjunction with extrabiblical sources.

The second source for knowledge of Canaanite religion was those classical texts that preserve descriptions of aspects of it. The best known of these are the *Phoenician History* of Philo Byblius, of which portions are preserved in Eusebius's *Praeparatio evangelica,* and *The Syrian Goddess,* attributed (perhaps falsely) to Lucian of Samothrace. The reliability of Philo Byblius, however, has been the subject of scholarly debate, and the present consensus is that the comparability of the *Phoenician History* with authentic Canaanite data should not be overstressed. At best, Philo's information probably sheds light on the religion of late hellenized Phoenicians, and offers no direct evidence for second-millennium Canaanite religion. The same generalization applies to (Pseudo-) Lucian, despite a few scholarly claims to the contrary.

Firsthand evidence for Canaanite culture in the second millennium BCE (or, in archaeological terms, the Middle Bronze and Late Bronze periods) comes from artifactual evidence found at many archaeological sites (more than sixty for the first part of the Middle Bronze period alone—mostly tombs) and from textual evidence stemming mainly from three great discoveries: (1) the eighteenth-century royal archives of "Amorite" Mari (Tell Hariri, on the Euphrates River near the present border between Syria and Iraq); (2) the diplomatic correspondence between several Levantine vassal princes and the pharoahs Amenophis III and IV (first half of the fourteenth century), found at Tell al-'Amarna (about 330 km south of Cairo on the east bank of the Nile); and (3) the mainly fourteenth- and thirteenth-century texts found at Ras Shamra (ancient Ugarit) and nearby Ras Ibn Hani, both within the present-day administrative district of Latakia, on the Mediterranean coast of Syria. The artifactual evidence is crucial for understanding material culture, socioeconomic developments, population movements, and the like, and provides considerable data about funerary practices. Most significant for the study of religion are the figurines, thought to represent gods and goddesses, that have been recovered in virtually every archaeological context. These will be discussed below with other manifestations of popular religion.

The ancient city of Mari was peripheral to both the Mesopotamian and the Levantine spheres of influence. Culturally and linguistically, it was clearly West Semitic, but to label it "Canaanite" goes beyond the evidence (the designation "Amorite" represents, to some extent, a scholarly compromise). The Mari texts are virtually all concerned with economic, juridical, and administrative matters. One text in particular testifies to the eclecticism and heterogeneity of Mari's religious cult in the eighteenth century. It lists the sacrificial sheep distributed among the various gods and temples of Mari, and the list of gods is a mixture of Semitic and non-Semitic deities from east and west, along with some gods perhaps unique to Mari. This list of diverse gods may be supplemented by the more than one hundred forty divine names (at least two dozen of which are West Semitic) attested as components of personal names in the Mari archives.

The most striking group of Mari texts is the small collection of so-called prophetic texts. These twenty-odd letters attest to a type of oracular speaking that shows significant affinities with biblical prophecies of a millennium later. Some of this oracular speaking seems to have been done by cultic personnel, and some apparently consisted of messages transmitted by the gods through ordinary people. In either case, it clearly deviated from the normal (and presumably normative) mode of divine intermediation, which was, as generally in the ancient Near East, divination in its various forms. Local temple officials probably felt that the extraordinary behavior, and the messages transmitted by it, had to be reported to higher authorities. It may be suggested, on the basis of these Mari texts and related evidence, that the phenomenon broadly termed *"prophecy"* represented a peculiar and peripheral kind of divine intermediation among the West Semites generally.

Most of the Amarna letters report on Levantine military, economic, and political matters to the Egyptian court. The letters were written in Babylonian, the diplomatic language of the period, but they regularly reveal the Canaanite character of their authors—in personal names, peculiar scribal practices, and, especially, the use of characteristic Canaanite vocabulary and turns of phrase. While none of the Amarna letters is directly concerned with religion, important information can be derived from the divine names and epithets mentioned in passing (and as components of personal names), and from Canaanite religious and liturgical clichés that have been incorporated into the epistolary style. For example, the son of Aziru, prince of Amurru, writes as follows to the Egyptian court: "You give me life, and you give me death. I look upon your face; you are indeed my lord. So let my lord hearken to his servant." Such expressions, which are frequent in the correspondence, are probably borrowed liturgical formulas, perhaps from lost Canaanite prayers that were probably comparable to the biblical psalms. A systematic study of all such formulas might shed considerable light on Canaanite religious conceptions of the mid-second millennium.

Without slighting the importance of the Mari and Amarna material, by far the most significant evidence for Canaanite religion in the second millennium is found at Ugarit. From the beginning of the millennium until the city's destruction at the hands of the Sea Peoples (c. 1180–1175 BCE), Ugarit was a thriving cosmopolitan trading center. In the Middle Bronze period (2000–1600; Level II of the Ras Shamra excavations), Ugarit underwent considerable expansion. During this period, two large temples (dedicated to the gods Baal and Dagan respectively; see below) were erected on top of older ruins, forming, in effect, an acropolis in the city. The pottery of the period is predominantly Canaanite, and other material evidence demonstrates that Ugarit was in contact with Egypt, the Aegean, and Mesopotamia. At the same time, Ugarit's population was augmented by an influx of Indo-European-speaking Hurrians from the northeast.

The best-attested period at Ugarit is the last two centuries of its existence (Late Bronze III, c. 1365–1180; Level I.3 of the Ras Shamra excavations). The Ugaritic texts date from this period, although some of the religious texts are undoubtedly older, and were merely written down at this time. One of the most important developments in human history was the invention, during the reign of Niqmad II (c. 1360–1330), of a cuneiform alphabetic script (the world's oldest alphabet) adapted to the Ugaritic language. It seems likely that this invention was specifically for the purpose of setting ancient religious documents in writing, since diplomatic and administrative texts could be, and often were, written in Akkadian. At the instigation of Niqmad II, the great mythological texts that are at the heart of the Ugaritic religion were incised on clay tablets. They were preserved in the library of the high priest, which was located on the acropolis near the two temples.

In addition to the mythological texts from the high priest's library, the excavations of this and several other archives of Ugarit and Ras Ibn Hani have turned up related mythological material, descriptive ritual texts, lists of sacrificial offerings, god-lists, prayers and liturgies, incantations, divinatory texts, and dedicatory inscriptions. These may be used, with due caution, as the basis of a description of Ugaritic religion.

DEITIES

The essential information about Ugarit's deities comes from what appears to be a canonical god-list. Two nearly identical copies of the basic list have been published, along with an Akkadian "translation." In addition, the list is incorporated, with minor variations, into a list of sacrificial offerings. This list shows that the basic cultic pantheon of Ugarit numbered thirty-three or thirty-four gods. One of the most controversial problems confronting Ugaritic scholarship is the imperfect correspondence between the god-list and the gods who are prominent in the mythological texts. The myths probably represent an older stratum of Ugaritic religion, and were undoubtedly "reinterpreted" in the light of subsequent developments in the cult.

Two reasons are generally given for the order of the gods in the list: either it reflects their relative importance, or else it gives the order in which their symbols were paraded in a cultic procession. The list begins with two or three Ils (El)—the sources are evenly split on the number. *Il* is the common Semitic word for "god"; it is the proper name of the head of the Ugaritic pantheon in the mythological texts. The first Il in the god-list is associated with Mount Sapan (Tsafon), the Canaanite Olympus, which was traditionally identified with Jebel al-Aqra, about fifty kilometers north of Ugarit at the mouth of the Orontes River. (The mountain was itself deified, and appears in the god-list in place 14/15.) In all likelihood, the term *sapan,* which means "north," was taken to be a metaphor for the god's temple (as in the Bible, Psalm 48:3), and not as a simple geographical designation. Thus the *Il* of *sapan* is the numen manifest in the sanctuary, which is the earthly representation of the divine abode. Sapan, it should be noted, is not the abode of Il in the mythological texts, but of Baal (see below).

The second Il is called *Ilib.* The Akkadian and Hurrian parallels show that this name is a portmanteau composed of the elements *il* ("god") and *ab* ("father"), but the precise significance of the combination is uncertain. Most likely the name denotes an ancestral spirit, the numen manifest in the Ugaritic cult of the dead. In the Ugaritic epic of Aqhat, the ancient worthy Danil, whose epithets mark him as one of the deified dead, seeks a son who will "erect a stela for his *ilib*"—that is, for the divine spirit of his dead father. The affinity of Il with the Ugaritic cult of the dead is shown in a mythological fragment in which the god participates in a *marzih* feast (an orgiastic revel comparable to the Greek *thiasos*), the ritual banquet of the funerary cult. Il drinks himself into a stupor (as is customary at such affairs), and has to be carried off by his faithful son. (This, too, is one of the duties of the son enumerated in the epic of Aqhat.)

The third Il is presumably to be identified with the head of the pantheon in the mythological texts. His epithets and activities in those, and in the cultic texts, provide a fair picture of his character. He is the father of the gods, who are called his "family" or "sons," and he is styled "father of humankind" and "builder of built ones." He may have been regarded as the creator of the world, but the Ugaritic evidence is inconclusive on this point. He bears the epithet "bull," a symbol of virility and power (although one mythological text casts some doubt on his sexual prowess). He is serene in his supremacy, a source of "eternal wisdom," "beneficent and benign"; a unique and problematic text that may be a prayer to Il seems even to hypostatize his "graciousness."

The three Ils comprise the three principal aspects of Ugaritic "godship," or numinous power, that are denoted by the term *il:* (1) it is the wise and sovereign power that brought gods and humans into being; (2) it abides in any sacred place; and (3) it is the tangible presence of the spirits of the dead.

The next deity on the list is Dagan. The Mari texts attest to his great importance in the Middle Euphrates region (especially Terqa). The most common explanation of his name relates it to the West Semitic word for "grain," but this is by no means certain; other (even non-Semitic) etymologies are possible. One of the two temples on the acropolis of Ugarit was evidently consecrated to Dagan. During excavations carried out in 1934, two inscribed stone slabs were found just outside the temple. The inscriptions, the only known examples of Ugaritic carved in stone, commemorate *pgr* sacrifices of a sheep and an ox offered to Dagan. Since so little is known of Dagan's character at Ugarit, and since the term *pgr* is controversial (perhaps "mortuary offering" is the best interpretation), it is not possible to say anything definitive about these stelae.

Despite his obvious prominence in the cult, Dagan plays no role in Ugaritic mythology. The god Baal bears the epithet "son of Dagan," but that is itself problematic, since Il was supposedly the father of the gods. Three explanations are possible: (1) Dagan was in some sense identified with or assimilated to Il; (2) the epithet represents a variant tradition of Baal's paternity; or (3) the epithet "son" is not to be taken literally but as an indication that Baal belongs to some class of gods exemplified by Dagan.

Following Dagan come seven Baals. The first is the Baal of Mount Sapan, who dwells in the same place as the Baal in the mythological texts (the "heights" or "recesses" of Sapan); the term *sapan* surely refers to the Baal temple of Ugarit as well. The Akkadian rendition of *Baal* is *Adad*, which is the name of the most prominent West Semitic mountain and weather god. The same Ugaritic "prayer" that mentions the graciousness of El also establishes the threefold identification of Adad (the variant Hadd occurs in the mythological texts) with Baal of Mount Sapan and Baal of Ugarit.

The significance of the other six Baals (none qualified by epithets and all identified with Adad) is uncertain, although sevenfold lists of all sorts, including divine heptads, are common throughout the ancient Near East: the number seven evidently denotes completeness or perfection. If the extra six Baals have some specific function, they might represent local manifestations or sanctuaries of Baal, separate cult symbols, or hypostatized attributes.

The name *Baal* is derived from the common Semitic noun meaning "lord, master, husband." The god's full title in the mythological texts is "prince, lord *(baal)* of the earth," and his principal epithet is "most powerful one" *(aliyan)*. He is also called "high one" *(aliy)* and "rider of the clouds," both names clearly illustrating his character as a weather god.

In contrast to the numinous Il, Baal represents the divine power that is immanent in the world, activating and effectuating things or phenomena. Given the paucity of rainfall in most of the Levant, it is not surprising that the lord of the storm is the most prominent god of this type (cf. the ubiquitous Phoenician Baal Shamem, "lord of the heavens," and his famous encounter with the Israelite god in *1 Kings* 18). On his shoulders rests the burden of bringing fertility and fecundity to the land, and as such he is venerated by the rest of the gods and declared their "king."

But the kind of god who is immanent in the natural world is also subject to its flux. Thus, in the mythological texts, Baal has three enemies. The first two, Yamm ("sea") and the desert gods who are called "devourers," represent the destructive potential inherent in nature. Baal succeeds in subduing Yamm (and undoubtedly also the "devourers"), but he is in turn defeated by his third and greatest adversary, Mot ("death"; never mentioned by this name in the cultic texts). Nothing that is in the world, gods included, can escape death.

Following the seven Baals, the god-list continues with Ars wa-Shamem ("earth and heaven"). Binomial deities are common in Ugaritic; they represent either a hendiadys (as in this case) or a composite of two related gods who have been assimilated to one another. This god's function is unknown; perhaps the domain over which Baal holds sway is deified. There are also two other geographical deities: Sapan (discussed above) and "Mountain and Valley" (significance unknown, unless it defines the domain of Athtar, the god occupying the preceding place on the god-list).

The remaining divine names on the list may be grouped in four categories: individual goddesses and gods who are known or at least mentioned in the mythological texts; collective terms that designate groups of lesser deities; Hurrian deities; and otherwise unknown or poorly attested gods.

The two most prominent goddesses in the mythological texts are Athirat (Asherah) and Anat. Athirat is the consort of Il, and as such she is the highest-ranking goddess in the pantheon. Her full title is "Lady Athirat of the sea" (or perhaps "the lady who treads the sea"). She is the mother of the gods, bearing the epithet "progenitress of the gods." She is also called Ilat ("goddess"), the feminine form of Il. Athirat's activities in the mythological texts are not always clear, but she seems to specialize in zealous intervention on behalf of her divine offspring.

In contrast to the maternal goddess Athirat, Anat is a violent goddess of sexual love and war, "sister" (perhaps consort) of Baal and vanquisher of Baal's enemy Mot. Her principal epithet is "maiden," a tribute to her youth, beauty, and desirability, but pugnacity is her primary trait in the mythological texts, as well as in the epic of Aqhat; there, she secures the magic bow of the title character by arranging his death.

Iconographic evidence from Ugarit and elsewhere may be associated with both of the principal divine pairs, Il/Athirat and Baal/Anat. The first two are represented as a royal pair, either standing or enthroned. Baal is typically depicted with his arm upraised in smiting position, and Anat is naked and voluptuous, sometimes standing on a lion's back, an Egyptian Hathor wig on her head, with arms upraised and plants or animals grasped in her hands. Only the Anat figures can be identified with any certainty, because of an Egyptian exemplar that bears the inscription "Qudshu-Ashtart-Anat."

Although the precise significance of Qudshu is uncertain (perhaps she is the same as Athirat?), the Egyptian inscription seems to demonstrate the fusion of the West Semitic Anat with the great Mesopotamian goddess Ishtar (Ugaritic Athtart; the biblical Ashtoret). This fusion is apparent in the binomial Athtart wa-Anat, which occurs in two Ugaritic incantation texts and is the ultimate source of the name of the first-millennium "Syrian goddess" Atargatis. In some mythological and cultic texts, as in the god-list, Athtart still has some independent status. (Paradoxically, in Israel it is Anat who has disappeared, evidently assimilated to Ashtoret.) Her beauty is proverbial, but her principal trait is pugnacity; like Anat, she is a divine huntress.

The textual and iconographic evidence suggests that a central feature of Ugaritic religion was the veneration of two divine pairs. One pair apparently symbolized kingly and queenly sovereignty over the world—Il and Athirat; the other represented brother and sister, caught in the flux and turmoil of the world, engaged in constant struggle for survival and supremacy—Baal and Anat.

There are three other Canaanite goddesses on the god-list. Shapash is the all-seeing sun (male in Mesopotamia, but female at Ugarit), "luminary of the gods." Pidray ("fat"?) and Arsay ("earth," perhaps, on the basis of the Akkadian parallel, having some connection with the netherworld) are two of the daughters of Baal; the third, Talay ("dew"), does not appear on the god-list. Two other non-Canaanite goddesses are on the list, undoubtedly via the Hurrians, although the deities themselves are not necessarily Hurrian in origin: Ushharay (Ishhara), the scorpion goddess, who appears in several cultic texts but never in the myths, and Dadmish, probably a warrior goddess but very poorly attested. The one remaining goddess on the list is Uthht (pronunciation uncertain; the sex of the deity is, in fact, only surmised from the feminine ending); possibly Mesopotamian in origin, and most likely signifying a deified incense burner.

Seven male deities remain on the god-list, all but one of whom are at least mentioned in the mythological texts. Yarikh is the moon god, and he figures prominently in a poem that describes his marriage to the moon goddess, Nikkal. This text is undoubtedly a Hurrian myth in Ugaritic guise. The other clearly astral god is Shalim (the divine element in the name of the city Jeru*salem* and of King *Solom*on), who represents the evening twilight or Venus as evening star. Since the root *sh-l-m* can signify "conclusion, completion," it is appropriate that Shalim is the last name on the list. Elsewhere, he is often paired with his sibling Shahr, who is the dawn or the planet Venus as morning star. The birth of the pair is described and celebrated in a Ugaritic poem.

Three of the gods play important roles in the mythological texts about Baal. Yamm is one of Baal's principal adversaries; he is identified with or accompanied by two fearsome sea monsters, Litan (the biblical Leviathan) and Tunnan (the biblical Tannin). The god Athtar (the masculine form of Athtart) is often associated with a prominent South Arabian astral deity, but the Akkadian translation of his name identifies him with the Hurrian warrior god Ashtabi. When Baal is killed by Mot, Athtar, styled "tyrant," is appointed king in his stead.

The god Kothar ("skilled one"; also known as Kothar wa-Hasis, "skilled and wise one") is the divine craftsman. In various sources he is a master builder, weapon maker, seaman, and magician. It has been suggested that he is the genius of technology.

The god Rashap (the biblical *Reshef,* which means both "pestilence" and "flame") is blamed in the epic of Kirta for the demise of part of the title character's family. But Rashap's real importance at Ugarit and Ras Ibn Hani emerges from the cultic texts, where he is the recipient of numerous offerings. In the late third millennium, he was one of the patron gods of the kings of Ebla. He also found his way to Egypt, where he was patron god of Amenophis II and one of the most popular gods in the cults of the nineteenth dynasty.

The Akkadian version of the Ugaritic god-list identifies Rashap with Nergal, the Mesopotamian king of the netherworld. That identification, along with other Canaanite and Egyptian evidence, leads me to suggest that Rashap is the god who, in one mythological text, is called Rapiu, the "healer," the eponymous patron of the deified dead, the *rapium* (the biblical *refa'im*). Most scholars, however, consider "Rapiu" to be an epithet of Il.

The remaining god on the list is Kinar, who is perhaps the deified lyre. Nothing is known about him, but he has been identified with the Cypriot hero Kinyras, father of Adonis.

Finally, the god-list includes four collective terms. The first, *kotharat,* designates a band of female divine singers and wet-nurses who appear on sad and joyful occasions in the Aqhat epic and the Nikkal poem, respectively (also, perhaps, in Psalm 68:7). Although their name suggests an affinity with the god Kothar, nothing further can be said about this. They bear an epithet that is problematic: the two most plausible translations are "daughters of joyous song, the swallows" and "shining daughters of the morning star [or the new moon]."

The next collective term apparently designates the "two allies of Baal," perhaps his messengers, Gapn ("vine") and Ugar ("field"). The third collective term is *puhr ilim,* the "assembly of the gods," which designates the host of lesser deities—unmentioned by name in the god-list—who constitute the progeny of Il and Athirat. In other texts, this assemblage bears other epithets, including "sons of Il" and "the family of the sons of Il"; the precise significance of these terms is much debated, but they all seem to pertain to the general Near Eastern notion of a "divine assembly" over which one god reigned supreme.

The last collective term is *malikum,* which literally means "kings." It designates the deified dead kings of Ugarit, the most important members of the larger assemblage of deified dead ancestors (*rapium,* mentioned above). The *malikum* are invoked by name in an extraordinary Ugaritic liturgy entitled the *Document of the Feast of the Protective Ancestral Spirits.* It may be inferred that the patron of the *malikum* was the ubiquitous Malik (biblical Molech), who is almost certainly to be equated with Death himself.

Many other deities who do not figure in the standard god-list are mentioned in various texts and as components of personal names. Huge, malleable pantheons characterized every major urban center of the ancient Near East, and Ugarit was no exception (see Johannes C. de Moor, "The Semitic Pantheon of Ugarit," *Ugarit-Forschungen* 2, 1970, pp. 185–228).

RITUALS AND CULTIC PERSONNEL

Most older descriptions of Canaanite religion explain it in terms of the seasonal cycle and concomitant fertility rites. The evidence for this characterization comes from first-millennium sources, especially the anti-"Canaanite" polemics of the Hebrew scriptures, and from the *a priori* claims of the "myth-and-ritual" approach to religion. When the mythic texts about the Ugaritic Baal were deciphered and pieced together, the tendency was naturally to make them conform to the older theories about Canaanite religion. Those texts were thus described as a mythic representation of the seasonal cycle, which was either recited as the accompaniment to fertility rites or served as the libretto of a fertility-cult drama.

Assuming that the biblical and related data are reliable, they evidently refer to local manifestations of first-millennium Phoenician cults (such as that of northern Israel). The simple assumption of continuity between second-millennium Canaan and first-millennium Phoenicia is unjustified—as is, more generally, the facile identification of "Canaanites" with "Phoenicians."

As for the myth-and-ritual claim, the seasonal interpretation of the Baal texts is by no means certain. There is no evidence that the Baal texts were ever used in conjunction with cultic activity. In fact, there is only one Ugaritic mythological text containing rubrics for ritual performance (discussed below); it apparently entails some sort of fertility rite, but one not necessarily connected with the seasonal cycle. Knowledge of the Ugaritic calendar and its fixed festivals is too scanty to permit the claim that Ugaritic religion was organized with respect to the agricultural year.

The Ugaritic ritual texts describe a highly organized sacrificial cult under the patronage of the king. The sacrifices seem to be of the gift or tribute type; that is, they were performed to curry favor with the gods, to secure their aid and protection. It is undeniable that offerings might have been made to deities (particularly chthonic ones) to promote the fertility of the land and the fecundity of the flocks. But the one mass public ritual that has survived, and the one attested prayer to Baal as well, both seem more concerned with protection from Ugarit's potential military opponents. In view of the shifting alliances and political instability that marked Ugarit's last two centuries, this concern seems only natural.

Most of the known Ugaritic rituals were performed by or on behalf of the king. The best-attested type of ritual is found in seven different texts. In it the king of Ugarit performs, at specified times, a ritual lustration to purify himself, and then offers a series of sacrifices to various deities. At sundown, the king "desacralizes" himself in a way that is not clear. The most interesting of these texts is evidently a prescriptive ritual to which is appended a prayer to Baal, perhaps recited by the queen, that seems to specify the occasion on which the rites were to be performed.

This text begins with a date formula and a list of offerings: "On the seventh day of the month of Ibalat [otherwise unknown]" sheep are offered to several gods, notable Baal and "the house of Baal of Ugarit." Then "the sun sets and the king performs the rite of desacralization." On the seventeenth day of the month, the king (re)purifies himself and makes another series of sacrifices, perhaps accompanied by a festal banquet (if this is the correct sense of the technical term *dbh*). (Another of the main sacrificial terms, *tb,* which seems to denote "gift offering," also occurs here.) The king remains in his purified state and continues the series of offerings on the eighteenth day. Then the text breaks off. The reverse of the tablet begins with broken references to rites performed on the second day (of what, is unspecified). On the fourth, birds are offered; on the fifth the king offers a *shlmm* sacrifice to Baal of Ugarit in the temple, along with the liver of an unspecified animal (which has presumably been used for divination) and an offering of precious metal. The *shlmm* offering, well attested in biblical Hebrew and Punic cultic texts, was probably the most common type of sacrifice at Ugarit. The term is traditionally translated "peace offering," but it seems actually to have been a "gift" or "tribute" to the god. In some texts (but not this one), the *shlmm* is described as a *shrp,* which probably signifies that it was wholly consumed by fire.

On the seventh day, at sundown, the king performs the ritual desacralization, evidently aided in this case by cultic functionaries called "desacralizers." Then the queen is anointed with a libation of "a *hin* [liquid measure] of oil of pacification for Baal"; the text concludes with the following prayer, perhaps recited by the queen:

> When a strong enemy assails your gates,
> A mighty foe attacks your walls,
> Raise your eyes unto Baal:
> "O Baal, chase the strong enemy from our gates,

The mighty foe from our walls.
A bull, O Baal, we consecrate;
A vow, O Baal, we dedicate;
A firstborn [?], O Baal, we consecrate;
A *htp* sacrifice, O Baal, we dedicate;
A tithe, O Baal, we tithe.
To the sanctuary of Baal let us ascend,
On the paths to the House of Baal let us walk."
Then Baal will hear your prayer,
He will chase the strong enemy from your gates,
The mighty foe from your walls.

None of the other royal rituals offers such specific information about its occasion as the one just described, but they all have the same basic character. Another group of texts merely lists the sacrificial offerings and the gods to whom they were offered. These texts sometimes begin with the rubric "when the king makes an offering," but they do not describe any accompanying rituals.

A second type of ritual is preserved in three texts that describe the transfer of cult statues from one place to another. The clearest of these begins "When Athtart of *hr* [meaning uncertain] enters into the sanctuary [?] of the king's house. . . ." It is not clear whether the term *king* refers to Ugarit's king or to a god (perhaps both?); the "house" could be a royal palace or temple. A group of offerings is then made in the "house of the stellar gods" (meaning uncertain), including oblations, vestments, gold, and sacrificial animals. The rites are repeated seven times. The remainder of the text describes essentially the same rituals as those performed for a different collection of gods (on a different occasion?), the poorly attested *gthrm*.

One substantial ritual text is unique in the corpus, and has been the subject of many studies. It is unique in its poetic/hymnic quality and in the acts it describes. It seems to depict a great public assembly in which the entire population of Ugarit, male and female, king and commoner alike, participated. The ritual appears to have been a mass expiation or purgation of sins, or some sort of mass purification rite, designed to protect Ugarit against its threatening neighbors. A parallel has been drawn between it and the Jewish Yom Kippur, the "day of purgation [of sin]." In the Ugaritic text, the men and women of the community are alternately summoned to offer sacrifices, which they do. While the sacrifices are performed the people sing, praying that their offerings will ascend to "the father of the sons of Il" (that is, to Il himself), to the "family of the sons of Il," to the "assembly of the sons of Il," and to *Thkmn wa-Shnm,* Il's son and attendant (the one who cares for him when he is drunk; in one of his epithets, Il is called "father of *Shnm*").

Only one mythological text, the poem about the birth of Shahr and Shalim (the *ilima naimima,* "gracious gods"), includes rubrics for ritual performance. These rubrics, interspersed throughout the poem, describe the activities of the king and queen, and of cultic functionaries called *aribuma* (some kind of priests?) and *thananuma* (members of the king's guard?). They offer sacrifices, participate in a banquet, and sing responsively to musical accompaniment. It seems almost certain that the poem itself was acted out as a type of ritual drama. It describes the subjugation of Death by some sort of pruning rite, followed by Il's sexual relations with Athirat and Rahmay ("womb" = Anat?). The poem concludes with the birth of Shahr and

Shalim, and their youthful activities. The text and its accompanying ritual may commemorate (or attempt to foster) the birth of a royal heir to the reigning king and queen of Ugarit; they bear some relation to Mesopotamian sacred marriage rites and to Hittite rituals designed to protect the life and vigor of the king and queen.

Most difficult to reconstruct, but obviously of great importance, was the Ugaritic cult of the dead. The dead were summoned, by a liturgy accompanied by offerings, to participate in a banquet. The banquet, which was apparently a drunken orgy, was intended to propitiate the dead and to solicit the aid and protection provided by their numinous power. The most important group of the deified dead was comprised of Ugarit's kings *(malikum)*. The larger assemblage, variously called "healers" *(rpim)*, "healers of the netherworld" *(rpi ars)*, "ancient healers" *(rpim qdmyn)*, "divine spirits" *(ilnym)*, and "assembly of Ditan/Didan" *(qbs dtn/ddn)*, included two men who are prominent in the epic texts, Danil and Kirta, as well as several other spirits who are identified by name in a liturgical invocation of the dead.

The funerary feast itself was called a *marzih* (or *marzi*), a feast. It was held at a special location: one text describes problems concerning the rental of a *marzih* hall; a poorly preserved fragment of the Aqhat epic suggests that the *marzih* was held at a sacred "threshing floor" or "plantation," perhaps within the royal palace.

Another important text invokes the god Rapiu, "king of eternity" (that is, of the netherworld). Rapiu is clearly the patron of the deified dead; at first he is invited to drink, and at the end of the text he is asked to exert his "strength, power, might, rule, and goodness" for the benefit of Ugarit. If Rapiu is indeed to be identified with Il, this text comports well with the mythological fragment that depicts Il getting drunk at a *marzih*.

Alongside the cult of the dead must be placed the texts that apparently describe the ritual offerings to the gods of the netherworld *(ilm ars)*. The clearest of these begins with an offering to Rashap and mentions several other chthonic deities. There is also a strange god-list that appears to include a collection of netherworld demons. Finally, an inscribed clay model of a liver may record a sacrifice offered to a person (or deity?) who is "in the tomb."

The considerable activity that took place in the Ugaritic cult demanded an extensive array of cultic personnel. Unfortunately, while the names of many cultic officials are known, their precise function is not. It can be assumed, of course, that "priests" participated in the royal rituals described above, but the ritual texts do not specify how. Apart from the "desacralizers," the *thananuma* and *aribuma* already mentioned, several other kinds of personnel figure prominently. Except for the queen, who participated in some rituals (one broken text from Ras Ibn Hani describes a "*dbh* [sacrificial rite] of the queen"), all the important cultic functionaries attested by name or title are male.

After the king, the highest-ranking religious official was probably the *rb khnm*, the "chief of the priests." Under him were orders or guilds of *khnm* ("priests"); the term corresponds to the Hebrew *kohanim*, but there is no necessary similarity of function. The priests either were connected with the palace or they earned their living at the many shrines in Ugarit and its environs. They appear on administrative lists of personnel and on a military payroll. Other administrative texts detail allotments of oil and wine to various shrines. One of the high priests is also designated *rb nqdm*, "chief of herdsmen." In all likelihood, there was a consecrated group of herdsmen whose task was to maintain the royal flocks to be used in the cult.

The second major category of priests is called *qdshm*, "devotees" (comparison with Hebrew *qedeshim*, "cult prostitutes," is almost certainly misleading). They appear only on administrative lists, in all but one case in conjunction with *khnm*. Nothing can be said about their function at Ugarit.

Two categories of cult functionaries are attested in Akkadian texts from Ugarit, but they have no certain Ugaritic equivalents. One is the *awilu baru*, which is either an omen priest or some sort of oracular seer; one of these men is also called "priest of Adad [i.e., of Baal]". The other, aptly characterized by Anson F. Rainey (1967) as "a sort of religious brotherhood" (p. 71), is "men of the *marzi/marzih*." Their activity was almost certainly related to the ritual feasts of the Ugaritic cult of the dead. Several other terms probably designated groups associated with the cult. There were singers, instrumentalists, and libation pourers who served as temple attendants, along with a group of uncertain function called *ytnm*, who may be compared with the problematic biblical *netinim*.

Finally, there is the well-attested and much-debated term *insh ilm*. Some scholars think that it is a divine name; others argue that it denotes cultic personnel. If the latter, then these people performed some function in the sacrificial rites, and seem to have been rewarded for their labor with "birds."

POPULAR RELIGION

As is generally the case in the ancient Near East, little can be said with any certainty about popular religion at Ugarit, since only kings, priests, and members of the elite are represented in the texts. The Ugaritic texts were apparently only a part of the larger cosmopolitan scribal tradition of Ugarit, which was modeled on the Babylonian scribal schools. The same scribes who produced the *Baal* texts were also trained to write in Babylonian cuneiform, and they copied Sumerian and Akkadian texts in almost every genre. Surviving evidence demonstrates that Ugarit's educated elite was conversant with the Mesopotamian Gilgamesh traditions, wisdom and proverbial literature, and legal formulas, although little of this material is reflected in texts in the Ugaritic language.

It is not at all certain, then, how much of the literary tradition might have filtered down to the commoners of Ugarit. Still, speculation about popular religion may be made in four areas: conceptions of gods reflected in personal names; the evidence of votive figurines; evidence for magic and divination; and possible religious, ethical, or "wisdom" teachings derived from the texts.

Popular conceptions of the gods may emerge from a consideration of personal names, since a great number of names are composites of divine names (or surrogates) and nominal or verbal elements. The standard collection of Ugaritic personal names, Frauke Gröndahl's *Die Personennamen der Texte aus Ugarit* (Rome, 1967), lists over fifty divine elements that appear in them. The most popular are Il, Baal, Ammu ("uncle," a surrogate for a divine name), Anat and her "masculine" equivalent Anu, Athtar, Yamm, Kothar, Malik, Pidr (masculine equivalent of Pidray?), Rapiu, Rashap, and Shapash. In some names, a god is described as father, mother, brother, sister, or uncle (e.g., *Rashapabi*, "Rashap is my father"). In others, the bearer of the name is the god's son, daughter, servant, or devotee (e.g., *Abdi-Rashap*, "servant of Rashap"). A large class of names describes characteristics of the gods; those composed with Il, for example, emphasize his kingship (*Ilimilku*, "Il is king") and justice

(*Danil,* "Il judges"; *Ilsdq,* "Il is just"), his creativity (*Yakunilu,* "Il establishes"; *Yab-niilu,* "Il builds") and his love (*Hnnil,* "Il is gracious").

The second class of evidence for popular religion comes from metal figurines that are generally thought to represent gods and goddesses. A comprehensive catalog of these figurines, compiled by Ora Negbi (1976), describes over seventeen hundred of them. They are considered to have been miniature copies of now-lost wooden cult statues, and were probably used as votive idols. The fact that so many have been found at cultic sites suggests that they had some ceremonial function. Negbi notes that these idols "may have been used as amulets for magic purposes in domestic and funerary cults as well" (p. 2).

As mentioned above, the figurines at Ugarit attest to the popularity of two distinct types of divine pairs, a kingly and queenly figure (Il and Athirat) and a smiting god and voluptuous goddess (Baal and Anat, with Anat occasionally portrayed as a war goddess). The latter pair is the better attested in Late Bronze Ugarit; figurines have been found in deposits from this period in and around both of the temples on the acropolis.

Some textual evidence has been recovered for magic and divination at Ugarit. There are two versions of a long and impressive incantation against the bite of a venomous serpent; several important deities are summoned from their mythical abodes during the course of the incantations.

Inscribed clay models of lungs and livers show that extispicy (divination by the examination of animal viscera) was practiced at Ugarit. The practice was undoubtedly borrowed from Babylonia, but it was given a distinctive Canaanite cast by the incorporation of West Semitic sacrificial rites. Another borrowing from the Babylonians is attested in three omen texts that describe the predictive value of unusual human and animal births. These texts clearly parallel the famous Babylonian *shumma izbu* omen series; unfortunately, they are all quite fragmentary.

Finally, one very difficult text reports a divine oracle. It begins: "When the lord of the great/many gods [Il?] approached Ditan, the latter sought an oracle concerning the child." Some individual presumably wishes to inquire of Il about his (sick?) child. (A comparable episode occurs in the Kirta epic.) Il can be reached through an intermediary, Ditan, the eponymous patron of those deified dead known as the "assembly of Ditan." The text continues with a series of instructions (broken and unclear) that will enable the inquirer to obtain the desired oracular response. The text seems to conclude with several instructions, "and afterward there will be no suffering [?]".

Taken together, these texts indicate a lively interest in the mantic arts at Ugarit. There is practically no evidence, however, about the specialists who practiced those arts; perhaps that is because they operated on the periphery of the official cultic institutions.

The most problematic aspect of popular religion is the interpretation of the Ugaritic religious texts. Assuming that they were in some way normative and that they were diffused orally, they would embody the religious "teachings" of Ugarit. There are, however, no surviving interpretations of the texts or expositions of religious doctrine that explain what those teachings might have been or what impact they had on the life of a community of believers. The Ugaritic mythic and epic texts (as opposed to the descriptive ritual texts) can be read as homilies on the nature of the world in which people live. Ancient readers or hearers of these texts would have sought their own place in the "cosmos" they describe. Ugaritic believers, like modern believers, would presumably have formulated a special application of sacred texts to their own lives.

The *Baal* texts punctualize eternal truths in a symbolic realm that is only superficially remote from human experience. The gods experience joy and mourning, battle and tranquillity, life and death, power and impotence. The mightiest of the gods confronts the world's challenges and surmounts them all, until he encounters Death, the one enemy to whom gods and humans alike succumb. Baal's triumphs and trials, furthermore, illustrate the contiguity and interrelationship of everything in the world: the gods, nature, the political order, and human life are all part of the same order. When Baal is vanquished, political order collapses and the earth turns infertile—not because Baal "symbolizes" order and fertility in some simplistic way, but because the intricate balance of the world has been subverted. The same upset of the natural order occurs when Kirta, a human king, becomes mortally ill.

Overarching the flux of the world, and apparently not subject to it, is the wise and beneficent Il. At critical moments in the *Baal* texts, the gods journey (or send emissaries) to him in order to obtain his favor and advice. After Kirta's family is annihilated by malevolent forces, Il comforts the king in a dream; later on, Il provides the cure for Kirta's terrible illness. And in the Aqhat epic, Baal implores Il to grant a son to the childless Danil. Il consents, and appears to Danil in a dream with the good news. In every case, Il manifests transcendent power that is wielded justly, in response to urgent pleas.

The epic texts (perhaps "historico-mythic" would be a better designation for them) *Aqhat* and *Kirta* parallel and supplement the mythic texts. They narrate the existential encounter of humans with the gods. Historical (or pseudohistorical) figures become exemplary or admonitory paradigms of human behavior.

The crises that move the plot of the *Aqhat* text demonstrate the conjunction and contiguity of the human and divine realms. Danil, who is, like Kirta, a man become god (one of the deified *rapium*—from the point of view of the reader, that is), is an embodiment of that contiguity. Danil is clearly an ideal type, pious and just; he brings his plea for a son before the gods in humble obeisance, and he is rewarded. The incubation rite performed by Danil at the beginning of the story seems to be a model of personal piety.

Other aspects of the *Aqhat* text suggest ethical teachings as well. The long-sought son, Aqhat, is presented as the archetypical huntsman, recipient of a magic bow fashioned by the craftsman god Kothar. But the bow is not an unequivocal blessing: it arouses the envy of Anat, and makes Aqhat so secure in his own power that he rudely dismisses the goddess. Aqhat's folly parallels Baal's when, secure in his new palace (also the work of Kothar), he presumptuously challenges Death. Even the cleverest invention affords no protection for one who oversteps his bounds and incurs divine wrath. Aqhat's death is avenged by his sister Pughat, a model of love and devotion, just as Baal's sister Anat acts on the god's behalf in the mythic texts.

The Kirta epic, like that of Aqhat, begins with its hero childless, this time because of catastrophe instead of impotence. Dramatic tension arises from the situation of a king without an heir, which could result in disruption of both the political and the natural order. The story conveys the fragility of power and the delicate relationship between humans and deities.

Kirta enjoys the favor of Il, "father of humankind," who calls the king "gracious one, lad of Il." Kirta is instructed to perform a series of rituals in order to secure victory in battle and a new wife. He does so faithfully, but he also stops to make a vow in the sanctuary of "Athirat of Tyre, goddess of the Sidonians." This act of personal piety leads to disaster: Kirta achieves his victory and builds a new family, but he is stricken with a mortal illness for his failure to fulfill the vow. His beneficent "father" Il intervenes once again in his behalf, but the story concludes with Kirta's son attempting to usurp the throne, accusing Kirta of unrighteousness (reason enough, evidently, to depose a king). The vicissitudes of kingship continue.

The texts are all firmly on the side of reward for virtue and piety, and punishment for wickedness, blasphemy, and folly. Yet even someone who is justly suffering the wrath of the gods may appeal to the gracious Il and be heard.

SURVIVALS

Survivals of Canaanite religion are observable in two first-millennium cultural spheres, the Levant and the Aegean. Phoenician religion, both in the Levant and in its wider Mediterranean sphere of influence, represents, to some extent, a continuation of Canaanite traditions. Northern Israel's official cult was among the Levantine successors of Canaanite religion. It has often been noted that biblical polemics against that cult (for example, in the *Book of Hosea*) are directed against a characteristically Canaanite feature—the idea that the god (in this case Yahveh = Baal) was immanent in nature and subject to its flux. The Israelite god was, on the other hand, comfortably assimilated to the transcendent Il.

In the Aegean area, the nature of Canaanite influence is more controversial. But there is compelling evidence for the existence of direct West Semitic contact with Mycenaean Greece, creating a legacy of Semitic names, literary motifs, and religious practices that became part of the Hellenic cultural heritage.

BIBLIOGRAPHY

There are excellent, comprehensive articles on Amarna, Mari, and Ras Shamra in the *Dictionnaire de la Bible, Supplément,* vol. 1, cols. 207–225 (by Édouard Dhorme); vol. 5, cols. 883–905 (by Charles F. Jean); and vol. 9, cols. 1124–1466, respectively (Paris, 1928–). The Ras Shamra article, by several distinguished experts, is magisterial—the best survey to be found anywhere. In English, the journal *Biblical Archaeologist* has published a number of good survey articles: on Mari by George E. Mendenhall, vol. 11 (February 1948), pp. 1–19, and by Herbert B. Huffmon, vol. 31 (December 1968), pp. 101–124 (on the "prophetic texts"); on Amarna by Edward F. Campbell, vol. 23 (February 1960), pp. 2–22; on Ugarit by H. L. Ginsberg, vol. 8 (May 1945), pp. 41–58, and by Anson F. Rainey, vol. 28 (December 1965), pp. 102–125. All of these articles have been reprinted in *The Biblical Archaeologist Reader,* edited by David Noel Freedman and G. Ernest Wright, vols. 2 and 3 (Garden City, N.Y., 1961–1970). More recently, *Biblical Archaeologist* 47 (June 1984) is a special issue devoted to Mari.

Turning specifically to Ugarit, an excellent popular introduction is Gabriel Saadé's *Ougarit: Métropole cananéenne* (Beirut, 1979). Saadé gives a thorough account of the excavations, with complete bibliographical information and many illustrations. Most of the technical information is derived from articles in the journal *Syria,* beginning with volume 10 (1929), and from the volumes in the series "Mission de Ras-Shamra," 9 vols., edited by Claude F.-A. Schaeffer (Paris, 1936–1968). Two other useful works on the archaeological data are Patty Gerstenblith's *The*

Levant at the Beginning of the Middle Bronze Age (Winona Lake, Ind., 1983) and Ora Negbi's *Canaanite Gods in Metal* (Tel Aviv, 1976).

A good detailed account of Ugarit's history is Mario Liverani's *Storia di Ugarit* (Rome, 1962), and an unsurpassed description of Ugaritic society is Anson F. Rainey's *The Social Structure of Ugarit* (in Hebrew; Jerusalem, 1967). Readers of English can consult Rainey's Ph.D. dissertation, "The Social Stratification of Ugarit" (Brandeis University, 1962).

On the study of Canaanite religion before the discovery of Ugarit, there is a fine survey by M. J. Mulder, "Von Seldon bis Schaeffer: Die Erforschung der kanaanäischen Götterwelt," in the leading scholarly journal devoted to Ugaritic studies, *Ugarit-Forschungen* 11 (1979): 655–671. The best general introduction to Canaanite religion is Hartmut Gese's "Die Religionen Altsyriens," in *Die Religionen Altsyriens, Altarabiens und der Mandäer* (Stuttgart, 1970), pp. 3–181. On the Canaanite gods, the standard work is still Marvin H. Pope and Wolfgang Röllig's "Syrien," in *Wörterbuch der Mythologie,* edited by H. W. Haussig, vol. 1 (Stuttgart, 1965), pp. 219–312. On the rituals and cultic personnel, an excellent presentation of the data is Jean-Michel de Tarragon's *Le culte à Ugarit* (Paris, 1980), which should be consulted alongside Paolo Xella's *I testi rituali di Ugarit* (Rome, 1981). There is an exceptionally interesting theoretical discussion of Canaanite religion by David L. Petersen and Mark Woodward in "Northwest Semitic Religion: A Study of Relational Structures," *Ugarit-Forschungen* 9 (1977): 232–248. The outstanding representative of the myth-and-ritual approach is Theodor H. Gaster's *Thespis,* 2d ed. (1961; New York, 1977).

There is not yet an adequately introduced and annotated English translation of the Ugaritic texts. The best English translations are those of H. L. Ginsberg, in J. B. Pritchard's *Ancient Near Eastern Texts relating to the Old Testament,* 3d ed. (Princeton, 1969), pp. 129–155, and those in J. C. L. Gibson's revision of G. R. Driver's *Canaanite Myths and Legends,* 2d ed. (Edinburgh, 1978). The serious student should consult *Textes ougaritiques,* translated and edited by André Caquot and others (Paris, 1974), and the even more comprehensive Spanish work by Gregorio del Olmo Lete, *Mitos y leyendas de Canaán según la tradición de Ugarit* (Madrid, 1981), complemented by the same author's *Interpretación de la mitología cananea* (Valencia, 1984). A more popular introduction and translation that is both readable and of high quality is Paolo Xella's *Gli antenati di Dio* (Verona, 1982). A comparable but inferior volume in English is *Stories from Ancient Canaan,* edited and translated by Michael D. Coogan (Philadelphia, 1978).

Works on Ugarit and the Bible are legion. The serious student is directed to *Ras Shamra Parallels,* edited by Loren R. Fischer, 2 vols. (Rome, 1972–1975). The contributions are uneven in quality, but the many proposed parallels are presented with full bibliographic information. A convenient survey of comparative studies is Peter C. Craigie's "Ugarit and the Bible," in *Ugarit in Retrospect,* edited by Gordon Douglas Young (Winona Lake, Ind., 1981), pp. 99–111. John Gray's *The Legacy of Canaan,* 2d ed. (Leiden, 1965), has become a standard work in this area; its great learning and originality are marred by eccentricity, especially in the translation of the Ugaritic texts. On the most important classical account of "Canaanite" religion, see the definitive work by Albert I. Baumgarten, *The Phoenician History of Philo of Byblos* (Leiden, 1981). Semitic influence on the Aegean world is one of the main topics of Cyrus H. Gordon's stimulating book *Before the Bible: The Common Background of Greek and Hebrew Civilizations* (London, 1962); a more technical work on the subject is Michael C. Astour's brilliant *Hellenosemitica* (Leiden, 1967).

6

ISRAELITE RELIGION

Moshe Weinfeld

This discussion of the religion of Israel pertains to the religion as presented in the literary sources of the Hebrew scriptures. These sources constitute a selection guided by certain normative principles and therefore do not always reflect the real circumstances of daily life. The religion of Israel described in the Hebrew Bible represents the view of the elite circles of the society of ancient Israel, such as priests, prophets, and scribes, who shaped the image of the ideal Israel. Furthermore, as will be shown below, even this ideal image of the religion of Israel underwent a process of development. However, despite this idealization, a continuous line of development of the religion of ancient Israel can be discerned, and it is this development that I shall attempt to delineate.

General Features

Unique in many ways, Israelite religion is most remarkable for its monotheism. The difference between monotheism and polytheism is not only in number—one god versus a plurality of gods—but in the character and nature of the deity. In contradistinction to the polytheistic system according to which gods are subject to biological rules (the existence of male and female in the divine sphere, which means procreation, struggle for survival, etc.), the God of Israel is transcendent, that is, beyond the sphere of nature and therefore not subject to physical and biological principles. In the biblical descriptions of the deity we never encounter any sexual feature, procreation, struggle for survival, or gaining of status. Theogony (genealogy of the gods) and theomachy (strife among the gods), which are almost indispensable in any polytheistic religion, are completely absent from the religion of Israel.

In what appears to be an exception, we are told that God subdued Rahab, the monster, during the creation period (*Is.* 51:9, *Ps.* 89:11, *Jb.* 26:12; verse citations are to the Masoretic text). However, this does not mean that Rahab existed outside the domain of the creator. Rahab could have been created by God, as were the other creatures, but in contrast to others he rebelled and therefore was crushed and defeated (cf. *Ps.* 74:12-14).

The transcendence of God explains the absence of mythology in the religion of Israel. Mythology, here defined as storytelling about gods and their life, activities, and adventures, is inconceivable in the monotheistic sphere. God's relation to men may be described in an anthropomorphic manner, but nothing is told about God's own self or body or about his personal activities and adventures. His actions, when depicted, are always presented in the framework of God's relationship to people or to his nation.

The transcendent character of the God of Israel explains, too, the objection of Israelite religion to magic, which was so prominent in polytheistic religions. The pagan prophet, according to ancient Israelite perception, resorts to various media in order to reveal the will of gods or to coerce them to do something for men. But the Hebrew scriptures express the Israelite belief that God's will cannot be revealed unless he himself wishes to do so; his will cannot be revealed through magic, which draws its power from mystic powers not subordinated to the deity. Indeed, the Israelite legislator, speaking about pagan diviners and the prohibition against pagan mantic devices (*Dt.* 18:9–12), adds an important explanation: "You must be wholehearted [*tamim,* "sincere"] with the Lord your God. Those nations that you are about to dispossess do indeed resort to soothsayers; to you, however, the Lord your God has not assigned the like" (*Dt.* 18:13–14). The use of magic presupposes reliance on ungodly forces, and that means "insincerity" toward God.

It is true that the biblical stories as well as the biblical cult contain magical elements. There are many allusions to the marvelous transformation of objects: the staffs of Moses and Aaron become serpents (*Ex.* 4:2–4, 7:9–10); Moses divides the sea with his staff (*Ex.* 14:16); Elisha's staff is supposed to revive the Shunammite's son (*2 Kgs.* 4:29); and the three arrows that Joash, the king of Israel, drove into the ground gave him three victories over Aram (*2 Kgs.* 13:14–19). However, all these acts are considered wondrous signs from God. The wonder is seen as "the hand" and power of God and not as originating in the action itself or in the power of the sorcerer, as was the case in pagan religions (cf. *Ex.* 4:1–4, 7:8–10, et al.). Thus, for example, Elisha's staff performs wonders only when accompanied by prayer (contrast *2 Kgs.* 4:29–31 with 4:32–35).

Another transcendent feature of Israelite monotheism is the prohibition against representing God by visual symbol or image: "You shall not make for yourself a sculptured image [*pesel*] or any likeness" (*Ex.* 20:4, *Dt.* 5:8, et al.). This is explained in *Deuteronomy* 4:15: "Be most careful [not to make for yourself a sculptured image], since you saw no shape when the Lord your God spoke to you at Horeb out of the fire." The god which is beyond nature and cosmos cannot be represented by anything earthly and natural.

It is this feature which makes the Israelite religion philosophical, as conceived by the Greeks. For example, it was the observation of Theophrastus (c. 372–287 BCE), a disciple of Aristotle, that "being philosophers by race, [the Jews] converse with each other about 'the Divine' [*to theion*]" (Menachem Stern, *Greek and Latin Authors on Jews and Judaism,* vol. 1, 1974, p. 10). "The Divine" denotes here the philosophical concept of the one force that governs the world in contrast to the popular belief in various mythical deities.

Historical Development until the Temple Cult

It is hard to know how and under what concrete circumstances the monotheistic belief crystallized and whether at its emergence the religion of Israel was already characterized by the negation of mythology as well as of magic and iconic represen- tation of the deity. According to Yeḥezkel Kaufmann in *History of the Religion of Israel* (trans. Moshe Greenberg, 1972), the sudden emergence of monotheism can- not be understood unless we suppose a radical revolutionary move under the lead- ership of Moses. Kaufmann compares this to the emergence of Islam, which, under the aegis of Muḥammad, succeeded in taking control of the whole Middle East in the course of twenty-five years. One must agree with Kaufmann that there is no clear evidence of an evolutionary process in the Israelite religion. The evolutionary ap- proach of the last century supposes that monotheism developed gradually from polytheism through henotheism (belief in one national god while not excluding the existence of gods of other nations) to monotheism. Real monotheism—according to this opinion—crystallized in Israel only during the times of the prophets, in the eighth century BCE. [*See* God, *article on* God in the Hebrew Scriptures.]

However, this supposition has little support in the literary-historical sources of the Bible. The documents and sources of the Bible, which represent a very broad spec- trum of opinions and beliefs rooted in various historical periods, do not show any trace of such polytheistic concepts as the origin of God (theogony), God's consort and family, or the gods' battle for survival (theomachy). By the same token, we do not find anything in these sources which alludes to the official religious use of magical devices for mantic purposes—as, for example, hepatoscopy (inspecting an animal's liver) or augury (deriving inferences from the behavior of birds and other omens), which was so prevalent in pagan religions.

It should be stressed that this article is concerned with the offical religious trend and not with popular religious life. In the popular religion, cultic practices prevailed that reflected pagan beliefs, especially beliefs connected with a divine power of fertility that was represented by the female characteristics of the deity. Archaeologi- cal excavations in Palestine revealed numerous female figurines that were used as amulets for securing fertility (see J. B. Pritchard, *Palestinian Figurines in Relation to Certain Goddesses Known through Literature,* London, 1943). Similarly, it was found that the Israelites worshiped the female goddess Asherah and the goddess of fertility Astarte (cf. *Jgs.* 2:13, 3:7; *1 Sm.* 7:4, 12:10; *1 Kgs.* 15:13; *2 Kgs.* 21:7, 23:6). In recent years inscriptions that date back to the ninth century BCE were discovered in Kuntil- let ʿAjrud (in southern Palestine) in which YHVH is being blessed next to Asherah— a positioning that suggests syncretic religious worship. Moreover, the worship of the Queen of Heaven (Ishtar?) was widespread in Judah during the end of the mo- narchic period (*Jer.* 7:18, 44:18). [*See* Astarte.]

All of these tendencies toward syncretism were strongly condemned by the prophets of the northern kingdom of Israel and the southern kingdom of Judah, who considered them aberrations from the pure monotheistic faith.

More complicated is the problem of the aniconic characteristics of Israelite reli- gion. Although erection of images is prohibited in the legitimate Israelite cult, as attested in the various legal codes of the Hebrew scriptures (*Ex.* 20:20, 23:24, 34:14, 34:17; *Lv.* 19:4, 26:1; *Dt.* 4:15ff., 5:8; et al.), the practice as such was not unheard of in ancient Israel. It is not the worship of the golden calf as told in *Exodus* 32 and in

1 Kings 12:28ff. which we have in mind, because, as investigation has shown, this worship cannot be considered idol worship. The iconic art of the ancient Near East shows that the calf or bull usually represented the pedestal of a god and not the deity itself. The latter was usually carved in human form. Indeed, the most appropriate place for an image of the deity, should this have existed, would have been the throne or the chariot of God, both represented by the Ark of the Covenant (cf. especially *Nm.* 10:35– 36). The Ark, which together with the cherubim represented the throne and the footstool of the deity (see Menahem Haran: "The Ark and the Cherubim: Their Symbolic Significance in Biblical Ritual," *Israel Exploration Journal* 9, 1959, pp. 35ff.), actually constitutes an empty throne: the god sitting on it is invisible, which attests to the antiquity of the aniconic principle in the religion of Israel.

On the other hand, the practice of image making in ancient Israel is described in the stories in *Judges* about Gideon and Micah. Gideon, the great judge of Israel, made an ephod (some sort of image) of gold and set it up in his town (*Jgs.* 8:27), and, similarly, the mother of Micah consecrated silver to make a sculptured image *(pesel)* and a molten image *(massekha)* to YHVH (*Jgs.* 17:3). However, it has been suggested that these events might be seen as deviations from the pure legitimate worship, as were other incidents in the history of Israel caused by Cannaanite influence (cf. the worship of Baal during the period of King Ahab [c. 874–853], *1 Kgs.* 19:18 et al.) and should not be considered a reflection of genuine Israelite religion. Indeed, as will be shown below, new evidence about the tribal setting in Sinai, the cradle of Israelite monotheism, tends to confirm the view that Israelite monotheism was aniconic from its beginning.

THE RELIGION OF THE PATRIARCHS

Tradition considers Abraham the father of Yahvistic monotheism but this has no basis in the Bible itself. On the contrary, the biblical documents show an awareness of a gap between the religion of the patriarchs and the Yahvistic national religion of Israel. The name of God, *Yahveh* (preserved only unvocalized in the texts, i.e., *YHVH*) is not known before Moses (*Ex.* 3:13f., 6:2ff.), and the nature of the patriarchal creed is completely different from that of Moses and later Israelites. The god of the patriarchs is tied to person and family; the god is called God of Abraham, Isaac, or Jacob or "the God of the father" (*Gn.* 26:24, 28:13, 31:42, 32:10, 46:3, 49:25), as is appropriate to a wandering family. When *El,* the generic designation of the god, occurs in the patriarchal stories, it is not of a national or universal character, as in later Israel; the name *El* is always bound to the place where the patriarch stays. In Jerusalem God's name is El-ʻElyon (*Gn.* 14:18f.); in Beersheba the name of the deity is El-ʻOlam (*Gn.* 21:33); in Bethel, El-Beit-El (*Gn.* 31:13); and in Shechem, El-elohei Yisraʼel (*Gn.* 33:20). The names of the patriarchal family do not contain the Yahvistic component, and there is no trace in the patriarchal religion of an established cult or of official cultic objects. It must be admitted, then, that the national concept of "Yahveh the god of Israel" does not apply to the patriarchal period. The very term *patriarchal period* has to be used with great caution, since Israel as such did not yet exist, and the descriptions of this period are based on anachronisms. At any rate, according to the descriptions themselves, the national creed and cult were still nonexistent.

HISTORICAL CIRCUMSTANCES OF THE BIRTH OF MONOTHEISM

According to the stories of *Exodus,* Mount Sinai or Horeb, which became the mountain of God's revelation to Israel, was hallowed before the revelation to Moses (*Ex.* 3:1; cf. Zeer Weisman, "The Mountain of God," *Tarbiz* 47, 1978, pp. 107–119). It is designated as Mountain of God, a geographical appellation, prior to any connection to Yahveh's theophany (*Ex.* 4:29). Furthermore, it was known as the Mountain of God to Jethro, the Midianite priest, Moses' father-in-law, and he went to this mountain in order to offer sacrifices and to celebrate (*Ex.* 18:12), which points to the fact that the Mountain of God was known to other nomadic tribes of the Sinai area. This is corroborated by the divine epithet "the god of the Hebrews" which occurs only in the stories of *Exodus* discussed here (*Ex.* 3:18, 5:3). This epithet refers to the god to whom the Hebrew tribes paid allegiance before their crystallization into Israel under Moses.

As is well known, the term *Hebrews ('Ivrim)* is associated with the term *Habiru,* which designates the nomadic population in the ancient Near East during the second millennium BCE. The "god of the Hebrews" was worshiped by all sorts of nomads in the area of Sinai and the Negev: the Midianites and Kenites, as well as the Israelites. Most important in this respect is the new, extrabiblical evidence which came to light in the last decades. In the Egyptian topographical lists of King Amenhotep III (1417–1379 BCE) discovered in the temple of Amon at Soleb in Nubia as well as in the list of King Ramses II (1304–1237 BCE) discovered at Amarah West, we find "the land of nomads [of] Yahveh," along with "the land of nomads [of] Seir" (see Raphael Gibeon, *Les bédouins Shosu des documents égyptiens,* Leiden, 1971, nos. 6a, 16a). A land of nomads associated with Yahveh alongside the land of Edom (Seir) reminds us of the old traditions of Israel, according to which Yahveh appeared from Sinai, Edom, Teman, Paran, and Midian (*Dt.* 33:2, *Jgs.* 5:4, *Hb.* 3:3–7). The fact that Yahveh's revelation is associated with places scattered over the whole Sinai Peninsula as well as over the Edomite territory east of Sinai seems to indicate that Yahveh was venerated by many nomads of Sinai and southern Palestine and that "the land of nomads of Yahveh" refers to the whole desert to the east of the delta. To be sure, the god revealed to Moses and adopted by the Israelites reflects a unique phenomenon. Monotheism did come out of Israel and not out of Edom or Midian. However, in the light of the new evidence, one must consider the existence of some kind of proto-Israelite belief in Yahveh in the wilderness region of Sinai and Edom (cf. S. Herrmann, "Der Name Jhw in den Inschriften von Soleb." *Fourth World Congress of Jewish Studies,* vol. 1, Jerusalem, 1967, pp. 213–216; B. Mazar, "Yahveh came out from Sinai," *Temples and High Places in Biblical Times: Proceedings of the Colloquium in Honor of the Centennial of Hebrew Union College–Jewish Institute of Religion, Jerusalem, 14–16 March 1977,* ed. A. Biran, 1981, pp. 5–9). The Egyptian inscriptions which speak about nomads living in the land of Yahveh make it easier for us to understand the biblical traditions about the connections between the Israelites, the Kenites, and the Midianites during their wanderings in Sinai. Moses marries the daughter of Jethro, the Midianite priest (*Ex.* 2:16ff., 3:1f.), and it is during his stay with Jethro that he visits the Mountain of God. According to *Exodus* 18:11, Jethro gives full recognition to the god Yahveh and even helps Moses to organize the judicial institutions of Israel (*Ex.* 18:14–27). On another occasion we find Moses proposing to his father-in-law to join him and serve as a guide for the Israelites in the wilderness (*Nm.* 10:29–32). In *Judges* 1:16 we hear that the Kenites of the clan of Jethro settled together with the tribe of Judah in the Negev.

All this shows that there were close relations between the Israelites and other nomads in the desert, and, as we have indicated above, Yahveh's appellation in *Exodus,* "the god of the Hebrews," seems to support this notion. Another important contribution to the problem discussed here is the archaeological findings in the area. Excavations at Timna, some 30 kilometers (19 miles) north of the Gulf of Aqabah, have shown that the Midianites who built a shrine on the top of an Egyptian sanctuary mutilated the statue of the Egyptian goddess Hathor and reused many objects from the original structure. According to the excavator, Benor Rothenberg, there is evidence of a tent-sanctuary the Midianites erected on the place of the Egyptian shrine, and this brings to mind the tabernacle of the Israelites in the desert (B. Rothenberg, "Timna," in *Encyclopedia of Archaeological Excavations in the Holy Land,* ed. Michael Avi-Yonah and Ephraim Stern, vol. 4, 1978).

In this Midianite sanctuary a copper snake was found, which reminds us of the copper serpent made by Moses and mounted on a standard (*Nm.* 21:4–9). This was the only votive object found in the sanctuary. The Egyptian representations of the goddess Hathor were effaced, and the central niche was left empty. All this should be interpreted as a reaction of the Midianite nomads against Egyptian religion and culture, not unlike the Israelite reaction against pagan idols. Israelite monotheism is described in *Exodus,* as emerging out of a wrestling with Egyptian religion and magic (cf. *Ex.* 7:8ff., 8:12f., 12:12). Indeed, the aniconic tendency of Israel's religion is characteristic not only of ancient Israel but also of other nomadic tribes in the wilderness of Sinai and southern Palestine and seems to have persisted down to the period of the Nabateans in the third to second century BCE.

The affinity of Israel's faith with the faith of their nomadic confederates is clearly expressed in the episode about Jehu, the king of Israel (c. 842–815 BCE) who, by his zeal for Yahveh and his opposition to the Canaanite Baal, asked Jehonadab the son of Rechab to cooperate with him (*2 Kgs.* 10:15–16). The Rechabites, who were associated with the Kenites (*1 Chr.* 2:55: cf. 4:12 [Septuagint]), preserved their nomadic way of life for hundreds of years (cf. Diodorus Siculus 9.9 on the first Nabateans). They were persistent in their zeal for Yahvism (see *2 Kgs.* 10:16), which was the faith of their ancestors, the nomads who lived in the land of Yahveh, according to the Egyptian inscriptions. In this connection it should be noted that the ninth-century BCE prophet Elijah who, like Jehu, opposed the Baal worship, made a pilgrimage to Sinai to express his zeal for Yahveh (*1 Kgs.* 19), and, as will be shown below, reestablished the cult of Mount Carmel according to the Mosaic principles and Sinaitic traditions. The trend in the ninth century against Baal stirred a movement which strove for a return to the old Mosaic worship.

EXODUS FROM EGYPT

Among the nomadic tribes in the land of Yahveh (that is, the Sinai Peninsula), the Israelites were under Egyptian control, and, as I have indicated, the religion of Israel actually took shape in the course of a struggle with Egyptian religion and culture. As shown above, the Midianites, who were close in their religion to the Israelites, also fought Egyptian cult and religion. The struggle of the Israelite tribes with the Egyptians comes to full expression in the story about the liberation of Israel from "the house of bondage"—that is, the Exodus, which became the hallowed Israelite epic.

Historical Background. Egyptian documents tell us about constant movements of nomads from Edom and other eastern regions into Egypt as well as of movements from Egypt into the desert. In one of these documents (Papyrus Anastasi VI) we read about the entrance of nomads into the pasturage of the delta: "We have finished letting the Shosu nomads of Edom pass the fortress . . . to keep them alive and to keep their cattle alive," (James B. Pritchard, *Ancient Near Eastern Texts relating to the Old Testament,* 3d ed., Princeton, 1969, p. 259), and in another we are told about the pursuit of runaway slaves (ibid.). This calls to mind the biblical traditions about the Israelite tribes entering Egypt in order to survive a famine (*Gn.* 45:7) and about their subsequent escape from slavery (*Ex.* 13–14). The Exodus stories may perhaps be traced back to a clash between a group of enslaved Hebrew nomads and the Egyptian authorities.

Biblical Account. According to biblical traditions, the leader of the Israelites was Moses, an Egyptian-born man (cf. *Ex.* 2:19) who was at odds with the Egyptian authorities and had been forced to flee to the desert. There he found shelter amongst the Midianites and married the daughter of the Midianite priest Jethro (compare the Egyptian prince Sinuhe, who fled Egypt and found shelter in the house of one of the leaders of an Asiatic tribe). His acquaintance with the Midianites and his previous associations with Egypt enabled him to conceive his plans for the liberation of his brethren from Egyptian slavery. Moses availed himself of his ties with the Midianites and Kenites in order to find his way in the wilderness of Sinai (cf. *Nm.* 10:29–32), and these ties were remembered for hundreds of years among the tribes of Israel (cf. 1 *Sm.* 15:6). Furthermore, according to *Exodus* 18:12, Moses and Aaron and the elders of Israel participated in the common sacrificial meal prepared by Jethro, the Midianite priest, and learned from him how to administer justice, which procedure Moses initiated among the Israelite tribes.

Religious Meaning Ascribed. The successful flight of the Israelites and their interpretation of it as divine salvation turned into the main vehicle of national-religious education. The God of Israel was always hailed as the one who redeemed the people from "the house of bondage" (see the prologue to the Ten Commandments, *Ex.* 20:1 and *Dt.* 5:6), and the events of the Exodus were recited to the children of Israel, especially during the festival of Passover, in order to teach them loyalty to God (*Ex.* 12:26–27, 13:8, 14–16; *Dt.* 6:20–25). The events of the Exodus were also recited during religious gatherings of the tribes when they recounted their glorious past and the divine help given them (*Dt.* 29:1–5; *Jos.* 24:5–7; 1 *Sm.* 12:6–8; etc.). Individual thanksgiving also opened with praises of God for his deliverance of Israel from Egypt (*Dt.* 26:5–9).

The liberation from Egyptian slavery was the reason behind the divine command for the abolishment of slavery within Israel—"For they are my servants, whom I freed from the land of Egypt, they may not give themselves over into slavery" (*Lv.* 25:22)—and was similarly used as motivation for not oppressing the stranger— "You shall not wrong a stranger or oppress him, for you were strangers in the land of Egypt" (*Ex.* 22:20; cf. *Ex.* 22:9); "You shall love the stranger, for you were strangers in the land of Egypt" (*Dt.* 10:19; cf. *Lv.* 19:34). The liberation from "the house of bondage" was considered an act of grace by the God of Israel for which the people were to express their gratitude by being loyal to God, that is, by keeping his commandments. This loyalty had to be endorsed by a solemn act: a covenant between God and Israel.

EARLY CULTIC WORSHIP

According to Pentateuchal sources, God revealed himself to the people on a specific mountain called Sinai or Horeb. However, ancient poems hail several places in the Sinai Desert as places of theophany. For example, *Deuteronomy* 33 speaks of YHVH coming from Sinai, Seir, and Mount Paran (33:2; cf. *Jgs.* 5:4-8). In *Habakkuk* 3 we read that God comes from Teman and from Mount Paran, and in the continuation of this poem Cushan and Midian are also mentioned. In all of these instances God sets out from his holy abode (on the mountain) to save his people, not to give laws as in the later prosaic sources. Furthermore, in these poems the deity sets out not from a single hallowed place (e.g., Sinai or Horeb) but from various places scattered throughout the Sinai Peninsula and the northwestern Arabian Desert. It seems that there were several holy mountains in this area that served the nomads who venerated YHVH.

This supposition can be supported by the excavations at Mount Karkom in the Negev (see Emmanuel Anati, "Has Mt. Sinai Been Found," *Biblical Archaeology Review* 11, 1985, pp. 42–57). This mountain constituted a sacred site for nearly a thousand years (3000 BCE to 2000 BCE) and displays features that characterize Mount Sinai as it is presented in the Pentateuchal tradition. At the foot of this mountain twelve standing stones were discovered. These stones are placed next to a structure that looks like an altar (cf. *Ex.* 24:4). A cleft was discovered in the mountain that is similar to the cleft in the rock, described in *Exodus* 33:22, in which Moses hides himself.

Such excavational findings suggest that the Sinai Desert was the site of a long tradition of cultic practices; Mount Sinai was only one of many cultic sites. The elaborate biblical descriptions of the cultic practices at Mount Sinai may reveal aspects of worship at such sites throughout the desert. The center of the tribal worship was the Mountain of God, ascent to which was allowed only to the priesthood and the elders (*Ex.* 24:1–2, 24:9, 24:14). Access to the godhead was the privilege of the prophet Moses alone (*Ex.* 3:5, 19:9–13, 19:20–22, 24:15, 33:21–23, 34:2ff.). Beneath the mountain stood an altar and twelve pillars (*Ex.* 24:4), where sacrificial rites were performed.

A reflection of this procedure may be found in the stories of the prophet Elijah, who tried to revive the old nomadic religion in defiance of that brought in by the Phoenicians (*1 Kgs.* 18–19). Like Moses, Elijah ascends Mount Horeb (*1 Kgs.* 19), and the divine revelation to him is similar to God's revelation to Moses in *Exodus* 33. Both stand at the opening of a cave or rock with their face hidden or wrapped (*Ex.* 33:22; cf. *Ex.* 3:6; *1 Kgs.* 19:13) while seeing God's "back" pass (*Ex.* 33:23, 34:6; *1 Kgs.* 19:11). Both fast forty days and forty nights before or during their encounter with the deity (*Ex.* 24:18, 34:28; *Dt.* 9:9ff.). They demonstrate their zeal toward God in a similar manner: Moses commands the killing of the men who violated the covenant and worshiped the golden calf (*Ex.* 32:37–38); Elijah slaughters the prophets of Baal out of zeal for Yahveh and his covenant with the children of Israel (*1 Kgs.* 18:40, 19:10, 19:14).

More instructive is the parallel of the cultic establishment by Moses at Sinai and by Elijah at Mount Carmel. Like Moses, who builds an altar at Sinai and erects twelve stone pillars there in order to mark the bond between God and Israel, Elijah restores the altar of Yahveh at Carmel with twelve stones, which represent the tribes of Israel, and performs the sacrificial rite, which symbolizes the presence of God and the reestablishment of the relationship with him (*1 Kgs.* 18:30ff.). Just as the people at Sinai confirm their bond with God by a solemn declaration of loyalty ("The people declared unanimously: 'Whatever Yahveh commanded we shall do,' " *Ex.* 24:3, 24:7; cf. *Ex.* 19:5), so the people gathered at Mount Carmel declare, "Yahveh alone is God" (*1 Kgs.* 18:39). Furthermore, the establishment of Yahveh's cult at Mount Carmel is strikingly similar to its establishment at the Tabernacle at Sinai. In the Priestly account of the dedication of the Tabernacle (*Lv.* 9:24), we read that when the people saw that the fire of Yahveh consumed the burnt offering, they fell on their faces and shouted (that is, they proclaimed in a hymnic way the praise of God). Similarly, we read of the ceremony at Mount Carmel that when all the people saw the fire of Yahveh consuming the burnt offering, and so on, they fell on their faces and said, "Yahveh alone is God, Yahveh alone is God" (*1 Kgs.* 18:39).

Though not all of these features may be traced to the time of Moses, it seems that most of them are rooted in the ancient nomadic reality of the Israelite tribes reflected in Mosaic tradition. In the Elijah stories there is a conscious tendency to reshape the religion as it was in the Mosaic period, which means that there was a strong awareness in Israel of the period of the Sinai revelation and its importance for the faith of the nation. In the light of the adduced parallels we may say that the Mosaic religion as presented in the Pentateuch was already a living tradition in the northern kingdom of Israel in the ninth century BCE. This implies that the kernel of this tradition goes back to premonarchic times, when tribal religion was fresh and dominant in the life of Israel and historically close to the Mosaic period.

COVENANT BETWEEN GOD AND ISRAEL

The covenant of Sinai, which became so central in the religion of Israel, denotes not a bilateral agreement between the deity and the people but rather a commitment by the people to keep the law of YHVH as it is inscribed on tablets and found in the "Book of the Covenant" (*Ex.* 24:3–8). The word *covenant* (Heb., *berit*) means a bond or obligation that is accompanied by a pledge or oath and that is validated by sanctions, dramatized curses, threats, and the like performed in specific cultic rites.

A very old Mosaic cultic rite not repeated in later periods is the blood covenant as described in *Exodus* 24:3–8. After Moses builds an altar at the foot of Mount Sinai and erects twelve stone pillars, he prepares sacrifices and uses the blood of the animal sacrifices for the covenantal ceremonies. Half of the blood he sprinkles on the altar (and, apparently, on the stone pillars), and the other half he puts into basins in order to sprinkle it over the people. Then he declares: "This is the blood of the covenant that the Lord [YHVH] has cut with you" (*Ex.* 24:8).

Blood covenantal ceremonies are attested in ancient nomadic societies. Herodotus (3.8), writing in the fifth century BCE, tells about covenantal procedures of the ancient Arabs. We read that the covenant was performed by taking blood of the participants' thumbs and smearing it on the holy stones which stood between them. A closer analogy to the Sinaitic blood ritual is found in a Ramesside ostracon of the twelfth century BCE. Here we read about a father reproaching his son for associating himself with the Semites of the delta by eating bread mixed with blood, that is, by making a pact with them (see Jaroslav Černy, "Reference to Blood Brotherhood among Semites in an Egyptian Text of the Ramesside Period," *Journal of Near Eastern Studies* 14, 1955, pp. 161–163). The fact that the blood ritual is found only in the Sinaitic ceremony may teach us that it belongs to the ancient nomadic reality and therefore reflects a Mosaic background.

REVELATION AT SINAI

In the description of the Sinaitic cult we find a clear distinction between the place of revelation on Mount Sinai and the place of worship below the mountain. This situation is reflected in the tradition about the tent of meeting *(ohel mo'ed)* at Sinai. According to *Exodus* 33:7–11, Moses pitches the tent of meeting outside the camp, and there it serves as a place of encounter between God and Moses. This contrasts with the later description of the Tabernacle by the Priestly source, which conceives the tent of meeting as the sanctuary in the middle of the camp, where Moses meets God (cf. *Ex.* 29:42–43; 40:34–35). The two phenomena, revelation and cult, which previously existed separately, amalgamated here, a situation which prevailed in later times when prophecy and cult joined hands in the Israelite and Judahite temples.

The place of revelation, be it the top of the mountain or the tent outside the camp, was out of bounds to the people. Indeed, according to the Sinaitic tradition it was Moses alone who received the words of God (the Decalogue), and as mediator, he delivered them afterward to the people. Literary criticism shows that gradually the notion developed that all Israel witnessed the theophany at Sinai and received with tremor the Ten Commandments. The rest of the laws were given indirectly; that is, they were transmitted through Moses (*Ex.* 24:3, *Dt.* 5:28ff.). But the distinction between two kinds of divine legislation, a short one written on tablets *(luḥot)* and a longer one written on a "book" *(sefer)*, always prevailed. As described in *Exodus* 32, the Ten Commandments, the basic constitution of Israel, were written by God on the tablets, which were put into the Ark, which represented the footstool of the deity, as described above. As holy documents they were deposited, as it were, beneath the feet of God, a procedure known to us from other ancient Near Eastern cultures.

That the words written on the tablets of the covenant are identical with the commandments of *Exodus* 20 is explicitly said in *Deuteronomy* 5:19, 9:10, and 10:4, and there is no reason to suppose that this was differently understood in former times. A series of cultic commandments in *Exodus* 23:10–19 (paralleled in *Exodus* 34:10–26) has been considered the original Decalogue by some scholars, who see the traditional Decalogue (*Ex.* 20:1–14) as a later ethical decalogue inspired by prophetic circles. But there is no warrant for this supposition. The division of the series of laws in *Exodus* 23:10–19 and 34:10–26 into ten discrete commandments is highly controversial, and the idea that a "cultic decalogue" should be more ancient than an "ethical" one has no basis at all. There is nothing specifically prophetic in the ethical decalogue; on the contrary, one can show that the prophets drew upon it (see *Hos.* 4:2, *Jer.* 7:9) and not vice versa. The "ten words" written on the tablets (cf. also *Ex.* 34:27) should be seen as identical with the commandments in *Exodus* 20:2–17 (and *Dt.* 5:6–18), while the series of cultic laws in *Exodus* 23:10–19 and 34:10–26 belongs to the Book of the Covenant.

THE TEN COMMANDMENTS: THEIR ESSENCE AND FUNCTION

From the point of view of content and form there is no difference between the Ten Commandments and other laws. The various law codes of the Bible contain the same injunctions which are attested in the Decalogue in both its versions. The prohibitions against idolatry and swearing falsely, the observance of the Sabbath, the honoring of parents, and the prohibitions against murder, adultery theft, and false witness—all these appear again and again in the various laws of the Pentateuch. The only exception is the injunction against coveting a neighbor's property, and this is indeed indicative of the particular nature of the Decalogue.

Let me state the five most particular and most characteristic features of the Decalogue.

1. *Universality.* In contrast to the ordinary laws whose enactment depends on particular personal or social circumstances such as sacrifices offered in various conditions (e.g., priestly dues dependent on income; civil laws dependent on ownership of property; laws of matrimony dependent on family status, etc.), the ordinances of the Decalogue apply to everybody regardless of circumstances. Every Israelite is committed not to practice idolatry and not to swear falsely, to observe the Sabbath and honor his or her parents, not to murder, not to commit adultery, not to steal, not to give false witness, and not to covet, no matter what his or her personal status is or in what society or in which period he or she lives. The commandments have thus universal validity.

2. *Restrictive conditionality.* The commandments are for the most part formulated in the negative, and even the positive, such as observance of the Sabbath and honoring one's parents, are in fact prohibitions. The observance of the Sabbath is explained by way of a prohibition: "Six days you shall work but the seventh day is a Sabbath . . . you shall not do any work" (*Ex.* 20:9– 10). Similarly, the object of the commandment to honor one's parents is to prevent offense or insult to them, as implied by the various other laws concerning parents (cursing and beating in *Exodus* 21:15, 21:17, and in *Leviticus* 20:9; rebellion and disobedience in *Deuteronomy* 21:18–21). These negative conditions determine the moral obligations or restrictions demanded of every member of this special community governed by the Decalogue.

3. *Instructability.* The commandments are concisely formulated and contain a typological number of units (ten) easy to inculcate. Biblical scholarship long held that the original Decalogue was even shorter than the present version and was approximately like this:

1. I am the Lord your God, you shall have no other god beside me.
2. You shall not make for yourself a sculptured image.
3. You shall not swear falsely by the name of the Lord your God.
4. Remember to sanctify the Sabbath day.
5. Honor your father and your mother.
6. You shall not murder.
7. You shall not commit adultery.
8. You shall not steal.
9. You shall not bear false witness against your neighbor.
10. You shall not covet your neighbor's house.

That the present form of the Decalogue is expanded may be learned from the fact that the explanation of the Sabbath commandment in the version of the Decalogue in *Deuteronomy* is completely different from that in the version in *Exodus*. This shows that both authors had before them a short commandment which they expanded, each in his own way. The author of the *Exodus* version added an explanation of a sacral-cosmogonic nature, while the author of *Deuteronomy* added an explanation of a sociohumanistic nature. The terse structure and short form of the Decalogue, the typological number ten divided into two (commandments concerning man versus God and commandments concerning man versus his neighbor), enabled their engraving on two stone tablets and their learning by heart. This intimates that these commandments make up a set of fundamental conditions which every Israelite was obliged to know and to inculcate.

4. *Covenantal, nonlegislative nature.* The commandments are, as indicated, essentially categorical imperatives of universal validity; they are beyond a specific historical time and place and independent of circumstances. Therefore no punishment is prescribed, and no detailed definition of each crime is given. One might ask what kind of theft is meant in the eighth commandment and what would be the thief's punishment, but these questions are irrelevant since the commandments are not intended to represent legislation as such; rather, they constitute the formulation of God's decrees set as conditions for being part of the covenantal community. The tenth commandment, not to covet, is irrelevant for any court legislation since no court could enforce punishment for mere intention (cf. Bernard S. Jackson, *Essays in Jewish and Comparative Legal History,* Leiden, 1975, pp. 212ff.). It is a principle employed by God's justice for the holy community and not by jurisprudence of man. Only under the terms of a covenant with God could man be punished for violation of such a commandment. The commandments are given to the people and not applied to the court. Anyone who does not observe these commandments excludes himself from the community of the faithful.

5. *Personal, apodictic nature.* The commandments are formulated in the second person singular, as if they were directed personally to each and every member of the community. This formulation of "I and thou" is not found in the legal corpora in the ancient Near East and indeed looks strange in human jurisprudence. The latter is usually formulated in casuistic style, that is, stating the objective case (in the third person) and giving the terms of punishment for the violation. On the contrary, in the Decalogue we find the apodictic style, which addresses the listener in the second person and does not mention punishment at all. This bears the character of instructions given by a master to his pupils or by a lord to his vassals. Indeed, this style is prevalent throughout the Bible in the various instructions and adjurations of the highest king to his subjects. (See my "The Origin of the Apodictic Law," *Vetus Testamentum* 23, 1973, pp. 63–75.) It is rooted in the covenantal assembly, where the God of Israel confronts his subjects and addresses them personally.

The Decalogue is, then, distinguished by its concisely worded basic obligations directed at every member of the Israelite community and is an aspect of a special covenant with God. It is an Israelite creed similar to the Shema' declaration (*Dt.* 6:4), which also consists of an easily remembered verse containing an epitome of the monotheistic idea and serving as an external sign of identification for monotheistic believers. It is no accident that both the Decalogue and the Shema' were recited together in the Temple (*Tam.* 5.1). In *Deuteronomy* the whole Decalogue pericope (chap. 5) precedes the Shema' passage (*Dt.* 6:4f.), which opens Moses' discourse, so that the combination of both in liturgy has its roots in the tradition of *Deuteronomy* itself.

Though we do not have clear evidence of when the Decalogue was crystallized and accepted, it seems to be very old. It is referred to by the eighth century BCE prophet Hosea (*Hos.* 4:2) and later by Jeremiah (*Jer.* 7:9) and is cited in two ancient psalms (*Ps.* 50:7, 50:18–19, 81:9–11), and one cannot deny that it might date from the beginning of Israelite history; it may even be traced back to Moses, the founder of Israel's religious polity.

A clear parallel in the ancient world to such a phenomenon as Moses, the prophet who reveals divine commands to the people, is to be found in a Greek document of the Hellenistic period. In a private shrine of the goddess Agdistis in Philadelphia (modern-day Alaşehir), in Asia Minor, an oath inscribed in a foundation stone of the sanctuary was found which contains injunctions similar to the ethical part of the Decalogue: not to steal, not to murder, not to commit adultery, and so on. These were revealed in a dream by the goddess Agdistis to the prophet Dionysius, who inscribed them on the stela of the sanctuary (see F. Sokolowski, *Lois sacrées de l'Asie Mineure*, 1955, no. 20, ll. 20ff.). It is also said in the inscription that whoever will violate one of the mentioned commandments will not be allowed to enter the shrine. Although this document is of late origin (first century BCE), it undoubtedly reveals ancient religious practice which is typologically similar to that of the Decalogue: a concise set of commandments revealed by a god to his prophet, who is to transmit them to the believers.

The tablets containing the Decalogue thus constituted a kind of binding foundation-document for the Israelite community. With the disappearance of the Ark of the Covenant and the tablets of the covenant sometime during the existence of the First Temple, the Decalogue was freed from its connection to the concrete symbols to which it was previously attached. At sacred occasions and every morning in the Temple, the Decalogue was customarily read, and all who were present would commit themselves to the covenant by oath *(sacramentum)* (cf. Pliny's epistle on the Christians who make an oath [*sacramentum*] every morning not to steal, commit adultery, etc., which is, no doubt, an allusion to the Decalogue).

Despite the similarity in background between the Decalogue tradition and the oath of the worshipers at the temple in Philadelphia, there is a decisive difference between them: the basic religious demands that are included in the first pentad of the Decalogue are not found and are not expected to be found in the Philadelphia oath. The first five commandments have a peculiarly Israelite nature: the name YHVH is mentioned in each commandment, whereas the last five commandments are of a universal nature and do not mention the name YHVH.

THE LAW

Biblical law consists of different literary types, indicating varying backgrounds of formation. In the oldest Israelite law corpus, *Exodus* 21–23, referred to in the Bible as *sefer ha-berit* ("book of the covenant"), we can recognize three types of law: civil law (*Ex.* 21:1–22:16), sociomoral law (22:17–23:9), and cultic ordinances (23:10–19).

However, this distinction blurs in the later law corpora, where the laws mingle and blend, leaving little possibility of distinguishing between the various types. Furthermore, civil laws, which account for over half of the Book of the Covenant and make up the larger portions of Mesopotamian law codes, gradually diminish and disappear in the later law codes of the Bible, because the religious legislator in Israel is no longer concerned about them.

This blurring of borders between types of laws is also discernible in the form and formulation of the laws. While in the Book of the Covenant the civil laws use a style known as casuistic ("if . . . then"), which is predominant in the ancient Near Eastern law corpora, and the cultic and moral-ethical laws use primarily an imperative apodictic style ("you shall," "you shall not," "do not," etc.,), in the late collections the styles are mixed. A law commencing casuistically switches in midstream to the apodictic, and no distinction can be made between them (e.g., *Lv.* 22:18–22; *Dt.* 22:23–24).

Furthermore, the later codes, and especially the Deuteronomic code, crystallized in the seventh century BCE, tend to free themselves of their legalistic character and become humanistic, sermonizing, and rhetorical. Thus, explanations given add a moral motivation for obedience to the law, for example:

You shall not oppress a stranger, for you know the feelings of the stranger, having yourselves been strangers in the land of Egypt. (Ex. *23:9*)

Six days you shall do your work, but on the seventh day you shall cease from labor in order that your ox and your ass may rest and that you bondman and the stranger may be refreshed. (Ex. *23:12*)

You shall not rule over [your servant] ruthlessly, you shall fear your God. (Lv. *25:43*)

You shall not take bribes, for bribes bland the eyes of the discerning and upset the plan of the just. (Dt. *16:19;* cf. Ex. *23:8*)

Furthermore, the "laws" themselves sometimes lose their legal character because of their moralistic, sermonizing nature:

You shall not hate your kinsfolk in your heart . . . . Love your fellow as yourself. (Lv. *19:17–18*)

Do not harden your heart and shut your hand against your needy kinsman. Rather, you must open your hand and lend him sufficient for whatever he needs. (Dt. *15:7–8*)

Such demands, which are directed to one's heart, are in fact moralizing discourses and cannot be considered legislative. Even cultic-ritual laws are explained and motivated by inner religious and moral reasons. For example, the obligation to sprinkle the blood of the sacrifice is explained by the necessity to atone for the shedding of blood (*Lv.* 17:1–7). The prohibition against eating carcass is motivated by the notion of the holiness of Israel (*Dt.* 14:21), and the same motivation is given for the command to ban the Canaanites and to destroy the pagan cultic installations in the Land of Israel (*Dt.* 7:5).

COVENANT BETWEEN GOD AND ISRAEL

The obligation of Israel toward God to keep his law equals the pledge to show loyalty to him. Besides the Mosaic covenant, which is based on the promise to observe the laws, we find in *Joshua* 24 a covenant which stipulates exclusive loyalty to the one God. Joshua's covenant, which took place in Shechem, modern-day Nablus (cf. *Dt.* 27 and *Jos.* 8:30–35), is mainly concerned with the choice of the God of Israel and the observance of strict loyalty toward him: "He is a jealous God. . . . if you forsake the Lord and serve alien gods, . . . he will make an end of you" (*Jos.* 24:19–20). This covenant, which was concerned with loyalty and made at the entrance to the Promised Land, was especially necessary because of the exposure to Canaanite religion and the danger of religious contamination.

In fact, the Shechemite covenant described in *Joshua,* which is associated—as indicated—with the foundation ceremony between mounts Gerizim and Ebal (cf. *Dt.* 27, *Jos.* 8:30–35), is close in its character to the covenant of the plains of Moab, presented in *Deuteronomy.* This covenant takes place before the crossing into the Promised Land and is defined as an act of establishing a relationship between God and Israel (*Dt.* 26:17–19, 27:9–10, 29:12; see expecially *Dt.* 27:9: "This day you have become a people belonging to the Lord your God").

The two covenants presented in the Pentateuch, the one at Sinai (*Ex.* 19–24) and the other at the plains of Moab in *Deuteronomy,* were patterned after the type of covenant prevalent in the ancient Near East between suzerains and vassals. Thus we find treaties or, rather, loyalty oaths between the Hittite suzerain and his vassals that contain the following elements:

1. Title and name of the suzerain,
2. Historical introduction, in which the suzerain tells about the graces he bestowed upon his vassal which justify the demand for the vassal's loyalty,
3. The basic stipulation of allegiance,
4. Stipulations of the covenant,
5. Invocation of witnesses,
6. Blessings for keeping loyalty and curses for disloyalty,
7. The deposit of the cofenantal tablets in the sanctuary,
8. The recital of the covenant before the vassal and his subjects.

All these are reflected in the Pentateuchal covenants. First comes God's introduction of himself, then a historical introduction (*Ex.* 19:4, *Dt.* 1–11; cf. *Jos.* 24:2–13), the statement of the basic postulate of loyalty (*Ex.* 19:5–6, *Dt.* 6:4–7:26, 10:12–22; cf. *Jos.* 24:19–24), covenantal stipulations (*Ex.* 21–23, *Dt.* 12–26), invocation of witnesses (*Dt.* 4:26, 30:9, 31:28; cf. *Jos.* 24:22, 24:27), blessings and curses (*Ex.* 23:16–28, *Dt.* 28), the deposit of the tablets of the covenant and the Book of the Covenant (*Ex.* 25:21, *Dt.* 10:1–5, 31:24–26; cf. *Jos.* 24:26), and the recital of the covenant before the people (*Ex.* 24:7, *Dt.* 31:9–13).

The forms which served a political need in the ancient Near East came then to serve a religious purpose in Israel. The religious use of a political instrument was especially suitable to Israel because the religion of Israel was the only religion that demanded exclusive (monotheistic) loyalty; it precluded the possibility of multiple loyalties, such as were found in other religions where the believer was bound in diverse relationships to many gods. The stipulation in political treaties demanding exclusive loyalty to one king corresponds strikingly to the religious belief in one single, exclusive deity. The political imagery applied to the divine being also helped crystallize the concept of the kingship of God so that in Israel the relations between the people and their God were patterned after the conventional model of relations between a king and his subjects. Thus, for example, political loyalty was generally expressed by the term *love* (see my article, "The Loyalty Oath in the Ancient Near East," in *Ugarit Forschungen* 8, 1976: 383–384). The emperor demanding loyalty of his subjects enjoins: "Love the king of Assyria as you love yourselves" (see Donald. J. Wiseman, *Vassal Treaties of Esarhaddon,* London 1958, p. 49). Similarly, the worldly emperor demands love "with the whole heart and soul," thus placing in context *Deuteronomy* 6:5: "and you will love the Lord your God with all your heart and with all your soul." *Love* here, as in the treaties, means loyalty and absolute devotion.

The notion of exclusive loyalty that is characteristic of the monotheistic belief has been dressed not only in the metaphor of the relationship between suzerain and vassal but also in the metaphor of the relationships between father and son and husband and wife. Just as one can be faithful only to one suzerain, to one father, and to one husband, so one can be faithful only to the God of Israel and not to other gods as well. The prophets elaborated the husband-wife metaphor in describing the relations between God and Israel (*Hos.* 3, *Jer.* 3:1–10, *Ez.* 16, 23).

SPIRITUAL TRANSFORMATION OF CULTIC RITUALS

Cultic acts in pagan religions were performed in order to reenact events of the divine sphere, such as the celebration of the divine marriage *(hieros gamos),* the dramatization of the death of the young god (Tammuz) and his annual resurrection, the ceremonies of awakening the god, and so forth. These are not attested at all in Israelite religion. By the same token, no magic procedure is applied in Israel's ritual. The priest never used spells in order to drive out evil spirits, and no incantations were used in the Israelite cult. It is true, sacrifices and purification rituals were very common in ancient Israel, and the techniques of sprinkling blood and burning incense before the deity were practiced like in the pagan religion. We even find the scapegoat ritual on the Day of Atonement (*Lv.* 16). However, in contrast to the pagan cult, all these are not accompanied by spells and magical formulas, save the confession of sin (*Lv.* 16:21).

The festivals and rituals of the Israelites, many of which derived from the customs and celebrations of ancient Near Eastern peoples, especially those of Hittite-Hurrian origin (cf. Moshe Weinfeld, 1983), underwent a transformation when adapted to the religion of the Israelites. As opposed to the mytho-theogonic explanations of the ancient Near Eastern festivals, the Israelite festivals are given historical explanations. The harvest festival as well as the ingathering festival are, for example, associated with the Exodus (*Ex.* 23:15, *Lv.* 23:42–43). [*See* Sukkot]. Even the first-fruit ceremony, in which one would expect to hear about the god who fertilizes the earth and provides the crops, consists only of a thanksgiving prayer in which the liberation from Egypt and the grant of land by God are hailed (*Dt.* 26:5–10). [*See* Shavu'ot.]

The New Year signifies the creation of the world by God, as in other Near Eastern religions; but in contrast to the latter, the New Year festival in the religion of Israel does not commemorate the combat of the supreme god with his rivals, as we find in the Babylonian opic *Enuma elish,* which was recited in the New Year ritual. The New Year in Israel serves as a day of "rememberance before the Lord," indicating the beginning of God's rule over the world. It is called "day of acclamation" (*yom teru'ah, Nm.* 20:1; cf. *Lv.* 23:24) because of the blowing of the horn, which signifies the coronation of a new king. This is the day of God's ascent to the throne and of his salutation as king (cf. *Ps.* 47, 96699) and therefore bears a cosmic character. In the liturgy of this day there comes to expression the hope that all the nations will recognize the sovereignty of Israel's god-king and will abandon idolatry (see Sigmund Mowinckel, *The Psalms in Israel's Worship,* vol. 1, Oxford, 1962, pp. 101–189).

The severance of the cult from its mythological and magical background transforms the ritual into a series of actions symbolizing spiritual values. The tenth day of the New Year festival, Yom Kippur, whose main purpose was the purification for the sanctuary (cf. the *kuppuru* rites in the Mesopotamian New Year festival Akitu), becomes the Day of Atonement for the sins of the individual. The ceremony of purification itself (*Lv.* 16) has a lot in common with Hittite and Assyro-Babylonian purification ceremonies (see Weinfeld, 1983, pp. 111-114); however, the distinct feature of the Israelite atonement ceremony is the confession of the sins of the children of Israel (*Lv.* 16:30) and the injunction associated with it ot fast on this day (*Lv.* 16:29; cf. *Lv.* 23:27–32). [*See* Ro'sh ha-Shannah and Yom Kippur.]

A similar transformation from a cultic aspect to a spiritual-moral one may be recognized in the Sabbath. The Sabbath was originally seen as a reenactment of God's res during creation (*Gn.* 2:1–3; *Ex.* 20:11, 31:17). 20:11, 31:17). However, the institution of Shabbat in Israel became a covenantal sign that attested to the establishment of an eternal relationship between God and his people (*Ex.* 31:16–17). Elsewhere we find a moral-humanistic interpretation of the institution of Shabbat: it was instituted in order to give rest to the enslaved and deprived (*Ex.* 23:12) and was motivated by the liberation of Israel from Egyptian slavery (*Dt.* 5:15). The idea of resting every seventh day undoubtedly has roots in the ancient world, where certain days (connected with the lunar cycle) were considered unfit for human activities. In Israel, however, these days were dissociated from their ancient magical background and became sanctified days endowed with deep; moral-religious meaning. [*See* Shabbat.]

Other rituals, too, underwent similar transformations. Circumsion, an initiation rite known among various peoples, was explained in Israel as a sign of God's covenant with Abraham and as signifying the bond between God and Israel (*Gn.* 17:7ff.). The act of circumcision was gradually spiritualized and was applied to the heart, as, for example, in *Jeremiah* 4:4: "Circumcise your hearts to the Lord and remove the foreskins of your hearts" (cf. *Dt.* 10:16). Circumcision of heart means repentance, as becomes clear from *Deuteronomy* 30:6: "The Lord, your God, will circumcise your heart . . . so that you will love him with all your heart and soul."

Two more ancient Near Eastern symbols were transformed within Israelite religion. The amulets worn on the forehead (phylacteries) by the peoples of ancient Egypt and Syria were considered protective symbols of the deity with whom the believer was associated (see O. Keel, "Zeichen der Verbundenheit: Zur Vorgeschichte und Bedeutung der Forderungen von Deuteronomium 6, 8f. und Par.," *Orbis Biblicus et Orientalis* 38, 1981, pp. 159–240). In Israel the signs on the forehead and on the arm were conceived as a reminder of the belief in the uniqueness of God (*Dt.* 6:4–8) and in the gracious act of Exodus from Egypt (*Ex.* 13:9, 13:16). In the same way that these symbols developed into the *tefillin* (a pair of small boxes containing scriptural passages), the tassels of the garments that were worn by aristocratic people in the ancient Near East became the four-cornered *tsitstsit*, a sign of holiness in Israel. Like these two fundamental symbols of the faith, most of the rituals and customs of ancient Israel were explained in a similar manner and thus were freed of their primitive connotations.

Centralization of the Cult: The Great Turning Point

Although there had existed in Israel a central shrine since the times of the Judges (cf. the temple at Shiloh, *1 Samuel* 1–2), small chapels and altars were also allowed. We hear about the patriarchs building altars in various places in the land of Canaan (*Gn.* 12:7–8, 13:18, 26:25), and we also find that during the time of the judges altars were built in the fields and on rocks (*Jgs.* 6:24, 13:19; *1 Sam.* 19:35). These other shrines were not prohibited; on the contrary, from Elijah's words at his encounter with God at Horeb (*1 Kgs.* 19:10, 19:14), we learn that the destruction of an altar dedicated to Yahveh is tantamount to killing a prophet of Yahveh. Elijah himself is praised because of his restoration of an altar to Yahveh on Mount Carmel (*1 Kgs.* 18). We first hear about the liquidation of provincial sites and altars and worship on the one altar in Jerusalem in the time of Hezekiah, king of Judah (715–686 BCE). It was he who destroyed all the altars in the country and commanded the people to offer sacrifices only at the Temple of Jerusalem (*2 Kgs.* 18:4, 18:29). It was this same king who dared to smash the bronze serpent which Moses made in the desert and to which people had burned incense up to that time (*2 Kgs.* 18:4; cf. *Nm.* 21:8–9).

The act of Hezekiah was actually the culmination of a process which started in the northern kingdom of Israel in the ninth century. That was the period of the struggle initiated by the prophets aginst the Tyrian god, Baal (*1 Kgs.* 17–19, *2 Kgs.* 9–10). From this struggle emerged the polemic against the golden calves erected in Dan and in Bethel (*1 Kgs.* 12:28ff.) and, finally, an iconoclastic tendency which affected the high places and altars all over the country, developing further a tendency to purge Israelite religion of pagan elements. The Canaanite cult involved worship at high places which contained pillars *(matstsevot)* and wooden symbols *(asherot)* next to the altar. Such cultic objects were seen as idolatrous by Hezekiah and Josiah (r. 640–609) and were therefore prohibited for use in Israelite worship. The legal basis for their acts is found in *Deuteronomy,* the only book of the Pentateuch which demands centralization of worship in a chosen place and prohibits erection of altars, pillars, and wooden symbols (see *Dt.* 12, 16:21–22).

The abolition of the provincial sites created the proper atmosphere for the spiritualization of worship as reflected in *Deuteronomy.* Even the Temple in Jerusalem was now conceived not as the physical house of the Lord but as the house in which God establishes his name (*Dt.* 12:11, 12:21, et al.). Furthermore in the reform movement of Hezekiah and Josiah, which is reflected in *Deuteronomy,* there is a shift from sacrificial ritual to prayer. The author of *Deuteronomy* is not concerned with the cultic activities in the Temple, such as daily offerings, burning incense, kindling the lamp, and so on. On the other hand, he is very interested in worship that involves prayer (*Dt.* 21:7–9, 26:5–10, 26:13–15), because he sees in liturgy the most important form of worship. Indeed, the historiographer of *Kings,* who worked under the influence of *Deuteronomy,* describes the Solomonic Temple not as a place for sacrifices but as a place for prayer (*1 Kgs.* 8:30, 8:34, 8:36, 8:39, et al.). This anticipated the institution of the synagogue, which developed during the Second-Temple period.

THE RELIGION OF THE BOOK: SCRIBES AND WISE MEN

Hallowed as the "book of the *torah*" *(sefer ha-torah)* written by Moses (*Dt.* 31:9), *Deuteronomy* became the authoritative, sanctified guidebook for Israel. It was the first book canonized by royal authority and by a covenant between God and the nation, established by the people gathered in Jerusalem in 622 BCE, under the auspices of King Josiah (*2 Kgs.* 23:1-3). Only after other books were appended to *Deuteronomy* did the term *Torah* refer to the whole Pentateuch.

The canonization of holy scripture which started with *Deuteronomy* turned the Torah into an object of constant study. The Israelites were commanded to occupy themselves constantly (day and night) with the written book of the Torah and to teach it to their children (*Dt.* 31:11–13, *Jos.* 1:8, *Ps.* 1:2). It is not by accident that *Deuteronomy* is the only book in the Pentateuch which uses the verb *lamad/limed* ("teach, educate"). The verb is most characteristic of wisdom literature, which was studied in the schools of ancient Israel, and thus reveals the scribal-educative background of *Deuteronomy. Deuteronomy* is indeed the only book of the Pentateuch which enjoins the people to act "according to the written *torah*" (cf., e.g., *Dt.* 28:58). This implies that it is not enough to do the will of the Lord; one must comply with the Lord's will as it is written in the book. Hence the importance of studying the written word, which became so important in Judaism, Christianity, and Islam.

The sanctification of the holy writ brought with it the need for scribes and scholars who had the ability to deal with written documents. It is in the period of the canonization of *Deuteronomy* that we hear about scribes *(soferim)* and wise men *(ḥakhamim)* preoccupied with the written Torah (*Jer.* 8:8). After the return to Judah of many Jews from exile in Babylonia, the man who brought with him the book of the Torah and disseminated it in Judah was Ezra the scribe (*Ezr.* 7:6, 7:11). Since the scribes and wise men were preoccupied with education in general, they did not limit themselves to sacred literature but also taught wisdom literature. The latter consists of didactic instructions on the one hand and speculative treatises on justice in the world (e.g., the *Book of Job*) and the meaning of life (e.g., *Ecclesiastes*) on the other. It is true that wisdom literature is cosmopolitan in nature and therefore addresses man as such and does not refer at all to Israel or to other sacred national concepts. However, this did not deter the scribes and wise men in Israel from incorporating this literature into their lore.

Wisdom literature was canonized and turned into an integral part of the holy writ. Furthermore, it was identified with the revealed Torah (cf. *Sir.* 24). *Deuteronomy,* in which the subject of education plays a central role, defines *torah* as wisdom (*Dt.* 4:6), and as has been shown (Weinfeld, 1972, pp. 260ff.), contains a great many precepts borrowed from wisdom tradition. The amalgamation of the divine word of Torah with the rational values of wisdom turned the law of Israel, especially the Deuteronomic law, into a guide of high moral and humane standards. For example, rest on the Sabbath is explained here as including rest for the slave as well as for his master; similarly, the seventh year *(shemittah)* in *Deuteronomy* is not just for letting the land lie fallow but, also, for the release of the debts of the poor.

THE IMPACT OF PROPHECY UPON ISRAELITE RELIGION

Prophecy was an indispensable tool for any monarchic society in the ancient world. No independent ruler could go out to war or initiate an enterprise of national character without consulting a prophet. Israel was no different in this respect from other nations. The only major difference between Israelite and pagan prophecy was in the way of obtaining the oracle. In the pagan societies the prophets resorted to mechanical devices such as hepatoscopy or augury, whereas in Israel these were forbidden and only prophecy by means of intuition was legitimate.

The prophets were thus serving political and national needs, which is why it is no wonder that most of them were furthering in their prophecies the interests of the king and the people (e.g., *1 Kgs.* 22:12, *Jer.* 14:13–14, et al.). However, the classical prophets, as idealists, managed to free themselves from the professional group (see *Am.* 7:14) and proclaimed, when necessary, messages unfavorable for the king and the people. This made them unique in the ancient world. In their drive for justice and morality, they predicted punishment for the violation of justice, and their words were preserved since their predictions were understood to have been borne out. In their messages the classical prophets came in conflict with popular tradition. They rejected the accepted mode of formal divine worship (*Am.* 5:21, *Is.* 1:13, *Jer.* 7:21–22) and spoke sarcastically and cynically about its conventional institutions (*Am.* 4:4, 5:5; *Hos.* 4:15). They even predicted the destruction of the Temple, which the people considered blasphemous (*Jer.* 26).

However, the prophets also foresaw a new concept of an ideal future in their eschatological visions. Israel was seen as bearing a universal message destined to obliterate idolatry and to bring the gentiles to the one true God, the God of Israel (*Is.* 2:17–18; *Jer.* 3:17, 16:19–21; *Is.* 45:20–25, 56:1–8; *Zep.* 3:9; *Zec.* 2:15, 8:20–23; et al.). In the language of the anonymous prophet ("Second Isaiah") who was active during the Babylonian exile, Israel is designated to become a "light for the nations" so that God's salvation "may reach the ends of the earth" (*Is.* 49:6; cf. *Is.* 42:1–4, 51:4–5). During the same period another prophet envisions that many peoples shall come to seek the Lord in Jerusalem, and "ten men from nations of every tongue will take hold . . . of every Jew by a corner of his cloak and say: 'Let us go with you, for we have heard that God is with you'" (*Zec.* 8:20–23). These idealistic universal visions marked the beginning of a process which culminated in the spread of monotheism through the agencies of Judaism, Christianity, and Islam. They stood in conflict to a particularistic trend which developed during the return from the Babylonian exile in the times of Ezra and Nehemiah (the middle of the fifth century BCE) and which led to Ezra's expulsion of gentile women from the community of Israel (*Ezr.* 9–10).

The particularistic tendency, which expressed a national/ethnic fear of assimilation, was based on scripture enjoining Israel's separation from gentiles (*Ex.* 23:31–33, 34:12–16; *Lv.* 20:26; *Dt.* 7:3–4). These verses refer only to the Canaanite nations, but they were interpreted as being directed against all foreign nations (*Ezr.* 9:12, *Neh.* 13:1–3), and an ideology was based on the idea that the new congregation should represent "the holy seed" (*Ezr.* 9:2), uncontaminated by foreign blood. If this attitude had prevailed, no proselytism would have been possible. Thanks to the universalistic "prophetic" movement, which aspired to admit as many nations as possible into the sphere of Jewish religion (*Zec.* 2:15, 8:23), the particularistic trend was neutralized and proselytism became possible.

An anonymous prophet of this period ("Third Isaiah") even polemicizes with the isolationists and says, "Neither let the foreigner . . . say: 'The Lord will separate me [*navdel yovdilani*] from his people'" (*Is.* 56:3). The prophet employs the same words used by Ezra when revealing his isolationist tendencies: "And the seed of Israel separated themselves [*vayibadlu*] from all foreigners" (*Neh.* 9:2; cf. *Ezr.* 9:1–2). The Judaism of the Second-Temple period managed to reach a synthesis between the two opposing tendencies. Proselytizing was subject to the obligation to keep the law: a gentile could become an Israelite the moment he agreed to take upon himself the precepts of the Israelite religion as embodied in the Torah, especially circumcision (for men) and observance of the Sabbath (see *Isaiah* 56:4: "the eunuchs who keep my Sabbaths, . . . and hold fast to my covenant [through circumcision]").

THE CRYSTALLIZATION OF JUDAISM: THE POSTEXILIC PERIOD

The period of exile and restoration left its deep marks on the people and changed their spiritual character. The severance of the exiles from their land made it easier for them to get rid of the cultic habits associated with the land, such as high-place worship, the burning of incense on the roofs (*Jer.* 7:17–19, 44:15–19), child offering (*2 Kgs.* 23:10; *Jer.* 7:31, 19:5; et al.), and other customs rooted in the Canaanite culture. After the exile, pagan worship never returned to Israel.

Because the exiles were deprived of sacrificial worship as a result of the principle of centralization of worship in Jerusalem, the spiritual, abstract nature of the religion was enhanced. The shift from sacrifice to prayer was facilitated by the very act of centralization, as shown above; however, as long as sacrifice was being practiced in the chosen place in Jerusalem, religion was still tied to the Temple. In the religious vacuum created following the destruction of the First Temple, stress came to be laid on the spiritual side of religion, and thus the way was paved for the institution of the synagogue, which is based on prayer and the recital of holy scripture. We do not know how this institution developed; it is clear, however, that in the times of Ezra and Nehemiah (end of fifth century and beginning of the fourth century BCE) it started its existence in Jerusalem. In *Nehemiah* 8–9 we find all the components of synagogue worship:

1. The recital of scripture with all the pertinent procedure, such as the reader standing on the pulpit (*Neh.* 8:4) displaying the scroll to the people while they stand up (*Neh.* 8:5), the recitation of blessings before the start of the reading (*Neh.* 8:6), and the use of the Targum (an Aramaic translation and explanation of the Torah; *Neh.* 8:8).
2. The reading of the Torah on each one of the holy days (*Neh.* 8:18).
3. The summoning of the people to bless the Lord before starting the prayer (*Neh.* 9:5).
4. Communal prayer (*Neh.* 9:6–14), which contains the elements of the Sabbath and festival conventional prayer.
5. The confession of sin and supplication (*taḥanun*; *Neh.* 9:16–37).

All this leaves no doubt that the synagogue service was already taking shape in the fifth century BCE. Since the service as described in *Nehemiah* 8–9 was sponsored by the leadership of the exilic community, it is likely that the exiles brought with them the liturgy as it had crystallized in Babylonia. This suggestion might be supported by the fact that the whole pericope of *Nehemiah* 8–9, which describes in detail the service of the congregation during the first month, the month of the High Holy Days, does not allude at all to Temple worship, which was undoubtedly quite intensive in this season of the year. The author does not refer to the Temple worship (the Second Temple was in existence since 516 BCE) or comment on this omission since its procedure was performed by priests according to ancient conventional principles.

The relatively newly established synagogal liturgy contained a great deal of edifying material: the doctrines of creation and election (*Neh.* 9:6, 9:7), sin and repentance, and the observance of the Sabbath and the Torah (*Neh.* 9:13–14); thus the liturgy turned into an instrument for the education of the people. Second Temple Jewry was dominated by the Babylonian returnees who, as descendants of the preexilic Judahite aristocracy, managed to preserve the genuine tradition of classical Israel.

Another important factor which shaped the character of Second-Temple Judaism was the impact of prophecy. The fact that prophets of the First-Temple period had predicted the return to Zion after a period of exile added to the glorification of the prophets and to the trust in their words. People began to believe that the prophecies about Jerusalem as the spiritual center of the world would also be realized and that the nations would recognize the God of Israel and finally abandon their idolatrous vanities. This was supported by the exiles' physical encounter with idol worshipers in Babylonia. Convinced of the futility of idol worship (cf. *Is.* 54:6ff.), the exiles apparently tried to persuade their neighbors of it. Some of the enlightened foreigners seem to have been attracted by the peculiar but reasonable faith of the Jews and joined the Jewish congregation (*Is.* 56:1–8; see above), a first step in the spreading of monotheism, and one which prepared the ground for later proselytism and for Christianity. It was during these several centuries that the fundamental elements of Judaism were settled.

Observance of the Torah. The exiles took seriously not only the demand for exclusive loyalty to the God of Israel, which meant complete abolition of idolatry and syncretism, but also the positive commands of God embodied in the law of Moses. They felt obliged not only to fulfill the law in a general sense but to do exactly as written in the book. This demanded expert scribes and exegetes to investigate scripture and explain it to the people (see *Neh.* 8:8).

At this time the Tetrateuch, the first four books of the Pentateuch, was added to the "Book of the Torah," or *Deuteronomy,* which had been sanctified before the exile, with the reform of Josiah in 622 BCE. The Tetrateuch was composed of ancient documents that had already been codified in literary sources, such as the Yahvistic-Elohistic source and the Priestly code. After adding these sources to *Deuteronomy,* the name "Book of the Torah" was extended to the whole of the Pentateuch, namely, the Torah, which was thus also taken as comprising the "Book of Moses."

The Pentateuch, then, comprised various codes representing different schools or traditions and different periods which sometimes contradicted each other. However, all of them were equally obligatory. How then would one fulfill two contradictory laws? According to the Priestly code, for example, one has to set aside a tenth of his crop for the Levites (*Nm.* 18:21f.), while the Deuteronomic code (written after centralization of the cult) commands one to bring the tithe to Jerusalem and consume it in the presence of the Lord (*Dt.* 14:22ff.). These laws reflect different social and historical circumstances, but since both were considered to belong to the law of Moses, both were authoritative; therefore, in the Second-Temple period two types of tithe were introduced: the so-called first tithe, which was given to the Levites, and second tithe, which was consumed in Jerusalem.

No less a problem was the exact definition of the ancient law in order to apply it to life circumstances. Thus, for example, the commandment "you shall not do any work on the seventh day" (*Ex.* 20:9) is quite vague. What does *work* mean? Is drawing water from the well considered work (as in *Jubilees* 50.8)? Interpretation of the law split the people into sects; the most practical were the Pharisees, who fixed thirty-nine chief labors forbidden on the Sabbath (*Shab.* 7.2), and thus tried to adjust the law to life. The Essenes, however, were much more stringent in their understanding of work forbidden on the Sabbath. Before the Maccabean Revolt (166–164 BCE), making war was forbidden on the Sabbath; in the Maccabean times, when the nation fought for its existence, the people learned that it could not survive without permitting themselves to fight on the Sabbath.

The struggle for the correct interpretation of the Torah was actually the struggle to fulfill the will of the Lord, and in this goal all Jews were united.

The Fate of the Individual. The problem of individual retribution and the fact of the suffering righteous is mainly dealt with in wisdom literature: *Proverbs, Job,* and *Ecclesiastes.* In *Proverbs* the optimistic view prevails: everybody receives his reward in accordance with his deeds. If one sees a righteous man suffering and a wicked man succeeding, this perception is only an illusion. In the long run the righteous will be vindicated, and the evil will fail (*Prv.* 23:18, 24:14–20, et al.). The wisdom traditions of *Psalms* express this idea most explicitly:

> though the wicked sprout like grass
> though all evildoers blossom
> it is only that they may be destroyed forever.
> (*Ps.* 92:8; RSV 92:7)

> Do not be vexed by evil men;
> do not be incensed by wrongdoers;
> for they soon wither like grass,
> like verdure fade away.
> (*Ps.* 37:1–2)

A similar solution is reflected in the prosaic narrative of *Job*: Job, the righteous one, is restored to his former happiness after long suffering (1–2, 42:7–17).

A different philosophical solution is offered in the poetic section of *Job* (3:1–42:6). In this section the point is made that no one can understand the ways of God and that one should not expect any reward for his deeds. The true faith is one that is independent of material interest. A more skeptical, cynical solution to the problem is found in *Ecclesiastes,* in which everything is said to be predestined by God, and nothing can be changed by man. Hence, one should not complain but enjoy life as long as one can; otherwise everything in life is vanity.

A somewhat mystical response to the problem of seemingly unjust rewards is found in the religious lyrics of *Psalms,* especially in Psalm 73. The Psalmist is perplexed by the problem of the evildoers, "the ever-tranquil who amass wealth" (*Ps.* 73:12), but finds the answer in God's dwelling. Through his trust in God he feels completely secure:

> My body and my mind came to end,
> but God is my portion forever.
> They who are far from you are lost. . . .
> As for me, nearness to God is good.
> I have made the Lord God my refuge.
>
> (*Ps.* 73:26–28)

The eternal portion *(ḥeleq)* which the pious finds in God reminds one of the expression of later Judaism about the portion in the world to come. That there was in ancient Israel some belief in immortality or blessed posthumous existence may be learned from Psalm 16. The Psalmist opens his prayer with a declaration that he seeks refuge in God, a declaration found also at the end of Psalm 73. Then he speaks about the holy in the earth (the ghosts, *Ps.* 16:3), and in this connection he mentions that he will have no part of their bloody libations, a procedure well attested in the ancient world in connection with necromancy (cf. Theodor H. Gaster, *Myth, Legend, and Custom in the Old Testament,* vol. 2. 1975). Afterward we hear an exclamation, similar to the one in Psalm 73:26–28: "You, Lord, are my alloted portion [*ḥelqi*]. . . . Delightful is my inheritance." (*Ps.* 16:5–6). He expresses his hope that his body will rest secure and that God will not let him down into She'ol and will not cause him to see the pit (*Ps.* 16:10); on the contrary, he hopes that God will let him see his presence (literally, "face") in perfect joy (*Ps.* 16:11). Most instructive here is comparison of the concept of She'ol with that of the portion of the Lord. She'ol, "the world of shades" *(refa'im),* is here understood in a negative manner, not unlike the Geihinnom (Gehenna) of the Second-Temple period, and is actually the opposite of God's portion and inheritance, which is reserved for the pious. That such ideas prevailed in ancient Israel may be deduced from *Proverbs* 15:24, where we read: "For the knowledgeable [in God's knowledge] the path of life leads upward, in order to avoid She'ol below." This view is supported by *Ecclesiastes* 3:21, whose author questions the generally accepted premise by asking: "Who knows if the man's spirit does rise upward and if a beast's spirit does sink down into the earth?"

Human Nature and Destiny. The prevalent outlook in the Hebrew Bible is that "man's thoughts and inclinations are always evil" (*Gn.* 6:5); "his inclination is evil from his youth onwards" (*Gn.* 8:21). Yet the fact that man was created in the likeness of God (*Gn.* 1:27, 5:1; cf. *Ps.* 8:6) makes him potentially good. God implanted in him the striving toward good or the good inclination (cf. *yetser ṭov* in rabbinic literature) which complements the evil one (cf. the tree of the knowledge of good and evil in *Gn.* 2–3). Indeed, the prophets envisioned in the ideal future a type of man who is naturally good and, consequently, who will do no evil.

Isaiah describes the ideal man in the framework of his vision of eternal peace (*Is.* 11:1–9). A world of peace between man and animal will be filled with knowledge of the Lord as water covers the sea (*Is.* 11:9). Jeremiah predicted that in the days to come, when the new covenant *(berit ḥadash)* will be established with Israel, there will be no need for teaching one another because every man and child will know the Lord, that is, will know how to behave:

> I will put my law into their inmost being
> and inscribe it upon their hearts. . . .
> no longer will they need to teach one another
> and say to one another: "Know the Lord,"
> for all of them, from small to great,
> shall know me.   (*Jer.* 31:33–34)

Obedience to God and respect for one another will be part of human nature, and force will not be needed to impose God's law.

TRANSFORMATION TO SECOND-TEMPLE JUDAISM

The canonization of the Torah during the time of Ezra brought with it scribal activity and exegesis that marked the beginning of a new period. Over time, the religion gradually shifted away from the domain of the Temple and its functionaries. The will of God, expressed in holy scripture, could now be interpreted not only by the priests but by trained sages *(ḥakhamim)* and scribes *(soferim)*. This shift was due in part to the fact that after the destruction of the First Temple exiles in Babylonia had begun to base their worship on prayer and the recital of the Torah. Furthermore, Jews living outside the Land of Israel were not subject to many of the purity laws and taboos connected with the land of YHVH (see *Hos.* 9:3–5, *Am.* 7:17b; cf. *Jos.* 22:19, *1 Sm.* 26:19). What had been the Israelite religion became less dependent on the physical reality. For Jews living outside the land and for those who had returned, the spiritual dimension of Jewish religious life intensified as stress was laid on institutions of a spiritual nature that were unrelated or only symbolically related to Land and Temple—the Sabbath, synagogal service, religious ethical obligations, and the other fundaments of Judaism as it was to evolve.

[*Related articles include* Biblical Temple; God, *article on* God in the Hebrew Scriptures; Israelite Law; Priesthood, *article on* Jewish Priesthood; *and* Prophecy, *article on* Biblical Prophecy.]

BIBLIOGRAPHY

Albright, William F. *Yahweh and the Gods of Canaan.* London, 1968.

Alt, Albrecht. *Der Gott der Väter: Ein Beitrag zur Vorgeschichte der israelitischen Religion.* Stuttgart, 1929.

Cross, Frank Moore. *The Ancient Library of Qumrân and Modern Biblical Studies.* Rev. ed. Garden City, N.Y., 1961.

Cross, Frank Moore. *Canaanite Myth and Hebrew Epic: Essays in the History of the Religion of Israel.* Cambridge, Mass., 1973.

Eissfeldt, Otto. *The Old Testament: An Introduction.* Translated from the third German edition by Peter R. Ackroyd. Oxford, 1965.

Fohrer, Georg. *History of Israelite Religion.* Translated by David E. Green. Nashville, 1972.

Gaster, Theodor H. *Myth, Legend, and Custom in the Old Testament.* New York, 1969.

Kaufmann, Yeḥezkel. *History of the Religion of Israel* (in Hebrew). 8 vols. in 6. Jerusalem, 1937–1956. Translated by Moshe Greenberg as *The Religion of Israel: From Its Beginnings to the Babylonian Exile.* New York, 1972.

Mowinckel, Sigmund. *The Psalms in Israel's Worship.* 2 vols. Translated by D. R. Thomas. Oxford, 1962.

Noth, Martin. *Gesammelte Schriften zum Alten Testament.* Munich, 1960.

Pedersen, Johannes. *Israel: Its Life and Culture.* 4 pts. Translated by Aslaug Møller and Annie I. Fausbøll. Oxford, 1926–1947; reprint, Oxford, 1959.

Rad, Gerhard von. *Gesammelte Studien zum Alten Testament.* Munich, 1958.

Rad, Gerhard von. *Old Testament Theology.* 2 vols. Translated by D. M. G. Stalker. New York, 1962–1965.

Vaux, Roland de. *Les institutions de l'Ancien Testament.* 2d ed. Paris 1961. Translated by John McHugh as *Ancient Israel: Its Life and Institutions.* London, 1965.

Vaux, Roland de. *Histoire ancienne d'Israel* (1971). Translated by David Smith as *The Early History of Israel.* Philadelphia, 1978.

Weinfeld, Moshe. "The Covenant of Grant in the Old Testament and in the Ancient Near East." *Journal of the American Oriental Society* 90 (April–June 1970): 184–203.

Weinfeld, Moshe. *Deuteronomy and the Deuteronomic School. Oxford, 1972.*

Weinfeld, Moshe. "Social and Cultic Institutions in the Priestly Source against Their Ancient Near Eastern Background." In *Proceedings of the Eighth World Congress of Jewish Studies,* pp. 95–129. Jerusalem, 1983.

Wellhausen, Julius. *Prolegomena to the History of Israel.* Translated by J. Sutherland Black. Edinburgh, 1885. Reissued as *Prolegomena to the History of Ancient Israel.* New York, 1957.

Zimmerli, Walther. *Gottes Offenbarung: Gesammelte Aufsätze zum Alten Testament.* Munich, 1963.

7

IRANIAN RELIGIONS

GHERARDO GNOLI
Translated from Italian by Ughetta Fitzgerald Lubin

Because of the scarce and fragmented data in our possession, we do not know the religions of ancient Iran, other than Zoroastrianism, as organic systems endowed with a specific pantheon, a mythology, particular creeds, cosmogonic and cosmological ideas, and precise eschatological notions. We can postulate the existence of other religions only through a careful analysis of those elements contained within Zoroastrianism that can be linked to a pre-Zoroastrian paganism and through an Indo-Iranian comparison. That is to say, we have no sources, other than the Zoroastrian, for any Iranian religion. Some scholars have viewed as testimony of a non-Zoroastrian cult those few religious references found in the royal Achaemenid inscriptions (sixth to fourth century BCE), as well as Herodotus's mention of "the Persian religion" (1.131–132), although, as is well known, Herodotus never refers to Zarathushtra (Zoroaster). Given these meager materials, we cannot be sure that the cults referred to were not affected in some way or at some time by the Zoroastrian "reform." In fact, it is probably most prudent to consider the religion of the Achaemenids—whose inscriptions also never mention Zarathushtra—as belonging to the Zoroastrian tradition and as a stage in its troubled and complex historical development.

Having said this, it is nonetheless possible to reconstruct a few essential elements of ancient Iranian religions through traces of ideas and beliefs that appear to be independent of the Zoroastrian tradition. Some of these are completely original, but most are held in common with ancient, especially Vedic, India. Such elements pertain mainly to rituals, the pantheon, concepts of death and the afterlife, and cosmology.

Rituals included libations *(zaothra)*, offered both to Āpas ("water") and to Ātar ("fire"). The latter was called Agni by the Indians. The libations offered to water were a blend of three ingredients: milk and the juice or leaves of two plants. Those offered to fire were also a blend of three ingredients: dry fuel, incense, and animal fat. In both the libations to water and fire, called *āb-zōhr* and *ātakhsh-zōhr* in late Zoroastrian literature, we find the symbolism of the number three, which also occurs in a number of Brahmanic practices, as well as the blending of ingredients from the animal and vegetable worlds.

These offerings to water and fire, typical of a daily and familiar ritual, were also at the heart of the priestly ritual called the Yasna by the Iranians and Yajña by the Indians, from the root *yaz* ("sacrifice, worship"). Animal sacrifice was certainly practiced in the oldest Yasna and was accompanied by prayers that made it sacred and justified it as a religious act through which the spirits of the household animals being sacrificed became absorbed into a divine entity called Gēush Urvan, the "soul of the bull." Herbs also played an important role in the Yasna, and the priest who carried out the sacrifice held a bundle of herbs in his left hand, called a *baresman* by the Iranians. In time the bundle of herbs was discarded in favor of a bundle of consecrated twigs.

Undoubtedly, *haoma* (*soma* in Sanskrit) constituted a central element in the cult. The offering made to the waters at the conclusion of the Yasna was prepared by blending milk, the leaves of a plant, and the juice squeezed from the stems of a different plant. The substance's name, *haoma*, applied to both the sacrificial matter and its *yazata*, that is, the "being worthy of worship," or deity, whom it represented. *Haoma*, which was endowed with hallucinogenic and stimulating properties and was seen as a source of strength for warriors, inspiration for poets, and wisdom for priests, was extracted in a stone mortar during a preparatory ritual, after which the consecrated substance was consumed by the priests and by those taking part in the ceremony. [*See* Haoma *and* Yazatas.]

The premises, the instruments, and the ingredients for the ceremony were purified with water in a meticulous and careful way. Purifying and disinfectant properties were also attributed to cattle urine (*gōmez*), a substance that played an important role in the Zoroastrian ritual of the Great Purification, Bareshnūm, as well as in the initiation of priests and corpse-bearers, in accordance with practices and notions that were certainly Indo-Iranian in origin.

Libations offered to water and fire, essential components in the ceremonial aspects of the cult, cannot be understood without an awareness of the complex symbolism linked to those two elements, both in Zoroastrian and pre-Zoroastrian Iran, as well as in ancient India. The Indo-Iranian background is particularly evident in the symbolism of fire: in the three ritual fires and in the five natural fires found in Iranian and Indian thought. We can trace the concept of the three fires, those of priests, warriors, and farmers, as well as the concept of five fires burning before Ahura Mazdā, in the bodies of men, animals, plants, clouds, and the earth, respectively, to the Indo-Iranian background. Two *yazatas*, Apạm Napāt ("grandson [or son] of waters") and Nairyōsanha ("of manly utterance"), are linked to fire and have Indian counterparts in Apāṃ Napāt and Narāśaṃsā, an epithet for Agni, whose name also belongs to a different god in the Vedas.

Concerning the pantheon, an Indo-Iranian comparison provides considerable help in reconstructing the pre-Zoroastrian religious environment in Iran. There are many divine entities that derive from a common cultural heritage, although they do, at times, present significant differences. Particularly important in such comparisons is the section of the Avesta known as the *Yashts*, or hymns to the various *yazatas*, which mostly perpetuate the worship of gods from an ancient, pre-Zoroastrian cult through a veil of zoroastrianization after the fact. Worthy of mention, in addition to the cult gods Āpas, Ātar, Gēush Urvan, and Haoma, are the nature gods, such as Asman ("heaven"), Zam ("earth"), Hvar ("sun"), Māh ("moon"), and the two winds, Vāta and Vāyu. A juxtaposition with the Vedic religion clarifies many aspects of an ancient theology dating back to a period that we can definitely call proto-Indo-Iranian. According to some scholars, a few of these divine beings, as well as others well known to the Zoroastrian tradition, such as Zrwan (Zurwān) and Mithra, were originally high gods of Iranian religions other than the Zoroastrian and were thus in competition with Ahura Mazdā, the creator god of Zoroastrianism. [*See* Ahura Mazdā and Angra Mainyu.] Apart from a few specific details in the theories propounded by various scholars (H. S. Nyberg, Stig Wikander, Geo Widengren), and apart from the complex question of the so-called Zurvanist heresy, it is hard not to recognize a certain degree of verisimilitude in their reconstructions, as we find embedded in the Zoroastrian tradition, and not only in the *Yashts,* clear traces of a plurality of heterogeneous elements gradually absorbed and modified.

The Iranian pantheon, like the Indian, was subdivided into two main groups of divine beings, *ahuras* and *daivas*, although there exists sufficient evidence to hold that in Iran the latter word at one time indicated the gods in general. This can be inferred from the Avestan expression *daēva/mashya,* analogous to the Vedic *deva/martya,* to which correspond the Greek *theoi/andres (anthrōpoi)* and the Latin *dii/hominesque,* all of which mean "gods and men." *Daivas*, as gods of an ancient polytheism condemned by Zarathushtra, acquired negative connotations only with the Zoroastrian reform. This happened also with some of the Indo-Iranian gods, such as Indra, Saurva (Śarva in India), and Nānhaithya (Nāsatya in India). The term *ahura* ("lord"; *asura* in India), on the other hand, maintained its positive connotations and became part of the name of the supreme god of Zoroastrianism, Ahura Mazdā, as well as being attached to the name of some of the ancient gods from the Indo-Iranian pantheon, such as Mithra (Mitra in India) and Apąm Napāt. [*See* Ahuras *and* Daivas.]

We are not able to establish whether, behind the image of Ahura Mazdā, which was probably created by Zarathushtra himself, there lies the Vedic Indian god Varuṇa or an Indo-Iranian god named Ahura or Asura.This problem, however, is not critical, for even if Zarathushtra's god were a sublimation of the ancient Varuṇa by the Iranian prophet's great religious reform, Varuṇa would certainly have already attained a higher status than that of other gods, such as Mitra or the other sovereign gods of the Indo-Iranian pantheon (Dumézil, 1968–1973).

If the Iranian Mithra corresponds to the weaker Indian Mitra, then Anāhitā, the other great divine being of the triad mentioned in the Achaemenid inscriptions, corresponds to the Indian Sarasvatī, through the Avestan Aredvī Sūrā Anāhitā. [*See* Anāhitā.] The latter, however, presents some very complex problems. Most likely, this ancient Indo-Iranian goddess was subject at an early date to the influence of religious concepts belonging to the Anarian substratum of the Iranian world. Even Herodotus (1.131), speaks of an "Assyrian" and an "Arabian" origin of the great goddess, who certainly shows traits typical of the Great Goddess of the most ancient settled civilizations of the Near and Middle East. In fact, in attempting to reconstruct Iranian religions other than Zoroastrianism, one must rely heavily on elements obtained through an investigation of the Indo-Iranian background. One must, however, try to ascertain, with the help of archaeological findings, what part was played by the Anarian substratum, from the Elam civilization to the so-called Helmand civilization, which came to light in the 1960s during excavations at Shahr-i Sokhta, in Iranian Seistan. A thorough investigation into more recent times is also necessary in order to see whether there are to be found, among the religions of the Hindu Kush, between Nuristan and Dardistan, any fossilized remains of ancient proto-Indo-Aryan religions (Jettmar, 1975; Tucci, 1977).

An Indo-Iranian comparison also provides many other elements pertaining to the pantheon, as well as mythical figures and epos. The latter has been the object of particularly detailed study in recent decades (Dumézil, 1968–1973; Wikander, 1949–1950; Molé, 1953). In this context, we find cast in a leading role the Iranian god Verethraghna, whose Indian name, Vṛtrahan ("slayer of the dragon Vṛtra"), is an epithet of the god Indra. Behind the sacred figure of Verethraghna, who represented victory in the Zoroastrian tradition, was, most likely, the idea of overcoming an obstacle to the activity of the cosmos, which is manifest through the flow of waters.

In the cosmogony of pre-Zoroastrian Iran, we find signs of a myth of separation of heaven and earth, in which the figure of Vāyu, the god of wind and of the atmosphere, the intermediate zone, must have played an important role. It is likely also that the doctrine of seven consecutive creations, of the sky, of water, earth, vegetation, animal life, man, and fire, which we find in late sources, in fact dates from very ancient times.

Essential elements are also provided by an Indo-Iranian comparison in matters pertaining to cosmology. Both Iranians and Indians believed that the world was divided into seven regions, whose Avestan name was *karshvar* (Pahl., *kēshvar;* Skt., *dvīpa*), and that it was surrounded by a mountain range. The central region was called Khvaniratha in Iran and Jambūdvīpa in India, and at its center was a high mountain, called Mount Harā in Iran and Meru or Sumeru in India. South of the mountain was the Tree of All Seeds, just as, in Indian cosmography, we find the Jambū Tree south of Mount Meru. The Tree of All Seeds was thought to be at the center of the great sea Vourukasha, to the south of the mountain standing at the center of the world, also called, in Avestan, Hukairya ("of good activity") or, in Pahlavi, Hukar and Cagād i Dāidīg ("the lawful summit"). [*See also* Cosmology, *article on* Hindu and Jain Cosmologies.]

The views of death and of the afterlife in the most ancient Iranian religions, before the Zoroastrian reform, seem to have included the survival of the soul *(urvan).* After wandering around the earth for three days, the soul was thought to enter a gray existence in a subterranean world of shadows, ruled by Yima, the first king, or king of the Golden Age, and the first man ever to have died. (The figure of Yima seems to correspond, although not without some question, to the Indian Yama.) There also appears to have been a notion of survival of a sort of "double" of the soul, the *fravashi,* linked to a concept of immortality typical of an aristocratic and warrior society, in which were present the values of the Indo-Iranian *Männerbund* (Wikander, 1983). [*See* Fravashis.] There was, as well, the idea of a terrible trial to be overcome by the dead man's spirit: the crossing of Chinvat Bridge, a bridge that could become wider or narrower, to the width of a razor's edge, depending on whether the dead man had been just *(ashavant)* or evil *(dregvant).* There was probably a test, analogous to this trial after death, used in initiation rites (Nyberg, 1966). [*See* Chinvat Bridge.]

Traces of a common concept of initiation can be found in both Iran and India. It is related to the basic Indo-Iranian religious idea of *asha* (in the Avesta) or *ṛta* (in the Vedas), which remained central even in Zarathushtra's reform, although modified by partly new and different aspects. If we compare the Indian and the Iranian ideas, we can see clearly that a vision of *asha* (or of the sun, which, in turn, is the visible manifestation of the Vedic *ṛta*), was considered by both as a step in the spiritual fulfillment of the believer, who thus became *ashavan* (Av.; OPers., *artāvan*), that is, a participant in the supreme state of possessing *asha/ṛta*. In fact, the Indo-Iranian concept, which the Zoroastrian tradition transformed into one of the Amesha Spentas, contained various positive meanings, from that of truth (its exact translation) to that of a cosmic, ritual, and moral order. The Iranian *ashavan* (Pahl., *ahlaw/ ardā*[*y*]) and the Indian *ṛtāvan* stood, although with different shades of meaning, for "the initiate" and, more generally, for those who, alive or dead, would succeed in penetrating a dimension of being or existence different from the norm.

The idea of the need for an initiation in order to achieve the supreme state of *asha/ṛta,* held in common by the ancient Indo-Iranian world and by what we may call "Aryan mysticism" (Kuiper, 1964), was also linked to the experience of illumination and of the mystic light. The blessed state of *asha* manifests itself through light (*Yasna* 30.1), and *asha* is to be found in "solar dwellings" (*Yasna* 53.4, 32.2, 43.16). The initiate is, then, first of all a "seer," one who has access to the mysteries of the otherworld and who can contemplate a luminous epiphany.

The experience of a mystical light and a complex symbolism connecting spirit, light, and seed form part of a common Indo-Iranian heritage and constitute, therefore, specific elements of an ancient Iranian religion that precedes Zarathushtra's reform. It may not be pure coincidence that we find in the *Gāthās* no mention by Zarathushtra himself of the concept of *khvarenah* ("splendor"), which was a notable aspect of Iranian religious thinking; yet we see it becoming part of the Zoroastrian tradition, as, for example, in *Yashts* 19. Khvarenah is a luminous and irradiating force, a sort of igneous and solar fluid (Duchesne-Guillemin, 1962), that is found, mythologically, in water, in *haoma,* and (according to an anthropological concept found in the Pahlavi tradition) in semen. [*See* Khvarenah.]

Khvarenah is an attribute of Mithra, of royalty, of divine and heroic figures belonging to a national and religious tradition, of Yima, of Zarathushtra, and of the Saoshyant; it does not have an exact Indian counterpart but is found in a context that, both literally and in terms of mythological structure, is strictly analogous to the Indian. [*See* Saoshyant.] In the Indian tradition, we find concepts concerning light—its splendor, its activity, its energy, and its effects—such as *ojas* (Av., *aojah*), *varcas* (Av., *varecah*), and *tejas,* meaning, respectively, "strength," "energy," and "splendor," concepts that closely resemble some in Iranian anthropology. The same adjective is used to describe "splendor" in both Iran and India: *ughra* (Av.) and *ugra* (Skt.), meaning "strong."

The Iranian religions other than Zoroastrianism, can, as we have seen, be partially reconstructed, not as organic systems, but rather in some of their particular and characteristic elements: cult and pantheon, cosmogony and cosmology, individual eschatology, anthropology, and psychology, as well as a concept of the experience of initiation substantially common to the entire ancient Indo-Iranian world. Such a common heritage was handed down in ancient Iran by schools of sacred poetry, which left their mark both on Zarathushtra's *Gāthās* and on the *Yashts* of the Younger Avesta.

[*For discussion of Iranian religions in broader context, see* Indo-European Religions. *For discussion of particular Iranian religions, see* Magi; Manichaeism; Mazdakism; Mithraism; Zoroastrianism; *and* Zurvanism. *See also the biographies of Mani and Zarathushtra.*]

BIBLIOGRAPHY

Preeminent among general reference works on Iranian religions is H. S. Nyberg's monumental *Irans forntida religioner* (Stockholm, 1937), translated by Hans H. Schaeder as *Die Religionen des alten Iran* (1938); 2d ed., Osnabrück, 1966. Among other invaluable references are Geo Widengren's *Stand und Aufgaben der iranischen Religionsgeschichte* (Leiden, 1955); Jacques Duchesne-Guillemin's *La religion de l'Iran ancient* (Paris, 1962), translated as *Religion of Ancient Iran* (Bombay, 1973); Geo Widengren's *Die Religionen Irans* (Stuttgart, 1965), translated as *Les religions de l'Iran* (Paris, 1968); and Mary Boyce's *A History of Zoroastrianism,* vol. 1 (Leiden, 1975).

On particular aspects of Iranian religions, the following works are recommended. On ceremonials, see Mary Boyce's *"Ātaš-Zōhr* and *Āb-Zōhr," Journal of the Royal Asiatic Society* (1966): 100–118. For a discussion of the Iranian pantheon and an Indo-Iranian comparison, see Émile Benveniste and Louis Renou's *Vṛtra et Vṛthragna* (Paris, 1934) and Stig Wikander's *Vayu* (Uppsala, 1941). On epos, see Stig Wikander's "Sur le fonds commun indo-iranien des épopées de la Perse et de l'Inde," *La nouvelle Clio* 1–2 (1949–1950): 310–329; Marijan Molé's "L'épopée iranienne après Firdōsī," *La nouvelle Clio* (1953): 377–393; and Georges Dumézil's *Mythe et épopée,* 3 vols. (Paris, 1968–1973). On the religions of the Hindu Kush, see Karl Jettmar's *Die Religionen des Hindukush* (Stuttgart, 1975) and Giuseppe Tucci's "On Swāt: The Dards and Connected Problems," *East and West,* n.s. 27 (1977): 9–103.

For discussion of the common Indo-European background of some concepts of the most ancient cosmography, see G. M. Bongard-Levin and E. A. Grantovskii's *De la Scythie à l'Inde: Énigmes de l'histoire des anciens Aryens,* translated by Philippe Gignoux (Paris, 1981). On the concept of the Iranian *Männerbund,* see Stig Wikander's *Der arische Männerbund* (Lund, 1983) and my "Antico-persiano *anušya-* e gli immortali di Erodoto," in *Monumentum Georg Morgensterne,* vol. 1, "Acta Iranica," no. 21 (Leiden, 1981), pp. 266–280. For discussion of the concept of *asha* and Aryan mysticism, see F. B. J. Kuiper's "The Bliss of Aša," *Indo-Iranian Journal* 8 (1964): 96–129.

On initiation, see Jacques Duchesne-Guillemin's "L'initiation mazdéenne," in *Initiation: Contributions to the Theme . . .* edited by C. Jouco Bleeker (Leiden, 1965), pp. 112–118, and on the common Indo-Iranian background of initiation through possessing *asha* and the experience of light, see, in particular, my "Ašavan: Contributo allo studio del libro di Ardā Wirāz," in *Iranica,* edited by me and Adriano V. Rossi (Naples, 1979), pp. 387–452.

For comparison of the Indo-Iranian notions of *ojas/aojah, varcas/varecah,* and so on, see Jan Gonda's *Ancient-Indian 'ojas', Latin *augos', and the Indo-Iranian Nouns in -es/-os* (Utrecht, 1952), pp. 57–67, and my "Licht-Symbolik in Alt-Iran," *Antaios* 8 (1967): 528–549. On the ancient Iranian tradition of sacred poetry, which was Indo-Iranian (and, more generally, Indo-European) in origin, see the various contributions by J. Wackernagel, Hans H. Schaeder, and Paul Thieme to *Indogermanische Dichtersprache,* "Wege der Forschung," vol. 165, edited by R. Schmitt (Darmstadt, 1968).

8 ZOROASTRIANISM

GHERARDO GNOLI
Translated from Italian by Ughetta Fitzgerald Lubin

With a history of some three thousand years, Zoroastrianism is one of the most ancient living religions. It is the most important and best-known religion of ancient, or pre-Islamic, Iran. It takes its name from that of its founder, Zarathushtra (Zoroaster), who probably lived around the beginning of the first millennium BCE. It was, therefore, the religion of Iran under the rule of the Iranian-speaking Aryan populations, members of the Aryan or Indo-Iranian group of the more extended Indo-European family. Another name for Zoroastrianism, Mazdaism, is derived from the name of the religion's supreme god, Mazdā ("wise"), or Ahura Mazdā ("wise lord"). Some scholars believe that a non-Zoroastrian Mazdaism also existed, but this hypothesis is most likely without foundation, as all historically documented forms of Mazdaism, even those mentioned in the inscriptions of the Achaemenid rulers (sixth to fourth century BCE), appear to be Zoroastrian. Thus we can consider Zoroastrianism and Mazdaism synonymous.

The roots of Zoroastrianism can be located in an eastern Iranian, tribal, and basically pastoral society. The religion originated around 1000 BCE and developed further under the first Persian empire, but its clear conservatism and strong traditionalism appear to be manifestations of a cultural attitude that emerged during the Sasanid period (third to seventh century CE). The evolution and profound transformations of Zoroastrianism are the consequences of its history. It survived the Macedonian conquest and the periods of Seleucid and Greco-Bactrian overrule. After the Arab conquest, it was handed down from generation to generation, throughout the time of the Mongol empire and the local hegemony of Turkic and Persian Islamic rulers, all the way to today's small and poor communities of Iranian Zoroastrians. It was also passed down to the influential Parsi communities in India (Gujarat, Bombay, the Deccan) and in modern Pakistan.

As a result of its history, attempts have often been made to distinguish between various phases of Zoroastrianism and to endow each with a slightly different name. Thus it has been suggested that the religion contained in the *Gāthās*, the texts attributed to Zarathushtra himself, be called "Zarathushtrianism," that the contents of the Younger Avesta be called "Zarathushtricism," and that the religion of the Sasanid period be called "Zoroastrianism" (Gershevitch, 1964). These definitions should be extended to include the religion of the Zoroastrian communities in Iran and India today.

SOURCES

Zoroastrian scholarship has always had to contend with considerable difficulties because sources of knowledge about the religion, in particular those pertaining to its earliest period, are few and conflicting. The Avesta, a collection of texts gathered in writing during the fourth or the sixth century CE, has survived only in part, and it presents a heterogeneous picture. In addition to the *Gāthās,* attributed to Zarathushtra himself, we find texts with very diverse structures and goals, dating from many different periods and handed down orally for many centuries, perhaps even a thousand years or more. The main sections of the Avesta are the *Yasna* (Act of Worship), which contains the *Gāthās* (Songs); the *Yashts* (Hymns of Praise to the Divine Entities), dating from various periods and partially reflecting an Indo-Iranian background; the *Vendidad* (Code against Demons), which has survived in its entirety and which is basically a code of purity to be used in the struggle against the evil power of the *daivas*; the *Vispered* (Worship of All the Masters); the *Nyāyishn* and the *Gāh* (Periods of the Day), a sort of Zoroastrian breviary containing prayers for priests and laymen; and the *Khorda,* or Little Avesta, a prayer book comprising selections from other Avestan texts, for everyday use. There also exist fragments of Avestan texts, including parts of the *Hadhōkht Nask* (Book of Scriptures) and the *Aogemadaēchā* (We Accept), which are important for their concept of the afterlife; and the *Nīrangistān* (Precepts for the Organization of the Cult). The language of the Avesta, particularly the more archaic forms found in the *Gāthās,* is extremely difficult, and in some cases interpretation of the text is uncertain and the results of philological work far from satisfactory. Such difficulties are made all the more serious by problems related to the codification of the texts, as well as to their transmission, as they were transcribed in a fairly late alphabet, created ad hoc and derived, basically, from Aramaic.

Sources of equal importance are the Pahlavi books, written in Middle Persian and dating, more or less, from the ninth century CE, a period in which Zoroastrian religious literature was flourishing, especially in the province of Fārs. During this time Iran had mostly been totally converted to Islam, and the adherents of Zoroastrianism had become a minority. Some parts of the vast Pahlavi literature are extremely important, such as the *Zand* (Interpretation), an exegesis of Avestan texts with commentaries, translations, and glossaries; the *Bundahishn* (Book of Primordial Creation), or *Zand-Āgāhīh* (Knowledge from the Zand), which pertains to cosmogony, cosmology, and eschatology; the *Dēnkard* (Acts of Religion), a summary of the knowledge of the time (ninth to tenth century CE) concerning various subjects; the *Wizīdagīhā* (Selections) written by the priest Zādspram; *Dādistan ī Denīg* (Religious Judgments), in which the priest Mānushcihr answers ninety-two questions on various matters; *Dādistān ī Mēnōg ī Khrad* (Book of Judgments of the Spirit of Wisdom), a typical text of Zoroastrian wisdom literature (the *andarz*); *Shkand-gumānīg Wizār* (Doubt-destroying Exposition), an apology of Zoroastrianism, containing a critique of Islam, Judaism, Christianity, and Manichaeism, which were interpreted as dangerous and deviant; and *Ardā Wīrāz Nāmag* (Book of Ardā Wīrāz), a work, widely known in Zoroastrian communities, that contained a description of a trip to the hereafter and a vision of heaven and hell, written in the style of a mantic composition. Many other Pahlavi texts are also extremely important in the study of Zoroastrian doctrine during the Sasanid and post-Islamic periods.

Zoroastrian religious literature did not, however, come to an end after the flowering of the Pahlavi books under the Abbasid caliphate; it continued to develop, in the context of the communities in Iran and India, using new graphic systems, such as *pazand* and *parsi*, and new languages, such as Persian, Gujarati, and even Sanskrit. The Parsis of India developed a considerable body of religious literature, written in both Gujarati and English, beginning around the middle of the nineteenth century.

Although the inscriptions of the rulers from the two great Persian dynasties, the Achaemenid—especially Darius I (522–486 BCE), Xerxes (486–465 BCE), Artaxerxes II (402–359 BCE)—and the Sasanid—especially Shāpūr I (241–272 CE) and Narses (293–302 CE)—do not belong to the religious genre, they are nonetheless important for the study of the historical development of Zoroastrianism. Historical and doctrinal inscriptions are also significant, especially those of the high priest Kerdēr, an influential figure under the early Sasanid rulers. Kerdēr was one of the authors of the refounding of Zoroastrianism and helped transform it into the state religion during the third century CE.

In addition to Zoroastrian sources, mention should be made of the classical ones, Greek in particular, as well as the Christian and Muslim ones. Herodotus, Plutarch, Strabo, and Diogenes Laertius, for example, are very important for the study of pre-Sasanid Zoroastrianism, as were Christian sources (Armenian and Syriac, particularly the *Acts of the Martyrs*). Muslim sources, in both Arabic and Persian, are also valuable for the study of the Zoroastrian religion during and after the Sasanid period.

ORIGINS

Zoroastrianism originated in the eastern and south-central regions of the Iranian world, between the great mountain ranges of the Hindu Kush and Seistan, an area that today is divided between Iran and Afghanistan. According to one tradition, Zarathushtra came from Azerbaijan, but this theory has no historical foundation; apparently, during the Parthian or Sasanid period, the clergy of a local sanctuary claimed that the cult originated in their region in an attempt to confer a higher stature and authority upon their own traditions. Moreover, the hypothesis that Zarathushtra lived on the outskirts of northeastern Iran, in part of the province of Chorasmia, at the eve of the establishment of the empire of Cyrus II, is based on arguments that do not stand up to critical analysis. Current research on the religion's origin is based on geographical information contained in the Avesta, as well as on an evaluation of archaeological findings and on a reinterpretation of the few available sources.

The geographical boundaries of the Avesta define the eastern Iranian world and include all of modern Afghanistan as well as some neighboring regions. The text does not mention any regions, areas, or places in western Iran, Media, or Persia. We also notice a complete absence of information about both Medes and Persians during the first half of the first millennium BCE. Furthermore, there is no indication of familiarity with urban civilization. All this seems to confirm that the world from which Zoroastrianism emerged was distant, both in space and in time, from the Achaemenid empire and from the founding of the unitary monarchies of the Medes and the Persians during the eighth and seventh centuries BCE. Rather, Zoroastrianism grew out of a politically fragmented tribal society whose civilization centered upon oases rather than upon fixed urban settings—although in certain areas this tribal society superseded an urban civilization that had flourished in the third century BCE (such as the Hilmand civilization, which was brought to light by excavations in Shahr-i Sukhta in Iranian Seistan). The society was ruled by a warrior aristocracy, that is, by one of the three classes—priests, warriors, and shepherds—that made up the original social structure of the Arya.

Within this society, religion most likely revolved around young warrior *(mairya)* fraternities (the Aryan or Indo-Iranian *Männerbund*), with their bloody cults, violent gods, sacrificial rites, initiations, and ecstatic practices that climaxed in a state of "fury" called *aēshma*. Animal sacrifices, especially those involving the slaying of a bull *(gav)* and the ingestion of hallucinogenic substances such as *haoma*, were certainly widely practiced. Zarathushtra inveighs strongly against them in the *Gāthās*, by giving a voice to Gēush Urvan, the "soul of the bull" *(Yasna* 29), who is presented as the victim of the fury of evil masters, and by condemning *haoma* as the urine of a stimulating and hallucinogenic drug *(Yasna* 48.10, 32.14).

DISTINCTIVE CHARACTERISTICS

The primary innovation of Zoroastrianism, which sets it apart from the religions of other Indo-European peoples in the Near East and Central Asia, is its emphasis on monotheism. Its outstanding feature, in the religious context of the entire Indo-Mediterranean world, resides in its radical dualism. Both aspects are fundamental to Zarathushtra's philosophical and religious doctrine. Zarathushtra's high esteem for speculation caused the Greeks to view him more as a wise man than as the founder of a religion; they saw the author of the *Gāthās* as one of the highest and most significant representatives of "alien wisdom." Nor is it pure coincidence that he was mainly known for his dualistic teachings, as were his most direct disciples, the Magi.

Monotheism and dualism are closely linked in the *Gāthās*. They are not in conflict with each other, for monotheism is in opposition to polytheism, not to dualism (Pettazzoni, 1920). In fact, dualism, far from being a "protest against monotheism" (Henning, 1951), is a necessary and logical consequence thereof; its purpose is to explain the origins of evil. The basis of dualism is essentially ethical: the nature of the two opposing Zoroastrian spirits, Spenta Mainyu ("beneficent spirit") and Angra Mainyu ("hostile spirit"), who are twin children of Ahura Mazdā, results from the choice they made between "truth," *asha*, and the "lie," *druj*, between good thoughts, good words, and good deeds and evil thoughts, evil words, and evil deeds. The choices made by the two spirits *(Yasna* 30.5) lie at the root of Zoroastrian dualism, and they act as a prototype *(Yasna* 30.2, 49.3) of the choices that face each man as he decides whether to follow the path of truth or that of untruth (Gershevitch, 1964). The good or evil nature of the two spirits derives from his own moral choice and is not, as suggested by some scholars, innate, ontologically given, or predetermined.

The concept of Ahura Mazdā as the creator of heaven and earth, day and night, and light and darkness *(Yasna* 44.3–5), as well as the ethical context in which Zara-thushtra conceived his answer to the problem of evil, demonstrates that the prophet was an original thinker, a powerful religious figure who introduced radical changes to the spiritual and cultural world in which he was reared. He responded to a deeply formalistic and ritualistic religion by strongly and insistently praising human worth and dignity. Early Zoroastrianism set itself apart from the sacrificial cult of a society in which militaristic values were still pervasive. It advocated an inward-seeking religion and favored an intellectual cult rooted in the Indo-Iranian priestly tradition— that of "Aryan mysticism" (Kuiper, 1964)—which had high regard for thought and knowledge.

The original Zoroastrian message, however, was profoundly transformed by the first generations of the prophet's disciples. Later, elaborations by the clergy even went so far as to allow various aspects of the old polytheistic and ritualistic practices to reemerge, albeit with some limitations. Contact with other religions, as well as historical developments in Iran, also contributed to the evolution of the religion. Ultimately Zoroastrianism, which had arisen in reaction to an archaic and formalistic religion, absorbed many of the concepts and values that belonged to the very world it had rebelled against, in particular those elements not linked with the ideas, practices, and ethics of the warrior aristocracy. The result was a complex religious tradition that has persisted throughout thousands of years of Iranian history. Zoroastrianism is based on an ethical approach and tends toward abstraction. Halfway between a prophetic and monotheistic type of religion, it incorporates elements and beliefs that also belonged to the great monotheistic religions that arose to the west of the Iranian world. At the same time it is a ritualistic, somewhat polytheistic religion, rich in mythology. Nonetheless it formed a highly original model that excercised a great and deep influence well beyond the Iranian world, both to the east and to the west.

THEOLOGY, PANTHEON, AND PANDEMONIUM

In Zarathushtra's conception, a dualistic vision is almost a natural consequence of monotheism, for dualism explains the evil that resides in the world and afflicts it. The problem of evil and suffering is basic to Zoroastrian thought, and the urgent human necessity of providing an answer to the problem is reconciled with an abiding faith in the dignity and freedom of humanity by means of belief in the so-called myth of choice.

Within the dualistic vision of Zoroastrianism, it is not only Angra Mainyu and Spenta Mainyu who are confronted by moral choices. The *daiva*s ("gods," a term that in later Zoroastrianism became a generic reference for the demonic powers), who are the progeny of bad thought, untruth, and pride, became evil because they made the wrong choice. As a result, the *daiva*s serve as the inspiration of humanity, which is poised in the center of the struggle between the two opposite poles of truth and untruth, of good and evil, of life and nonlife. In the *Gāthās* we read:

The two primordial Spirits, who are twins, revealed themselves in a dream. They have two ways of thinking, of acting: the good and the bad. And, of the two, the one who acts well has made the right choice, not the one who does evil. And when these two spirits met, they established, at the beginning, life and nonlife, and the consequence, in the end, of the Worst Existence for evil, and Best Thought for good. The evil one of the two Spirits chose to do bad things, and the Most Bounteous Spirit, clothed in the hardest stones, chose Truth, as is also true for all those who constantly strive to please the Wise Lord with honest actions. The daiva *did not get to choose between the two, because the* Deceiver *approached them as they were making their decision. So they chose the Worst Thought, and then ran to join Wrath, and together with it they have afflicted the world and humanity.*

(Yasna 30.3–6)

Above and beyond the *daivas* and the two Mainyus is the Wise Lord, Ahura Mazdā, who was most likely created by Zarathushtra. The name itself has no parallel in India—apart from the first half, *ahura,* "lord" (Old Indian, *asura*)—and in this it differs from the names of many other deities or divine entities derived from the ancient Iranian pantheon. Ahura Mazdā's existence may have owed something, at least in part, to the Varuṇa of Vedic India or to an Indo-Iranian *ahura* or *asura,* which we might be able to reconstruct by using a comparative method. Yet Ahura Mazdā presents unique features that can only be explained by Zarathushtra's concept of divinity and by his particular intuitions. Zarathushtra's creation of Ahura Mazdā reveals that the prophet was a great religious reformer, a wise man in search of knowledge and enlightenment, rather than a follower of any traditional doctrine. Here Zarathushtra addresses his god:

This I ask you, oh Lord, answer me truthfully: who was created father of the Truth, at the very beginning? Who set the course for the sun and the stars? Who, if not yourself, causes the moon to wax and wane? This, and other things, oh Wise One, I want to know from you. This I ask you, oh Lord, answer me truthfully: who holds down the earth and up the sky so that it does not fall? Who [set down] waters and plants? Who harnessed the two steeds to the wind and to the clouds? Who, oh Wise One, is the Creator of Good Thought? This I ask you, oh Lord, answer me truthfully. Which craftsman wrought sleep and wakefulness? Who is responsible for morning, noon, and night, to remind the wise man of his duties? This I ask you, oh Lord, answer me truthfully if what I say is true: will Devotion strengthen Truth by its action? Did you, as good thought, institute Power? For whom did you make the cow a giver of prosperity? This I ask you, oh Lord, answer me truthfully: who created Devotion, and anointed it with Power? Who made the son respectful of his father in his own heart? I am the one who seeks, through these questions, to make you known, oh Wise One, as Good Thought, as the Creator of all things.

(Yasna 44.3–7)

In the passage quoted above we find terms such as Truth, Good (or Best) Thought, Devotion, and Power. These, together with others, such as Wholeness and Immortality (or Long Life), as well as the Wise Lord or, rather, his beneficent spirit, form a group of seven "beneficent immortals," the Amesha Spentas, who are of fundamental importance for understanding Zarathushtra's thought. They are mentioned again and again in the *Gāthās,* sometimes in reference to a divine subject, that is, the Wise Lord, and sometimes to a human subject, that is, Zarathushtra or other men. The seven are Vohu Manah ("good thought"), Asha Vahishta ("best truth"), Khshathra Vairya ("desirable dominion"), Spenta Ārmaiti ("beneficent devotion"), Haurvatāt ("wholeness"), and Ameretāt ("immortality"). These are entities as well as abstract concepts, aspects, or virtues of the Wise Lord and of the man who follows truth, or *asha* (Vedic, *ṛta*). Theological speculation after the *Gāthās* has arranged them by codifying their order and their attributes and is also probably responsible for devising for them a system of interrelations, based on an analysis of the physical world. Thus Vohu Manah is traditionally linked with cattle, Asha with fire, Khshathra with metals, and Ārmaiti with earth. According to Georges Dumézil's theory of the Indo-European tripartite ideology, subscribed to by a number of scholars of Iranian studies (e.g., Jacques Duchesne-Guillemin and Geo Widengren), an analysis of the Amesha Spenta system reveals what appears to be the typical framework of functional tripartition. In other words, Asha and Vohu Manah would appear to be Zoroastrian substitutes for the two main Aryan deities, Varuṇa and Mitra, representing the first function, that of magical and juridical sovereignty. Khshathra Vairya corresponds to Indra, representing the warrior function; Haurvatat and Ameretāt, of the Nāsatya couple, together with Ārmaiti, a polyvalent entity, conform to the function of fertility and fruitfulness.

It is not easy to understand the Zoroastrian concept of the beneficent immortals who form the retinue of the Wise Lord. In order to comprehend its meaning, one should probably keep in mind the double structure of opposites—good and evil, spirit and matter—that characterizes the Amesha Spentas, their interrelations, and their reciprocal conditioning. Their dual character—they are both divine and human—can perhaps be explained by a mystical experience. In this experience, Zarathushtra, or the man "who possesses *asha*" *(ashavan),* assumes divine virtues and powers while in a state of ecstasy called *maga* and, in so doing, joins the beneficent immortals and becomes identified, in a way, with the beneficent spirit who made the right choice. We should, of course, view the Zoroastrian language, however greatly innovative, in the context of the priestly tradition clearly identified as Aryan mysticism. The *Gāthās* shows us an inner religiosity, one that allowed ample space for individual experience.

Sraosha ("obedience'), the lord of prayer, is by his nature analogous to the entities in the *Gāthās*. He is particularly important both in the *Gāthās* and in later Zoroastrian tradition, where he protects against the evil of death and judges the soul after death. The other divine or superhuman beings of Zoroastrianism are essentially different from those in the *Gāthās*. Most are old deities from the Indo-Iranian pantheon, dominated by the figure of the Wise Lord. Because he was the only god in the Gathic message, the Wise Lord was subsequently, and increasingly, viewed as the supreme, although not the only, god of later Zoroastrianism. In the later form of the religion, monotheism became diluted, and with time it came to represent more of a tendency than a reality. This is made clear by older documents—other than the *Gāthās*—both religious ones, such as the Younger Avesta, and secular ones, such as the royal Achaemenid inscriptions, as well as by the Greek sources concerning the Persian religion, Zarathushtra, and the Magi.

Zoroastrianism did not integrate all of the ancient gods into its pantheon. Only those not thought to be in contrast with the main tenets of the prophet's new religion were absorbed into it. For the most part, the ancient *daiva*s censured by Zarathushtra remained outside of the new pantheon, but a few deities, who had probably been widely and deeply venerated, reappeared in Zoroastrianism. Their features and aspects, however, were partly modified, partly kept intact, and generally only thinly disguised under a veil of zoroastrianization. Thus the ancient gods became *yazata*s ("ones worthy of worship") in the new religion; in a language more secular and less priestly and theological, they can be called *baga*s, as in the Achaemenid inscriptions.

This major development in Zoroastrianism, that is, the tendency to reabsorb many elements from the Indo-Iranian "pagan" religion, even animal sacrifice and the cult of haoma, was the result of a long historical process that began in the eastern regions of Iran during the pre-Achaemenid period. The evolution took place over a number of centuries and was brought about by priestly groups that at first were eastern and can be called, for lack of a more precise definition, "Avestan priests," that is, *āthravan*s or *athaurvan*s (Old Indian, *átharvan*), "found in the Avesta," and later western, that is, the magi. Their theological elaborations led to a precise structuring of a pantheon and a pandemonium; each is characterized by analogous hierarchical structures and precise interrelations between the worlds of good, or of *asha*, and that of evil, or *druj*, so that each positive or beneficent entity has a corresponding negative or maleficent entity.

Not even the Zoroastrian doctrine of the beneficent immortals was left untouched. The Amesha Spentas, which had been mere abstractions and aspects of a divine entity, or qualities of those who attain the status of *ashavan* ("possessor of *asha*"), became full beings, in line with a tendency to angelicize that can be found throughout the entire history of religion in Iran. Within this framework, a significant development was the demonization of ancient Indo-Iranian gods, such as Indra, Nānhaithya, and Saurva; Indra, in particular, became a symmetrical opposite of Khshathra Vairya and the probable usurper of the role of the Indo-Iranian Vṛthraghna.

The *Yasht* section of the Avesta is the principal and most clear evidence available to us regarding the process of zoroastrianization of ancient deities within a new cultural context, dominated by the figure of the supreme god, Ahura Mazdā. The *Yasht*s are hymns dedicated to the various beings worthy of worship: Ahura Mazdā himself, the Amesha Spentas as a group, Asha Vahishta, Amaretāt, and Aredvī Sūrā Anāhitā, a goddess also known to us through the Achaemenid inscriptions, who corresponded to the Indian Sarasvatī; Hvare Khshaēta (the "brightly shining" sun); Māh ("the moon"); Tishtrya, the star Sirius, a rain god; Druvāspā ("possessing sound horses"), a female *yazata*, closely associated with Gēush Urvan; Mithra, who also appears in the Achaemenid inscriptions; and Sraosha and Rashnu, who, together with Mithra, judge the soul after death. Also considered worthy of reverence are the *fravashi*s, or spirits of the soul, whose worship was probably a surviving trace of an ancient cult of the spirits of the dead and of a concept of immortality typical of a warrior society; Verethraghna ("smiting of resistance"), the *yazata* of victory; Vayu ("wind"), the *yazata* of the wind; *daēnā*, the etymology of which is uncertain, probably meaning "image," as well as "conscience," "self," and "religion"; Ashi ("reward, recompense"), a female *yazata* of abundance and fertility; Arshtāt, a female *yazata* personifying justice, the companion of Mithra; Khvarenah ("splendor"), a *yazata* personifying an igneous and luminous energy, seen as a vital force, and the bearer of success and fortune, traditionally linked with royalty; Haoma, personifying the object of the sacrifice and worshiped as the "priest of the sacrifice," whose hymn is preserved in the *Yasna* section (9.10, 9.11); and, finally, the star Vanant (Vega).

Of all these entities, Anāhitā and Mithra are certainly the most important, forming a triad when joined with Ahura Mazdā. The two also appear in the Achaemenid inscriptions, beginning with those of Artaxerxes II. During the Achaemenid period, Anāhitā was seen as a great goddess whose worship, according to Herodotus, was adopted by the Persians from the Assyrians and the Arabs. She descended from the great Near Eastern female deities, who were linked to the functions of fertility and fruitfulness, as well as to royalty. Mithra, on the other hand, had already become a solar deity, the god of covenants and of light, prior to the diffusion of his cult to Rome, where it became a mystery religion. Throughout the deity's history, both within and outside of Iran, Mithra maintained regal and militaristic attributes. Both Mithra and Anāhitā show signs of a very strong influence of religious concepts from Mesopotamia, Asia Minor, and, more in general, the Near East.

Accounts given by Herodotus concerning Persian religion show a picture similar to that found in the Younger Avesta. Herodotus (1.131–132) asserts that the Persians were not in the habit of building statues, temples, or altars, and that they would offer sacrifices from high places, in the open air, to "Zeus" (Ahura Mazdā), a name by which they called the entire sky, the sun, the moon, the earth, fire, water, and the wind. He adds that they would not carry out a sacrifice without the attendance of a Magus, a priest of the Magi, who chanted a "theogony" during the ceremony. This account refers to western Iran at the middle of the fifth century; thus it was written about five hundred years after Zoroastrianism originated.

COSMOGONY AND COSMOLOGY

Zoroastrian cosmogony contemplates three basic moments: the creation of the world, the revelation of the Mazdean "good religion," and the final transfiguration. Although most ancient texts do not present the cosmogonic doctrine systematically, it can be reconstructed with the aid of the Pahlavi religious literature, in which the three cosmogonic moments are called, respectively, Bundahishn ("creation"); Gumēzishn (the mingling of the two opposing spirits); and Wizārishn (their final separation). Everything that exists does so in a double state, the mental, or spiritual (Pahl., *mēnōg*), and the physical, or material (Pahl., *gētīg*). The spiritual state also possesses an embryonic, seminal value in relation to the material one, which is almost like its fruit. According to the Pahlavi literature, only the evil spirit is incapable of transforming its creation from the spiritual to the physical state because it is innately sterile and destructive. Material existence is therefore not seen as negative in itself; rather, in the state of "mixture," it is contaminated by the aggressive activity unleashed against it by the evil spirit. In the *Gāthās*, too (*Yasna* 30.4), life and non-life, good and evil, result from the meeting of the two spirits.

The world was created in six consecutive stages. First, the sky was made of stone and rock crystal, then water, earth, vegetation, animal life, and humanity were formed. The earth is surrounded by a great mountain range, Harā Berezaiti ("high Harā"; Pahl., Harburz; Pers., Alburz), which is linked, through subterranean roots, with Mount Harā, located at the center of the earth. The first and largest of the seven areas in which the earth is divided is a region called Khvaniratha; it is the only one inhabited by man. The remaining six sections of the world (Pahl., *kēshwar*) surround the Khvaniratha. From Mount Harā descend waters that flow into the Vourukasha ("having many inlets") Sea, which covers a third of the earth toward the south and has at its own center a mountain made of the same matter as the sky. Two great rivers, Good Dāityā and Ranhā, originate in the Vourukasha Sea, and they mark the eastern and western borders of the Khvaniratha *kēshwar*. Mount Harā, also known as Hukairya ("of good activity"), is thus the highest spot on earth, and from it the souls of the dead depart on their heavenly voyage. In the middle of the Vourukasha Sea is found the "tree of all seeds," as well as another tree that is endowed with healing powers and confers immortality. It is identified as "white haoma," the "chief of plants."

Gav-aēvō-dāta (Pahl., Gaw-ī-ēw-dād), or "uniquely created bull," who was killed by the evil spirit, and Gaya-maretan (Pahl., Gayōmard), or "mortal life," also killed by Ahriman, were the prototypes, respectively, of animals and men. From their seed there originated all manner of good animals, as well as the first human couple, Mashya and Mashyānag.

The Indo-Iranian background of many of these doctrines is evident. We are reminded, for example, of Mount Meru or Sumeru in Indian mythology and cosmography; of the seven *dvīpas*, which echo the seven *kēshwars*; of the Jambū Tree, to the south of Mount Meru; and of Mārtānda ("mortal seed"), whose myth contains some important analogies with that of Gayōmard.

The most original aspects of Zoroastrian doctrine lie not so much in its cosmological conclusions as in its history of the cosmos and in its teachings concerning the two states of *mēnōg* ("spiritual") and *gētīg* ("material") and the three stages of Bundahishn, Gumēzishn, and Wizārishn. In particular, the notion of the two states, which is also analogous in some of its aspects to a number of Greek ideas (a fact that has led to speculation concerning Greek influences, either Platonic or Aristotelian, as the doctrine is recorded systematically only in relatively late texts), is nonetheless rooted in very early Zoroastrianism. We find traces of it even in the *Gāthās*, which describe the two states of being and of life as "spiritual" and "with bones," that is, "endowed with a body." In fact, the concept of two worlds or two existences is deeply rooted in all of Zoroastrian thought.

The teachings concerning the three stages are also original in specific ways. The first stage involves the separation of the two spirits in the *mēnōg;* the second stage is that of their mingling, in the *gētīg;* the third is that of their final separation, in a state of perfect purity, *abēzagīh,* in which man will live in his future body, *tan īpasēn.* According to these teachings, purity and separation are one and the same, which probably helps to explain the Zoroastrian path to spiritual realization. The initiate, the man who possesses *asha (ashavan),* can, through the power that results from his state of purity—which, in the *Gāthās*, seems to be what is called *maga*—obtain the benefits of a spiritual existence, that is, enlightenment and an intellectual vision. Through such a process the initiate may come to resemble, in life, the man who is blessed after death.

ESCHATOLOGY AND SOTERIOLOGY

The history of the cosmos is a sacred one, and it develops through three high points, each with its own protagonist: Gayamaretan, Zarathushtra, and Saoshyant (Pahl., Sōshans), or the future savior. These figures, however, are only the main characters, representing the beginning, the middle, and the end. A host of other figures, heroes, and defenders of the faith, organized in a complicated sequence and in groups and dynasties that are, for the most part, mythical, fills the sacred history of Zoroastrianism. With time and historical changes, these other figures became increasingly identified with history itself and with the fate of Iran, following a process that is clearly exemplified during the Sasanid period.

The Zoroastrian eschatological doctrine was not developed suddenly; rather, it underwent a sequence of theological reworkings. Its core, however, can already be seen in the *Gāthās,* where it certainly reflects Indo-Iranian or, at least, pre-Zoroastrian concepts of the individual.

The Avesta teaches that after death the soul can reach Heaven, or the Infinite Lights *(Anagra Raocha),* by following three steps, a succession of increasingly bright and intense lights: the Stars (good thoughts, *humata*), the Moon (good words, *hūkhta*), and the Sun (good deeds, *hvarshta*). In order to undertake the celestial journey, the soul must undergo a dramatic trial: the crossing of the Chinvat Bridge, the "bridge of separation." Only those souls who have been deemed just by Mithra, Sraosha, and Rashnu will be able to cross the bridge; the souls of the evil will fall into Hell, for the bridge will narrow to the width of a razor's edge when they attempt to cross it. Three days after death and the painful separation of the soul from the body, the just will meet their *daēnā,* the image of their own self, who will be disguised as a beautiful fifteen-year-old girl. There is an intermediate area for those who do not deserve either Heaven or Hell because the total weight of their good thoughts, good words, and good deeds is equal to that of their bad thoughts, bad words, and bad deeds. These souls remain in a sort of limbo called Hamistagān ("region of the mixed"), a dwelling place of shadows where there is neither joy nor torment.

Even as early as in the *Gāthās* the collective eschatology is dominated by the notion of an ordeal by fire. Fire, a son of Ahura Mazdā, is Asha's instrument, and good men will be separated from the evil by a torrent of fire, like a river of molten metal. At that time the Last Judgment will take place, and Frashōkereti (Pahl., Frashgird) will "transfigure" existence and "rehabilitate" the world and life. Then the dead will come back to life, with indestructible bodies clad in glory. The sacrificial ceremony performed by the savior (the Saoshyant), who will use the fat or marrow of a miraculous cow, blended with white *haoma* (rather than the yellow kind used in regular ceremonies), will bring about the final transfiguration and the resurrection of the bodies.

This version of the doctrine, probably the result of a relatively late elaboration, is codified in the Pahlavi texts. Its premises, however, are ancient and can be found in the teachings of the *Gāthās.* They represent a yearning for a transfiguration of our beings and of life and are strongly fueled by eschatological hope. Zarathushtra himself exclaimed, "If only we could be the ones to transfigure the world!" (*Yasna* 30.9).

The idea of a future savior is, in any case, an archaic one, appearing in one of the oldest hymns (*Yashts* 19.86–96). According to later tradition, the savior is born of a virgin who was impregnated by the seed of Zarathushtra while she was bathing in the waters where it was deposited (the great Hāmūn-i-Hilmand Basin, in Iranian Seistan). One legend holds that there will be three saviors: Ukhshyaterera ("he who makes truth grow"), Ukhshyatnemah ("he who makes reverence grow"), and Astvatereta ("he who embodies truth"). All three saviors, each the son of Zarathushtra, will appear at three different times, each at the end of one of the last three millennia in the history of the cosfmos (there are twelve millennia in total). According to the *Bundahishn,* the twelve-thousand-year period is subdivided into four segments, each lasting three thousand years. The first period is that of the creation made by Ōhrmazd (the Pahlavi form for Ahura Mazdā) in the *mnōg* ("ideal") stage; during this time, Ahriman (the Pahlavi form for Angra Mainyu), starts his struggle against the forces of good. The second period, which resulted from an agreement between the two opponents to establish a period of nine thousand years in which to mingle, witnesses Ōhrmazd's transformation of his creation from the *mēnōg* stage to the *gētīg*. The third period begins with Ahriman's attack against the world created by Ōhrmazd, after which the latter creates the *fravashi* of the prophet. The fourth begins with the revelation to the prophet of the "good religion," an event that takes place in the year 9000 of the history of the world and continues with the advent of the three saviors at the end of each millennium.

In this complex body of eschatological and cosmological doctrines, known to us through a literature that is rather late in its traditional versions, we see what appear to be foreign influences, especially Western ones (Babylonian or Hellenistic). There is no doubt, however, that eschatological hope and the faith in a future savior were among the earliest components of Zoroastrianism and that they exercised a widespread and deep influence on other religions outside of the Iranian world.

CUSTOMS, RITUALS, FESTIVALS

Despite its original antiritualistic character, Zoroastrianism soon became a religion in which ceremony played a leading role. It is not possible to know which religious rituals were recommended by the prophet to his disciples in addition to prayer. The importance of prayer was always fundamental, and some forms, particularly revered ones, have lasted through the centuries, for example, a type of traditional *manthra* (Skt., *mantra*) that is endowed with magical powers. The main prayers are Ahuna Vairya, Airyēmā Ishyō, Ashem Vohū, Yenhē Hātąm. Even in modern times, the day of a pious Zoroastrian is divided into five prayer periods. Most likely, alongside the recitation of the *manthra,* Zarathushtra recommended meditating before the only basic symbol of the new religion—fire.

Although modified to fit the tenets of the Zoroastrian message, the old ritualism reemerged and asserted itself anew during the first centuries of the new faith. The reemergence most likely took place before the advent of the great Achaemenid empire. Animal sacrifice became accepted again, although only in forms that could be seen as compatible with the new ethical values, and even the *haoma* cult was reestablished. In fact, Haoma became a *yazata* in the new Zoroastrian pantheon. This reconstruction of the earliest history of Zoroastrianism, the result of traditional scholarship, must still be considered valid, despite claims by some scholars (Marijan Molé, Mary Boyce) that it is fundamentally incorrect.

The strongest analogy with Vedic sacrifice and its ideology is to be found in the cult of *haoma.* Like the Indian *soma,* which is also Soma, a divine being, the Iranian *haoma* is an immortalizing potion, one that brings various benefits, such as inspiration, victory, fertility, and riches, to the person performing the sacrifice. We do not know whether *haoma* was originally a mushroom or a plant of some kind, but Zoroastrians have traditionally used a species of *Ephedra* in the sacrificial ceremony. Using a mortar, they extract the juice from the plant, then drink this liquid while a complex set of rituals is performed. *Haoma* was also given to the dying, functioning as a kind of viaticum that would allow them to obtain immortality and to be resurrected. The *haoma* sacrifice is seen in some ways as a precursor of the eschatological one, in which the future savior is to prepare the ambrosia with white *haoma.*

Herodotus's statement that Persians did not use statues, temples, or altars as part of their religious worship is basically confirmed by archaeological evidence. We must, of course, keep in mind that the absence of temples resembling the Greek or

Babylonian ones does not preclude the existence of other sacred areas dedicated to religious ceremonies, such as those with outdoor fences and altars. We learn of anthropomorphic images of a deity only under the rule of Artaxerxes II, who put up statues of the goddess Anāhitā in the main centers of his empire, reflecting the influence of Near Eastern religious concepts and cults. In fact, some scholars have seen this move by Artaxerxes II as the initial cause of a religious struggle that lasted many centuries (Boyce, 1975) and opposed "houses of idols" (Pahl., *uzdēs kadag*) to "houses of fire" (Pahl., *ātakhsh kadag;* Pers., *āteshgāh*). The latter, typically built on the model of a *cahār tāq* ("four arches"), became widespread during the Sasanid period.

The tendency to reject anthropomorphic representations of divine entities is typical of later Zoroastrianism. During the Sasanid period we find anthropomorphic representations of Ōhrmazd, Mihr (Mithra), and Anāhīd (Anāhitā) in large rupestrian reliefs in Fārs; during the Achaemenid period, in addition to the accounts of statues of the goddess Anāhitā, we find torsos of Ahura Mazdā, emerging from a disk or a winged ring from which there emerge, as well, two paws and a bird tail. This symbol, of ancient Egyptian origin, was widespread, and it was the subject of a number of different interpretations throughout the Near East; it was found among the Hittites, Phoenicians, Syrians, Urartians, Assyrians, and Babylonians. We can state with certainty that the winged disk represents Ahura Mazdā despite the divergent opinions of some scholars and some Parsis, the latter concerned about preserving the aniconic coherence of their religion. Other traditional symbols of Zoroastrianism are the fire altars and the *barsom* (Av., *baresman*), a ritual object consisting originally of a bunch of herbs and later of a bundle of consecrated twigs.

The complex Zoroastrian rituals involve many of the most significant moments in the lives of the faithful. Thus we find initiation rites, Naojot (a term deriving from an older one indicating a "new birth"), in which a child, at age seven or ten, is fitted with a shirt, *sadre,* and girded with a cord called *kustī.* Zoroastrians also celebrate marriage rituals, as well as purification rituals (e.g., Pādyāb, ablution; Nāhn, bath; Bareshnūm, the great purification for the initiation of priests and corpse-bearers), in which an important part is played by *gōmez,* consecrated urine, originally cow's urine, following Indo-Iranian practices and ideas. Funeral rites (for example, Zōhr ī ātash, in which animal fat is poured onto the fire, obviously reminiscent of some ancient animal sacrifice) take place in the *dakhmas,* the "towers of silence," and are meant to free the soul of the dead man from the demon of corpses (Druj ī Nasu) and to assist it along its heavenly journey, which begins four days after death. Confession of one's sins is made during Patet, a ritual of penance. Also important in the Zoroastrian liturgy are the rituals surrounding the founding of an *āteshgah* and the consecration of a *dakhma.* These involve the entire community.

But Yasna ("sacrifice"; Skt., *yajñah*), the sacrifice of *haoma* before a fire, performed in a different room from that where the fire is usually kept, is the main Zoroastrian liturgy. The Yasna is preceded by a preparatory rite, the Paragra, which consists of a number of meticulous ritual operations and ends with the preparation of the sacrificial liquor. The ritual is performed by two priests, known as the *zōt* (Av., *zaotar;* Skt., *hotṛ*) and the *rāspī.* The former recites the *Yasna*—that is, the seventy-two chapters included in this section of the Avesta—and the latter fuels the ceremonial fire. The entire ceremony takes place in twelve stages, during which the

Yasna is recited in a rhythmical way. The sacrifice is commissioned by the faithful and is carried out for their intentions.

Fire is not only the main symbol of Zoroastrianism; it is also the most venerable witness of the Yasna. It is the object of the priest's address and of the offering of the *haoma*. In Iran, as in India, there are three ritual fires: *farrbay,* the fire of priests; *gushnasp,* the fire of warriors; and *burzēn mihr,* the fire of farmers. There are also five natural fires, which reside, respectively, in front of Ahura Mazdā, in the bodies of men and animals, in plants, in clouds, and in the earth. Thus, fire is a vital element and is present in all of nature. Two divine entities are associated with it: Apạm Napāt ("grandson" or "son of the water"), the *ahura* "who created male human beings," and Nairyōsanha (Pahl., Neryōsang, "of manly utterance"), the *yazata* of prayer. Also related to fire is the concept of *khvarenah* (Pahl., *khwarrah, farr*), meaning "splendor" or "divine grace" and represented as an igneous fluid and vital seed (Duchesne-Guillemin, 1962). This is a basic concept in the cosmogony, in the eschatology, and in the psychology of Zoroastrianism. Because of the symbolic values they attribute to fire, Zoroastrians have been erroneously considered fire worshipers, especially by the Muslims.

A strongly ritualistic religion, Zoroastrianism marked the year with a series of fixed holidays, thus incorporating traditional ways and customs that were hard to eradicate. But there have always been problems connected with this calendar, throughout thousands of years of history, and many things, especially those from the earliest times, are still far from clear to us. We do know for certain, however, that a lunar-solar calendar, whose roots are clearly Babylonian, was adopted under the Achaemenids. But, most likely under Artaxerxes I in 441 BCE, a Zoroastrian calendar came into use. Under the Sasanids, the year was divided into 365 days, into 12 months of 30 days, to the last of which were added 5 days, each dedicated to a group of *Gāthās* (*Gāh*-days). This, of course, did not prevent confusion or the superimposition of dates, which, in turn, caused modifications, attempts at reform, and drawn-out debates that continue even into the twentieth century in Parsi communities.

The first month of the year was dedicated to the *fravashis*, the spirits of the just, who were originally thought to be transcendental doubles of the soul. Zoroastrians believed in the *fravashis* of the dead, of the living, and of the yet unborn. According to a most likely pre-Zoroastrian tradition, the *fravashis* returned to earth at the end of the year, before the vernal equinox, the Nō Rūz ("new day"), or the first month of the new year. Zoroastrians also celebrated six additional great feasts: Maidhyōizaremaya ("midspring"); Maidhyōishema ("midsummer"); Patishahya ("bringing in the corn"); Ayathrima ("the homecoming"); Maidhyāirya ("midwinter"). Also very important were the feast of Mithra (Mithrakāna), the god to whom the seventh month was dedicated, held at the beginning of the second half of the year (autumnal equinox), and that of Tīrī (Av., Tishtrya), a deity who corresponds to the star Sirius, to whom was dedicated the fourth month.

Nō Rūz probably originated as an ancient pan-Iranian celebration of the vernal equinox and was later adopted and modified by Zoroastrianism. It was connected to the legend of Yima (the New Persian Jamshīd), the first king, who had reigned over the earth in an ancient golden age. An important figure in ancient Iran's religious and national tradition, Yima appears to correspond (but not without question) to the Indian figure of Yama, the lord of hell. The "new day" of the new year, a day of good auspices and of renewal of creation and of life, was celebrated with a joyous feast. During the Achaemenid period, the feast acquired special relevance, becoming associated with the concept of royalty.

HISTORICAL DEVELOPMENT

While the *Gāthās* contain the original teachings of Zarathushtra, the Younger Avesta shows how Zoroastrianism synthesized its new ideas with older beliefs and traditions, always, however, maintaining precise theological standards. Thus the concepts that were absorbed by the new Zoroastrian religion were undoubtedly deeply rooted in the Iranian religions of the first half of the first millennium BCE, but they were reinterpreted in a way that did not conflict with the ethical and spiritual values originally advocated by Zarathushtra. That is, in the terminology of the "tripartite ideology" of Georges Dumézil, the religion absorbed those elements reflecting the values of the first and third functions, priests and shepherds (later farmers), rather than those reflecting ideologies and attitudes typical of the second, the warrior, function. The violent and aggressive character of some deities of the ancient Iranian and Indo-Iranian pantheon, such as Indra, irretrievably condemned them to be downgraded to the role of *daivas*, or demons. At the same time, whatever positive elements could be perceived in the warrior values were put in the service of the new faith and attributed to gods from the other two functions, in particular the first. Such is the case with Mithra, who is, in Iran, strongly marked by warrior traits yet also has positive qualities, for he is the god of light and the guardian of truth and order in the cosmos.

These first syntheses were carried out by the Avestan priests in pre-Achaemenid times and were handed down through the Magi during the entire period of the Achaemenid empire. The mediation of the Magi was important from a historical point of view, and it marked an important stage in the development of Zoroastrianism. On the one hand, the Magi ensured the transmission and survival of the religion throughout the entire Iranian or iranized world; on the other, they modified Zoroastrianism in a deep way, not only from a philosophical and theological point of view (i.e., the dualistic doctrine) but also from a more general point of view. They widened its scope and allowed it to interpret other religious traditions, especially the Near Eastern ones. They opened it to syncretism and to eclecticism, a development that acquired considerable importance when the Mesopotamian civilization was encountered. Political elements, of course, played a part in these developments: they were strongly fostered by the great supranational Achaemenid empire, whose rulers needed to affirm a concept of royalty that could fit into the political universalism of the Persians without conflicting with the cultural, social, and religious traditions found in other countries of their vast empire. The concept of royalty that emerged during Achaemenid rule, which was transmitted, under various guises, to later Iranian and non-Iranian dynasties, was as far from the ideologies and the values of the archaic world of early Zoroastrianism as it was close to the millenarian, monarchic traditions of Near Eastern societies.

The most important change made by the Magi, however, was their modification of the doctrine of dualism. According to the original doctrine, the beginning of everything, the root of the conflict between the forces of good and evil, could be traced to the principle of Time as Destiny (Pahl., Zurwān). No one, not even the human soul, can escape this principle. The Magi's new formulation, however, no longer considered Ahura Mazdā as the transcending principle but, rather, placed him in a lesser role as one of the two opposing spirits. Thus was born Zurvanism, whose existence is documented by sources from the Sasanid period, as well as by Christian, Armenian, and Syriac sources and by Greek sources referring to the Achaemenid and Parthian periods. Zurvanism must have been an earlier expression of the new Iranian dualism. It seems to indicate a tendency, originating inside Zoroastrianism, to reconcile the original Zoroastrian dualistic inspiration with Babylonian astral religiosity as well as with Mesopotamian demonology. The tendency was the result of an encounter between the western Magi and the Chaldeans, the Babylonian priesthood known for its occultism. (The meeting also produced Mithraism during the Parthian period.) Time was thus endowed with an overpowering and regulating authority.

The Seleucid period (Greco-Bactrian in the easternmost areas of the Iranian world and later Parthian) was characterized by Hellenistic influences. These were partly accepted, partly rejected by the Parthians. The resistance developed after the break in tradition caused by Alexander the Great's conquest of Iran. The break, however, proved not to be radical, as Zoroastrianism survived. In the end, in fact, its basic tenets, its soteriological inspiration, as well as its dualistic approach, exercised a deep influence far beyond the Iranian world. This influence extended even into the Judeo-Christian and Buddhist cultural areas, possibly contributing to the development of the Mahāyāna (Great Vehicle) Buddhist pantheon. Some aspects of the Zoroastrian religion even spread east of the Parthian territories to the Kushan empire, as we can see, for example, by the coin iconography of that dynasty.

The Sasanid period witnessed the refoundation of Zoroastrianism. The religious traditions that had survived the break caused by the Greco-Macedonian hegemony— and partly connected to the concepts and ideology of royalty that flourished during the Achaemenid period, especially in Fārs—were elaborated in the context of a vast reorganization, codification, and canonization of tradition. This was carried out by priests of the *mōbad* (from the ancient *magupati,* "master of the Magi") and *hērbad* (Av., *aēthrapaiti*), who were based in the power centers of the new dynasty, the most influential shrines of western Iran, Media, Shīz (Takht-i Sulaiman) and of Fārs and Stakhr (near Persepolis). Several outstanding figures emerged as the creators and defenders of the new orthodoxy, such as Tōsar, during the reign of Ardashīr I (224–241 CE); Kerdēr, under the first rulers, from Ardashīr I to Wahrām II (276–293); and Ādurbād ī Mahraspandān, under Shāpūr II (309–379). Thanks to the refounding, Zoroastrianism acquired new connotations: it became a religion in the service of the ruling classes, the warrior aristocracy and the clergy, as well as the crown. It became a hierarchically organized state religion, an epic and nationalistic tradition increasingly identified with the Iranian nation. From a universal religion, which had shown its best throughout the Parthian period, Zoroastrianism was transformed into a national religion. The "good religion" (Pahl., *wēh-dēn*), and Iran became, in a certain sense, synonymous.

The nationalistic evolution of Zoroastrianism continued even after the Arab conquest of the Sasanid empire. Zoroastrian communities that survived the first centuries of Islam, as well as the priests who were responsible for the flowering of the Pahlavi religious literature, kept alive the memory of the imperial era in Iran as a happy time for the "good religion" and for the doctrine of the future savior and the apocalypse. They railed against Arabs, Romans, and Turks, planting in the mind of the faithful the dangerous certainty of revenge. In fact, during the Sasanid period Zoroastrianism had not been able to hold up against other universalistic religions. If it did succeed in stifling Manichaean universalism in Iran during the third century (as it also later suppressed the Mazdakite movement), it was nonetheless not able to mount effective opposition against the spread of Christianity, the Nestorian church in particular, and, later, of Islam.

Uprisings against Arab domination, for example, the revolt in the city of Shīrāz in 979, not only failed but also resulted in harsh repressive measures. By the tenth century, Zoroastrians began to leave Iran and head for India, where they today form a small but flourishing community known as the Parsis ("Persians"). Along with the reduced Zoroastrian community in Iran (found especially in the regions of Yazd and Kermān), the Parsis have perpetuated the ancient religion of Zarathushtra to this very day, notwithstanding the deep transformations brought about by complex and varied events throughout three millennia of history.

Thus the communities in Iran and India, the two main branches of modern Zoroastrianism, evolved throughout many centuries into separate and independent forms. The first lasting contacts between the Parsis of India and the Zoroastrians of Iran were made around the end of the fifteenth century, through the traditional exchange of *rivāyat,* texts providing answers to liturgical and doctrinal questions. Although the Iranian communities remained isolated for centuries, holding together in a hostile environment, the Indian ones were able to excercise considerable influence on the society in which they had settled, not only from a social and political point of view (aided later by the position of privilege they acquired under the British rule of India), but also from a religious one. This is shown by the presence of Zoroastrian ideas in the syncretic and archaizing religious reform carried out by the emperor Akbar around the last quarter of the sixteenth century.

The history of the Parsi communities in India, which have their main center in Bombay, is characterized principally by two phenomena. The first phenomenon is their contact with other religious traditions (Hinduism, Islam, Christianity), as well as with forms of modern spiritualism, such as theosophy, astrology, esotericism. This has led to considerable problems of a theological and doctrinal nature, especially concerning monotheism and dualism, and has resulted in a number of revisions. The second is the dialogue—sometimes struggle—between the conservative and the reform-oriented tendencies within the Parsis. The cult of the dead and questions related to the calendar and to feast days are traditional subjects of debate within the Indian communities. Moreover, the rediscovery of the Avesta in the eighteenth century and the resulting studies by Western philologists have also, in some instances more directly than in others, caused divisive doctrinal conflicts among the Persis in their interpretation of traditional teachings.

After the end of the British rule in India, and at the birth of the Indian union and of Pakistan, the Parsis found themselves divided into Indian communities (the vast majority) and Pakistani communities in Karachi, Lahore, and Quetta (in 1976, there were about 5,000 members). There is also a small Parsi community in Sri Lanka. In 1976, it was estimated that the world's Zoroastrian population numbered 130,000, of whom, in addition to the ones just mentioned, 82,000 were in India, 25,000 in Iran, and most of the others in North America. Zoroastrians from around the world have been able to meet and to establish working relationships at international symposia and conferences, as in Tehran in 1960 and in Bombay in 1964, 1978, and 1985. Modern Zoroastrianism is characterized by its lack of a proselytizing impulse. Historical reasons have contributed, especially among the Parsi communities, to such an attitude, which was also related to the fear of an influx from the lower castes. Historically Zoroastrians have never shown a great interest in conversions, except in the earliest times. In India, the Parsis eventually became a sort of caste, one that became economically strong within Indian society. They are also perceived as a group that sees religion as strictly linked to birth and lineage. This perception was fostered by their custom of marriage between blood relatives, generally cousins, in accordance with Zoroastrian tradition, which in ancient times recommended marriage even between brothers and sisters.

Zoroastrian communities show great vitality and, very often, a considerable interest in the study and interpretation of their millenarian religious tradition. In Bombay, in particular, there are various institutions, even secular ones, devoted to the study of the religion, and they have valued the scholarship of Western philology of the past three centuries. In addition, religious institutions have arisen in Bombay and Naosari for the special purpose of teaching the religion to future priests.

[*For further discussion of Zoroastrianism, see* Ahura Mazdā and Angra Mainyu; Ahuras; Airyana Vaejah; Amesha Spentas; Anāhitā; Ateshgah; Avesta; Chinvat Bridge; Daivas; Dahkma; Frashōkereti; Fravashis; Haoma; Khvarenah; Magi; Saoshyant; *and* Yazatas. *See also the biography of Zarathushtra.*]

BIBLIOGRAPHY

The best of relatively recent works on Zoroastrianism are Jacques Duchesne-Guillemin's *La religion de l'Iran ancien* (Paris, 1962); Geo Widengren's *Die Religionen Irans* (Stuttgart, 1965), translated as *Les religions de l'Iran* (Paris, 1968); and Mary Boyce's *A History of Zoroastrianism,* 2 vols. to date (Leiden, 1975–1982). These works are very different from each other, both in approach and in method, and for this reason the careful reader will be able to get a fairly full picture of the rich and complex series of problems involved in the study of Zoroastrianism.

Classic works, again very different from each other in approach and method, are Herman Lommel's *Die Religion Zarathustras nach dem Awesta dargestellt* (Tübingen, 1930) and H. S. Nyberg's *Irans forntida religioner* (Stockholm, 1937), translated as *Die Religionen des alten Iran* (1938; 2d ed., Osnabrück, 1966). Lommel's work is a faithful reconstruction of ancient Zoroastrianism, more philological than historical-religious; Nyberg's study, also based on a careful philological analysis of the sources, is more involved with historical and religious problems, and its approach is highly original, if somewhat controversial.

Other Swedish scholars, following the guidelines traced by Nyberg, have contributed in a significant fashion to the study of the earliest Iranian religions, from both a philological and a historical-religious point of view. Notable are Geo Widengren's *Hochgottglaube im alten Iran* (Uppsala, 1938) and Stig Wikander's *Feuerpriester in Kleinasien und Iran* (Lund, 1946).

As the result of long and demanding work, gathered for the most part in the *Archäologische Mitteilungen aus Iran* in 1929–1930, Ernst Herzfeld, an archaeologist and historian of Iran, published, some years later, a vast reconstruction of the religion of ancient Iran: *Zoroaster and His World,* 2 vols. (1947; reprint, New York, 1973). Although vast in scope, Herzfeld's work is not systematic but is, rather, a fragmented account in independent chapters.

Against the conclusions expressed by Herzfeld concerning Zarathushtra and the early period, as well as against the main theses of Nyberg, W. B. Henning, one of the foremost authorities in Iranian philology, published the texts of some of his own lectures in *Zoroaster: Politician or Witch-Doctor?* (Oxford, 1951). Nyberg's position was later defended, however, by Geo Widengren, from his own original point of view, in two long articles published in *Numen* and later in his *Stand und Aufgaben der iranischen Religionsgeschichte* (Leiden, 1955). Nyberg himself defended his position in his introduction to the second printing of his *Religionen des alten Iran* (Osnabrück, 1966).

One of the new elements in Widengren's work, as well as in that of Jacques Duchesne-Guillemin, is the acceptance of Georges Dumézil's theory of a tripartite Indo-European ideology, and of its applicability to Iran and Zoroastrianism. Dumézil has offered a number of contributions along these lines, of which the most famous is still *Naissance d'archanges* (Paris, 1945), in which he interprets the Zoroastrian system of the Amesha Spentas in the light of his theory.

Preceding Widengren in his application of the Dumézilian theory to Zoroastrianism was Jacques Duchesne-Guillemin in his *Zoroastre: Étude critique avec une traduction commentée des Gâthâ* (Paris, 1948), which he followed, a decade later, with *The Western Response to Zoroaster* (Oxford, 1958). The latter work is extremely clear yet, at the same time, critical and problematical. Dumézil's theory is also applied in a rather original way to ancient Iran by Marijan Molé in *Culte, mythe et cosmologie dans l'Iran ancien* (Paris, 1963), in which he tries to provide a structural, rather than a historical, picture of the entire Zoroastrian tradition.

Following in the footsteps of Henning's work, Ilya Gershevitch gives a clear and perceptive reconstruction of the Zoroastrian teachings and of the early development of Zoroastrianism in a short but fundamental article: "Zoroaster's Own Contribution," *Journal of Near Eastern Studies* 23 (1964): 12–38.

A number of works concerned with particular problems and subjects are nevertheless important for general Zoroastrian studies. Among them are Émile Benveniste's *The Persian Religion according to the Chief Greek Texts* (Paris, 1929), which presents an interpretation of the main Greek sources so as to allow the reconstruction of the historical development of religion in ancient Iran, and H. W. Bailey's *Zoroastrian Problems in the Ninth-Century Books* (Oxford, 1943), which deals with various subjects on the basis of an extraordinarily erudite understanding of the Pahlavi literature of the ninth century CE. Also to be numbered among essential works is R. C. Zaehner's *Zurvan: A Zoroastrian Dilemma* (Oxford, 1955), a reexamination, after more than twenty years, of the question of Zurvanism that had been so masterfully tackled by Nyberg in his "Questions de cosmogonie et de cosmologie mazdéennes," *Journal asiatique* (1929): 193–310 and (1931): 1–134, 193–244. Zurvanism was later the subject of Ugo Bianchi, in his *Zamān i Ōhrmazd: Lo zoroastrismo nelle sue origini e nella sua essenza* (Turin, 1958), as well as of other scholars.

Works that, to a certain extent, show their age but that are nonetheless useful as general references are J. H. Moulton's *Early Zoroastrianism* (London, 1913), M. N. Dhalla's *Zoroastrian Theology* (New York, 1914), Raffaele Pettazzoni's *La religione di Zarathustra nella storia religiosa dell'Iran* (Bologna, 1920), and M. N. Dhalla's *History of Zoroastrianism* (New York, 1938). Good for its second part is another book by R. C. Zaehner, *The Dawn and Twilight of Zoroastrianism* (1961; reprint, London, 1976), originally published in the same year as Walther Hinz's *Zarathustra* (Stuttgart, 1961) and Jacques Duchesne-Guillemin's *Symbolik des Parsismus* (Stuttgart, 1961), a consideration of all aspects of Zoroastrian symbolism.

General works on Zoroastrianism written with more of a popularizing intent include Marijan Molé's *L'Iran ancien* (Paris, 1965); Jacques Duchesne-Guillemin's "L'Iran antique et Zoroastre" and "L'église sassanide et le mazdéisme," in *Histoire des religions,* edited by Henri-Charles Puech, vol. 1 (Paris, 1970), pp. 625–694, and vol. 2 (Paris, 1973), pp. 3–32, respectively; and Mircea Eliade's "Zarathustra and the Iranian Religion" and "New Iranian Syntheses," in his *A History of Religious Ideas,* vol. 1 (Chicago, 1978), pp. 302–333, and vol. 2 (Chicago, 1982), pp. 306–329, respectively. Other useful works are Jivanji Jamshedji Modi's *The Religious Ceremonies and Customs of the Parsees,* 2d ed. (Bombay, 1937), and Louis H. Gray's *The Foundations of the Iranian Religions* (Bombay, 1929), which is particularly helpful on the listing of the members of the Zoroastrian pantheon and pandemonium.

In addition to *A History of Zoroastrianism,* her *magnum opus,* Mary Boyce has produced a number of other valuable works on Zoroastrianism. In *A Persian Stronghold of Zoroastrianism* (Oxford, 1977), she paints an interesting and accurate picture of the religion in today's Iranian communities. In *Zoroastrians: Their Religious Beliefs and Practices* (London, 1979), she gives a clear and useful synthesis of the medieval period, the post-Islamic period, and the modern era of the Zoroastrian religion, both in Iran and in India. And in *Textual Sources for the Study of Zoroastrianism* (Manchester, 1984), she has gathered a vast selection of translated texts from various periods and sources.

Two of my own works are dedicated to questions relating to the origins and early development of Iranian religion from Zarathushtra to the third century CE: *Zoroaster's Time and Homeland: A Study on the Origins of Mazdeism and Related Problems* (Naples, 1980) and *De Zoroastre à Mani: Quatre leçons au Collège de France* (Paris, 1985).

Important chapters concerning Zoroastrianism and particular subjects pertaining to the religious history of ancient Iran are to be found in *The Cambridge History of Iran,* vol. 2, edited by Ilya Gershevitch, and vol. 3, edited by Ehsan Yarshater (Cambridge, 1983), in particular the contributions of Martin Schwartz, Yarshater, Boyce, Carsten Colpe, and Duchesne-Guillemin. This volume of *The Cambridge History of Iran* covers the Seleucid, Parthian, and Sasanid periods; a volume dedicated to the Achaemenid period is forthcoming.

TWO

GRECO-ROMAN RELIGIONS

9

AEGEAN
RELIGIONS

OLIVIER PELON
Translated from French by Anne Marzin

The Aegean world is composed of regions limited in area but geographically and culturally very diverse, whose evolution proceeded in an irregular and more or less independent fashion: whereas the Cyclades, the island microcosm situated between Europe and Asia, flourished as early as the third millennium BCE, Crete reached its apogee in the first half of the second millennium, and the continent, where the Greeks seem to have settled shortly before 2000 BCE, achieved a great civilization at Mycenae only in the second half of the same millennium. Although related, the religions of the Aegean that developed around these three poles preserved an undeniable regional originality.

Cycladic Religion

The Cycladic religion of the Early Bronze Age (third millennium BCE) remains difficult to define even after a century of research. Archaeological data are severely lacking, as no religious architecture has been identified with any certainty. A stone pyxis (boxlike vase) from Melos perhaps provides us with an image of a Cycladic sanctuary: the vase is made up of a set of seven cylindrical receptacles grouped in a square around a central space to which there is access through a kind of roofed porch. An Aegean parallel, but of a later date, is offered by the palatial silo building on the site of Mallia in Crete. On the other hand, the multiplicity of the recipients relates this vase to the series of kernoi, or offering vases, that were common in the Cyclades at that time.

Especially well known from the Cycladic civilization are the small marble "idols," generally found in a funerary context. The majority are nude female figures, related, despite their slender, elongated forms, to the voluptuous Neolithic fertility figurines of continental Europe. The Cycladic idols do not seem to have served as cult statues. Yet a silver diadem from Syros may represent a religious scene involving two animals and two bird-headed feminine figures with raised arms, separated by stellar motifs. Comparable symbols decorate a type of vase whose function is not well established, the terra-cotta "frying pan." These flat, wide vases with their bifid handles bear on their reverse an incised decoration: a boat against a background of connected spirals and a pubic triangle between stylized plants on an example from Syros, and a stellar motif and pubic triangle on another. The belief in a feminine principle of fertility linked with the celestial and marine worlds and undoubtedly related to Oriental models appears to be an established fact, even though the forms of worship are unknown to us.

After 2000 BCE the Cyclades seem to have lost their religious autonomy. The site of Akrotiri on the island of Thera, once buried under volcanic ashes, has revealed a series of frescoes that, though inspired by Crete, display a certain originality. While some of the women depicted follow the ritual style of the Minoans, with flounced skirts and bared breasts, a young priestess carrying offerings is clothed in an ample tunic. However, a scene portraying the ritual gathering of crocuses and the presence on the site of stone horns of consecration betray the extent of Minoan influence.

Religious architecture, until then nonexistent, developed at Keos and Melos. A small temple built at Hagia Irini was closer in plan, with its antechamber, interior room, and annexes, to the constructions of the continent than to those of Crete. One of the annexes was crowded with female terra-cotta statues whose naked, ample breasts and long skirts recall the Cretan prototypes. It has been supposed that they belonged to a cult of Dionysos, whereas at Phylakopi a goddess seems to have been worshiped in the form of a figurine decorated in the ceramic style of Mycenae, thus probably indicating a religious takeover from the continent.

Minoan Religion

Crete remained relatively independent of the neighboring Cyclades during the entire Early Bronze Age. An original Cretan civilization did not reach its height until the beginning of the second millennium BCE, with the building of the palaces attributed to the more or less mythical Minos. Yet no clean break with the preceding period is discernible at that time, especially as far as religion is concerned.

PLACES OF WORSHIP

It is usually maintained that, in contrast to the contemporaneous Near East and Egypt, large constructions of a religious nature were unknown in Minoan Crete. Supposedly, a temple conceived as a monumental dwelling for the divinity was a notion foreign to the Minoans, whose architecture therefore in no way foreshadowed the sacred buildings of Classical Greece. However, without equating the Minoan palace with the Oriental temple, which was at the same time residence of the god, lodging for the priests, and center of many economic activities, one cannot forget that the palace gave a monumental setting to certain religious manifestations.

Still, an important architectural framework was not necessary to the cult, and wherever architecture does appear, it is usually very modest. It is often necessary to turn to figured depictions, the only surviving evidence we have. Thus on a gold ring from Isopata, four female figures can be seen wearing the ritual dress, with exposed breasts and flounced skirts, and dancing in a landscape flowered with clusters of lilies. Probably this is a replica of a Knossian fresco in which a group of women in similar attire are shown in the middle of a wood. In other representations, architecture, though present, plays only a secondary role in the form of a small structure out of which grows a tree—clearly, no mere figurative schematization. One may well imagine, therefore, that at least some of the Minoan rites took place in a context of rocks, trees, or landscape unmodified by human intervention.

The same spirit pervades the two great categories of Minoan places of worship: peak sanctuaries and caves. The cave offers a crude natural setting that nature itself has transformed by decorating it with strangely shaped, more or less anthropomorphic or zoomorphic concretions in which, from a very early period, the Minoans saw manifestations of the divinity. Some of these caves are particularly well known: the cave of Kamares in the Ida mountain chain, the cave of Arkalochori, and finally the cave of Psychro, also called the Diktaean Cave. The last-mentioned presents an interesting arrangement. In the upper room a quadrangular altar made of rough-hewn stones was surrounded by offerings: stone libation tables, clay vases, and a double ax of bronze, mingled with animal bones and ashes. In an adjoining room other offerings were deposited inside a rectangular *temenos* (sacred enclosure), among them some bronze weapons. Finally, in a lower room in the vicinity of a small pond, one finds spear points, double axes, and bronze figurines intentionally wedged into the interstices of the stalactites. Another cave, at Skotino, has been interpreted as the actual labyrinth of Greek mythology; it may be significant that it is still used each year in July for feasts in honor of Hagia Paraskevi, whose chapel stands on the edge of the chasm.

Undeniably, the peak sanctuaries bring to mind the high places of Canaan. On a sealing from Knossos a feminine form appears on a mountaintop flanked by two lions and holding out a javelin or scepter to a worshiper arching his back in the Cretan attitude of adoration. One of the sanctuaries is depicted on a stone vase from the palace of Zakros: in a mountainous landscape overrun by wild goats, a tripartite construction surmounted by horns of consecration, ibexes, and birds rises within a walled enclosure of squared blocks. A fragment from Knossos shows a worshiper in comparable surroundings placing on a rock a basket filled with offerings. Archaeological evidence is less precise: although some installations have been discovered on the mountaintops at Petsofas near Palaikastro, on the Kofinas in the Asteroussia Mountains, and on Mount Juktas near Knossos, no elaborate architecture has been found. At Petsofas a terrace of large blocks supported a building with several rooms. Our conception of the sanctuary on Mount Juktas has been modified by recent findings: instead of the three rooms identified by Arthur Evans within an enclosure of large blocks, the sanctuary is composed of at least three terraces juxtaposed on the hillside with a stepped altar at the top, on the edge of a deep crevice in the rock. At Petsofas as on Mount Juktas, human or animal figurines of various sizes fill the layer of offerings that, here also, is mixed with ashes and charcoal, the remains of ritual fires; often only parts of the human body are deposited here as ex-votos, and little clay balls seem to prefigure the prayer pellets of Buddhism.

For a long time it was believed that caves and summits were the only public places where rites were celebrated (Nilsson, 1927). It now appears that, in the cities as well as in the country, the Minoans built more or less important religious edifices that functioned independently of other buildings. On the southern coast of the island the settlement of Myrtos, from the prepalatial period, presents a set of four unpretentious rooms in which a low base of stones and clay supported a feminine figurine, evidently an object of collective worship. At Mallia, a group of three rooms dating from the period of the first palaces shows no evidence of architectural progress, but on the floor of the main room there was a rectangular offering table, blackened by fire, to which one could have easy access from the neighboring street. This recalls a similar arrangement in a small room in the first palace of Phaistos that was also accessible from the outside through an opening in the west facade.

Outside the towns, the "country villa" of Kannia near Gortyna (if, as its discoverer believes, it has not undergone modification) represents an even more imposing building in which, out of twenty-seven rooms, five appear to have had a religious purpose, making it more akin to a large sanctuary than to a private house. More recently, near Arkhanes on the northern foothills of Mount Juktas, beside the Minoan road leading from Knossos to the peak sanctuary, a construction has been discovered with three rooms opening onto a corridor; clay feet, a vase decorated with a bull in relief, and an incised dagger found on a human skeleton endow the site with unquestionable religious significance. As for the sanctuary of Kato Syme near Viannos, it presents features heretofore unique: a building of several rooms situated in a mountain gorge far from any populated area, on the edge of a spring and at the foot of a steep cliff—a site used until Roman times for sacrifices and burnt offerings in honor of a divine couple.

But the religious building *par excellence* in Crete is the palace, although it did not have exactly the same functions as the Mesopotamian temple. Struck by the religious aura that pervaded the edifice he was uncovering at Knossos, Arthur Evans (1901) named it the "palace-sanctuary" and identified it with the labyrinth of Greek legend, the residence of the monstrous Minotaur. The other palaces, at Phaistos, Mallia, and Zakros, while not absolutely identical to that at Knossos, are remarkably similar. To the west (except at Zakros), a wide esplanade is crossed by stone-paved causeways leading to the main entrances and to a "theatral area" (Knossos, Phaistos); at Knossos, two altar bases emphasize the religious function of this courtyard. Inside the edifice, another rectangular court served as a theater for great popular spectacles, as proved by tiers of steps on the sides and, at Mallia, by a hollow altar, or *bothros,* dug in the center. The frescoes covering the walls of the palace at Knossos evoke the rites that took place there: processions, offerings, bullfights. The palatial architecture, with its recesses of the facade, porticoes, and wide staircases, conferred a true monumentality upon the ceremonies for which it served as setting.

The building itself concealed in its maze many rooms or places with a religious function. Evans recognized very early at Knossos the particular role of the pillar rooms that, according to him, were in fact cult chambers with offerings placed around a pillar marked with sacred signs. Similarly, small rooms with the floor on a lower level, which are also present in certain houses and generally adjoin ceremonial halls, must have been used as lustral areas, according to the most plausible interpretation. Finally, sanctuary rooms proper, often accompanied by storerooms for sacred objects or offerings, initially contained the effigy of the divinity.

GODS AND SACRED SYMBOLS

The divinity remains difficult to identify with any certainty among the representations in use in Minoan Crete, owing to the absence of a distinctive sign comparable to the horns adorning the headdresses of the gods and goddesses of Mesopotamia from the middle of the third millennium BCE. Thus, following Evans, the double image of a snake goddess was often recognized in the two faience figurines found in the Temple Repositories of Knossos, west of the central courtyard, but they could also be worshipers or priestesses decked out with the attributes of the goddess herself: flounced skirt, open bodice, snakes, and leopard. There seems to be a clear filiation, however, with later figurines from Gazi and Karphi, whose nature is emphasized by the sacred symbols attached to the headdress: poppy blossoms, horns of consecration, and birds.

That these are cult statues seems to be proved by the above-mentioned figurine from Myrtos, found toppled from its base. Twenty-one centimeters high, holding a pitcher under her arm, she belongs to a group of contemporary images of a fertility goddess. The often accentuated breasts and a painted or incised representation of the pubic triangle emphasize their nature; the figurines from Knossos as well as those from Gazi and Karphi are but a later disguise.

Attempts have been made to distinguish in the Cretan pantheon several goddesses with different attributes according to scenes in which a feminine figure seems to play a specific role: snake goddess, mountain goddess, war goddess, sea goddess, goddess of the hunt, tree goddess. The absence of any intelligible text from this period does not help to clarify the situation. Later texts from the Greek period mention several names of pre-Hellenic formation—*Britomartis* ("the sweet virgin"), *Diktynna,* ("the lady of Dikte"), and *Ariadne* ("the very holy")—all of which may be diverse epithets of the same divinity. As Stylianos Alexiou correctly noted in *Minoïkos politismos* (Minoan Civilization; 1964), "it would be vain to expect a logical classification in a spiritual context governed by emotion and intuition" (pp. 64–65).

However, a male god appears next to the goddess, but always in a subordinate position. On a gold ring from Knossos the god is shown as a diminutive figure with a staff in his hand who descends from heaven in answer to the prayers of a female worshiper standing in front of a column and a small sanctuary. Intaglios from Kydonia grant him a more important place, either between a winged goat and a demon of fertility or slaying two lions. On a sealing from Knossos, like the goddess herself he strides forward, wearing a tall, pointed tiara, armed with shield and spear, and accompanied by a lioness. In Greek texts he is named Velchanos or Hyakinthos and is assimilated to Zeus, but Zeus as a child or adolescent. The Minoan goddess, on the other hand, seems to survive in the Classical pantheon sometimes with the features of Artemis or Demeter, sometimes with those of Athena or Aphrodite, diversified forms of the same entity. In his article "Aegean Religion," D. G. Hogarth seems to have been right in defining the relationship between the goddess and the god as a "dual monotheism" (*Encyclopaedia of Religion and Ethics,* edited by James Hastings, vol. 1, 1908, p. 143).

But if the same divine being can easily embody different functions, he can appear as well under different aspects without changing his function. At Çatal Hüyük in Neolithic Anatolia, the feminine principle of fertility is represented sometimes in human form and sometimes symbolically by plaster reliefs of breasts, while the male principle appears sometimes as a bull's or ram's head but also as horns set into benches or small brick pillars. Similarly, in Crete a bird generally identified as a dove takes the place of the goddess, and a bull, that of the god. As for the snake, it has been diversely interpreted. A genius of the house, according to some (Nilsson,

1927), it would be the attribute of "the household goddess." But as a subterranean animal that sheds its skin, it would more likely be the symbol of the chthonic and reviviscent function of the Minoan goddess.

Moreover, the Minoan religion uses a whole range of religious symbols whose meaning is not always clear to us. Among them, the double ax occupies a place apart: sometimes a sign accompanying the goddess as shown on the seals of Knossos, where it dominates the goddess herself, it can also be her substitute and be worshiped in the same way. One of the possible etymologies of *labyrinth* is the word *labrus,* which designated the ax in Lydian. The labyrinth of the legend, generally identified with the palace of Knossos, would then be the House of the Double Ax. Numerous bronze examples of double axes were set in stone bases there, and images of them were incised on the blocks of the walls or on the pillars of the crypts. [*See also* Labyrinth.]

The question of the pillar or column, that is, of architectural support, is more doubtful. Indeed, Evans (1901) considered that the pillar, like the tree, was an aniconic representation of the divinity and therefore an object of worship for the votaries. Others, in particular Nilsson (1927), have thought that the pillar was not sacred in itself but could possibly become so in a certain context. It is nonetheless true that at Knossos, in the crypts of the palace and of the Royal-Villa, small basins set in the floor at the foot of the central pillar can be explained only as libation receptacles for ritual ceremonies, and that the gold ring mentioned earlier represents a worshiper standing before an isolated column in mystical expectation.

As for the horns of consecration, they emphasize the sacred character of a building, scene, or object. The three representations, on a bronze votive tablet from the Diktaean Cave, of a branch rising from a pair of horns show the importance of the sign even in popular imagery. Although rarer, the sacred knot, the flounced skirt, the figure-of-eight shield, and the helmet appear to have an undeniable but more specific relationship with the divinity.

CULT CEREMONIES

We have little information concerning the Minoan priesthood other than a few representations in which the priest is distinguished by his long, Syrian-type dress and fenestrated ax. It is likely that the priests and priestesses usually wore the same attire as both the gods themselves and ordinary worshipers: for the women, flounced skirts leaving the torso nude, and for the men, mere loincloths. Evans (1921) put forward the hypothesis of a "priest-king" with both political and religious functions, who was obliged to have his powers renewed by the divinity every nine years. Although subsequent criticism has demolished Evans's view that the Knossian Priest-King Fresco depicts such a figure, he can undoubtedly be recognized in certain other scenes portraying him as a young man with long hair, wearing bracelets and necklaces and sometimes holding a long stick or spear.

The encounter with the divinity, for the faithful as well as for the king, is an attested episode in the Minoan cult. On the sealing from Knossos already mentioned, the goddess is seen standing on a mountain peak; a worshiper, perhaps the priest-king himself, faces her, his body strongly arched backward and his hand raised to his face. This is the attitude of adoration, also found in bronze or clay statuettes: in the presence of the divinity, the worshiper must protect his eyes from her brightness. Central to the cult, this act was made possible only by the epiphany, or visible manifestation, of the goddess, which was the goal of the entire ritual.

As in Near Eastern religions, the first of these rites consisted in the offering of perishable foodstuffs, solid or liquid, in baskets or vases. One must distinguish, from the typological and functional points of view, between the altar and the offering table. The altar, which could have been simply an uncut rock, was often made of a more or less cubic block of stone with concave sides; in the palace of Mallia it was carved with two signs: a star and a cross. More monumental altars, with or without steps, are also found in the courts of the palaces and in the peak sanctuaries (Mount Juktas). A fragment of a pyxis from Knossos depicts one of these altars: the main part in squared-off stone is surmounted by a coping and by horns of consecration. As for the offering table, which appeared in various shapes and dimensions, in stone or clay, with or without legs, it generally included a large hollow for liquid offerings or libations. The rim of one of these, from Phaistos, is incised with a repeated motif of bovines and spirals, illustrating the use made of it, that is, the offering of the blood of sacrificed animals. Another, at Mallia, bears unmistakable traces of fire, which relate it to combustion pits like the one found in the central court of the palace. Similar to the offering table were the stone blocks with numerous hollows. The most elaborate of these stones, in the palace of Mallia, is circular in form and provided with a deep central hollow and thirty-four peripheral ones: it was placed on a small terrace in the corner of the central court to receive the first fruits of the harvest, according to a rite that prefigures the *panspermia* of the Classical period.

Libation ceremonies were performed using jugs and special vases, or rhytons; these, either conical or ovoid in shape, were pierced at the bottom to let the liquid flow out. Several of these stone vases bear decorations in relief that demonstrate an undeniable relationship with the cult; others, in stone or terra-cotta, represent the head of an animal, a lioness or bull, the bull's head probably meant for the blood of that animal.

The sacrifice is a particular form of libation ceremony in which the poured liquid is the blood of the victim. The rest of the animal was burned, as is proved by the bones found in layers of deposit in sanctuaries or sacrificial pits. The bull was the sacrificial animal *par excellence* in accordance with a tradition deeply rooted in the Near Eastern past; at the end of acrobatic bull games it must have been put to death with a double ax, probably in the central court of the palace. As for human sacrifice, in the absence of any incontestable data, one can only observe that the Cretans seem to have practiced it in one form or another, if the legend of Theseus and the Minotaur is to be believed.

Ritual processions ordinarily accompanied the offering of gifts to the divinity. Both on a fragment of a stone vase and on the walls of the Knossian palace, a file of hieratic figures carry cups and rhytons. Processions may also have borne the god's statue or the high priest in the oriental manner in a palanquin, as in the terra-cotta model discovered at Knossos, or the palanquin represented in a fresco painting. In this respect the stone-paved causeways that cross the western esplanades of the palaces seem to mark the requisite approaches to the main entrances and central court: thus at Knossos one of these walks leads to the West Porch, where the Corridor of the Procession begins, named after the paintings that decorate its walls. On a stone rhyton from Hagia Triada called the Harvesters' Vase, peasants carrying pitchforks on their shoulders march joyously to the music of a sistrum, led by a curious figure dressed in a cloak of scales, a prefiguration, in a way, of the Attic *kōmoi* of the Dionysian cult.

The dances often illustrated on intaglios and wall paintings were probably also ritual ceremonies. So famous were these dances in antiquity that Homer had them depicted on the shield of Achilles. The relationship between cult and physical movement, even acrobatics, was even stronger than in the Near East. Various exercises, wrestling matches, and bullfights fit into this context. Bullfights clearly had a particular importance, to judge by the number of representations. Before the death of the bull, young boys and girls took part in dangerous competitions like the one depicted in the fresco from Knossos known as the Taureador Fresco: they would somersault over the back of the wild animal just as the inhabitants of Çatal Hüyük in Anatolia had done during the Neolithic period. The distant echo of these games has come down to us as the legend of Theseus, who came from Athens to be fed with other youths to the Minotaur.

The profound unity of these cult manifestations, apparently so diverse, seems to have been ensured by their link with the vegetation cycle. Evans (1901) supposed the existence of a veritable tree cult, and after him Axel W. Persson thought that he could recognize in Crete traces of a New Year festival modeled on Oriental lines (*The Religion of Greece in Prehistoric Times,* 1942). We may assume in any case that the Minoan goddess was essentially a goddess of nature in all its forms—heavenly, earthly, subterranean, marine, animal, vegetal—of which she represented the creative force. In numerous scenes figures of men or women are seen dancing wildly, bowing low, or kneeling near a tree or small plants springing up from a shrine or a large pithos (earthenware cask); they seem to be celebrating successive episodes of the vegetation cycle: the birth, growth, and decline of nature, whose death induces funerary mourning on the part of the officiants.

FUNERARY CULT

It is in this light that the obvious link between divine worship and funerary cult in Minoan Crete must be understood. There was no fundamental difference between them; in practice, they were probably more or less indistinguishable. Pierre Demargne has rightly demonstrated, through the study of objects deposited in tombs, that the goddess of the dead and the goddess of fertility were one and the same (*Mélanges Gustave Glotz,* vol. 1, 1932, pp. 305–314). At Chryssolakkos, the princely necropolis of Mallia, one finds both a stone with hollows resembling the one in the palace, and a curious hollowed-out altar that seems to bring into close relationship, through the libation ritual, the world of the living and the world of the dead. The famous sarcophagus of Hagia Triada, from a rather late period, presents the most complete illustration of ceremonies in honor of the dead, which nothing differentiates from the usual cult ceremonies. On one side, near an altar associated with a basket of fruit and a libation pitcher and in front of a small shrine enclosing the sacred tree, a bull is sacrificed to the sound of a flute. On the other side of the sarcophagus, officiating priests and priestesses pour libations to the music of a harp and bring offerings to the dead person standing before his tomb. The scene is dominated by sacred signs: horns of consecration crowning the shrine, and double axes standing on their shafts and topped by birds. The same symbols, by themselves, are constantly represented on postpalatial sarcophagi, in combination with stylized flowers evoking the renewal of life. For the Cretans, as for every primitive mentality, the death of man is a normal part of the great cycle of nature, so that the same rites are necessary to bring about the rebirth of being and the revival of vegetation.

Mycenaean Religion

Nothing precise can be said about the divinities and cults of the continent before the Mycenaean period. The image of a fertility goddess seems to appear in the numerous representations from the Neolithic period of a naked female figure with hypertrophied forms, but the rites that were practiced are still unknown to us, in the absence of any cult installations. Even this image vanishes at the beginning of the Bronze Age, and thus the existence of a cult at this period, though probable, remains problematic until the appearance of the "shaft grave" culture in Mycenae and the rise of Minoan influence on the continent.

DATA FROM THE TABLETS

For a long time no distinction was made between the Mycenaean and Minoan civilizations, especially where religion was concerned. Indeed, in the view of Evans (1921–1936), the Minoans imposed on the Mycenaeans their way of life, their art, their ideas, and their rites. Even though there was mounting opposition to this theory of colonization, Cretan influence was hardly disputed until the deciphering of the Linear B script in 1953, which threw a whole new light on the matter by revealing a pantheon entirely different from that of the Minoans.

The tablets inscribed in Linear B are economic documents and give only indirect indications about the religion, in the form of lists of offerings to a god. Still, it is clear that the supremacy of a great goddess is replaced in the Mycenaean world by that of a male god who bears the name of the great god of the Classical Greeks: Zeus. Around him the pantheon of Olympian divinities was already taking shape: Hera, Athana Potnia (Athena), Enyalios (Ares), Paiawon (Apollo), Poseidaon (Poseidon), perhaps even Hermes and Dionysos; the hierarchies are not identical, however, as Poseidon played a preeminent role at Pylos. Some of these gods seem to mask older divinities whose attributes they took over. At Knossos, Zeus Diktaios ("of Mount Dikte") appears to have had the functions of the goddess of Mount Dikte, Diktynna, while the name *Potnia* ("lady, mistress"), used without other qualification, seems to express the personality of the Great Mother of pre-Hellenic days. As for the "Lady of the Labyrinth," her appellation apparently relates her to the palace of Knossos.

The offerings listed were varied and the quantities often considerable, in particular vegetable products such as barley, olives, and wine. Also offered were animals—cattle, sheep, and pigs—and humans of both sexes, as well as objects of value. As for the religious ceremonies, these remain for the most part obscure: in addition to offerings, mention is made of human sacrifices that are probably reflected in Greek mythology.

One term has been variously interpreted: *wa-na-ka*. It is undeniable that it constitutes the prototype of the word *anax,* which in the Homeric poems is usually applied to the chief of the Achaeans, Agamemnon. But on certain tablets it seems to be the epithet of a god, which has led some to the bold supposition that the Mycenaean king might have been divine in nature.

ARCHAEOLOGICAL DATA

The image that archaeology gives of the Mycenaean religion is no closer to Minoan reality. None of the great types of Cretan sanctuaries has been detected in continental Greece other than perhaps a peak sanctuary on Mount Kinortion at Epidaurus, and possible natural places of worship characterized by hoards of figurines remote from any constructions (the sanctuary of Marmaria at Delphi). The Mycenaean palace presents none of the features of the palaces of Crete: it is built not around a central court but around an enclosed hall or *megaron* to which a religious function, among others, must be attributed. Preceded by a two-columned porch between the antas and by a shallow vestibule, it anticipates the ground plan of the first Greek temples. In the center was a great circular hearth. At Pylos, near the royal throne, a drain joining two cavities together might have been used to receive libations. In addition, small offering tables were found under the porch or near the hearth. It is very likely, therefore, that the royal palace was the principal place of worship in the Mycenaean city, and that the king, though his divine nature remains subject to controversy, played a significant role in the ceremonies. At Mycenae, as if to emphasize this idea, the great gateway to the citadel that enclosed the palace was decorated with an eloquent relief: rearing face to face, two lions, their forepaws resting on a small Cretan altar, symmetrically flank a column with its capital, the sacralized symbol of the palace and of royal power.

However, sanctuaries did exist independently of the palaces, as the discovery of a true cult complex on the acropolis of Mycenae has recently proved. Located on the western slope not far from Grave Circle A, it consists of several sacred buildings with various installations for sacrifices, offerings, and libations. The "temple," comprising a vestibule, a cult room, and a raised annex accessible from an off-center staircase, has yielded an abundant series of figurines, mostly feminine, with raised arms and highly unusual characteristics: their heads, with strongly modeled features, are set on tubular bodies, and they are generally covered with a uniform layer of paint. The discovery of one of these in the main room on a stepped bench next to a small offering table shows their indisputably sacred character. Coiled clay snakes no doubt stress the chthonic aspect of the divinity represented. In a neighboring room, a fresco portrays a seated goddess holding two sheaves of wheat in a gesture that has no true parallel in Crete. Access to this religious quarter was afforded by a dog-legged processional approach, which demonstrates the importance of the area to the city. The arrangement seems very different from the cult installations of Minoan Crete, and the *megaron* plan was widely used, recalling in humbler form the great hall of the royal palace.

ICONOGRAPHY

Mycenaean iconography remains, on the other hand, practically identical to that of Minoan Crete. In the royal graves of Grave Circle A, to be sure, the figure of a naked goddess surrounded by birds was discovered, associating the Cretan theme of a divine bird with ritual nudity, probably Oriental in origin and unknown in Crete.

Yet in the same grave there was a silver pin with a gold head ornamented with a Cretan-type goddess in a flounced skirt and with bared breasts. Furthermore, at a later date human figures, animals, and symbols are so alike on the continent and in Crete that sometimes the best illustrations of certain incontestably Minoan scenes come from Mycenaean sites, such as the above-mentioned scene, on a ring from Mycenae, of the offering of gifts to the goddess. The goddess with the sheaves from the cult center is herself Cretan in spirit, even though she finds a closer parallel in an ivory carving from Minet-el-Beida in Syria. Yet everything leads one to believe that this iconographic repertoire covers a totally different reality. It is as if the Mycenaeans had disguised their relationship with the divinity in a language of symbols and themes borrowed from Crete, which for them were hardly more than material for artistic variations deprived of their original meaning.

FUNERARY CULT

The existence of a funerary cult on the continent appears much less certain than in Crete, even if one rejects the altogether negative position of G. E. Mylonas (1966). The concave altar found by Schliemann in Grave Circle A at Mycenae is undoubtedly associated with a late modification of the circle and attests to a cult of the dead only for the thirteenth century BCE. The expeditious treatment that the Mycenaeans usually inflicted on the oldest remains in the tombs bears witness to a fundamental impiety toward ancestors, whether of common or princely extraction. Concentrated around those great funerary constructions, the tholos graves, or beehive tombs, however, are signs of a particular veneration that seems to contain the seeds of the hero cult of the following period.

BIBLIOGRAPHY

Our knowledge of the Cycladic religion suffers from a dearth of archaeological and figured data from the Early Bronze Age. The most recent comprehensive study is that of Olof Höckmann, "Cycladic Religion," in *Art and Culture of the Cyclades in the Third Millennium B.C.,* edited by Jürgen Thimme, Pat Getz-Preziosi, and Brinna Otto (Chicago, 1977), an exhibition catalog accompanied by developments concerning the main aspects of the Cycladic culture. The religious significance of the frescoes of Thera is analyzed with new documentation in the work of Nanno Marinatos, *Art and Religion in Thera* (Athens, 1984).

It is because of the wealth of iconographic material that the Minoan religion has been the most explored of the Aegean religions ever since the first discoveries of Arthur Evans in Crete. His first book, *The Mycenaean Tree and Pillar Cult and Its Mediterranean Relations* (London, 1901), brings together a good many scenes of which he proposes a coherent exegesis within the framework of a pillar and vegetation cult. His outstanding publication, *The Palace of Minos,* 4 vols. plus index (London, 1921–1936), remains to this day a fundamental work owing to the abundant material presented and the penetrating character of his analyses, even though they are biased toward a religious interpretation.

Martin P. Nilsson's great work, *The Minoan-Mycenaean Religion and Its Survival in Greek Religion* (1927), 2d ed. rev. (Lund, 1950), gives a systematic account of all the information available at that date and presents a more critical view of religious manifestations in the Aegean in the third and second millennia, but his observations are somewhat weakened by his assimilation of the Minoan with the Mycenaean religion. Another comprehensive review is Charles Picard's *Les religions préhelléniques: Crète et Mycènes* (Paris, 1948), which groups material on the question in a convenient fashion but without illustrations. Each of these works must be supplemented by the well-informed synthesis of Emily Townsend Vermeule, *Götterkult,* in volume 3 of "Archeologia Homerica" (Göttingen, 1974); the drafting of the text goes back to 1963 and does not take into account the latest discoveries, in particular those of the frescoes of Thera and the cult center of Mycenae.

The interpretations of Evans, already discussed by Nilsson, have been strongly challenged by new analyses of archaeological data tending toward a more or less complete desacralization of the installations or architectural structures considered by him as sacred. This tendency is particularly noticeable in the article of Luisa Banti, "I culti minoici e greci di Haghia Triada (Creta)," *Annuario della Scuola Archeologica di Atene* 3– 5 (1941–1943): 9–74, and in the work of Bogdan Rutkowski, *Cult Places in the Aegean World* (Wroclaw, 1972).

In addition, new iconographic studies of the rich repertoire of Minoan representations with a religious character have been made by Friedrich Matz in his *Göttererscheinung und Kultbild im minoischen Kreta* (Wiesbaden, 1958), and more recently by Rutkowski in his *Frühgriechische Kultdarstellungen* (Berlin, 1981). The relationship between the Aegean and the Greek religions, already studied by Nilsson, was reexamined for Crete by R. F. Willetts in *Cretan Cults and Festivals* (New York, 1963) and, with the addition of Oriental antecedents, by B. C. Dietrich in *The Origins of Greek Religion* (Berlin and New York, 1974).

The great discovery in the field of Aegean religions has been the deciphering of the Linear B script by Michael Ventris and John Chadwick in 1953; its repercussions on our knowledge of the Mycenaean religion are brought to the fore in their joint publication, *Documents in Mycenaean Greek* (Cambridge, 1959). Since that date, commentaries of limited scope have been devoted to the Mycenaean religion in the context of more general works, such as George E. Mylonas's *Mycenae and the Mycenaean Age* (Princeton, 1966), Chadwick's *The Mycenaean World* (Cambridge, 1976), and J. T. Hooker's *Mycenaean Greece* (London, 1976). Following the discoveries made in Mycenae by Lord William Taylour and himself, Mylonas has drawn up a useful review of all the findings on the question as far as architecture is concerned, *Mycenaean Religion: Temples, Altars, and Temenea,* in volume 39 of *Proceedings of the Academy of Athens* (Athens, 1977).

10   GREEK RELIGION

JEAN-PIERRE VERNANT
Translated from French by Anne Marzin

The Greek religion of the Archaic and Classical periods (eighth–fourth century BCE) presented several characteristic traits that should be borne in mind. Like other polytheistic cults, Greek religion was a stranger to any form of revelation: it knew neither prophet nor messiah. It was deeply rooted in a tradition in which religion was intimately interwoven with all the other elements of Hellenic civilization, all that gave to the Greece of the city-states its distinctive character: from the language, the gestures, and the manner of living, feeling, and thinking to the system of values and the rules of communal life. This religious tradition was neither uniform nor strictly defined; its nature was not dogmatic in any way. It had no sacerdotal cast, no specialized clergy, no church, and no sacred book in which the truth was fixed once and for all. It had no creed that gave the faithful a coherent set of beliefs about the beyond.

MYTHOLOGY AND RELIGION

On what basis, then, did the deep-seated religious convictions of the Greeks lie, and how were they expressed? As their beliefs were not based on doctrine, they did not entail for the devout any obligation to adhere, for fear of impiety, on all points and to the letter to a body of defined truths. It sufficed for a person performing rites to give credence to a vast repertory of stories learned in childhood. Each of these stories existed in many versions, allowing a wide margin of interpretation. It was within the context of this narrative tradition that beliefs about the gods developed and that a consensus emerged as to their nature, their role, and their requirements. Rejecting this core of common beliefs would have been, for a Greek, like giving up the Greek language or the Greek way of life. However, for all that, the Greeks were fully aware that other languages and other religions existed. They could, without falling into disbelief, remain objective enough about their own religious system to engage in a free and critical reflection on it, and they did not hesitate to do so.

But how did they preserve and transmit this mass of traditional "knowledge" about the social reality of the otherworld—the families of the gods, their genealogies, their adventures, their conflicts or agreements, their powers, their spheres and modes of action, their prerogatives, and the honors that were due them? Where language was concerned, essentially in two ways. First, through a purely oral tradition maintained in each household, especially by women: nurses' tales or old grandmothers' fables, as Plato called them, were absorbed by children from the cradle. These stories, or *muthoi*—which were all the more familiar for having been heard by children at the age when they were learning to speak—helped shape the mental framework in which the Greeks imagined the divine, situated it, and conceived it.

As adults, the Greeks learned about the world of the gods through the voices of the poets. Through the tales about the gods, the remoteness and strangeness of the otherworld took a familiar, intelligible form. Performed with a musical instrument, the poets' songs were not heard in private, intimate surroundings, as were the tales told to children, but at banquets, official festivities, and important competitions and games. The rise of a written narrative tradition modified and preserved the very ancient tradition of oral poetry and came to occupy a central place in the social and spiritual life of Greece. The poets' songs were not a luxury reserved for the learned elite, nor were they merely personal entertainment for an audience; they functioned as a real institution that kept alive the social memory, as an instrument for the preservation and communication of knowledge. As a verbal form that could be memorized easily, poetry expressed and fixed the fundamental traits that went beyond the particularities of each city and were the foundation of a common culture for all of Hellas—especially those traits reflected in religious representations of the gods proper, daemons, heroes, or the dead. Had it not been for all the works of the epic, lyrical, and dramatic poetry, we could speak of Greek cults in the plural instead of a unified Greek religion. In this respect, Homer and Hesiod played prominent roles: their narratives about the divine beings acquired an almost canonical value and functioned as sources of reference for the authors who came after them as well as for the public that listened to or read them.

Certainly, the poets that succeeded Homer and Hesiod were not as influential. As long as the city-state remained alive, however, poetic activity continued to act as a mirror, reflecting the image of the inhabitants and allowing them to perceive their dependence on the sacred and to define themselves with reference to the immortal. Poetic activity gave the community of mortals its cohesiveness, its continuity, and its permanence.

Consequently, a problem arises for the historian of religions. If poetry was the vehicle through which the attributes of divine creatures, their roles, and their relationships with mortal creatures were expressed, and if it fell to each poet to present, with occasional modifications, the divine and heroic legends that, taken together, constituted an encyclopedia of knowledge about the otherworld, should these poetic tales and dramatized narrations be considered as religious documents or be given a purely literary value? That is, do myths and mythology, in the forms given them by Greek civilization, belong to the field of religion or to that of literary history?

For the scholars of the Renaissance, as for the great majority of the scholars of the nineteenth century, the reply was self-evident. In their eyes, Greek religion was, above all, an abundant treasure of legendary tales transmitted to us by the Greek authors (assisted by the Romans) in which the spirit of paganism remained alive long enough to offer the modern reader in a Christian world the surest path to a clear view of ancient polytheism.

Actually, in taking this standpoint, they simply walked in the footsteps of the ancients. In the sixth century BCE, Theagenes of Rhegium and Hekataios inaugurated a critical approach to the traditional myths, as recounted by Homer in particular. They subjected these stories to a reasoned examination or applied to them a method of allegorical exegesis. In the fifth century, work was begun that would be systematically pursued in essentially two directions. First, chroniclers undertook the collection and inventory of all the legendary oral traditions peculiar to a city or a sanctuary. Like the atthidographs of Athens, these scholars attempted to set down in writing the history of a city and its people from its earliest beginnings, going back to the fabulous time when the gods mingled with men, intervening directly in their affairs to found cities and to beget the first reigning dynasties. Thus was made possible, from the Hellenistic period onward, the enterprise of scholarly compilation that led to the drafting of veritable repertories of mythology: the *Bibliotheca* of "Apollodorus," the *Fabulae* and *Poetica Astronomica* of Hyginus, book 5 of the *Bibliotheca historica* of Diodorus Siculus, the *Metamorphoses* of Antoninus Liberalis, the three miscellaneous collections known as the Mythographi Vaticani.

Parallel to this effort, which aimed at a systematic summary of the legends common to all Greeks, there became apparent a certain hesitation and uneasiness— already perceptible among the poets—about how much credit should be accorded to the scandalous episodes that seemed incompatible with the eminent dignity of the divine. But it was with the development of history and philosophy that interrogation reached full scale; from then on criticism assailed myth in general. Subjected to the investigations of the historian and the reasonings of the philosopher, the fable, as fable, was deemed incompetent to speak of the divine in a valid and authentic fashion. Thus, at the same time that they applied themselves, with the greatest care, to setting down their legendary heritage, the Greeks were led to challenge the myths, sometimes in the most radical manner, and to raise the problem of the truth—or falsehood—of the myth. The solutions varied from rejection, or pure and simple negation, of the myths to the multiple forms of interpretation that permitted them to be "saved"; for example, a banal reading might be replaced with learned hermeneutics that brought to light a secret lesson underlying a narrative and analogous to those fundamental truths—the privilege of the wise—which, when known, reveal the only real sure access to the divine. Yet, from one point of view, no matter if the ancients were carefully collecting myths, if they interpreted or criticized them or even rejected them in the name of another, truer kind of knowledge—it all came down to recognizing the role generally assigned to myths in the Greek city-state, namely, to function as instruments of information about the otherworld.

During the first half of the twentieth century, however, historians of Greek religion took a new direction. Many refused to consider the legendary traditions as strictly religious documents that could be useful as evidence of the real state of the beliefs and feelings of the faithful. For these scholars, religion lay in the organization of the cult, the calendar of sacred festivals, the liturgies celebrated for each god in his sanctuaries. Next to these ritual practices, which constitute the "real" religious comportments, the myth appears as a literary outgrowth, a mere fabulation. As a more or less gratuitous fantasy of the poets, myth could be only remotely related to the inner convictions of the believer, who was engaged in the concrete practice of cult ceremonies and in a series of daily acts that brought him into direct contact with the sacred and made him a pious man.

In the chapter on Greece in *Histoire générale des religions* (1944), A.-J. Festugière warned the reader in these terms:

> *No doubt poets and sculptors, obeying the requisites of their art, were inclined to represent a society of highly characterized gods; form, attributes, genealogy, history, everything is clearly defined, but the cult and popular feeling reveal other tendencies. Thus, from the beginning, the field of the religious is enclosed. In order to understand fully the true Greek religion, forgetting therefore the mythology of the poets and of art, let us turn to the cult—to the earliest cults.*

What are the reasons for this exclusive bias in favor of the cult and for the importance attributed to its most archaic elements? There are two, very distinct reasons. The first is of a general nature and has to do with the personal philosophy of the scholar and with his idea of religion. The second is a response to more technical requirements: the progress of classical studies—in particular, the strides made in archaeology and epigraphy—opened new areas of investigation, besides the mythological field, to students of antiquity. These advances led scholars to call into question, and sometimes even modify profoundly, the image of Greek religion furnished by literary tradition alone.

Today, the rejection of mythology is based on an anti-intellectualist presumption in religious matters. Scholars of this standpoint believe that behind the diversity of religions—just as beyond the plurality of the gods of polytheism—lies a common element that forms the primitive and universal core of all religious experience. This common element, of course, cannot be found in the always multiple and varying constructions that the mind elaborates in its attempt to picture the divine; it is placed, therefore, outside of intelligence, in the sacred terror that man feels each time he is compelled to recognize, in its irrecusable strangeness, the presence of the supernatural. The Greeks had a word for this effective, immediate, and irrational reaction in the presence of the sacred: *thambos* ("reverential awe"). Such awe would be the basis of the earliest cults, the diverse forms taken by the rites answering, from the same origin, to the multiplicity of circumstances and human needs.

Similarly, it is supposed that behind the variety of names, figures, and functions proper to each divinity, a ritual brought into play the same general experience of the divine, considered a suprahuman power *(kreitton)*. This indeterminate divine being (Gr., *theion,* or *daimonion*), underlying the specific manifestations of particular gods, took diverse forms according to the desires and fears to which the cult had to respond. From this common fabric of the divine, the poets, in turn, cut singular characters; they brought them to life, imagining for each a series of dramatic adventures in what Festugière does not hesitate to call a "divine novel." On the other hand, for every act of the cult, there is no other god but the one invoked. From the moment he is addressed, "in him is concentrated all divine force; he alone is considered. Most certainly, in theory he is not the only god since there are others and one knows it. But in practice, in the actual state of mind of the worshiper, the god invoked supplants at that moment all the others" (Festugière, 1944, p. 50).

Thus the refusal of some scholars to take myth into account becomes clear: it leads exactly to that which from the beginning was meant, more or less consciously, to be proved. By effacing the differences and the oppositions that distinguish the gods from one another, any true difference is effaced between polytheisms of the Greek type and Christian monotheism, which then becomes a model. This flattening out of religious realities to make them fit a single mold cannot satisfy the historian. Must not his first concern be, on the contrary, to define the specific traits that give each great religion a character of its own and that make it, in its unicity, an entirely original system? Apart from reverential awe and a diffused feeling of the divine, the Greek religion presents itself as a vast symbolic construction, complex and coherent, that allows room for thought, as well as feeling, on all levels and in all aspects, including the cult. Myth played its part in this system in the same way as ritual practices and representations of the divine. Indeed, myth, rite, and figurative portrayals were the three modes of expression—verbal, gestural, and iconic—by which the Greeks manifested their religious experience. Each constituted a specific language that, even in its association with the two others, responded to particular needs and functioned autonomously.

The work of Georges Dumézil and Claude Lévi-Strauss on myth led to a totally different presentation of the problem of Greek mythology: How should the texts be read? What status did they assume in Greek religious life? The days when one could discuss myth as if it were a poet's individual fantasy, a free and gratuitous romantic invention, are gone. Even in the variations to which it lent itself, a myth obeyed the severe constraints of the community. During the Hellenistic period, when an author, such as Callimachus, wrote a new version of a legendary theme, he was not free to modify the elements or to recompose the scenario as he pleased. He belonged to a tradition; whether he conformed to it exactly or deviated on a certain point, he was restrained and supported by it and had to refer to it, at least implicitly, if he wanted the public to hear his tale. As Louis Gernet (1932) noted, even when a narrator seemed to have completely invented a tale, he was actually working according to the rules of a "legendary imagination" that had its own functioning, internal necessities, and coherence. Without even knowing it, the author was obliged to submit to the rules of the play of associations, oppositions, and homologies that had been established by a series of previous versions of the tale and that composed the conceptual framework common to the type of narrative. To have meaning, each variation of a myth had to be linked to, as well as compared with, the other variations. Together, they composed one semantic space, whose particular configuration appears as the characteristic mark of Greek legendary tradition. By analyzing a myth in all its versions, or a corpus of diverse myths centered around the same theme, we are able to explore this structured and organized mental space.

Interpretation of a myth, therefore, operates along lines different from those characterizing the study of literature and must meet other goals. It seeks to determine the conceptual architecture of the very composition of the fable, the important frameworks of clas-sification that are involved, the choices made in the division and the coding of reality, and the network of relationships that the story, by its narrative procedures, establishes between the various elements of the plot. In short, the mythologist seeks to reconstitute what Dumézil calls the "ideology," that is, the conceptualization and appreciation of the great forces that in their mutual relationships and their perfect equilibrium govern the natural and supernatural worlds, men, and society and makes them what they ought to be.

In this sense myth, which should not be confused with ritual or subordinated to it, does not conflict with ritual as much as has been supposed. In its verbal form, myth is more explicit than rite, more didactic, more apt to theorize. It thus contains the germ of that knowledge that—on another level of language and thought—is the concern of philosophy when it formulates its assertions using concepts and terms that are removed from any reference to the gods of the common religion. The cult is more engaged in considerations of a utilitarian nature. But it is no less symbolic: a ritual ceremony unfolds according to a scenario whose episodes are as strictly organized and as fraught with meaning as the sequences of a narrative. Every detail of this mise-en-scène, in which the worshiper in defined circumstances undertakes to act out his relationship with one god or another, has an intellectual dimension and goal: it implies a certain idea of the god, the conditions for his approach, and the results that the various participants, according to their role and status, have the right to expect from this means of entering into symbolic commerce with the divinity.

Figurative representation is of the same nature. Although it is true that during the Classical period the Greeks gave a privileged place in their temples to the great anthropomorphic statues of the gods, they were familiar with all the forms of divine manifestation: aniconic symbols, either natural objects, such as a tree or a rough stone, or products shaped by the human hand (e.g., a post, a pillar, a scepter); diverse iconic figures, such as a small, rough-hewn idol whose form was completely hidden by clothes; monstrous figures mingling the bestial and the human; a simple mask whose hollow face and fascinating eyes evoked the divine; a fully human statue. These figures were not all equivalent, nor were they indiscriminately suited to all the gods or to all aspects of the same god. Each had its own way of translating certain aspects of the divine, of "making present" the beyond, of locating and inserting the sacred in the space of the here and now. Thus, a pillar or post driven into the ground had neither the same function nor the same symbolic value as an idol that was ritually moved from one place to another; as an image locked away in a secret repository, its legs bound to prevent its escape; or as a great cult statue whose permanent installation in a temple demonstrated the lasting presence of the god in his house. Each form of representation implied for the specific divinity a particular way of making himself known to man and of exercising, through his images, his supernatural powers.

If, following various modalities, myth, image, and ritual all operate on the same level of symbolic thought, it is understandable that they combine to make each religion a complete whole in which, to quote Dumézil in *L'héritage indo-européen à Rome* (Paris, 1949, p. 64), "concepts, images and actions fit together and by their relations form a kind of net in which, potentially, all the matter of human experience must be caught and distributed."

THE WORLD OF THE GODS

To find the lines of the net, to pick out the configurations shaped by its meshes: such must be the historian's task. In the case of Greek religion, this proves to be far more difficult than with the other Indo-European religions, in which the pattern of the three functions—sovereignty, war, and fertility—is maintained. Where it is clearly attested, this structure serves as the framework and keystone of the entire edifice and provides a unity that seems to be lacking in Greek religion.

Indeed, Greek religion presents an organization so complex that it excludes recourse to a single reading code for the entire system. To be sure, a Greek god is defined by the set of relationships that unite or put him in opposition to other divinities of the pantheon, but the theological structures thus brought to light are too numerous and, especially, too diverse to be integrated into the same pattern.

According to the city, the sanctuary, or the moment, each god enters into a varied network of combinations with the others. Groups of gods do not conform to a single model that is more important than others; they are organized into a plurality of configurations that do not correspond exactly but compose a table with several entries and many axes, the reading of which varies according to the starting point and the perspective adopted.

Take the example of Zeus. His name clearly reveals his origin, based on the same Indo-European root (meaning "to shine") as Latin *dies/deus* and the Vedic *dyeus.* Like the Indian Dyaus Pitṛ or the Roman Jupiter (Iovpater), Father Zeus (Zeus Pater) is the direct descendant of the great Indo-European sky god. However, the gap between the status of the Zeus of Greece and that of his corresponding manifestations in India and in Rome is so evident, so marked, that even when comparing the most assuredly similar gods one is compelled to recognize that the Indo-European tradition has completely disappeared from the Greek religious system.

Zeus does not appear in any trifunctional group comparable to the pre-Capitoline Jupiter-Mars-Quirinus, in which sovereignty (Jupiter) is contrasted with the action of the warrior (Mars) and the functions of fertility and prosperity (Quirinus). Nor is he associated, as Mitra is with Varuṇa, with a sovereign power that expresses not only legal and juridical aspects but also the values of magic and violence. Ouranos, the dark night sky, who has sometimes been compared with Varuṇa, is paired in myth with Gaia, the earth, not with Zeus.

As sovereign, Zeus embodies greater strength than all the other gods. He is the supreme power: with Zeus on one side and all the assembled Olympians on the other, it is Zeus who prevails. Confronted by Kronos, whom he dethroned, and the Titan gods, whom he fought and imprisoned, Zeus represents justice, the fair distribution of honors and offices, respect for the privileges to which each person is entitled, concern for what is due even to the weakest. In him and by him, order and power, law and violence are reconciled and conjoined. "All kings come from Zeus," wrote Hesiod in the seventh century BCE, not to oppose monarch, warrior, and peasant, but to affirm that there is no true king among men who does not set himself the task of quietly making justice triumph. "From Zeus are the kings," echoes Callimachus four centuries later, but this kinship between kings and the royalty of Zeus does not fit into a trifunctional framework. It crowns a series of similar statements that link a particular category of men to the divinity who acts as its patron: blacksmiths to Hephaistos, soldiers to Ares, hunters to Artemis, and singers accompanied by the lyre to Phoibos (Apollo).

When Zeus enters into the composition of a triad, as he does with Poseidon and Hades, it is to delimit by their apportionment the cosmic levels, or domains: the heavens to Zeus, the sea to Poseidon, the subterranean world to Hades, the surface of the earth to all three. When he is paired with a goddess, the dyad thus formed brings out different aspects of the sovereign god, depending on the female divinity who is his counterpart. Joined with Gaia ("earth"), for example, Zeus is the celestial principle, male and generative, whose fertilizing rain reaches deep in the ground to animate young sprouts of vegetation. United with Hera in a lawful marriage that engenders a legitimate line, Zeus becomes the patron of the institution of matrimony, which, by civilizing the union of man and woman, serves as the foundation of every social organization; the couple formed by the king and queen is the exemplary model. Associated with Metis, his first wife (whom he swallowed and assimilated entirely), Zeus the king is identified with cunning intelligence and with the underhanded shrewdness needed to win power and to keep it. He is able to ensure the permanence of his reign and to protect his throne from traps, snares, and surprises, for he is always prompt to foresee the unexpected and to ward off dangers. Taking Themis for his second wife, he fixes, once and for all, the order of the seasons, the balance of human groups in the city (order and balance represented by the Horai, daughters of Zeus and Themis), and the ineluctable course of the Fates (the Moirai). He becomes cosmic law, social harmony, and destiny.

Father of the gods and men, as he is designated already in the *Iliad*—not because he sired or created all beings but because he exercises over each of them an authority as absolute as that of the head of a family over his household—Zeus shares with Apollo the epithet *patrōios* ("the ancestral"). Together with Athena Apatouria, Zeus, as Phratrios, ensures the integration of individuals into the diverse groups that compose the civic community. In the cities of Ionia, he makes of all the citizens authentic brothers, celebrating in their respective phratries, as in one family, the festival of the Apaturia, that is, of those who acknowledge themselves children of the same father. In Athens, joined with Athena Polias, Zeus is Polieus, patron of the city. Master and guarantor of political life, Zeus forms a couple with the goddess, whose function as titulary power of Athens is more precise and, one might say, more localized. Athena watches over her city as a particular city distinguished from the other Greek city-states. She favors Athens, according it the dual privileges of concord within the city and victory outside of it.

Celestial and judicious wielder of supreme power, founder of order, guarantor of justice, governor of marriage, father and ancestor, and patron of the city, the tableau of the sovereignty of Zeus includes still other dimensions. His authority is domestic as well as political. In close connivance with Hestia, Zeus has supreme control not only over each private hearth—that fixed center where the family has its roots—but also over the common household of the state in the heart of the city, the Hestia Koinē, where the ruling magistrates keep watch. Zeus Herkeios, the god of the courtyard and the household, circumscribes the domain within which the head of the house has the right to exercise his power; Zeus Klarios, the divider of estates, delineates and sets boundaries, leaving Apollo and Hermes in charge of protecting the gates and controlling the entries.

As Zeus Hikesios and Zeus Xenios, he receives the suppliant and the guest, introduces them into the unfamiliar house, and ensures their safety by welcoming them to the household altar, although he does not assimilate them entirely to the members of the family. Zeus Ktesios, the guardian of possession and wealth, watches over the property of the head of the house. As an Olympian and a celestial god, Zeus opposes Hades; yet as Ktesios, Zeus's altar is deep in the cellar, and he takes on the appearance of a serpent, the most chthonic of animals. The sovereign can thus incorporate that chthonic part of the universe normally controlled by the powers of the underworld but occasionally incarnated by Zeus himself in a kind of internal tension, polarity, or even a double image. The celestial Zeus, who sits at the summit of the shining ether, is mirrored by a Zeus Chthonios, Zeus Katachthonios, Zeus Meilichios, a Zeus of the dark underworld, who is present in the depths of the earth where he nurtures, in the proximity of the dead, the riches or retributions that are ready, if he is willing, to surge into the light led by the chthonic Hermes.

Zeus connects heaven and earth by means of the rain (Zeus Ombrios, Huetios, Ikmaios, "rainy," "damp"), the winds (Zeus Ourios, Euanemos, "windy," "of a good wind"), and the lightning (Zeus Astrapaios, Bronton, Keraunios, "wielder of thunderbolts," "thunderer"). He ensures communication between high and low through signs and oracles, which transmit messages from the gods of heaven to mortals on the earth. According to the Greeks, their most ancient oracle was an oracle of Zeus at Dodona. There he established his sanctuary at the site of a great oak, which belonged to him and which rose straight as the tallest column toward heaven. The rustling of the leaves of the sacred oak above their heads provided the consultants with the answer to their questions to the sovereign of heaven. Moreover, when Apollo pronounces his oracles in the sanctuary of Delphi, he speaks not so much for himself as in the name of his father, with whom he remains associated and, in his oracular function, seems to obey. Apollo is a prophet, but he is the prophet of Zeus: he voices only the will and decrees of the Olympian so that here—at the navel of the world—the word of the king and father may resound in the ears of those who can hear.

The different epithets of Zeus, wide as their range may be, are not incompatible. They all belong to one field and emphasize its multiple dimensions. Taken together, they define the contours of divine sovereignty as conceived by the Greeks; they mark its boundaries and delimit its constituent domains; they indicate the various aspects that the power of the king-god may assume and exercise in more or less close alliance (according to circumstances) with the other divinities.

An entirely different matter is the Zeus of Crete, the Kretagenes, Diktaios, or Idaios, the youthful god whose infancy was associated with the Curetes, with their dances and orgiastic rites and the din of their clashing weapons. It was said of this Zeus that he was born in Crete and that he also died there; his tomb was shown on the island. But the Greek Zeus, in spite of his many facets, can have nothing in common with a dying god. In the *Hymn to Zeus,* Callimachus firmly rejects the tradition of these stories as foreign to his god, "ever great, ever king." The real Zeus was not born in Crete, as those lying Cretans told it: "They have gone so far as to build you a tomb, O King; Nay, you never died; You are for eternity."

In the eyes of the Greeks, immortality, which sets a rigorous boundary between the gods and men, was such a fundamental trait of the divine that the ruler of Olympus could in no way be likened to one of the Oriental deities who die and are reborn. During the second millennium, the framework of the Indo-European religious system, whose influence is reflected in the name of Zeus, may well have collapsed among those people speaking a Greek dialect, who came in successive waves to settle Helladic soil and whose presence is attested as far as Knossos in Crete from the end of the fifteenth century BCE. Contacts, exchanges, and intermixing were numerous and continuous. There were borrowings from the Aegean and Minoan religions, just as there were from the Oriental and Thraco-Phrygian cults when the Greeks later expanded throughout the Mediterranean. Nevertheless, between the fourteenth and the twelfth centuries, most of the gods revered by the Achaeans—and whose names figure on the Linear B tablets from Knossos and Pylos—are the same ones encountered in the classical Greek pantheon: Zeus, Poseidon, Enualios (Ares), Paean (Apollo), Dionysos, Hera, Athena, Artemis, and the Two Queens, that is, Demeter and Kore.

The religious world of the Indo-European invaders of Greece could well have been modified and opened to foreign influences, but while it assimilated some concepts, it kept its specificity and the distinctive features of its own gods. From the religion of the Mycenaeans to that of the age of Homer, during those obscure centuries that followed the fall or the decline of the Achaean kingdoms after the twelfth century, continuity was not only marked by the persistence of the names of the gods and cult places. The continuity of certain festivals celebrated by the Ionians on both shores of the Mediterranean proves that these festivals must already have been customary in the eleventh century at the outset of the first wave of colonization, whose point of departure may have been Athens, the only Mycenaean site to remain intact, and which established groups of emigrants on the coast of Asia Minor to found Greek cities.

This permanence of Greek religion must not be misleading, however. The religious world evoked by Homer is no more representative of the religion of an earlier period than the world of the Homeric poems is representative of the world of the Mycenaean kings, whose exploits the bard, after an interval of four centuries, undertook to evoke. During this time a whole series of changes and innovations were introduced: behind apparent continuities was a veritable rupture (that the epic text effaces but whose extent can be measured through archaeological research and a reading of the tablets).

THE CIVIC RELIGION

Between the eleventh and eighth centuries, technical, economic, and demographic changes led to what the English archaeologist Anthony Snodgrass called the "structural revolution," which gave rise to the city-state *(polis)*. The Greek religious system was profoundly reorganized during this time in response to the new forms of social life introduced by the *polis*. Within the context of a religion that from then on was essentially civic, remodeled beliefs and rites satisfied a dual and complementary obligation. First of all, they fulfilled the specific needs of each group of people, who constituted a city bound to a specific territory. The city was placed under the patronage of its own special gods, who endowed it with a unique religious physiognomy. Every city had its own divinity or divinities, whose functions were to cement the body of citizens into a true community; to unite into one whole all the civic space, including the urban center and the *chora,* or rural area; and to look after the integrity of the state—the people and the land—in the presence of other cities. Second, the development of an epic literature cut off from any local roots, the construction of great common sanctuaries, and the institution of pan-Hellenic games and panegyrics established and reinforced, on a religious level, legendary traditions, cycles of festivals, and a pantheon that would be recognized equally throughout all of Hellas.

Without assessing all the religious innovations brought about during the Archaic period, the most important should be mentioned. The first was the emergence of the temple as a construction independent of the human habitat, whether houses or royal palaces. With its walls delimiting a sacred enclosure *(temenos)* and its exterior altar, the temple became an edifice separated from profane ground. The god came to reside there permanently through the intermediacy of his great anthropomorphic cult statue. Unlike domestic altars and private sanctuaries, this house of the god was the common property of all citizens.

To mark and confirm its legitimate authority over a territory, each city built a temple in a precise place: in the center of the city, the acropolis or agora, the gates of the walls surrounding the urban area, or in the zone of the *agros* and the *eschatiai*—the wilderness that separated each Greek city from its neighbors. The construction of a network of sanctuaries within, around, and outside the city not only punctuated the space with holy places but also marked the course of ritual processions, from the center to the periphery and back. These processions, which mobilized all or a part of the population on fixed dates, aimed at shaping the surface of the land according to a religious order.

Through the mediation of its civic gods (installed in their temples), the community established a kind of symbiosis between the people and their land, as if the citizens were the children of an earth from which they had sprung forth in the beginning and which, by virtue of this relationship with those who inhabited it, was itself promoted to the rank of "earth of the city." This explains the bitterness of the conflicts, between the eighth and the sixth centuries, that pitted neighboring cities against each other in the appropriation of cult places on those borders that were held in common by more than one *polis*. The occupation of the sanctuary and its religious annexation to the urban center were equivalent to legitimate possession. When it founded its temples, the *polis* rooted them firmly in the world of the gods so that its territorial base would have an unshakable foundation.

Another innovation with partly comparable significance left its mark on the religious system. During the eighth century, it became customary to put into service Mycenaean buildings, usually funerary, that had been abandoned for centuries. Once they were fitted out, they served as cult places where funeral honors were rendered to legendary figures who, although they usually had no relationship to these edifices, were claimed as ancestors by their "progeny," noble families or groups of phratries. Like the epic heroes whose names they carried, these mythical ancestors belonged to a distant past, to a time different from the present, and constituted a category of supernatural powers distinct from both the *theoi*, or gods proper, and the ordinary dead. Even more than the cult of the gods (even the civic gods), the cult of heroes had both civic and territorial value. It was associated with a specific place, a tomb with the subterranean presence of the dead person, whose remains were often brought home from a distant land.

The tombs and cults of the hero, through the prestige of the figure honored, served as glorious symbols and talismans for the community. The location of the tombs was sometimes kept secret because the welfare of the state depended on their safety. Installed in the heart of the city in the middle of the agora, they gave substance to the memory of the legendary founder of the city (the tutelary hero or, in the case of a colony, the colonizing hero), or they patronized the various components of the civic body (tribes, phratries, and demes). Disseminated to various points of the territory, the cults consecrated the affinities that united the members of the rural areas and villages (the *kōmai*). In all cases their function was to assemble a group around an exclusive cult that appears to have been strictly implanted in precise points of the land.

The spread of the cult of the hero did not just comply with the new social needs that arose with the city; the adoration of the heroes had a properly religious significance. Different from the divine cult, which was obligatory for everyone and permanent in character, and also from the funerary rites, which were limited in time as well as to a narrow circle of relatives, the heroic institution affected the general stability of the cult system.

For the Greeks, there was a radical opposition between the gods, who were the beneficiaries of the cult, and men, who were its servants. Strangers to the transience that defines the existence of men, the gods were the *athanatoi* ("the immortals"). Men, on the other hand, were the *brotoi* ("the mortals"), doomed to sickness, old age, and death. Consequently, the funeral honors paid to the dead were placed on a different level from the sacrifices and devotions demanded by the gods as their share of honor, their special privilege. The narrow strips of material decorating the tombs, the offerings of cakes for the dead person, the libations of water, milk, honey, or wine that had to be renewed on the third, ninth, and thirtieth day after the funeral and again each year on the festival of the Genesia appear to have been the temporary continuation of the funeral ceremony and mourning practices rather than acts of veneration toward the higher powers. [*See* Genesia.] The intent of opening the doors of Hades to the dead person was to make him disappear forever from this world, where he no longer had a place. At the same time, through the various procedures of commemoration, the funeral transformed his absence into a presence in the memory of the survivors—an ambiguous, paradoxical presence, as of one who is absent, relegated to the realm of shadows, reduced henceforth to the social status of a dead man by the funeral rites. Even this status, however, is destined to sink into oblivion as the cycle of generations is renewed.

The heroes were quite another matter. To be sure, they belonged to the race of men and thus knew suffering and death. But a whole series of traits distinguished them, even in death, from the throng of ordinary dead. The heroes had lived during the period that constituted the "old days" for the Greeks, a bygone era when men were taller, stronger, more beautiful. Thus the bones of a hero could be recognized by their gigantic size. It was this race of men, later extinct, whose exploits were sung in epic poetry. Celebrated by the bards, the names of the heroes—unlike the names of ordinary men, which faded into the indistinct and forgotten mass of the nameless—remained alive forever, in radiant glory, in the memory of all the Greeks. The race of heroes formed the legendary past of the Greece of the city-states and the roots of the families, groups, and communities of the Hellenes.

Although they were men, these ancestors seemed in many ways nearer to the gods, less cut off from the divine, than the rest of humanity. In their day, the gods still mingled readily with mortals, inviting themselves to the homes of men, eating at their tables, and even slipping into their beds to unite with them and—by mixing the two races, the mortal and the immortal—to beget beautiful children. The heroic figures whose names survived and whose cults were celebrated at their tombs were very often presented as the fruit of these amorous encounters between the divinities and human beings of both sexes. They were, as Hesiod said, "the divine race of heroes called demigods." If their birth sometimes endowed them with a semidivine origin, their death also placed them above the human condition. Instead of descending into the darkness of Hades, they were "abducted" or transported by means of divine favor—some during their lifetime but most of them after death—to a special, separate place on the Isles of the Blessed, where they continued to enjoy in permanent felicity a life comparable to that of the gods.

Although it did not bridge the immeasurable gulf that separates men from the gods, heroic status seemed to open the prospect of the promotion of a mortal to a rank that, if not divine, was at least close to divinity. However, during the entire Classical period, this possibility remained strictly confined to a narrow sector. It was thwarted, not to say repressed, by the religious system itself. Indeed, piety, like wisdom, enjoined man not to pretend to be the equal of a god; the precepts of Delphi—"know who you are, know thyself"—have no other meaning than that. Man must accept his limits. Therefore, apart from the great legendary figures, such as Achilles, Theseus, Orestes, and Herakles, the status of the hero was restricted to the first founders of the colonies or to persons, such as Lysander of Samos and Timoleon of Syracuse, who had acquired exemplary symbolic worth in the eyes of a city.

We know of few cases of men who were heroized during the Classical period. They never concerned a living person but always one who after his death appeared to bear a *numen* (or formidable sacral power) because of his extraordinary physical characteristics (size, strength, and beauty), the circumstances of his death (if he had been struck by lightning or had disappeared leaving no trace), or the misdeeds attributed to his ghost, which it seemed necessary to appease. For example, in the middle of the fifth century, the boxer Cleomedes of Astypalaia, who was exceptionally strong, killed his adversary in combat. Denied a prize by the decision of the jury, he returned home mad with rage. He vented his fury on a pillar that held up the ceiling of a school, and the roof caved in on the children. Pursued by a crowd that wanted to stone him, Cleomedes hid in a chest in the sanctuary of Athena, locking the lid on himself. His pursuers succeeded in forcing it open, but the chest was empty: no Cleomedes, living or dead, was to be found. The Pythia, when consulted, advised the establishment of a hero cult in honor of the boxer, whose strength, fury, misdeeds, and death set him above ordinary mortals. Sacrifices were to be made to him as "no longer a mortal." But the oracle manifested her reservations by also proclaiming that Cleomedes was the last of the heroes.

However much the heroes constituted, through the honors paid to them, a category of superior beings, their role, their power, and the domains in which they intervened did not interfere with those of the gods. They never played the role of intermediary between earth and heaven; they were not intercessors but indigenous powers, bound to the spot of ground where they had their subterranean homes. Their efficacy adhered to their tombs and to their bones; there were anonymous heroes designated only by the names of the places where their tombs were established, such as the hero of Marathon. This local quality was accompanied by a strict specialization. Many heroes had no other realities than the narrow function to which they were dedicated and which defined them entirely. For example, at Olympia, at the bend of the track, competitors offered sacrifices at the tomb of the hero Taraxippos, the Frightener of Horses. Similarly, there were doctor heroes, doormen, cook, fly-catcher heroes, a hero of meals, of the broad bean, of saffron, a hero to mix water and wine or to grind the grain.

If the city could group into the same category of cults the highly individualized figures of heroes of long ago, whose legendary biographies were fixed in their epics, of exceptional contemporaries, of anonymous dead of whom all that remained were funerary monuments, and of all sorts of functional daemons, it was because inside their tombs they manifested the same contacts with the subterranean powers, shared the same characteristic of territorial localization, and could be used as political symbols. Instituted by the emerging city, bound to the land that it protected and to the groups of citizens that it patronized, the cult of the hero did not, in the Hellenistic period, lead to the divinization of human figures, nor did it lead to the establishment of a cult of sovereigns: these phenomena were the product of a different religious mentality. Inseparable from the *polis,* the hero cult declined with it.

The appearance of the hero cult, however, was not without consequences. By its newness it led to an effort to define and categorize more strictly the various supernatural powers. Plutarch noted that Hesiod was the first, in the seventh century, to make a clear distinction between the different classes of divine beings, which he divided into four groups: gods, daemons, heroes, and the dead. Taken up again by the Pythagoreans and by Plato, this nomenclature of the divinities to whom men owed veneration was common enough in the fourth century to appear in the requests that the consultants addressed to the oracle of Dodona. On one of the inscriptions that have been found, a certain Euandros and his wife question the oracle about which "of the gods, or heroes, or daemons" they must sacrifice to and address their prayers to.

THE SACRIFICIAL PRACTICES

To find his bearings in the practice of the cult, the believer, therefore, had to take into account the hierarchical order that presided in the society of the beyond. At the top of the hierarchy were the *theoi,* both great and small, who made up the race of the blessed immortals. These were the Olympians, grouped under the authority of Zeus. As a rule they were celestial divinities, although some of them, such as Poseidon and Demeter, bore chthonic aspects. There was indeed a god of the underworld (Hades), but he was in fact the only one who had neither temple nor cult. The gods were made present in this world in the spaces that belonged to them: first of all, in the temples where they resided but also in the places and the objects that were consecrated to them and that, specified as *hiera* ("sacred"), could be subject to interdiction. These include the sacred groves, springs, and mountain peaks; an area surrounded by walls or boundary markers *(temenos);* crossroads, trees, stones, and obelisks. The temple, the building reserved as the dwelling of the god, did not serve as a place of worship. The faithful assembled to celebrate the rites at the exterior alter *(bōmos),* a square block of masonry. Around it and upon it was performed the central rite of the Greek religion, the burnt offering *(thusia),* the analysis of which is essential.

This was normally a blood sacrifice implying the eating of the victim: a domestic animal, crowned and decked with ribbons, was led in procession to the altar to the sound of flutes. It was showered with water and fistfuls of barley seeds, which were scattered on the ground and on the altar as well as on the participants, who also wore crowns. The head of the victim was then lifted up and its throat cut with a *machaira,* a large knife concealed under the seeds in the *kanoun,* or ritual basket. The blood that gushed onto the altar was caught in a receptacle. The animal was cut open and its entrails, especially the liver, were drawn out and examined to see if the gods accepted the sacrifice. If accepted, the victim was immediately carved. The long bones, entirely stripped of flesh, were laid on the altar. Covered with fat, they were consumed with herbs and spices by the flames and, in the form of sweet-smelling smoke, rose toward heaven and the gods. Certain internal morsels *(splagchna)* were put on spits and roasted over the same fire that had sent to the divinity his share, thus establishing a link between the sacred powers for whom the sacrifice was intended and the performers of the rite for whom the roasted meat was reserved. The rest of the meat was boiled in caldrons, divided into equal parts, and eaten by the participants on the spot, taken home, or distributed outside to the community at large. The parts that were thought to confer honor, such as the tongue or the hide, went to the priest who presided at the ceremony, though his presence was not always indispensable.

As a rule, any citizen, if he was not impure, had full authority to perform sacrifices. The religious significance of this must be defined by bringing out its theological implications. From the start, however, several points are essential. Certain divinities and certain rituals, such as that of Apollo Genetor in Delphi and Zeus Hupatos in Attica, required, instead of a blood sacrifice, food oblations: fruit, palms, grain, porridge *(pelanos)*, and cakes sprinkled with water, milk, honey, or oil; no blood or even wine was offered. There were cases in which this type of offering, usually consumed by fire but sometimes simply deposited on the altar without being burned *(apura)*, was characterized by marked opposition to customary practice. Considered pure sacrifices, unlike those involving the killing of living creatures, they served as models for sectarian movements. Orphics and Pythagoreans referred to them in advocating a ritual behavior and an attitude toward the divine that, in rejecting the blood sacrifice as impious, diverged from the official cult and appeared foreign to the civic religion.

In addition, blood sacrifice itself took two different forms according to whether it addressed the heavenly and Olympian gods or the chthonic and infernal ones. The language already made a distinction between them: for the first, the Greeks employed the term *thuein;* for the second, *enagizein* or *sphattein.*

The *thusia,* as we have seen, was centered on an elevated altar, the *bōmos.* The chthonic sacrifice had only a low altar (the *eschara*) with a hole in it to let the blood pour out into the earth. Normally the celebration took place at night over a ritual pit *(bothros)* that opened the way to the underworld. The animal was immolated with its head lowered toward the earth, which would be inundated with its blood. Once its throat was cut, the victim was no longer the object of ritual handling; because it was offered in holocaust, it was burned entirely without the celebrants having the right to touch it or to eat it. In this kind of rite, in which the offering is destroyed in order to be delivered in its entirety to the beyond, it was less a matter of establishing with the divinity a regular commerce of exchange in mutual confidence than of warding off the sinister forces, of placating a formidable power who would approach without harm only if defenses and precautions were taken. One might say that it was a ritual of aversion rather than one of reconciliation or contact. Understandably, its use was reserved for the cult of the chthonic and infernal deities, for expiatory rites, or for sacrifices offered to heroes and to the dead in their tombs.

In the Olympian sacrifice, the orientation toward the heavenly divinities was marked not only by the light of day, the presence of an altar, and the blood gushing upward when the throat of the victim was cut. A fundamental feature of the ritual was that it was inseparably an offering to the gods and a festive meal for the human participants. Although the climax of the event was undoubtedly the moment that, punctuated by the ritual cry *(ololugmos),* life abandoned the animal and passed into the world of the gods, all the parts of the animal, carefully gathered and treated, were meant for the people, who ate them together. The immolation itself took place in an atmosphere of sumptuous and joyful ceremony. The entire staging of the ritual—from the procession in which the untied animal was led freely and in great pomp to the concealment of the knife in the basket to the shudder by which the sprayed animal, sprinkled with an ablution, was supposed to give its assent to the immolation—was designed to efface any traces of violence and murder and to bring to the fore aspects of peaceful solemnity and happy festivity. Furthermore, in the economy of the *thusia,* the procedures for cutting up the victim, for roasting or boiling the pieces, for their orderly distribution in equal parts, and for their consumption, either on the spot or elsewhere, were no less important than the ritual killing. The alimentary function of the rite is expressed in a vocabulary that makes no distinction between sacrificer and butcher. The word *hiereion,* which designates an animal as sacrificial victim, at the same time qualifies it as an animal to be butchered, as one suitable for eating. Since the Greeks ate meat only on the occasion of sacrifices and in conformity with sacrificial rules, the *thusia* was simultaneously a religious ceremony in which a pious offering, often accompanied by prayer, was addressed to the gods; a ritualized cooking of food according to the norms that the gods required of humans; and an act of social communion that reinforced, through the consumption of the parts of one victim, the bonds that were to unite all citizens and make them equal.

As the central moment of the cult, the sacrifice was an indispensable part of communal life (whether family or state) and illustrated the tight interdependence of the religious and the social orders in the Greece of the city-states. The function of the sacrifice was not to wrest the sacrificer or the participants away from their families and civic groups or from their ordinary activities in the human world but, on the contrary, to install them in the requisite positions and patterns, to integrate them into the city and mundane existence in conformity with an order of the world presided over by the gods (i.e., "intraworld" religion, in the sense given by Max Weber, or "political" religion, in the Greek understanding of the term). The sacred and the profane did not constitute two radically opposite, mutually exclusive categories. Between the "sacred" in its entirely forbidden aspect and its fully accessible one a multiplicity of configurations and gradations existed. In addition to those realities dedicated to a god and reserved for his use, the sacred was also to be experienced by way of objects, living creatures, natural phenomena, and both the everyday events of private life—eating a meal, departing on a journey, welcoming a guest—and the more solemn occasions of public life. Without any special preparation, every head of a family was qualified to assume religious functions in his home. Each head of a household was pure as long as he had not committed any misdeed that defiled him. In this sense, purity did not have to be acquired or obtained; it constituted the normal state of the citizen.

As far as the city was concerned, there was no division between the priesthood and the magistracy. There were priesthoods that were devolved and practiced as magistracies, and every magistrate was endowed by virtue of his duties with a character of holiness. For any political power to be exercised, for any common decision to be valid, a sacrifice was required. In war as in peace, before giving battle as well as when convening an assembly or inaugurating a magistrate, the performance of a sacrifice was just as necessary as it was during the great religious festivals of the sacred calendar. As Marcel Detienne so accurately observes in *La cuisine du sacrifice en pays grec:* "Until a late period, a city such as Athens maintained the office of archon-king—one of whose major functions was to administer all of the sacrifices instituted by the ancestors, that is, all the ritual gestures that guaranteed the harmonious operation of society" (Detienne, 1980, p. 10).

If the *thusia* was indispensable for ensuring the validity of social undertakings, it was because the sacrificial fire, by causing the fragrant smoke of the burning fat and bones to rise toward heaven while at the same time cooking man's portion, opened the lines of communication between the gods and the participants in the rites. By immolating a victim, burning the bones, and eating the flesh according to ritual rules, the Greeks instituted and maintained with the divine a contact without which their entire existence, left to itself and emptied of meaning, would have collapsed. This contact was not a communion; even in a symbolic form, the Greeks did not eat the god in order to identify with him and to participate in his strength. They consumed a victim, a domestic animal, and ate a part different from that offered to the gods. The link established by the sacrifice emphasized and confirmed the extreme distance that separated mortals and immortals, even when they communicated.

Myths about the origin of the sacrifice are most precise in this respect. They bring to light the theological meanings of the ritual. It was the Titan Prometheus, son of Iapetus, who was said to have instituted the first sacrifice, thus establishing forever the model to which humans were to conform in honoring the gods. This took place during the time when gods and men were not yet separate but lived together, feasted at the same tables, and shared the same felicity far from all evils and afflictions. Men were still unacquainted with the necessity of work, sickness, old age, fatigue, death, and women. Zeus had been promoted king of heaven and had carried out an equitable distribution of honors and privileges. The time had come to define in precise terms the forms of life appropriate for men and for gods.

Prometheus was assigned the task. He brought before the assembled gods and men a great steer, killed it, and cut it up. The boundary that exists between gods and men follows, therefore, the line of division between the parts of the immolated beast that went to the gods and those that went to men. The sacrifice thus appears as the act that, as its first accomplishment, consecrated the distinction of divine and human status. But Prometheus, in rebellion against the king of the gods, tried to deceive him for the benefit of men. Each of the two parts prepared by the Titan was a ruse, a lure. The first, camouflaged in appetizing fat, contained only the the bare bones; the second, concealed in the skin and stomach and disgusting in appearance, constituted all that was edible in the animal.

Honor to whom honor is due: it was for Zeus, in the name of the gods, to be the first to choose a portion of the sacrifice. He saw the trap but pretended to be tricked, the better to take his revenge. He chose, therefore, the outwardly enticing portion, the one that concealed the inedible bones under a thin covering of fat. For this reason, men burned the white bones of the victim for the gods, then divided the meat, the portion that Zeus did not choose, among themselves. Prometheus had imagined that in allotting the flesh to humans he was reserving the best part for them. But shrewd as he was, he failed to suspect that he was giving them a poisoned gift. By eating the meat, men sentenced themselves to death. Driven by their hunger, they behaved from then on like all the animals that inhabit the earth, the water, or the air. If they take pleasure in devouring the flesh of an animal that has lost its life, if they have an imperious need for food, it is because their hunger, never appeased but constantly renewed, is the mark of a creature whose strength fails gradually, who is doomed to weariness, old age, and death. By contenting themselves with the smoke from the bones and living off smells and fragrances, the gods bore witness that they belonged to a race whose nature was entirely different from that of men. They, the immortals, were everlasting and eternally young; their being contained nothing perishable and had no contact with the realm of the corruptible.

But the vengeance of the angry Zeus did not stop here. Even before he created out of the earth and water the first woman, Pandora, who introduced among men all the woes hitherto unknown to them—birth from procreation, fatigue, toil, sickness, age, and death—he decided, as retribution for the Titan's partiality toward mankind, to never again allow men access to the celestial fire. Deprived of fire, were men thus obliged to eat raw meat like beasts? Prometheus then stole a spark, a seed of fire, in the hollow of a stick, and brought it down to earth. Although they would no longer have the flash of the thunderbolt at their disposal, men were given a technical fire, more fragile and mortal, one that would have to be preserved by constant feeding. By cooking their food, this second fire—contingent and artificial, in comparison with the heavenly fire—differentiates men from animals and establishes them in a civilized life. Of all the animals, only men share the possession of fire with the gods. Thus it is fire that unites man to the divine by rising toward heaven from the lighted altars. [See Fire.] But this fire, celestial in origin and destination, is also, in its all-consuming ardor, as perishable as the living creatures subjected to the necessity of eating. The frontier between gods and men is both bridged by the sacrificial fire, which unites them, and accentuated by the contrast between the heavenly fire in the hands of Zeus and the fire that Prometheus's theft made available to mankind. Furthermore, the function of the sacrificial fire is to mark the portion of the victim belonging to the gods (totally consumed in the flames) and that of men (cooked just enough not to be eaten raw).

The ambiguous relationship between men and gods in the sacrifice was coupled with an equally equivocal relationship between men and animals. In order to live, both must eat, whether their food be animal or vegetable, and so they are equally perishable. But it is only man who eats his food cooked according to rules and after having offered in honor to the gods the animal's life, dedicated to them with the bones. If the barley seeds showered on the head of the victim and on the altar were associated with the blood sacrifice, the reason was that cereals, as a specifically human food involving agricultural labor, represented in the Greek view the paradigm of cultivated plants symbolizing, in contrast to a savage existence, civilized life. Cooked three times (by an internal process that assists the cultivation, by the action of the sun, and by the human hand that turns it into bread), cereal was an analogue to the sacrificial victim, the domestic animal whose flesh had to be ritually roasted or boiled before it was eaten.

In the Promethean myth, sacrifice comes into being as the result of the Titan's rebellion against Zeus at a time when men and gods needed to separate and establish their respective destinies. The moral of the story states that one could not hope to dupe the sovereign god. Prometheus tried to deceive Zeus; man must pay the price of his failure. To perform a sacrifice was both to commemorate the adventure of the Titan, the founder of the rite, and to accept its lesson. It was to recognize that through the accomplishment of the sacrifice and all that it entailed—the Promethean fire, the necessity of work and of women and marriage in order to have children, the condition of suffering, old age, and death—Zeus situated man between animals and gods for all time. In the sacrifice, man submitted to the will of Zeus, who made of mortals and immortals two separate and distinct races. Communication with the divine was instituted in the course of a festive ceremonial, a meal recalling the fact that the commensality of former times was no more: gods and men no longer lived together, no longer ate at the same tables. Man could not sacrifice according to the model established by Prometheus and at the same time pretend in any way to equal the gods. The rite itself, the object of which was to join gods and men together, sanctioned the insurmountable barrier that separated them.

By means of its alimentary rules, sacrifice established man in his proper state, midway between the savagery of animals that devour one another's raw flesh and the perpetual bliss of the gods, who never know hunger, weariness, or death because they find nourishment in sweet smells and ambrosia. This concern for precise delimitations, for exact apportionment, closely unites the sacrifice, both in ritual and in myth, to cereal agriculture and to marriage, both of which likewise define the particular position of civilized man. Just as, to survive, he must eat the cooked meat of a domestic animal sacrificed according to the rules, so man must feed on *sitos,* the cooked flour of regularly cultivated domestic plants. In order to survive as a race, man must father a son by union with a woman, whom marriage has drawn out of savagery and domesticated by setting her in the conjugal home. By reason of this same exigency of equilibrium in the Greek sacrifice, the sacrificer, the victim, and the god—although associated in the rite—were never confused.

The fact that this powerful theology should have its base on the level of alimentary procedures indicates that the dietary vagaries of the Orphics and Pythagoreans, as well as certain Dionysian practices, had a specifically theological significance and constituted profound divergences in religious orientation. Vegetarianism was a rejection of blood sacrifice, which was believed to be like the murder of a close relation; *omophagia* and *diasparagmos* of the Bacchantes—that is, the devouring of the raw flesh of a hunted animal that had been torn to pieces while still alive— inverted the normal values of sacrifice. [*See* Omophagia.] But whether sacrifice was circumvented, on the one hand, by feeding like the gods on entirely pure dishes and even on smells or, on the other, by destroying the barriers between men and animals maintained by sacrificial practice, so that a state of complete communion was realized—one that could be called either a return to the sweet familiarity of all creatures during the Golden Age or a fall into the chaotic confusion of savagery—in either case, it was a question of instituting, whether by individual asceticism or by collective frenzy, a type of relationship with the divine that the official religion excluded and forbade. Furthermore, although employing opposing means with opposite implications, the normal distinctions between sacrificer, victim, and divinity became blurred and disappeared. The analysis of sacrificial cuisine thus leads to an understanding of the more or less eccentric—sometimes integrated and sometimes marginal—positions occupied by various sects, religious movements, or philosophical attitudes, all of which were at odds both with the regular forms of the traditional cult and with the institutional framework of the city-state and all that it implied concerning the religious and social status of man.

GREEK MYSTICISM

Blood sacrifice and public cult were not the only expressions of Greek piety. Various movements and groups, more or less deviant and marginal, more or less closed and

secret, expressed different religious aspirations. Some were entirely or partly integrated into the civic cult; others remained foreign to it. All of them contributed in
various ways to paving the way toward a Greek "mysticism" marked by the search
for a more direct, more intimate, and more personal contact with the gods. This
mysticism was sometimes associated with the quest for immortality, which was either
granted after death through the special favor of a divinity or obtained by the observance of the discipline of a pure life reserved for the initiated and giving them the
privilege of liberating, even during their earthly existence, the particle of the divine
present in each.

In this context, a clear distinction must be made between three kinds of religious
phenomena during the Classical period. Certain terms, such as *teletē, orgia, mustai,*
and *bakchoi,* are used in reference to all three, yet the phenomena they designate
cannot in any way be considered identical. Despite some points of contact, they were
not religious realities of the same order; nor did they have the same status or the
same goals.

First, there were the mysteries. [*See* Mystery Religions.] Those of Eleusis, exemplary in their prestige and their widespread influence, constituted in Attica a well-
defined group of cults. Officially recognized by the city, they were organized under
its control and supervision. They remained, however, on the fringe of the state because of their initiatory and secret nature and their mode of recruiting (they were
open to all Greeks and based not on social status but on the personal choice of the
individual).

Next there was the Dionysian religion. The cults associated with Dionysos were
an integral part of the civic religion, and the festivals in honor of the god had their
place like any other in the sacred calendar. But as god of *mania,* or divine madness—because of his way of taking possession of his followers through the collective
trance ritually practiced in the *thiasoi* and because of his sudden intrusion here
below in epiphanic revelation—Dionysos introduced into the very heart of the religion of which he was a part an experience of the supernatural that was foreign and,
in many ways, contrary to the spirit of the official cult. [*See* Dionysos].

Finally, there was what is called Orphism. Orphism involved neither a specific
cult, nor devotion to an individual deity, nor a community of believers organized
into a sect as in Pythagoreanism, whatever links might have existed between the two
movements. Orphism was a nebulous phenomenon that included, on the one hand,
a tradition of sacred books attributed to Orpheus and Musaios (comprising theogonies, cosmogonies, and heterodox anthropogonies) and, on the other, the appearance of itinerant priests who advocated a style of existence that was contrary to the
norm, a vegetarian diet, and who had at their disposal healing techniques and formulas for purification in this life and salvation in the next. In these circles, the
central preoccupation and discussion focused on the destiny of the soul after death,
a subject to which the Greeks were not accustomed.

What was the relationship of each of these three great religious phenomena to a
cult system based on the respect of *nomoi,* the socially recognized rules of the city?
Neither in beliefs nor in practices did the mysteries contradict the civic religion.
Instead, they completed it by adding a new dimension suited to satisfying needs that
the civic religion could not fulfill. The goddesses Demeter and Kore (Persephone),
who together with several acolytes patronized the Eleusinian cycle, were great fig-

ures of the pantheon, and the narrative of the abduction of Kore by Hades, with all its consequences (including the founding of the *orgia,* the secret rites of Eleusis), is one of the basic legends of the Greeks. The candidate had to take a series of steps to attain the ultimate goal of initiation—from the preliminary stage of the Lesser Mysteries of Agrai to renewed participation in the Greater Mysteries at Eleusis, the *mustēs* having to wait until the following year to acquire the rank of *epoptēs.* The entire ceremony (at Athens itself, at Phaleron for the ritual bath in the sea, and on the road from Athens to Eleusis in a procession that followed the sacred objects and included the Eleusinian clergy, the magistrates of Athens, the *mustai,* foreign delegations, and throngs of spectators) took place in full daylight before the eyes of everyone. The archon-king, in the name of the state, was in charge of the public celebration of the Greater Mysteries, and even the traditional families of the Eumolpides and the Kérukes, who had a special relationship with the two goddesses, were responsible to the city, which had the authority to regulate by decree the details of the festivities.

Only when the *mustai* had entered the sanctuary was secrecy imposed and nothing allowed to escape to the outside world. The interdiction was sufficiently powerful to be respected for centuries. But although the mysteries have kept some of their secrets till this day, some points about them can be considered certain. There was no teaching, nothing resembling an esoteric doctrine, at Eleusis. Aristotle's testimony on this subject is decisive: "Those who are initiated have not to learn something but to feel emotions and to be in a certain frame of mind." Plutarch describes the mood of the initiates, which ranged from anxiety to rapture. Such inner emotional upheaval was brought about by the *drōmena,* things played and mimed; by the *legomena,* ritual formuals that were pronounced; and by the *deiknumena,* things shown and exhibited. It is probable that they were related to the passion of Demeter, the descent of Kore into the underworld, and the fate of the dead in Hades. It is certain that after the final illumination at the end of initiation, the believer felt that he had been inwardly transformed. From then on, he was bound to the goddesses in a close personal relationship of intimate connivance and familiarity. He had become one of the elect, certain to have a fate different from the ordinary in this life and in the next. Blessed, asserts the *Hymn to Demeter,* is he who has had the full vision of these mysteries; the uninitiated, the profane, would not know such a destiny after they died and went to the realm of the shades. Although they neither presented a new conception of the soul nor broke with the traditional image of Hades, the mysteries opened the prospect of continuing a happier existence in the underworld. This privilege was available to believers who freely decided to submit to initiation and to follow a ritual course, each stage of which marked a new progress toward a state of religious purity.

On returning home to his family and to his professional and civic activities, nothing distinguished the initiate either from what he had been before or from those who had not undergone initiation—no external sign, no mark of recognition, not even a slight modification in his way of life. He returned to the city and settled down again to do what he had always done with no other change but his conviction that through this religious experience he would be among the elect after his death: for him, there would be light, joy, dancing, and song in the world of darkness. These hopes concerning the hereafter would later be nourished and developed among the sects, which would also borrow the symbolism of the mysteries, their secrecy, and their hierarchical system. But in the city that patronized them, the mysteries became part of the official religion.

At first glance, the status of Dionysism may seem comparable to that of the mysteries. This cult also consisted of *teletai* and *orgia,* initiations and secret rites open only to those who were invested as *bakchoi.* But the winter festivals of Dionysos at Athens—Oschoporia, rural Dionysia, Lenaea, Anthesteria, urban Dionysia—did not form a coherent and self-contained whole or a closed cycle as they did at Eleusis; they were instead a discontinuous series spread throughout the calendar along with the festivals of the other gods and revealing the same norms of celebration. All of them were official ceremonies, fully civic in character. Some of them carried an element of secrecy and required specialized religious personnel, for example, the annual marriage of the queen, the wife of the archon-king, to Dionysos, which was performed in the Boucoleion during the Anthesteria. The Gerarai, a group of fourteen women, who assisted the queen in her role as wife of the god, performed secret rites in the sanctuary of Dionysos in the marshes, but they did this "in the name of the city" and "following its traditions." The people themselves prescribed the procedures of the wedding and ensured their safety by having them engraved on a stele. Thus the queen's secret marriage was equivalent to the official recognition by the city of the divinity of Dionysos. It consecrated the union of the civic community with the god and represented his integration into the religious order of the community.

The Thyiads, or Bacchantes, of Athens, women who participated in the orgiastic rites of Dionysos, met their counterparts from Delphi at Mount Parnassus every three years. They performed their secret rites in the name of the city. They were not a segregated group of initiates, a marginal sisterhood of the elect, or a sect of deviants: they formed an official female cult, entrusted by the city with the task of representing it before the Delphians. They operated according to the framework of the cult rendered to Dionysos in the sanctuary of Apollo. There is no evidence of private Dionysian associations that recruited adepts to celebrate secretly a specific cult under the protection of the god in Attica, or even in continental Greece, in the fifth century, as was the case several centuries later with the Iobakchoi. Toward the fifth century, when the city of Magnesia, on the Meander River, decided to organize a cult dedicated to Dionysos, it founded, after consulting Delphi, three *thiasoi* (three official female colleges placed under the direction of qualified priestesses who had come from Thebes especially for that purpose).

What then constituted, in comparison with the other gods, the originality of Dionysos and his cult? Dionysism, unlike the mysteries, did not exist as an extension of the civic religion. Instead, it expressed the city's official recognition of a religion that in many ways eluded the city, contradicting it and going beyond its control. It established, in the midst of public life, a religious behavior that displayed aspects of eccentricity in an allusive, symbolic form or in an open manner.

Even in the world of the Olympian gods, to which he had been admitted, Dionysos personified, as expressed so well by Louis Gernet, the presence of the Other. He did not confirm and reinforce the human and social order by making it sacred. Dionysos called this order into question; indeed, he shattered it. In so doing he revealed another side of the sacred, one that was no longer regular, stable, and defined but strange, elusive, and disconcerting. As the only Greek god endowed with the power of *māyā* ("magic"), Dionysos transcends all forms and evades all definitions; he assumes all aspects without confining himself to any one. Like a conjurer, he playes with appearances and blurs the boundaries between the fantastic and the real. Ubiquitous, he is never to be found where he is but always here, there, and nowhere at the same time. As soon as he appears, the distinct categories and clear oppositions that give the world its coherence and rationality fade, merge, and pass from one to the other. He is at once both male and female. By suddenly appearing among men, he introduces the supernatural in the midst of the natural and unites heaven and earth. Young and old, wild and civilized, near and far, beyond and here-below are joined in him and by him. Even more, he abolishes the distance that separates the gods from men and men from animals.

When the Maenads give themselves over to the frenzy of the trance, the god takes possession of them, subjugating and directing them as he pleases. In frenzy and enthusiasm, the human creature plays the god, and the god, who is within the believer, plays the human. The frontiers between them are suddenly blurred or obliterated in a proximity through which man is estranged from his daily existence or ordinary life, alienated from himself, and transported to a distant elsewhere. This contiguity with the divine, accomplished by the trance, is accompanied by a new familiarity with animal savagery. On the mountains and in the woods, far from their homes and from cities and cultivated lands, the Maenads play with serpents and suckle the young of animals as their own, but they also pursue, attack, and tear to pieces living animals (*diasparagmos*) and devour their raw flesh (*omophagia*). Through their eating behavior, they assimilate themselves to wild beasts that—unlike men, who eat bread and the cooked meat of ritually sacrificed domestic animals— eat one another and lap up each other's blood, knowing no rule or law but only the hunger that drives them.

Maenadism, which was limited to women, carried in its sudden outburst two opposing aspects. For the faithful, in happy communion with the god, it brought the supernatural joy of momentary escape to a kind of Golden Age where all living creatures meet again, mingled like brothers and sisters. However, for those women (and cities) who rejected the god and who had to be constrained by punishment, *mania* led to the horror and madness of the most atrocious of pollutions: a return to the chaos of a lawless world in which maddened women tear apart the bodies of their own children as if the children were animals and devour their flesh. A dual god, combining in his person two facets, Dionysos, as he proclaims in *The Bacchae* of Euripides, is both "the most terrible and the most gentle."

In order that he may show himself beneficent in his gentleness, Dionysos—whose strangeness, irrepressible exuberance, and intrusive dynamism seem to threaten the stability of the civic religion—must be welcomed into the city, acknowledged as belonging to it, and assured a place beside the other gods in the public cult. The entire community must solemnly celebrate the festivals of Dionysos: for its women, it must organize a form of controlled and ritualized trance within the framework of the official *thiasoi,* promoted public institutions; for its men, an estrangement from the normal course of things in the joyfulness of a revelry consisting of wine and drunkenness, games and festivities, masquerades and disguises; and, finally, it must found the theater on whose stage illusion acquires substance and comes to life and the imaginary is displayed as if it were reality. In each case, the integration of Dionysos into the city and its religion meant installing the Other, with all honors, in the heart of the social establishment.

Ecstasy, enthusiasm, and possession; the joy of wine and festival; the pleasures of love; the exaltation of life in its outpouring and unexpectedness; the gaiety of masks and disguises; the happiness of everyday life—Dionysos can bring all of these if men and cities are willing to recognize him. But never does he come to announce a better fate in the hereafter. He does not advocate flight from the world, nor does he teach renunciation or offer the soul access to immortality through an escetic way of life. He conjures up the many faces of the Other in this life and world, around us and within us. He opens before us, on this earth and even in the framework of the city, the way of escape toward a disconcerting strangeness. Dionysos teaches or forces us to become other than what we ordinarily are.

Undoubtedly, it was this need to escape, this nostalgia for a complete union with the divine, that—even more than his descent into the underworld in search of his mother, Semele—explains the fact that Dionysos could be associated, sometimes quite closely, with the mysteries of the two Eleusinian goddesses. When the wife of the archon-king went to celebrate her marriage with Dionysos, she was assisted by the sacred herald of Eleusis; and, at the Lenaea, perhaps the most ancient of the Attic festivals of Dionysos, it was the torchbearer of Eleusis who led the invocation taken up by the public: "Iacchos, son of Semele." The god was present at Eleusis as early as the fifth century and had a discreet presence and a minor role even in those places where he had neither temple nor priest. He intervened as the figure of Iacchos, to whom he was assimilated and whose function was to preside over the procession from Athens to Eleusis during the Greater Mysteries. Iacchos was the personification of the joyful ritual cry given by the cortege of *mustai* in an atmosphere of hope and festivity. In the representations of a hereafter to which the faithful of the god of *mania* seemed quite indifferent (with the exception perhaps of those in southern Italy), Iacchos was imagined as leading the blessed chorus of initiates in the underworld while Dionysos led his *thiasoi* of Bacchantes on earth. [*See* Dionysos.]

The problems of Orphism are of another order. [*See* Orpheus.] This religious movement, in all of its diverse forms, belonged essentially to late Hellenism, in the course of which it took on increasing importance. But several discoveries during the twentieth century have confirmed that Orphism had a role in the religion of the Classical period. Let us begin with the first aspect of Orphism: a tradition of written texts and sacred books. The papyrus of Derveni, found in 1962 in a tomb near Salonika, proves that theogonies from the sixth century may have been known to pre-Socratic philosophers and to have partly inspired Empedocles. Thus Orphism's principal feature appears from its beginning: a doctrinal form that opposed it to the mysteries and to Dionysian religion, as well as to the official cult, while relating it to philosophy. These theogonies are known to us in many versions, but the basic orientation is the same: they take an opposite view from that of the Hesiodic tradition. For Hesiod, the divine world is organized in a linear progression leading from disorder to order, from an original state of indistinct confusion to a differentiated world organized into a hierarchy under the immutable authority of Zeus. For the followers of Orphism, the reverse was true: in the beginning the first principle, primordial Egg or Night, expresses perfect unity, the plenitude of a self-contained totality. But the nature of "being" deteriorates as its unity is divided and dislocated, producing distinct forms and separate individuals. To this cycle of dispersion there must succeed a cycle during which the parts are reintegrated into the unity of the whole. This is to take place during the sixth generation with the coming of the Orphic Dionysos, whose reign represents a restoration of the One, the recovery of the lost plenitude.

But Dionysos does not just play a part in a theogony that substitutes for the progressive emergence of a differentiated order a fall into division, followed (as if redeemed) by a reintegration into the whole. According to one tale, Dionysos, who had been dismembered and devoured by the Titans, was reconstituted from his heart, which had been preserved intact; the Titans were then struck down by Zeus's thunderbolt, and the human race was born from their ashes. This story, to which Pindar, Herodotus, and Plato seem to make allusions, is attested in the Hellenistic period. In it, Dionysos himself assumes the double cycle of dispersion and reunification in the course of a "passion" that directly engages the life of man since it mythically founds the misfortune of the human condition and, at the same time, offers mortals the prospect of salvation. Born from the ashes of the Titans, the human race carries as a legacy the guilt of having dismembered the body of the god. But by purifying himself of the ancestral offense by performing rites and observing the Orphic way of life, by abstaining from all meat to avoid the impurity of the blood sacrifice—which the city sanctifies but which recalls for the Orphics the monstrous feast of the Titans—each man, having kept within himself a particle of Dionysos, can return to the lost unity, join the god, and find a Golden Age type of life in the hereafter.

The Orphic theogonies therefore led to an anthropogony and a soteriology that gave them their true meaning. In the sacred literature of Orphism, the doctrinal aspect cannot be separated from the quest for salvation: the adoption of a pure life, the avoidance of any kind of pollution, and the choice of a vegetarian diet expressed the desire to escape the common fate of finitude and death and to be wholly united with the divine. The refusal of blood sacrifice was more than just a deviance from common practice, for vegetarianism contradicted precisely what sacrifice implied: the existence of an impassable gulf between men and gods, even in the ritual through which they communicate. The individual search for salvation was situated outside the civic religion. As a spiritual movement, Orphism was external and foreign to the city, to its rules and to its values.

Its influence was nonetheless exercised along several lines. From the fifth century on, certain Orphic writings seem to have concerned Eleusis, and whatever the differences, or rather the oppositions, between the Dionysos of the official cult and the one of the Orphic writings, assimilation between the two might have occurred quite early. In *Hippolytus,* Euripides suggests such an assimilation when he makes Theseus speak of the young man "playing the Bacchant under the direction of Orpheus," and Herodotus attributes the interdiction from being buried in woolen clothes to "the cults called orphic and bacchic." These convergences are not decisive, however, as the term *Bacchic* is not reserved exclusively for Dionysian rituals. The only evidence of a direct encounter between Dionysos and the Orphics, and at the same time of an eschatological dimension to Dionysos, is to be found on the fringes of Greece, on the edges of the Black Sea, in the Olbia of the fifth century. Here, the words *Dionusos Orphikoi,* followed by *bios thanatos bios* ("life death life"), were discovered on bone plates. But, as has been observed, this puzzle remains more enigmatic than enlightening, and in the present state of documentation, its singular character attests to the peculiarities of religious life in the Scythian environment of the colony of Olbia.

In fact, Orphism had two major impacts on the religious mentality of the Greeks during the Classical period. On the level of popular piety, it nourished the anxieties and the practices of the superstitious, who were obsessed with the fear of impurity and disease. Theophrastus, in his *The Superstitious Man,* shows the protagonist going every month to renew his initiation and discovering, together with his wife and children, the Orpheotelestai. Plato, for his part, described the Orpheotelestai as beggar priests and itinerant holy men who took money for their alleged competence in performing purifications and initiations (*katharmoi* and *teletai*) for both the living and the dead. These marginal priests, who made their way from city to city and based their science of secret rites and incantations on the authority of the books of Musaios and Orpheus, were readily identified as a band of magicians and charlatans who exploited public credibility.

But on another, more intellectual level, the Orphic writings belonged, along with others, to the movement that, in modifying the framework of the religious experience, shifted the direction of Greek spiritual life. Orphism, like Pythagoreanism, belonged to a tradition of outstanding figures with exceptional prestige and powers. From the seventh century on, these "god-men" used their abilities to purify the cities; they have sometimes been defined as representing a Greek version of shamanism. [*See* Shamanism.] In the middle of the fifth century, Empedocles testified to the vitality of these maguses, who were capable of commanding the winds and of bringing the dead back from Hades and who presented themselves, not as mortals, but as gods. A striking characteristic of these singular figures—who included not only Epimenides and Empedocles but also a number of inspired and more or less legendary missionaries, such as Abaris, Aristeas, and Hermotimos—was that their disciplined lives, spiritual exercises in the control and concentration of their breathing, and techniques of asceticism and recollection of former lives placed them under the patronage, not of Dionysos, but of Apollo, a Hyperborean Apollo, the god of ecstatic inspiration and purifications.

In the collective trance of the Dionysian *thiasos,* the god came down to take possession of his group of worshipers, riding them and making them dance and jump about according to his will. Those who were possessed did not leave this world, but they were made different by the power that inhabited them. In contrast, among the god-men, for all their diversity, it was the human individual who took the initiative, set the tone, and passed to the other side. Thanks to the exceptional powers that he had succeeded in acquiring, a god-man could leave his body, abandoned as if in a cataleptic sleep, and travel freely into the other world, then return with the memory of all that he had seen in the beyond.

This type of man, by the way of life that he had chosen and his techniques of ecstasy, demonstrated the presence of a supernatural element within him, an element foreign to earthly life, a being from another world, in exile, a soul *(psuchē)* who was no longer, as in Homer, a shadow without force or an insubstantial reflection but instead a *dàimon,* or "spirit," a power related to the divine and longing to return to it.

To possess the control and mastery of this *psuchē,* to isolate it from the body, to focus it in itself, to purify it, to liberate it, and by means of it to return to the heavenly place for which the heart still yearns—such may have been the object and the end of the religious experience in this tradition of thought. However, as long as the city-state remained alive, no sect, religious practice, or organized group expressed the need to leave the body and to flee the world in order to achieve an intimate and personal union with the divine. The renouncer was unknown to the traditional Greek religion. It was philosophy that relayed this concept by interpreting in its own terms the themes of asceticism and of purification of the soul and its immortality.

For the oracle of Delphi, "know thyself" meant "know that you are not a god and do not commit the sin of pretending to become one." For Socrates and Plato, who adopted the maxim as their own, it meant: know the god who, in you, is yourself; try to become, as much as is possible, a likeness of the god.

BIBLIOGRAPHY

General Works

Bianchi, Ugo. *La religione greca.* Turin, 1975. For the general reader, this book presents the results of a number of erudite studies on Greek religion (those, for example, of Wilamowitz, Nilsson, Pettazzoni, Guthrie, Kern, Kerényi, et al.) and includes a methodical bibliography and a large number of significant illustrations.

Burkert, Walter. *Griechische Religion der archaischen und klassischen Epoche.* Stuttgart, 1977. Translated as *Greek Religion* (Cambridge, Mass., 1985). This synthesis, supported by an abundant bibliography, covers both the Archaic and Classical periods, examining Minoan and Homeric religion, the ritual, the principal divinities, hero cults, cults of the chthonic deities, the place of religion in the city, the mysteries, and the "religion of the philosophers."

Festugière, A.-J. "La Grèce: La religion." In *Histoire générale des religions,* edited by Maxime Gorce and Raoul Mortier, vol. 2, pp. 27–147. Paris, 1944. A general portrayal of ancient Greek religion, organized under four principal headings: origins, the Olympians, the organization of the divine, and the emergence of the individual.

Gernet, Louis, and André Boulanger. *Le génie grec dans la religion.* Paris, 1932. Reprinted in 1969 with a complementary bibliography. Discusses the complex origins of religious concepts in ancient Greece, the rise of civic religion, and the transformation of religious feeling and the decline of the gods of Olympus during the Hellenistic period.

Nilsson, Martin P. *Den grekiska religionens historia.* 2 vols. Stockholm, 1921. Translated by F. J. Fielden as *A History of Greek Religion* (1925); 2d ed., Oxford, 1949), with a preface by James G. Frazer.

Nilsson, Martin P. *Geschichte der griechischen Religion* (1941–1957). 2 vols. 3d rev. ed. Munich, 1967–1974. The basic "manual" for any study of the religion of ancient Greece; a truly comprehensive work, indispensable, especially for its wealth of documentation.

Vian, Francis. "La religion grecque à l'époque archaïque et classique." In *Histoire des religions,* edited by Henri-Charles Puech, vol. 1, pp. 489–577. Paris, 1970. A general study of the formation of Greek religion and its basic components: the nature and agrarian cults, the religion of the family and the city, the federative and pan-Hellenic cults, and the mysteries and ecstatic cults.

Gods and Heroes

Brelich, Angelo. *Gli eroi greci.* Rome, 1958. From the viewpoint of a general history of religions, this book analyzes the role of the Greek heroes in myth and cult and examines their relations with other mythical figures in order to bring out the specific morphology of the Greek hero.

Farnell, Lewis R. *Greek Hero Cults and Ideas of Immortality* (1921). Oxford, 1970. An investigation of the origin of the Greek heroes, proposing a compromise theory between the thesis of Erwin Rohde, who considered the heroes as spirits of the dead, and that of Hermann Usener, who upheld the theory of a divine origin of the heroes.

Guthrie, W. K. C. *The Greeks and Their Gods.* London, 1950. A still useful work on Greek religion, conceived and written for nonspecialists.

Kerényi, Károly. *The Heroes of the Greeks.* Translated by H. J. Rose. London, 1959. Discusses the life, exploits, and deaths of the Greek heroes.

Otto, Walter F. *Die Götter Griechenlands: Das Bild des Göttlichen im Spiegel des griechischen Geistes.* Bonn, 1929. Translated by Moses Hadas as *The Homeric Gods: The Spiritual Significance of Greek Religion* (1954; Boston, 1964). A study of the nature and essence of the gods of Homer, who is treated as a great religious reformer.

Séchan, Louis, and Pierre Lévêque. *Les grandes divinités de la Grèce.* Paris, 1966. A complete scientific file on the principal figures of the Greek pantheon, whose origins, cult manifestations, and figurative representations are analyzed by the authors.

Myth and Ritual

Burkert, Walter. *Structure and History in Greek Mythology and Ritual.* Berkeley, 1979. An analysis of the concepts of myth and ritual from a historical perspective, which seeks to demonstrate the existence of a continuous but constantly transformed tradition from primeval times, through the Paleolithic period, to the Greek and Oriental civilizations.

Detienne, Marcel. *L'invention de la mythologie.* Paris, 1981. Through the study of the status of the "fable" in the eighteenth century, the discourse of the mythologists of the nineteenth century, and the place of myth in ancient Greek society, the author makes an epistemological investigation of mythology, reconsidered as an object of knowledge as well as an object of culture.

Deubner, Ludwig. *Attische Feste* (1932). Hildesheim, 1966. The most complete discussion of the festivals of Attica, indispensable for the wealth of texts cited; places iconographic material in relationship to certain festivals.

Farnell, Lewis R. *The Cults of the Greek States* (1896–1909). 5 vols. New Rochelle, N.Y., 1977. A veritable "encyclopedia" of Greek cults, invaluable for the broad range of materials brought together and analyzed under the name of each divinity of Greece.

Kirk, G. S. *Myth: Its Meaning and Functions in Ancient and Other Cultures.* Berkeley, 1970. Studying the relationship between myth, ritual, and fable, the limits of the structuralist theory of Claude Lévi-Strauss, as well as the specific character of Mesopotamian and Greek myths, the author examines the status of myths as expressions of the subconscious and as universal symbols.

Nilsson, Martin P. *Griechische Feste von religiöser Bedeutung: Mit Ausschluss der Attischen* (1906). Stuttgart, 1957. The best-documented study of the festivals of ancient Greece, with the exception of Attic festivals, classified and analyzed under the name of each divinity.

Parke, H. W. *Festivals of the Athenians.* Ithaca, N.Y., 1977. A description of the festivals of the ancient Athenians, analyzed according to the calendar; accessible to nonspecialists of the Greek world.

Rudhardt, Jean. *Notions fondamentales de la pensée religieuse et actes constitutifs du culte dans la Grèce classique.* Geneva, 1958. A pertinent analysis of the notion of the divine;

beliefs concerning the gods, the dead, and the heroes; and the acts of the cult (dances, ritual meals, purifications, religious songs, prayers, sacrifices, etc.).

Vernant, Jean-Pierre. *Mythe et pensée chez les Grecs* (1965). 2 vols. 3d ed. Paris, 1971. Translated as *Myth and Thought among the Greeks* (London, 1983).

Vernant, Jean-Pierre. *Mythe et société en Grèce ancienne*. Paris, 1974. Translated as *Myth and Society in Ancient Greece* (Atlantic Highlands, N.J., 1980). Attempts to determine the intellectual code proper to the Greek myth and to define the logical form that the myth brings into play (a logic of ambiguity, equivocality, and polarity); examines the relationship between the intellectual framework brought out by structural analysis and the sociohistorical context in which myth was produced.

Divination and Oracles

Bouché-Leclercq, Auguste. *Histoire de la divination dans l'antiquité* (1879–1882). 4 vols. Brussels, 1963; New York, 1975. The fundamental book on ancient divination, although outdated on numerous points.

Parke, H. W., and D. E. W. Wormell. *The Delphic Oracle*. 2 vols. Oxford, 1956. The most complete synthesis devoted to the oracle of Delphi, treating all the ancient accounts in the light of archaeological discoveries.

Sacrifice

Burkert, Walter. *Homo Necans: Interpretationen altgriechischer Opferriten und Mythen*. Berlin, 1972. Translated by Peter Bing as *Homo Necans: The Anthropology of Ancient Greek Sacrificial Ritual and Myth* (Berkeley, 1983). Continuing the work of Karl Meuli, the author attempts to articulate a general theory of sacrifice in which the ritual murder of the victim is central to the entire ceremony.

Casabona, Jean. *Recherches sur le vocabulaire des sacrifices en grec, des origines à la fin de l'époque classique*. Aix-en-Provence, 1966. An excellent semantic study of the vocabulary of sacrifice and libations, supported by a meticulous examination of literary texts (from Homer to Xenophon) and epigraphic texts.

Detienne, Marcel, and Jean-Pierre Vernant, eds. *La cuisine du sacrifice en pays grec*. Paris, 1980. An anthropological analysis of the Greek sacrifice as a ritual and civic act situated in the center of the alimentary practices and politico-religious thinking of the city; leads to questioning the pertinence of a Judeo-Christian model pretending to be unitarian and universal. With contributions by Jean-Louis Durand, Stella Georgoudi, François Hartog, and Jesper Svenbro.

Meuli, Karl. "Griechische Opferbräuche." In *Phyllobolia für Peter von der Mühli zum 60. Geburtstage*, edited by Olof Gigon and Karl Meuli, pp. 185–288. Basel, 1946. A comparison between the "Olympian sacrifice" of the Greeks and certain rites of the hunting and herding peoples of northeastern Europe and northern Asia; discerns a sacrificial structure originating in this primitive world and surviving in ancient Greece.

Reverdin, Olivier, ed. *Le sacrifice dans l'antiquité*. Geneva, 1981. Contributors approach questions of method, not in a theoretical and general manner, but through the study of a choice of specific and varied sacrificial rites.

Mysteries, Dionysism, Orphism

Guthrie, W. K. C. *Orpheus and Greek Religion: A Study of the Orphic Movement*. 2d ed., rev. London, 1952. A study of Orpheus and Orphic beliefs, in which the author tries to analyze and assess the influence of Orphism on the life and thought of the Greeks.

Jeanmaire, Henri. *Dionysos: Histoire du culte de Bacchus.* 2 vols. Paris, 1951. A study devoted to the major institutions and the characteristic elements of the Dionysian religion as it was constituted especially in the Archaic period; also analyzes the development of the Dionysian myth and mystic speculation in the Hellenistic and Greco-Roman environment.

Kerényi, Károly. *Dionysos: Archetypal Image of the Indestructible Life.* Translated by Ralph Mannheim. Princeton, 1976. Considering the Dionysian element as a chapter of the religious history of Europe, the author retraces the itinerary of the Dionysian religion from "the Minoan period to the Roman empire" with the aid of linguistic, archaeological, philosophical, and psychological research; includes 146 illustrations and a rich bibliography.

Linforth, Ivan M. *The Arts of Orpheus* (1941). New York, 1973. A critical study of texts relating to Orphism and the legend of Orpheus as well as the myth of Dionysos.

Mylonas, George E. *Eleusis and the Eleusinian Mysteries.* Princeton, 1961. An archaeological study of the sanctuary and mysteries of Eleusis, retracing the history of the cult from the first houses of the Bronze Age to the imperial era of Rome.

Otto, Walter F. *Dionysos: Mythos und Kultus.* Frankfurt, 1933. Translated by Robert B. Palmer as *Dionysos: Myth and Cult* (Bloomington, Ind., 1965). Emphasizes the Archaic and pan-Hellenic character of this "god of paradox" and the theme of his "persecution" as well as the typology of his multiple epiphanies.

Sabbatucci, Dario. *Saggio sul misticismo greco.* Rome, 1965. An essay on the Greek concepts of salvation and Orphism, Pythagoreanism, Dionysism, and Eleusinism as alternatives to the politico-religious system of the city.

11 ROMAN RELIGION TO 100 BCE

ROBERT SCHILLING
Translated from French by Paul C. Duggan

Prior to the Roman unification, the Italian peninsula contained many different ethnic groups. Their influence on religious civilization varies from one to another. In this context a historian tends to highlight three great centers of culture: the Etruscans, established mainly to the north of the right bank of the Tiber; the Greeks of Magna Graecia, located to the south of the Volturno River; and the Latins, located to the south of the lower course of the Tiber up to the confines of Magna Graecia. These borders, however, are only approximate, since they fluctuated in reaction to historical changes.

Here the discussion will concern only the Latins and Rome, since they constitute the essential element of the Indo-European presence on the peninsula. Yet it is necessary to indicate the existence in Campania of the Oscans, who left behind important documents of juridical and religious interest (the *tabula Bantina* of the city of Bantia; the *cippus Abellanus* concerning the towns of Abella and Nola; and the bronze plaque of Agnone with its precepts from sacred law). We should also not forget that the poet Ennius (239–169 BCE) stated that he had three souls, since he knew Greek, Oscan, and Latin (Aulus Gellius, *Noctes Atticae* 17.17). As for the Umbrians, located to the east of Etruria, they left an even richer legacy. Thanks to discovered inscriptions, and above all to the impressive document of the Eugubine Plaques, we are able to know their formulas of prayer as well as the names of their divinities. We now know about the liturgy required for the consecration of the city, about the prescriptions for the lustration of the people, about the sacrifices to be offered according to different places and divinities invoked, about divination by the observation of birds, and about prescriptions for the inauguration of the *templum* or the *pomerium* (religious boundary). One can see that the Osco-Umbrian documentation will sometimes provide valuable comparisons with the Latin data.

Let us return to the domain of the Latins and describe its expansion. At the beginning of the first millennium BCE (between the end of the Bronze Age and the beginning of the Iron Age) these people inhabited Latium Vetus (Old Latium), which extended to the south of the lower course of the Tiber up to the Pontine plain (*Pomptinus ager:* Livy, 6.5.2). This territory was bordered on the northwest by the Tiber and the land of the Etruscans and on the northeast by the Sabine area. On the east it was bounded by the Alban chain from the mountains of Palombara, Tivoli (Tibur), Palestrina (Praeneste), and Cori (Cora) as far as Terracina (Anxur) and Circeo (Circei), and to the west was the shore of the Tyrrhenian Sea. Within this area are the hills that served as habitats, such as Alba Longa, regarded as the most ancient Latin city, or Monte Cavo (Mons Albanus), which was the seat of a federal cult of Jupiter Latiaris.

This Latium Vetus, or Latium Antiquum, was augmented later on by the Latium Adiectum, or Latium Novum (New Latium), formed by the territories won by the Romans of the historical epoch (starting with the sixth century BCE) from the Volsci, the Aequi, the Hernici, and the Aurunci (see Pliny the Elder, *Historia naturalis* 3.68–70). Traditionally the Latins are called *populi Latini* ("Latin peoples") or by the collective noun *nomen Latinum* ("Latin nation"). They occupied the hills, which were easier to defend, in autonomous groups more or less bound to one another, a system termed *vicatim* ("by small villages"). These territorial associations were based essentially on religious bonds. Thus a feeling of community was created that was carried over into the historical epoch by the development of federations based on common cults: those around the sanctuary of Jupiter Latiaris on Mons Albanus, for example, or around the sanctuary of Diana Aricina located in "the sacred grove" of Aricia (Nemus Dianae). Another federal cult would play an exceptional role in history, because it held privileged ties with the Romans. It was centered at Lavinium, which Varro (*De lingua Latina* 5.144) identifies as the religious metropolis of Rome: ". . . Lavinium: . . . ibi di Penates nostri" ("Lavinium: there are our household gods"). Recent excavations have uncovered the site, which includes a necropolis going back to the tenth century BCE. There are also ruins of ramparts dating from the sixth century, the vestiges of a house of worship flanked by thirteen altars, and a mausoleum (it could be a *hērōion* in memory of Aeneas) that houses an archaic tomb from the seventh century BCE.

In the archaic period, the cradle of the future Rome was no more than one village among others. Various stages occurred before the official foundation of the Urbs ("city"), on 21 April 753 BCE (feast day of the Parilia, dedicated to shepherds and flocks) at the summit of what is now the Palatine. The *regio Palatina* ("Palatine region") was subdivided into three knolls, the most important of which was the Palatium, the other two being Cermalus and the Velia. (Regarding the concept of *Roma quadrata,* the expression appears already in Ennius's *Annals* 123 as a "city in four parts", it seems to constitute a projection into the past of the principle of orthogonal division that the Romans later applied in their urban design.)

We have evidence of a second phase, thanks to the topographical grid that corresponds to the feast of the Septimontium, celebrated on 11 December. The three knolls of the Palatine region (Palatium, Cermalus, Velia) are joined with the three knolls of the Esquiline group (Fagutal, Oppius, Cispius) along with the Subura (the Caelius was added later to this list of seven names). These are the stages of the procession that the abridger Sextus Pompeius Festus outlines for this feast, but in a different order probably in line with the liturgical itinerary. The list is borrowed, as is known, from the scholar M. Verrius Flaccus: Palatium, Velia, Fagutal, Subura, Cermalus, Oppius, Caelius, Cispius.

In the third stage of topographical development the city was divided into four regions: Palatina, Esquilina, Suburana, and Collina, the last comprising the Quirinal and the Viminal. Surrounding walls were constructed. Tradition attributes these initiatives to the next to last king, Servius Tullius. This has been confirmed, in that recent archaeological discoveries have verified a notable territorial extension of the city during the sixth century. As for the ramparts, if the date of the wall made by Servius in *opus quadratum* should be advanced to the fourth century, after the burning of Rome by the Gauls, the existence of walls in the sixth century is nonetheless established by the vestiges of an *agger* found on the Quirinal. The discovery at Lavinium of a rampart in *opus quadratum* dating from the sixth century leads, analogously to the Roman situation, to the same conclusion.

These, then, were the stages of the city's formation. Nevertheless, the Romans of the classical period preferred a simpler scheme in the form of a diptych: the "providential" passage from the "savage" state to the "civilized" state. The narrative by Cicero follows this form (*De republica* 2.4). He first evokes the divine origin of the twins Romulus and Remus (born of the god Mars and the Vestal Virgin Rhea Silvia), who were left exposed on the banks of the Tiber by their granduncle Amulius, king of Alba Longa, but were then miraculously saved by the intervention of a nursing wolf. The author then draws a contrast between the pastoral phase, which saw the assertion of the authority of Romulus (the elimination of Remus is passed over in silence), and the civilizing phase of the city's founder. During this period (from the eighth to the seventh century) Rome did not yet impose itself upon the Latin world, which contained several remarkable centers, *clara oppida* (Pliny the Elder, *Historia naturalis* 3.68). We can mention in passing the ones that archaeology has brought to light: Satricum, Antium (Anzio), Ardea, Lavinium (Pratica di Mare), Politorium (perhaps Castel di Decima), Ficana, and Praeneste (Palestrina).

It is possible to give some detail of the conditions of life in these population centers. They drew their sustenance mainly from animal husbandry and from the exploitation of natural resources (salt, fruit, and game). Their inhabitants progressively took up agriculture in pace with the clearing of the woods and the draining of the marshes, at the same time making pottery and iron tools. Their language belonged to the Indo-European family. The first document in the Latin language may be the inscription on the golden brooch of Praeneste, dated at the end of the seventh century: "manios med fhefhaked numasioi" (in classical Latin: "Manius me fecit Numerio," "Manius made me for Numerius.") However, the authenticity of this inscription has recently been strongly contested. (see M. Guarducci, *La cosidetta Fibula Prenestina,* Rome, 1980). As regards their rites, it was believed for a long time that the Indo-European invaders practicing cremation could be contrasted with the aborigines practicing burial, with the latter chronologically preceding the former. This picture no longer corresponds to the facts. Archaeology has revealed that the practice of cremation (end of the Bronze Age and beginning of the Iron Age) almost always preceded burial (late Iron Age: eighth to seventh century), with no ethnic significance attached to these usages.

In this community of Latins, Rome became progressively preponderant, once it had established its political and religious foundations. Tradition ascribes this growth on a shared basis to the first two kings, Romulus and Numa Pompilius. This preponderance was extended by the destruction of Alba Longa under the third king, Tullus Hostilius, and by the conquest of the coastal regions as far as Ostia, at the mouth of the Tiber. In the course of these operations, centers such as Tellenae, Ficana, and Politorium were wiped out. If it is true that Politorium corresponds to the modern city of Castel di Decima, the recent excavations in that locality would confirm tradition; indeed, they have brought to light a necropolis containing tombs dating from the eighth century into the end of the seventh—the *terminus* indicated by Livy (1.33.3) for the destruction of Politorium by the fourth king, Ancus Marcius.

Yet, once she became the mistress of Latium, Rome herself was subjected by the Etruscans. The last three kings, Tarquin the Elder (Tarquinius Priscus), Servius Tullius, and Tarquin the Proud (Tarquinius Superbus) are all presumed to be of Etruscan origin. After the expulsion of the last Etruscan king (in 509 BCE), Roman power wasted no time in consolidating itself, thanks to the victory gained (in 499 or 496) over the Latins at Lake Regillus. This was followed in 493 by the establishment of an alliance of "eternal peace" between the two parties, namely, the treaty of Spurius Cassius. The establishment of a federal cult of the Latin Diana on the Aventine no doubt falls within this same period of time. From then on, all Italy was destined sooner or later to acknowledge Roman law. One last revolt by Latins who took up arms during the first Samnite war (343–341 BCE) was put down with finality. The Latin league was dissolved in 338 BCE, and the Latins were incorporated into the Roman community.

DIVINITIES OF THE ARCHAIC PERIOD

The Latin word designating divinity has an Indo-European origin. *Deus,* which phonetically comes from the ancient *deivos* (just as *dea* comes from *deiva*), means "heavenly being." In line with this etymology, *deus* and *dea* represent for the Latins powers in relation to the luminous sky *(divum),* in opposition to man *(homo),* who is bound to the earth *(humus), homo* itself being a derivative of an Indo-European word meaning "earth." One immediate consequence of this is the fact that the Latin noun is distinguished from its Greek homologue *theos,* which takes its meaning from a different etymology: *theos* probably is connected with the prototype **thesos,* which refers to the sphere of the sacred (Benveniste), though no one has been able to specify the limits of its meaning. We note, however, that this difference of vocabulary between the Latin and the Greek in naming the divinity fades at the level of the supreme god: *Iuppiter (*Iou-pater,* with **Iou-* deriving from **dyeu-*) and *Zeus (*dyeus)* both go back to the same Indo-European root.

It also follows that the Latins represented the divinity as an individual and personal being. This linguistic fact at once discredits the "animist" notion that would postulate a pre-deist phase in Rome that would have preceded the advent of the personal divinity. The erroneous utilization of the word *numen,* arbitrarily confused with the Melanesian term *mana,* has fizzled out, as shown by Georges Dumézil.

How did Romans depict their gods? A remark by Varro (quoted by Augustine, *De civitate Dei* 4.31) deserves attention: "For more than 170 years, the Romans worshiped their gods without statues. If this custom had prevailed, the gods would be honored in a purer fashion." This reference to a lost state of purity *(castitas)* is an indirect criticism of the Hellenic anthropomorphism that attributed human passions and vices to the gods, as in Homer's *Iliad* or in Hesiod's *Theogony.*

Indeed, the native Roman divinities lack the embellishments of a mythology that is more or less abundant with picturesque variations. They were mainly defined by their specific competence, far from any tie with the human condition. (Georg Wissowa, 1912, had already observed that there was no marriage or union between gods and goddesses at Rome.) This fact is particularly verified by the existence of many divinized abstractions, such as Fides, the goddess of good faith, who received each year the common homage of three major priests. They would come in an open chariot to her chapel to ask her to preserve harmonious relations within the city. Also, Ceres, the etymology of whose name places her in charge of growth (especially of grains), appears as the background to the feast of the Cerialia, which was celebrated annually on 19 April. These, then, are not minor divinities, nor is Consus, the god of grain storage (*condere*, "to store"), who was celebrated at the time of the Consualia on 21 August, as well as at the time of the Opiconsiva on 25 August, when he was in association with Ops, the goddess who watched over abundance. As for Janus, god of beginnings and of passages, and Vesta, the goddess of the sacred fire, their importance in the Roman liturgy was such, as reported by Cicero (*De natura deorum* 2.67), that the former shared in the beginning of every religious ceremony, while the latter was invoked at the end.

Did this tendency toward divinized abstraction lend itself to excesses? One readily cites the example of the minor specialist gods that assisted Ceres in her functions, according to Fabius Pictor (quoted by Servius Danielis, *Ad Georgica* 1.21): Vervactor (for the plowing of fallow land), Reparator (for the renewal of cultivation), Imporcitor (for marking out the furrows), Insitor (for sowing), Obarator (for plowing the surface), Occator (for harrowing), Sarritor (for weeding), Subruncinator (for hoeing), Messor (for harvesting), Convector (for carting the harvest), Conditor (for storage), Promitor (for distribution). Another group of minor divinities gave Augustine (*De civitate Dei* 6.9.264–265) occasion for sarcastic comments in detailing its list. This group included lesser divine entities who were regarded as aiding the husband on his wedding night: Virginensis (to loosen the belt of the young virgin), Subigus (to subdue her), and Prema (to embrace her). "And what is the goddess Pertunda [from *pertundere*, "to penetrate"] doing here? Let her blush, let her flee! Let her leave the husband something to do! It is really a disgrace that someone else besides himself is fulfilling the duty that this goddess's name embodies."

What can be said about all this? Whatever the merit of these lists of specialized divinities (the first one, transmitted by Servius, is guaranteed by the quality of the source: Fabius Pictor, the author of books on pontifical law, contemporary with Cato the Elder), one can observe that they name only secondary entities that are served by no particular priest (even though the Roman institution recognized the *flamines minores*, the "lesser priests"). Nor did they appear in the liturgical calendar. Moreover, these entities moved in the wake of top-level divinities. This trait is expressly brought out by the list of lesser specialists who gravitate toward Ceres: the *flamen* (priest) of this goddess invokes them when he offers, during the Cerialia, the sacrifice to Tellus ("earth") and to Ceres. Everything indicates that the same applies to the list drawn up by Augustine: all those names fit easily within the circle of Juno Pronuba, protectress of marriages. Also, one can grant that these lesser gods constitute an inferior category of *di humiliores*. Most of the time they fall under the banner of the greatest among them, after the manner of clients who place themselves under the protection of a *patronus*. In this sense they share, as Georges Dumézil puts it, in the *"familia* of a great god." In any case, they demonstrate the analytic abilities of pontifical experts and their concern for accompanying each phase of an activity with a religious factor. Finally, this tendency to divine miniaturization corresponds to a kind of luxuriant manifestation of the inclination of Roman pontiffs toward abstract analysis.

These divine abstractions exist in both masculine and feminine forms, without any interference between the two. The apparent exceptions are only illusory. Thus it is that Faunus has no feminine counterpart. (His name's meaning is uncertain; it has sometimes been compared by the ancients with *fari*, "to talk," as in Varro, *De lingua Latina* 7.36, and sometimes with *favere*, "to be favorable," as in Servius Danielis, *Ad Georgica* 1.10; this god had been assimilated to the Greek Pan, as is confirmed by the location of his temple, erected in 194 BCE on the Isle of the Tiber, i.e., in the extrapomerial zone.) Indeed, Fauna seems to be an artificial construction of syncretic casuistry that attempted to associate her with Faunus as either wife or sister or daughter (Wissowa, 1912). Her name was later confused with Fatua and with Bona Dea (an appellation also used in turn by Damia, a goddess originating in Tarentum).

The same holds true for Pales, the goddess whose feast, the Parilia, occurred on 21 April, the anniversary of the foundation of Rome. (In contrast, two Pales appear on the date of 7 July on the pre-Julian calendar of the town of Antium. Nothing prevents us from considering these as two goddesses liable for distinct tasks, the protection of different categories of animals: small and large livestock.) The god Pales, mentioned by Varro (quoted by Servius, *Ad Georgica* 3.1), belongs to the Etruscan pantheon and has no liturgical place in Rome.

How then is one to understand the expression "sive deus sive dea" ("whether god or goddess"), which is found in many prayers? It does not reflect uncertainty about the gender of a possibly epicene divinity but rather uncertainty about the identity of the divinity that one is addressing. In Cato's example the peasant, careful not to make a mistake in the form of address when pruning a *lucus* ("sacred grove"), where he does not know the protective divinity, envisions the two possibilities: he thus invokes either a god or a goddess.

The same prudence is evident in the precautionary formula inserted by the pontiffs, cited by Servius (*Ad Aeneidem* 2.351): "Et pontifices ita precabantur: Jupiter Optime Maxime, sive quo alio nomine te appellari volueris" ("And the pontiffs uttered this prayer: Jupiter, Best and Greatest, or whatever be the name by which you choose to be called"). This formula is all the more instructive in that it provides for the case in which Jupiter, while well identified by his Capitoline titles, might by chance desire some other name.

Since a Roman divinity is essentially defined by its action, even a single manifestation of this action suffices for the existence of the divinity to be acknowledged. Such would be an exceptional, but significant, case. In vain a voice once called out on the Via Nova in the silence of the night to announce the approach of the Gauls. The Romans later reproached themselves for their culpable negligence and erected a sanctuary to the voice under the name of Aius Locutius ("he who talks, he who tells"; Livy, 5.32.6; 50.5; 52.11). Similarly, a *fanum* (shrine) was constructed outside of the Porta Capena to the god Rediculus. This was because Hannibal in his march on Rome had retreated, overcome by apparitions, from that place.

All the divinities of autochthonous background had a privilege: their sanctuaries were allowed within the pomerial zone. What was this pomerium? According to Varro (*De lingua Latina* 5.143), it was a circle within the surrounding wall marked by stones and describing the limit inside of which urban auspices had to be taken. Rome included sectors outside the pomerial zone that were still part of the city: the Aventine Hill, which had been outside the city of the four regions (its incorporation into the city was attributed by tradition sometimes to Romulus and sometimes to

Ancus Marcius), remained outside the pomerial zone until the time of Claudius (first century CE) even though it was surrounded by what was called "Servius's wall."

The same extrapomerial status held true for the Field of Mars, which owed its name to the military exercises that were conducted on its esplanade. Yet here there occurs a further practice that lies at the root of Roman law. On this emplacement there was an altar consecrated to Mars from time immemorial. It is mentioned by the "royal" law of Numa in relation to the distribution of the *spolia opima,* spoils taken from an enemy's general slain by one's own army commander, and was completed later on by the erection of a temple (in 138 BCE). The assemblies of military centuries *(comitia centuriata)* were also held there. In addition, every five years the purification of the people *(lustrum)* was celebrated there by the sacrifice of the *suovetaurilia,* the set of three victims—boar, ram, and bull—that had been paraded beforehand around the assembly of citizens. The presence of the old Mars outside the *pomerium* (similarly, another temple of Mars, constructed in 338 BCE to the south of Rome outside the Porta Capena, was also outside the pomerial zone) was in strict conformity with the distinction established between the *imperium domi,* the jurisdiction of civil power circumscribed by the pomerial zone, and the *imperium militiae* that could not show itself except outside this zone. This is why it was necessary to take other auspices when one wanted to go from one zone to another. If one failed to do so, every official act was nullified. This misfortune befell the father of the Gracchi, T. Sempronius Gracchus, during his presidency of the *comitia centuriata.* While going back and forth between the Senate and the Field of Mars, he forgot to take the military auspices again; as a result, the election of consuls that took place in the midst of the assemblies when he returned was rejected by the Senate (see Cicero, *De divinatione* 1.33 and 2.11). The delimitation of Roman sacral space by the pomerial line explains the distribution of the sanctuaries. Vesta, the goddess of the public hearth, could only be situated at the heart of the city within the pomerium, whereas a new arrival, such as Juno Regina, originating in Veii, was received, as an outsider, in a temple built on the Aventine (in 392 BCE).

Does this territorial distribution of the sanctuaries into zones *intra* and *extra pomerium* correspond in any way to the distinction made by the ancients between *di indigetes* and *di novensiles?* These expressions appear (though in reverse order) within the old formula of the *devotio* (quoted by Livy, 8.9.6) by which a Roman general "devoted himself"—in other words, consecrated himself, and the enemy army as well, to the *di manes* (the underworld gods) cited at the end of a list of other divinities. The meaning of these two terms is debated. It appears that many ancients and some moderns (among them Wissowa) yielded to a semantic slip by confusing *indigetes* with *indigenae,* thus interpreting the *di indigetes* as the "indigenous" gods, as opposed to more recent divinities. Although this confusion is philologically unacceptable, it still conveys a contrast that seems real. It seems likely that *novensiles* (*-siles* coming from *-sides,* just as *lacrima* comes from *dacrima,* as attested in Livius Andronicus) can be explained as deriving from *novus* and *insidere* in order to designate the "newly-resident" gods. As for the *indigetes,* I would connect the term with *indigitare* ("to recite ritually") and *indigitamenta* ("collection of litanies"). Thus the expression would designate the divinities invoked since time immemorial by preference. The Vergilian formula *di patrii indigetes* (*Georgics* 1.498) would thus be explained: far from being an idle repetition with *patrii, indigetes* adds a note of confidence drawn forth in permanent fervor.

Among the archaic divinities there were some who were split off, so to speak, in the course of time, so that their identity was not preserved except in the name of the feast that honored them. Even this element often remains obscure if no light is shed on it from elsewhere. This is where Indo-European comparative studies have shown themselves to be especially fruitful, thanks to the labors of Georges Dumézil. A few examples will suffice.

Roman calendars mark the date of 21 December as the feast of the Divalia, directed toward a goddess Angerona, about whom not much is known. A breakthrough was achieved by Theodor Mommsen, in his work *Römisches Staatsrecht* (1871–1888), when he underscored the coincidence of the feast with the winter solstice (an account of the calendar of Praeneste, successfully restored by that scholar, justified the celebration of the feast by the coming of the solar year). Georges Dumézil (1974) attempted to go further in explaining the name of the goddess by referring to the *angusti dies* of the solstice, a time when the light is *angusta,* or "restricted" (Macrobius, *Saturnalia* 1.21.15). He thus seeks to clarify its action (in conformity with the dynamic of divinized abstractions) as directed toward easing the passage through these *angustiae,* "a sadly brief period of time." As for the goddess herself, he remarked that she appeared with "her mouth gagged and sealed, a finger on her lips, in a gesture that commands silence." He understands this gesture of silence, advised in India and in Scandinavian mythology, as a means of concentration for gaining magical efficacy. In the mythologies, silence is placed at the service of the threatened sun.

The second example is even more suggestive, to the extent that it brings out the meaning of a liturgy that had become incomprehensible to the Romans of the classical period. It deals with the Matralia on 11 June in honor of Mater Matuta. Here again, the name of the divinity, however transparent (she is identified with the goddess Aurora by Lucretius 5.656), and the nearness of her feast to the summer solstice have not prevented certain scholars from forgetting these data and from seeing in Mater Matuta anything more than a simple mother goddess or benevolent mother. It is true that the liturgy of her feast could appear as mysterious as one wished.

On 11 June Roman matrons gathered in the goddess's temple. (This sanctuary, built in 396 BCE by M. Furius Camillus, replaced an earlier structure. According to tradition as reported by Livy [5.19.6], it took the place of a temple constructed by Servius Tullius. Recent excavations have uncovered two temples in the northern part of the Forum Boarium. One is attributed to Mater Matuta and the other to Fortuna, dating from the fifth to the fourth century. One of them contains an older stratum, datable to the end of the sixth century, the time of Servius Tullius.) During the ceremony, the matrons would carry in their arms not their own children but the children of their sisters. Having already sent a servant girl into the temple ahead of time, they now began to beat her with switches before casting her outside. These rites could not but appear strange in the absence of an explanatory ideology. Now, as Georges Dumézil has observed, the goddess Aurora is one of the most striking figures of the *Rgveda,* where she appears nursing and licking a child, who is either "both her own and that of her sister, the Night" (India is not embarrassed by such contradictory conceptions) or "of the latter alone."

All this occurs as if Rome had done nothing but retain the most logical form of the mythologem: Aurora cherishing the child of her sister, the Night. But the myth has disappeared here; only the rite has survived. Once a year, the matrons perform actions inspired by some kind of sympathetic magic that Aurora is supposed to do every day. They throw a slave out of the temple; in the *Rgveda*, Aurora "chases away the black formlessness . . . the shadows." The matrons carry their nephews and nieces but not their own children; the Vedic Aurora accepts with an affectionate eagerness the child of her sister, Night.

This ceremony occurs on 11 June, and

> *the nearness of the summer solstice is not happenstance. It is at the point when the days, as if weary, reduce to nearly nothing their growth and soon set about declining, that the goddess Aurora becomes most interesting for the people, just as, at the end of the disturbing process of shortening at the winter solstice, it is Angerona who arouses interest, the goddess who lengthens at last the days that become angusti."*   (Dumézil, 1974, p. 344)

The example of the Matralia shows in a significant way that in Rome a rite could be preserved in spite of the loss of its underlying myth. In this connection, it is interesting to take note of the "theologian" Ovid's reaction to this exegetical problem. Given his and his contemporaries' ignorance of this Indo-European mythologem, he could only search through the skein of Greek mythology. Thanks to syncretism, he was able to settle on a comparison of Mater Matuta with the Greek goddess Ino/Leukothea. In search of a fable adaptable to the liturgical plan of 11 June, he chanced upon a matching outline. Indeed, Ino/Leukothea, who proved to be a kindly nurse for her nephew Bacchus (son of her sister Semele), was a malicious mother toward her own children. Ovid thus "justified" the liturgy of the Matralia by means of this parallel in addressing this exhortation to the mothers of Latium: "Let the mothers piously invoke the goddess not for their own offspring, for she did not bring any luck as a mother. Let them rather plead with her for the children of others, since she was of more service to her nephew Bacchus than to her own children" (*Fasti* 6.559–562).

Thus the archaic divinities, who survived only by virtue of the Romans' liturgical conservatism, have recovered their true identity thanks to Indo-European comparative studies. Nor is this the only benefit that can be credited to these studies, whose decisive contribution concerns the fundamental structures of religious heritage. Wissowa (1912) had already brought out the importance in Roman religion of the triad of Jupiter-Mars-Quirinus, who appears at the point of convergence of several factors and proceeds from the ancient priestly hierarchy as transmitted by Festus, who set down the following hierarchy: the king, the *flamen Dialis*, the *flamen Martialis*, the *flamen Quirinalis*, the *pontifex maximus*. Framed by the king and the grand pontiff, the three major *flamines* (the *flamines maiores*) bring into relief the gods to which they are respectively attached: Jupiter, Mars, and Quirinus. Their close union is emphasized by the ritual in which, once a year, they would go together to the chapel of Fides, to venerate the goddess of good faith. [*See* Flamen *and* Pontifex.]

The same triad is manifest in the interior arrangement of the Regia, or "king's house," which under the republic became the official seat of the pontifical college. Indeed, this building housed three different cults in addition to the cults of Janus and Juno, who were honored respectively as ushers of the year and of the month: the cult of Jupiter, associated with all the *nundinae* ("market days"); that of Mars, in the *sacrarium Martis*; and, in another chapel, the cult of Ops Consiva (abundance personified) in conjunction with Consus, the god of the storage *(condere)* of grains. This last goddess belongs to the group of agrarian divinities headed by Quirinus (whose *flamen* could substitute for any absent priest from within the whole of the jurisdiction of Quirinus: thus, in Ovid's *Fasti* 4.910 we learn that the *flamen Quirinalis* officiated in the ceremonies of Robigus, or Robigo, the divinity invoked against mildew in grains).

The same triad of Jupiter, Mars, and Quirinus is found after Janus, the god of passage, and before the divinities invoked by reason of particular circumstances in the old hymn of the *devotio* (Livy, 8.9.6) that a Roman general uttered in order to consecrate himself, at the same time as the enemy army, to the *di manes*.

The triad also appears in the regulations provided by the ancient royal law of Numa Pompilius for the distribution of the *spolia opima*. The first of these spoils were offered to Jupiter Feretrius, the second to Mars, the third to Janus Quirinus. The ternary scheme is clearly supported by the document, despite some difficulties of interpretation. The meaning of *Feretrius* (derived from *ferire* ("to smile") or from *ferre* ("to carry")) is not certain. As for the expression *Janus Quirinus*, I have offered the explanation that the presence of Janus comes from his role as the initiator of the peacemaking function of Quirinus in opposition to the fury of Mars Gradivus. The tertiary scheme appears finally in the threefold patronage of the college of Salian priests ("who are under the protection of Jupiter, Mars and Quirinus"; Servius, *Ad Aeneidem* 8.663).

This cluster of Roman elements is confirmed by a parallel structure in the Umbrian pantheon: in the town of Iguvium, as in Rome, there existed a grouping of three gods—Iou, Mart, Vofiono—all bearing the common epithet Grabovio (its meaning obscure). This similarity between the two pantheons is all the more apparent since *Vofiono* is the exact linguistic equivalent of *Quirinus,* even to its adjectival form *-no-,* derived from a nominal root.

Let us return to the arrangement of this triad that, in Rome as in Iguvium, constituted a fundamental base for the archaic pantheon. The remarkable part is that it presents an order of three gods that correspond, in the Indo-European world, to three diversified functions. Jupiter embodies sovereignty in its magical and juridical aspects, which in Vedic India belong respectively to Varuna and Mithra; Mars embodies power (his physical and military attributes are similar to Indra in India); Quirinus (**Couirio-no,* the god of the community of citizens in time of peace) is connected with fruitfulness and with prosperity in its pastoral and agrarian forms. As Dumézil has demonstrated, this triad shows the survival of the characteristic tripartite ideology of the Indo-European world, which considered the hierarchical structuring of these three complementary functions to be indispensable for the prosperity of society. Despite a later evolution that would progressively fossilize their offices as the pantheon was opened to new gods, the three major *flamines* would remain the unimpeachable witnesses of this Indo-European heritage in Rome.

If, thanks to Roman conservatism and to comparative analysis, we can go back to some extent into prehistory, it is nonetheless true that Rome did not delay—indeed, it moved sooner than one would have thought until recently—in entering into history. The political event placed by tradition toward the end of the sixth century BCE, namely, the presence of the three kings who were of Etruscan origin (Tarquin the Elder, Servius Tullius, and Tarquin the Proud), involved a religious repercussion. The ancient masculine triad was replaced by a new triad in which Jupiter's masculine associates were replaced by two goddesses, Juno and Minerva. It is significant that goddesses replaced gods: Etruscan society accorded to women a more important social status than did Indo-European society. That these goddesses were none other than Juno and Minerva can be explained not only by the fact that their Etruscan homologues Uni and Mernva held respectable places in their pantheon but perhaps also by their meeting a two-sided need: to renew without destroying.

In a certain sense, did they not renew things with the abilities of their predecessors? Juno, the patroness of *iuniores* (especially of youth available for battle), succeeded Mars, the god of war; Minerva, the protectress of artisans and crafts, succeeded Quirinus, the god overseeing economic activity. The keystone of the triad remained immovable, even though Jupiter took on the traits of Tinia, as illustrated by the Etruscan artist Vulca of Veii.

Indeed, theological novelty brought about innovation at the levels of statuary and urban design: the era of aniconic divinities, mourned by Varro, was definitively over. Terra-cotta statues now came to be used by the believers, divine figures that remained within residences. One point is worthy of note: the temple built on the Capitoline Hill in honor of the new triad of Jupiter, Juno, and Minerva likewise marked the transition from the royal to the republican period. According to tradition, the construction of the Capitoline temple (the sanctuary of Jupiter, the Best, the Greatest) was begun under the Tarquins, while the dedication was performed by the consul M. Horatius Pulvillus in the first year of the republic (509 BCE). Jupiter Optimus Maximus sits on his throne in the central *cella* (shrine), flanked by Minerva on his right and by Juno on his left.

THE REPUBLICAN PERIOD

A new era began with the expulsion of the last king, Tarquin the Proud, and with the institution of the republic. One comment is immediately required: the political change did not provoke any religious upheaval, and this contrast is indicative of the Roman mentality. In fact, the Capitoline triad was not called into question, in spite of its strong Etruscan connotation. Moreover, the title of king was maintained on the religious level. On that account, the official designation from then on was *rex sacrorum* or *rex sacrificulus;* in other words, a king limited to his liturgical functions but stripped of his political privileges. This point of prudence is explained by observing the care that the Romans took to avoid irritating their gods with untimely interventions in the realm of the sacred.

This care lies at the very root of their attitude toward the gods, and it is admirably expressed in the word *religio.* If the modern languages of the Western world (both Romance and Germanic) have failed to translate this word and have settled on a simple copy thereof *(religion, religione),* the reason lies in the fact that this idiom is untranslatable. Indeed, in the ancient world there was no Greek equivalent. All the expressions that one can bring to mind by analogy—*sethas* (respect for the gods), *proskunāsis* (adoration), *peulasthea* (reverential fear), *thrāskea* (cult)—are far from filling the semantic range of *religio.* Careful examination shows that the Latins, who were not concerned with philological rigor, connected *religio* more with the verb *religare* ("to tie"), alluding to the bonds between gods and men, than with the verb *relegere* ("to take up again with care"). Such as it is, *religio* expresses a fundamental preoccupation manifested in two complementary ways: the care to avoid divine wrath; the desire to win the benevolence and favor of the gods. It was the Romans' inner conviction that, without the accord of the gods, they could not succeed in their endeavors. This explains the solemn declaration of a Cicero (*De natura deorum* 2.3) proclaiming the Roman people to be "the most religious in the world."

This preoccupation is evident throughout Livy's history. Roman accomplishments rise and fall in complete rhythm with the disfavor or favor evinced by the gods. A revealing example is furnished in the episode of the Romans' desperation following upon the sack of Rome by the Gauls (in 390 BCE). Overwhelmed, they were nearly resolved to abandon the ruins of their city, at the instigation of their tribunes, in order to emigrate to Veii. It was then that M. Furius Camillus, the predestined leader—*dux fatalis*—and dictator who conquered Veii (in 396), and now the restorer of the situation in Rome (in 390), lit upon the decisive argument that inspired the mood reversal of the assembly: to abandon Rome, many times endowed with heavenly blessings since its origins, would be to commit sacrilege. In the course of his address, Camillus had called to mind this permanent lesson for the benefit of his listeners: "For consider the events of these last years, whether successes or reversals. You will find that everything succeeded when we followed the gods, and everything failed when we scorned them" (Livy, 5.51.4).

Under these conditions, it was essential for the Roman state authorities to know the divine will and to be able to consult it whenever necessary. To this end, there existed an indigenous institution especially charged with this mission: augury. [*See* Divination.] *Augur* (derived from an old neuter root **augus,* which Dumézil translates as "the fullness of mystical power" and which yields the noun *augurium* as well as the adjective *augustus*) designates the priest in charge of obtaining the *augurium,* or sign of supernatural manifestation, by performing the *auspicium,* the observation (*specere*) of birds (*aves*). Everyone knows that Rome was founded as a consequence of the *auspicium* of Romulus, who had benefited from the sight of twelve vultures. The augur during the historical epoch was a specialist in the interpretation of signs sent by Jupiter. The god was to assist the magistrate, the sole possessor of the right to take the auspices.

Later on, Rome did not hesitate to resort to other techniques, borrowed from its neighbors in Etruria or Magna Graecia: the *haruspicinae disciplina* ("lore of the haruspex"), the consultation of the Sibylline Books. This accumulation is explained simply: the desire to benefit from new techniques, all the more seductive the more they appeared to be fruitful. Let us focus on this point. The traditional augur could do nothing more than *constat,* verify the presence or absence of favorable auspices. The Etruscan soothsayer, in contrast, boasted of being able to foretell the future, either by examining the entrails of sacrificed animals or by observing lightning or by interpreting marvels. To this end, he would use respectively the *libri haruspicini,* the *libri fulgurales,* and the *libri rituales.* The first method, divining by examination of entrails, was especially in vogue. It featured, among the *exta* ("entrails") used, the liver, which was considered a microcosm of the macrocosm that was the world. Every lesion detected in some part of the former allowed an inference on the fate of the latter. One celebrated example of entrail-reading is narrated by Livy (8.9.1s) at the time of the battle of Veseris, launched in 340 BCE against the Latins: the soothsayer announced a happy result for the consul Manlius, but an unhappy one for the consul Decius.

The Sibylline Books, which had been introduced, according to tradition, under Tarquin the Proud, purported to contain prophetic verses. [*See* Sibylline Oracles.] These books, kept in the temple of Jupiter Capitoline (later, they would be transferred by Augustus to the sanctuary of Apollo Palatine) could be consulted, upon order of the Senate, by the priests specialized in that office, the *viri sacris faciundis*. The measures advocated by these priests (often the introduction of new divinities) were submitted to the evaluation of the senate, which would make the final decision. The sibyl was far from enjoying a liberty comparable to that of the oracle of Delphi: her responses were always subject to senatorial censorship. There is no need to stress further the benefit that the Romans hoped to gain from these techniques of foreign origin. This cluster of methods is moreover instructive to the extent that it reveals a fundamental trait of Roman polytheism. Founded upon a conservative tradition, it was perpetually open to enrichment and renewal. This double character made it resemble Janus Bifrons ("Janus the two-faced"), one face turned toward the past and the other to the future.

Therefore it is possible to recognize in the Roman pantheon different levels that were formed under the influence of different factors. Certain cults staked out, so to speak, the city's topographical development. Others reflected the struggle for influence within Roman society. Still others corresponded to the expansion of the Roman republic within and beyond the Italian peninsula.

One major cleavage allows us to identify very ancient cults that were linked to the territorial expansion of Rome. The first, the Lupercalia, celebrated on 15 February, delimited the very cradle of the city. On that date "the old Palatine stronghold ringed by a human flock" (Varro, *De lingua Latina*), was purified by naked Luperci (a variety of wolf-men, dressed in loincloths), who, armed with whips, would flog the public. Everything about this ceremony—the "savage" rite (see Cicero, *Pro Caelio* 26) and the territorial circumscription—demonstrates its extreme archaism.

The feast of Septimontium on 11 December designated, as its name suggested, a more extended territory. It involved no one except the inhabitants of the *montes* ("mountains"). These seven mountains (which are not to be confused with the seven hills of the future Rome) are the following: the knolls of the Palatium, the Germalus, the Velia (which together would make up the Palatine), the Fagutal, the Oppius, the Cespius (which three would be absorbed by the Esquiline), and the Caelius (S. Pompeius Festus, while still asserting the number of seven *montes*, adds the Subura to this list). This amounted, then, to an intermediary stage between the primitive nucleus and the organized city. One will note the use of the word *mons* to designate these knolls, as opposed to *collis*, which would be reserved for referring to the northern hills.

The feast of the Argei, which required two separate rituals at two different times (on 16 and 17 March and on 14 May), marks the last stage. It involved a procession in March in which mannequins made of rushes (Ovid, *Fasti* 5.621) were carried around to the twenty-seven chapels prepared for this purpose. On 14 May they were taken out of the chapels in order to be cast into the Tiber from the top of a bridge, the Pons Sublicius, in the presence of the pontiff and the Vestal Virgins. There are different opinions on the meaning of the ceremony. Wissowa saw in it a ritual of substitution taking the place of human sacrifices. (A note by Varro, *De lingua Latina* 7.44, specifies that these mannequins were human in shape.) However, Kurt Latte prefers to compare these mannequins of rushes to *oscilla* (figurines or small masks that were hung from trees), which absorbed the impurities that were to be purged from the city. The itinerary of the procession shows that it corresponds to the final stage of the city's development, the Rome of the *quattuor regiones* ("four regions"). Varro outlined the procession as follows: it proceeded through the heights of the Caelius, the Esquiline, the Viminal, the Quirinal, and the Palatine, and encircled the Forum—henceforth located in the heart of the city.

Other cults reflect, so to speak, the specific aspirations of the two classes that formed the basis of Roman society, the patricians and the plebeians. One observes an antagonism between the two classes that is evident not only on economic, social, and political levels but also on the religious level. We can recall that up until 300 BCE only the patricians were allowed to discharge as an official function the great traditional priesthoods, such as the pontificate and the augury. At that date a kind of religious equality was established by a law (the Lex Ogulnia), which, in providing members for these two colleges, reserved a good half of the seats for plebeians. Nevertheless, the patricians kept for themselves the privilege of admittance to the archaic priesthoods: the *rex sacrorum,* the three major *flamines,* and the Salii.

This rivalry between the two classes explains diverse cult initiatives that are nonetheless not necessarily mutually exclusive. In the critical phases of the city's history, they were able to coexist in a way that was satisfactory to both parties. A particularly convincing example comes to us from the beginning of the fifth century, when one individual strove to balance the two tendencies. It was the time when, according to Livy (2.18.3), "a coalition of thirty tribes" was formed against Rome. The situation induced the Romans to name a dictator, Aulus Postumius, who was vested with full powers, in place of the two consuls.

He had two problems to resolve: to stabilize the food supply, which had been disrupted by the state of war, and to confront the enemy in decisive combat. He successfully accomplished his twofold mission. The victory he won over the Latins (in 499 BCE) near Lake Regillus is celebrated in the annals. This battle entered a critical phase when the infantry failed to hold its ground. On that account, the dictator decided to send in the Roman cavalry and, at the same time, made a vow to build a temple dedicated to Castor. He thus combined, according to Livy's expression, "human and divine" means. He did so because this god, of Greek origin, was the patron of horsemen, by virtue of an old Indo-European tradition that associated him with the art of horsemanship. Before going into the campaign, the dictator took another step toward easing the difficulties surrounding the food supply: he made a vow to build a temple to the Roman triad of Ceres-Liber-Libera, the names of which barely disguised the Greek divinities Demeter-Dionysos-Kore.

The victory enabled Castor to become a Roman god and to acquire a temple above the Forum: the Aedes Castoris (dedicated in 484 by the dictator's son; Pollux was not to join his brother until the beginning of the empire, and even then the name Aedes Castorum recalled the original primacy of Castor). Since the harvests were abundant, Aulus Postumius also fulfilled his vow to the triad of Ceres-Liber-Libera by dedicating a sanctuary. This was a source of great satisfaction for the plebeians, for the sanctuary was entrusted to their charge and served as a meeting place for *aediles* (plebeian officials).

Thus, circumstances had moved Aulus Postumius to achieve a skillful balance by the concomitant foundation of a patrician cult and a plebeian cult. Only the placement of the sanctuaries revealed a difference of status: Castor was installed inside the pomerium, in the heart of the Forum, while Ceres and her associates had to be located outside of the pomerium, near the Circus Maximus.

Lastly, other cults owed their introduction to the expansion of Rome beyond its frontiers. In this connection, it helps to distinguish the cults of federal character from the isolated cults. Since time immemorial, there existed in Italy liturgical celebrations that united several cities. These ceremonies were presided over by cities that owed this honor to their prestige at the time. In the course of events, all concluded by bowing to Roman authority. Nevertheless, the ascendancy of the Urbs (Rome) was not always achieved in the same way or under the same conditions. The Romans' capacity for adaptation to different circumstances is evident here in an especially remarkable way, as illustrated by the following three cases.

One of the most ancient federal cults presupposes the original preeminence of the ancient city of Alba Longa: the *Feriae Latinae* ("Latin holidays") were celebrated at the summit of the Alban Hills in honor of Jupiter Latiaris. In earlier times, the Latins had been granted equal footing in sharing in the sacrifice, which consisted of a white bull (this detail, coming from Arnobius in *Adversus nationes* 2.68, would show that the ordinary rule, which provided a castrated victim for Jupiter, did not apply here). Once the consecrated entrails *(exta)* were offered to the god, all in attendance would share the meat, demonstrating thus their bonds of community. After the destruction of Alba Longa, Rome quite naturally picked up the thread of tradition by incorporating the Feriae Latinae as a movable feast in its liturgical calendar. Still, the attitude of the Romans was selective: even though they transferred the entire Alban population to Rome itself, they kept the Alban celebrations in their usual locations. They simply built a temple to Jupiter Latiaris where previously there was only a *lucus,* a sacred grove. During the historical epoch, the Roman consuls, accompanied by representatives of the state, would make their way to the federal sanctuary shortly after assuming their responsibilities and would preside there over the ceremonies. The Feriae Latinae had come under Roman control.

The conduct of the Romans was very different with regard to the federal cult of Diana. Tradition places this cult at Aricia near Lake Nemi, which is known as the *speculum Dianae,* "mirror of Diana" (Servius, *Ad Aeneidem* 7.515). An archaic rite determined that the priest of Diana's sacred grove, called the *rex nemorensis,* could hold office there until he was killed by his successor in single combat. During the historical period, this odd priesthood attracted only fugitive slaves. The federal altar had been consecrated to Diana by the Latin dictator Egerius Laevius, a native of Tusculum. Tusculum was the center of a federation of Latin towns (established perhaps after the disappearance of Alba Longa). When the cult came under Roman authority, it was transferred into the city on the extrapomerial hill of the Aventine. It had nothing there at first except an altar, then a temple that Varro acknowledges as having federal status: *commune Latinorum templum.* Yet this status was only one of appearance, since no assembly of Latin cities is recorded as ever having occurred on the Aventine during the Roman period, any more than at Aricia. Another point is significant: the anniversary of the temple fell on the ides of August and bore the name *Dies Servorum* ("slaves' day"). Whatever interpretation one gives to this designation, the fact remains that the cult of Diana was not of concern either on the Aventine or in Aricia. This time Rome had reduced a federal cult to a suitable level. In contrast with Jupiter Latiaris, Diana, whose name is a semantic homologue of

Jupiter (since both names were formed from the root **diu;* she signified nocturnal light, just as he signified the light of day), was doomed to fade gradually away. Identified with Artemis, she would be invoked in Horace's *Carmen saeculare* as the sister of Apollo.

The relations that Rome held with Lavinium were very different. In the Roman mind, Lavinium had the same resonance as the Alban Hills, judging from the discourse that Livy attributes to the dictator Camillus. Camillus did not hesitate to put these two high places on the same level: "Our ancestors entrusted to us the celebration of religious ceremonies on Mount Alban and in Lavinium." In reality, the latter ranked higher than the former. Varro (*De lingua Latina* 5.144) specifies it as the source of Roman lineage and the cradle of the Roman *penates:* Lavinium benefited from a continual deference on the part of the Romans after the treaty that tradition traced back to the time of T. Tatius (Livy, 1.14.2). This deference was evident in the ritual processions of higher magistrates to the *penates* and to Vesta as they entered their office and as they left it. The deference was likewise evident in the annual pilgrimages by the pontiffs and the consuls to the sanctuary of Aeneas Indiges, which Ascanius is reputed to have built for his divinized father. If one considers that Lavinium was also the cradle of the religion of Venus, who was understood according to Trojan legend to be the *Aeneadum genetrix* ("mother of the descendants of Aeneas"), one can imagine that this exceptional site exerted in every way a great attraction for the Romans. Archaeology has recently made an important contribution concerning the territory of Lavinium by bringing to light, among other things, a *hērōin* (temple) from the fourth century BCE, constructed upon an archaic tomb (which its discoverer, Pado Sommella, identifies as the mausoleum of Aeneas) and a set of thirteen altars, of which twelve were in use in the middle of the fourth century. They may have served a new Latin federation presided over by Rome. Indeed, Rome did not stop at destroying the Latin confederation in 338 BCE, but also reinforced the privileges of Lavinium. For Lavinium, as Livy points out (8.11.15), had added to its titles the merit of loyalty by refusing to join the Latin revolt. It brought even more renown upon itself as a pilgrimage center. Thus Rome's attitude toward federal cults was definitively shown under three very different aspects: sometimes she assumed one (Alba Longa), sometimes she restricted one (Aricia), and sometimes she exalted one (Lavinium).

Just as varied was the Romans' behavior toward the divinities that they intended to introduce into their pantheon. By definition, polytheism lent itself to this sort of openness, when the traditional gods proved to be inadequate in a critical situation. Here again circumstances inspired the Romans' attitude. An early example is demonstrated by the entry of Castor into Rome, as related above. One recalls that the dictator Aulus Postumius, alarmed by the weakness of his infantry, had turned to the patron god of horsemen at the same time that he sent his cavalry into battle. He had made a vow to erect a temple to the god. The exceptional feature of this *votum* ("vow") was that Castor became installed right in the Forum, thus within the pomerial zone. He was exempted from the rule that located the residence of new divinities outside this area. Perhaps one of the reasons for this exception was the long-standing acclimatization of Castor to Latium (a dedication engraved on a bronze plaque dating from the sixth century BCE, found in Lavinium, mentions Castor and Pollux). Another reason was the importance of the occasion (it would have been the end of the young Roman republic had the Romans fallen at Lake Regillus to the Latins, who were emboldened by the exiled king, Tarquin). In any event, Castor, the god of a class (the *equites*), became the god of a nation (the Romans).

There were also other ways for foreign gods to be introduced into the Roman pantheon. When the Romans had trouble with an enemy city, they had the *evocatio* at their disposal. It consisted of a kind of abduction of divine power at the adversary's expense and to Rome's benefit. A famous case (and also unique in the annals) is seen in the siege of Veii (in 396 BCE). The war against that Etruscan city seemed endless. It was to last ten years, as long as the Trojan war. Struck by marvels ("Lake Alban had risen to an unaccustomed level without rain or any other cause"; Livy, 5.15.2), the Romans named M. Furius Camillus as dictator. In addition to his military successes, he achieved fame by addressing directly the city's protective divinity, Uni (the Etruscan homologue of Juno): "Juno Regina, who resides now in Veii, I pray that you will follow us after our victory into our city, which will soon be yours; you will there have a temple worthy of your majesty" (Livy, 5.21.3). In this way Juno Regina acquired a temple on the Aventine, as a divinity of outside origin, while still continuing to sit, as a national divinity, on the Capitolium at the side of Jupiter.

Finally, there was one other procedure: the capture, pure and simple, of a foreign divinity. *A priori,* this arrogant attitude can seem strange on the part of a people imbued with "religious" respect toward the supernatural world (by way of explaining the *evocatio,* Macrobius in *Saturnalia* 3.9.2 had advanced precisely this reason: "Quod . . . nefas aestimarent deos habere captivos," "They regarded it as sacrilege to make prisoners of the gods"). However, the seizure of Falerii in 241 BCE resulted in captivity for its goddess, who was then given a small shrine in Rome at the foot of the slope of Caelius, under the name of Minerva Capta (Ovid, *Fasti* 3.837). Apparently Rome no longer thought it necessary to treat the vanquished with caution, whether men or gods. She was adopting to her own advantage the *vae victis* formerly pronounced against her by a Gaulish chief.

INFLUENCES OF HELLENISM

The Greek influence played very quickly upon Rome both indirectly and directly. Indirectly, by means of the Etruscans, to the extent that the Etruscan pantheon was itself hellenized, with allowance made for its own specificity. Directly, by the nearness of Magna Graecia, while contact was taking place with continental Greece and Asia Minor. This influence contributed to anthropomorphism in conceiving the divine, above all once syncretism had established a table of equivalences between Greek and Italic divinities. How is *syncretism* defined? As a consequence of a mistaken etymology that confused *sugkrētismos* ("federation") with *sugkrēsis* ("mixture"), as Stig Wikander has shown, the term came to mean a "mixture of myths and religions." In this way the parallel connection between the Greek triad Demeter-Dionysos-Kore and the Latin triad Ceres-Liber-Libera (explained above) is ascribable to syncretist interpretation. Instead of remaining an abstract concept of "creative" force *(creare),* Ceres was more or less identified with a Demeter in human form and enhanced by a moving legend (Demeter in search of her daughter Kore, abducted by Pluto). This "new" Ceres was made into a statue which, according to Pliny the Elder, was "the first bronze statue made in Rome." Consequently, she gained a "house," the temple built in 493 BCE to the triad near the Circus Maximus. The temple was decorated with the painting and sculptures of Damophilos and Gorgasos, two celebrated Greek artists. In this instance, hellenization had consisted in overlaying an Italic abstraction with an image and a legend. There is only a hellenization by contamination between homologous divinities. [*See* Syncretism.]

Yet some Greek gods came into Rome outside of any process of contamination. This fact has already been examined in the case of Castor. The same held true for Apollo. His introduction was due to an epidemic. Indeed it was not the god of the Muses, nor the sun god, nor the prophet god who would later be the patron of the Sibylline Books (these titles would appear in the *Carmen saeculare* by Horace during the time of Augustus) and to whom the Romans had appealed for aid at the beginning of the fifth century; rather, this Apollo was the healing god. His temple, dedicated in 433 "pro valetudine populi" ("for the people's health"), was dedicated in 431 in the Flaminian Meadows at the southwest of the Capitol, within a sector that already bore the name Apollinare ("Apollo's enclosure"; Livy, 4.25.3, 40.51.4). The oldest invocation used in the prayers of the Vestals were directed to the "physician": Apollo Medice, Apollo Paean (Macrobius, *Saturnalia* 1.17.15).

This introduction had been recommended by the Sibylline Books that were consulted upon orders of the Senate by the *viri sacris faciundis.* The striking thing in the cases of Castor and Apollo lies in the circumstances surrounding their manifestations. In both instances there was an imperative necessity: for the former, the essential situation was in a crucial battle; for the latter, it was an alarming pestilence. In contrast with Castor, who was introduced by the lone initiative of the dictator Aulus Postumius, Apollo entered Rome as a consequence of a consultation with the Sibylline Books. This procedure would be put to use more and more, and, as a result, the Romans became familiar with a new form of devotion, the *lectisternia,* which had more significance on the emotional level than was usual in Roman worship. This worship consisted essentially in a canonical prayer followed by the offering of consecrated entrails (the *exta*) to the divinity (the distinction between *exta*—comprising the lungs, the heart, the liver, the gall bladder, and the peritoneum—and the *viscera,* flesh given over for profane consumption, is fundamental in Roman liturgy). The sacrificial ceremony was celebrated by qualified magistrates and priests around the altar, placed in front of the temple. On the contrary, in the *ritus Graecus* statues of the deities reposing on cushions *(pulvinaria)* were exposed within the temples on ceremonial beds *(lectisternia).* Men, women, and children could approach them and offer them food and prayers in a fervent supplication (see Livy, 24.10.13; 32.1.14) often presided over by the *viri sacris faciundis* (cf. Livy, 4.21.5).

The first *lectisternium* was celebrated in 399 BCE at the injunction of the Sibylline Books that had been consulted by the *viri sacris faciundis* upon order of the Senate, which was worried about a persistent epidemic in Rome. It joined in heterogeneous pairs Apollo and Latona, Hercules and Diana, Mercury and Neptune (Livy, 5.13.4–6). Outwardly, half of the names were of purely Greek origin (Apollo, Latona, Hercules) and the other half of Latin origin. In reality, even these last names applied to Hellenic divinities: Diana/Artemis, Mercury/Hermes, Neptune/Poseidon. The healing god Apollo, accompanied by his mother Latona, was at the head of the list during this period of epidemic.

Much more dramatic circumstances—Hannibal at the walls of Rome—instigated in 217 BCE the last and most celebrated *lectisternium* in the history of the republic (Livy, 22.10.9). On this occasion, the Romans for the first time adopted the Greek plan of a set of twelve deities divided into six couples in the following order: Jupiter and Juno, Neptune and Minerva, Mars and Venus, Apollo and Diana, Vulcan and Vesta, Mercury and Ceres. This ceremony would remain unique (one cannot regard as a parallel the merry parody organized by Augustus during a *cena* where the twelve dinner companions disguised themselves as gods and goddesses (see Suetonius, *Augustus* 70). Without a doubt, the Greek inspiration is evident in this list, presenting couples of gods and goddesses (the idea of grouping twelve principal deities would be repeated later by the installation of gilded bronze statues of the *di consentes* in the niches located below the Portico at the foot of the Capitolium).

Yet it is necessary to avoid misunderstanding the meaning of the coupling here. The Greek model appeared in outline after the first four couples: Zeus-Hera, Poseidon-Athena; Ares-Aphrodite, Apollo-Artemis. It could suggest a conjugal meaning for Jupiter and Juno and an erotic meaning for Mars and Venus, but nothing of the kind would apply for the association of Neptune and Minerva (which evokes the rivalry of Poseidon and Athena in giving a name to Athens), nor for Apollo and Diana/Artemis, who were brother and sister. One can also wonder if the Romans were not still more heedful of the representative value of these divine pairs. Only a functional bond makes sense for the two last couples, in Rome as well as in Greece: fire for Vulcan and Vesta, economic activity (commerce and grain) for Mercury and Ceres. As for the couples that seemed most to bear the stamp of Hellenism, they were explained perfectly in accord with Roman norms. Thus Jupiter and Juno were associated here, just as they had been in the Capitoline cult since the sixth century. Nor did Venus and Mars form a couple in Rome in the strict sense of the term. Mars, father of Romulus, is the old Italic god, while Venus, mother of Aeneas, appeared as the protectress of the Romans-Aeneades. In a word, Rome knew how to utilize the Greek plan to her own ends without in turn submitting to it. She joined together the two essential personages of her history: Aeneas, the founder of the nation, and Romulus, founder of the city.

This example makes manifest a constant attitude. Nothing is more significant in this connection than the introduction of the cult of Venus Erycina. Once again the circumstantial cause was the imperative need for supplementary divine aid. It was during the Second Punic War (218–210), after the disaster of Trasimene in 217 BCE. Named as dictator, Q. Fabius Maximus (who would bear the surname *Cunctator*, or "delayer") obtained from the Senate a consultation with the Sibylline Books, which prescribed, among other measures, a promise to provide a temple dedicated to Venus Erycina (Livy, 22.9.7–11). This choice becomes clear when one recalls that, at the time of the First Punic War, the consul Lucius Junius had "recognized" Venus, the mother of Aeneas, in the Aphrodite of Mount Eryx, which he had succeeded in occupying from the start (248 BCE) up till the victorious finish. Thus the dictator who was struggling with the same enemy (the Carthaginians) as before, ought to vow to the same goddess—as a pledge of victory—a temple, which was dedicated in 215 on the Capitolium. It was the "Trojan light" that earned for Venus Erycina, "mother of the Aeneades," this majestic entry to the summit of the Capitolium, which was included at that date within the pomerial zone.

Some ten years later, the oriental goddess Cybele was introduced on the same basis. Once more, marvels had impressed religious awareness: "two suns were seen; intermittent flashes had streaked through the night; a trail of fire reached from east to west. . ." (Livy, 29.14.3). An oracle drawn from the Sibylline Books had predicted "the day when an enemy of foreign race would bring war to Italian soil, he could be defeated and banished from Italy, if the Mater Idaea were carried from Pessinus to Rome" (Livy, 29.10.5). In this way the Magna Mater (alias Cybele), honored as a "Trojan" ancestor despite her primitive nature (she was represented by a black sacred stone), was solemnly received in Rome in 204 BCE and was installed on the Palatine. Until the building of her own temple, which was dedicated in 191 BCE, she was provisionally lodged in the temple of Victoria.

The entry of these two goddesses, understood in terms of the "Trojan light," is instructive on another account as well. In spite of the considerable honors that she accorded them (far from treating them as outsiders, she installed them on the prestigious hills of the Capitoline and the Palatine), Rome did not neglect to subject their cults to discreet censorship. She treated Venus Erycina in two ways: in the temple on the Capitoline (dedicated in 215) she venerated her as a Roman goddess. However, in the extrapomerial temple, built later outside of the Porta Collina and dedicated in 181, she considered her to be a foreign goddess, covered by the statute of the *peregrina sacra* ("foreign rites") which allowed for tolerance of certain original customs. The temple of Venus Erycina outside the Porta Collina admitted, as an extension of the one on Mount Eryx, the presence of prostitutes in imitation of the sacred courtesans on the Sicilian mountain. The restraints were even stricter for the Magna Mater Idaea. Her cult could be practiced only by the Galli, the eunuch-priests, to the exclusion of Roman citizens. It was placed under the police surveillance of the urban praetor.

The affair of the Bacchanals in 186 BCE can be explained in similar fashion. Rome's action was not directed against the god Bacchus when in 186 BCE she forbade the Bacchanalia by a Senate decree. (Engraved on a bronze plaque, this valuable document, found in 1640 in the Abruzzi region, is kept in the Vienna Museum; it is illuminated by the ample report in Livy, 39.8–18.) Bacchus was present not only in Magna Graecia (at Cumae, an inscription dating from the first half of the fifth century establishes the existence of a burial ground reserved for Bacchants) but also in Etruria, where he was rendered as Fufluns, and in Latium, where he was rendered as Liber, the god celebrated in the Liberalia of 17 March. Following a denunciation, alarm had been created by the secret gatherings (Livy, 39.8.3) that reeked of scandals involving both men and women. The Bacchants were accused of taking part in criminal orgies in a milieu marked by "the groans of victims amid debaucheries and murders." The prohibition was dictated out of a concern for public order, the best proof of which is the fact that the Senate decree did not abolish the authorized celebration of the mysteries of Bacchus (for a limited—no more than five—number of participants) on condition of being subject to the permission and control of the officials. In conformity with Roman traditions, the distinction was made between *coniuratio* ("conspiracy") and *religio*.

PUBLIC WORSHIP

The aim of public worship (the *sacra publica*) was to assure or to restore the "benevolence and grace of the gods," which the Romans considered indispensable for the state's well-being. To that end, the calendar days were divided into profane days *(dies profesti)* and days reserved for the gods *(dies festi* or *feriae)*, and thus for liturgical celebrations. [*See* Fasti.] However, if one looks at a Roman calendar, one observes that the list of days contains some other signs. When the days are profane, they are marked by the letter *F (fasti)*; when they pertain to the gods, by *N (nefasti)*. This presentation does not call in question the division of "profane" and "sacred" times. It simply changes the perspective as to when "divine" becomes "human." Indeed, for the Romans, the day is *fastus* when it is *fas* ("religiously licit") to engage in profane occupations, *nefastus* when it is *nefas* ("religiously prohibited") to do so, since the day belongs to the gods. (In reality, the analytical spirit of the pontiffs came up with yet a third category of *C* days *(comitiales)*, which, while profane, lent themselves in addition to the *comitia*, or "assemblies." Further, there are other rarely used letters, such as the three *dies fissi* (half *nefasti*, half *fasti*). The *dies religiosi* (or *atri*) are outside these categories: they are dates that commemorate public misfortunes, such as 18 July, the Dies Alliensis (commemorating the disaster of the battle of Allia in 390 BCE).

The republican calendar (called *fasti*) divided the ferial days over the course of twelve months. Each month was marked by the *calendae* (the first day), the *nonae*, and the *idus* (the last two fell respectively on the fifth or seventh, and the thirteenth or the fifteenth, according to whether they were ordinary months or March, May, July, or October). The feasts were fixed *(stativae)* or movable *(conceptivae)* or organized around some particular circumstance. The letters *(N, F, C)* of the different days, as well as the forty-five most important feasts that stand out in capital letters in the stone calendars, go back to the most ancient period, that of the institution of the lunar-solar calendar attributed to Numa.

The Roman liturgy developed in line with an order of feasts consecrated to particular deities. An overlap was therefore possible: since the ides, "days of full light," were always dedicated to Jupiter, the sacrifice of the Equus October ("horse of October") on 15 December coincided with them. This liturgy was punctuated by the rhythm of seasons for the agrarian celebrations (especially in April and in July-August) and by the schedule of training for military campaigns. Thus it is interesting to note that the month of March contained nearly all the feasts marking the opening of martial activities, just as in the month of October the feasts marked their closing. In March there was registered on the calends a sacrifice to the god Mars; the blessing of horses on the Equirria on 27 February and 14 March; and the blessing of arms on the Quinquatrus and of trumpets on the Tubilustrium on 19 March. In addition, there was the Agonium Martiale on 17 March. The month of October displayed a comparable list. On 1 October, a rite of purification was performed for the Tigillum Sororium; on the ides, the sacrifice of the Equus October offered to Mars; and on 19 October, the Armilustrium, or purification of arms. In both March and October the Salii, carrying lances *(hastae)* and shields *(ancilia)* roamed the city performing martial dances.

The feasts of archaic character continued to be celebrated, while at the same time, the *ritus graecus* produced a more emotional liturgy. The *supplicatio* (organized in 207 BCE, following upon a miracle) in honor of Juno Regina of the Aventine make a particularly memorable impression with an innovation: twenty-seven girls sang a hymn composed especially for the occasion by the poet Livius Andronicus (Livy, 27.37.7–15).

Besides the liturgical feasts, it is also necessary to cite the *ludi*, games consisting essentially of chariot races. They went back to an old tradition represented by the Equirria. The new *ludi* replaced the *bigae*, teams of two horses, with the *quadrigae*, teams of four, for the races in the Circus Maximus and included various performances: riders leaping from one horse to another, fights with wrestlers and boxers. (The gladiator fights, which were Etruscan in origin, appeared in 264 BCE for private funeral feasts, but they did not become part of the public games until the end of the second century BCE.) These competitions were soon complemented by other spectacles: pantomimes and dances accompanied by the flute. The principal ones were the Ludi Magni or Ludi Romani, celebrated from the fifteenth through the eighteenth of September after the ides that coincided with the anniversary of the temple of Jupiter Capitoline. (It is known that an interval, *dies postriduanus*—the fourteenth of September in this instance—had to separate the ides from another feast day.) Considered to have been instituted by Tarquin the Elder (Livy, 1.35.9), they became annual events starting in 367 BCE, which is the date that saw the creation of the curule magistracy *(aediles curules)*. The Ludi Plebei, a kind of plebeian reply to preceding games, were instituted later: they are mentioned for the first time in 216 BCE (Livy, 23.30.17). They took place in the Circus Flaminius, involved the same kind of games as the Ludi Romani, and were celebrated around the time of the ides of November. It is also noteworthy that the Ludi Romani and the Ludi Plebei were both held around the ides (of September or November) and dedicated to Jupiter, to whom a sacrificial meal, the Epulum Jovis, was offered. The public worship was conducted by a corps of specialized priests. While the *rex sacrorum* and the three major *flamines* appeared more and more as archaic characters, the *pontifex maximus* (the last of the ancient *ordo sacerdotum*) became the first in importance under the republic. He was the one to preside over the pontifical college in the Regia, or "king's house" of times past. He was the one to name the *rex sacrorum,* the *flamines maiores,* and the Vestal Virgins. He was attended by a college of pontiffs that grew from three to nine members (the Lex Ogulnia of 300 BCE), then to fifteen (the Lex Cornelia of 82 BCE), and finally to sixteen (the Lex Julia of 46 BCE). He had the upper hand in respect to the calendar, the public rites, and the temple laws.

As for the Vestal Virgins, residing near the Regia in the Atrium Vestae under the direction of a *virgo maxima,* their essential mission was to maintain the public hearth in the Aedes Vestae. They were six in number. Their service lasted thirty years and enjoyed great prestige (Cicero, *Pro Fonteio* 48). Their liturgical importance is confirmed by two significant points. Once a year, they would make their way to the king in order to ask him: "Are you vigilant, king? Be vigilant!" On another solemn occasion, the *virgo maxima* mounted the Capitolium in the company of the *pontifex maximus* (Horace, *Carmina* 3.30.8).

The Augures ("augurs") made up the second college. Their official title served as a clear definition: "The augurs of the state are the interpreters of the almighty Jupiter." In having recourse to the *auspicium,* divination by means of the observation of birds, they discerned the *augurium* (the presence of the heavenly blessing), specifically of the **augus* ("fullness of mystical power" in Georges Dumézil's translation). It also fell upon them to inaugurate both persons (the *rex sacrorum* and the three *flamines maiores*) and buildings *(templa).* Their college's structure evolved like that of the pontifical college: beginning with three, the number of augurs grew to six, to nine (in 300 BCE), then to fifteen (under Sulla), and finally to sixteen (under Julius Caesar).

The *viri sacris faciundis,* "men in charge of the celebration of sacrifices," were responsible for safeguarding and for consulting the Sibylline Books by order of the Senate. There were at first two of them, then ten (beginning in 367 BCE), and finally fifteen. The Epulones were created in 196 BCE in order to relieve the pontiffs of some of their obligations. In particular, it was their duty to organize the sacrificial supper, the Epulum Jovis, at the Ludi Romani and the Ludi Plebei. They numbered three at first, then seven, and finally ten.

The plebeians' access to these four kinds of priesthoods was acquired gradually. The Lex Licinia Sextiae of 367 BCE assigned to them half of the ten seats of the *viri sacris faciundis*. In 300 BCE the Lex Ogulnia admitted the plebeians to a half-share in the colleges of the pontiffs and the augurs. In 103 BCE the Lex Domitia de Sacerdotiis established the principle of election of these priests by seventeen tribes chosen by lot, using a list of candidates presented by each college involved. From then on this method of recruitment was used (instead of co-optation) for the *sacerdotum quattuor amplissima collegia.*

In addition to the four *collegia,* it is worth mentioning the fraternities that, for their part, confirm the liking in Rome for priestly specialization. The twenty Fetiales saw to the protection of Rome in her foreign relations, especially with regard to declarations of war and conclusion of peace treaties. The twenty-four Salii (twelve Salii Palatini and twelve Salii Collini) were the dancer-priests who opened the season of war in March and closed it in October. The twenty-four Luperci (twelve Fabiani and twelve Quinctiales) acted only in the rites of the Lupercalia on 15 February. The twelve Arval Brothers were in charge of the blessing of the fields *(arva)*. They disappeared before the end of the republic but were restored by Augustus. (In their *Acta* they recorded the ancient liturgical chant, known as the *Carmen Arvale*.) [*See* Arval Brothers.]

PRIVATE WORSHIP

The expression *Populus Romanus Quiritium* ("the citizens of Rome") attests in itself to the power of collective bonds: the individual does not exist except as a member of the community. The best proof of it is that the Latin grammarians have insisted on only one instance in which *Quirites* had a singular form: when the citizen left the community through death. Then, "a herald declared in the funeral notice: this Quiris has passed away."

Within this community there were smaller groups such as the *curia,* the *gens,* and the *familia.* It was within the bosom of the family, placed under the authority of the *pater familias,* that the first private forms of worship were celebrated. The day of birth *(dies natalis)* and the day of purification (*dies lustricus:* the ninth day for boys, the eighth for girls, when the infant received its name) were the family feasts. In the atrium of the family home, the infant would acquire the habit of honoring the household gods (the *lar familiaris* and the *di penates*). The allusion made in the *Aulularia* (v. 24s) by Plautus to the young daughter, who every day would bring "some gift such as incense, wine, or garlands" to the *lar familiaris,* shows that personal devotion was not unknown in Rome. Livy (26.19.5) cites a more illustrious example of this kind about P. Cornelius Scipio, the future conqueror of Hannibal. "After he received the *toga virilis,* he undertook no action, whether public or private, without going right away to the Capitolium. Once he reached the sanctuary, he remained there in contemplation, normally all alone in private for some time" (it is true that a rumor attributed divine ancestry to Scipio, something he very carefully neither confirmed nor denied). [*See* Lares.]

The taking of the *toga virilis,* or *pura* (as opposed to the *toga praetexta,* bordered with a purple ribbon and worn by children), generally took place at age seventeen during the feast of the Liberalia on 17 March. Before this point, the *puer* ("boy") had offered his *bulla* (a golden amulet) to the *lar familiaris* (under the republic, the plural *lares familiares* often designated, by way of extension, the group of divinities in the home: Lar, *penates,* Vesta. From then on, he was a *iuvenis.* He would go up to the Capitolium to offer a sacrifice and leave an offering in the sanctuary of the goddess Iuventas. Another family feast occurred on the birthday of the father of the family in honor of his genius. A warm atmosphere brought together the whole family (including the servants) at least twice a year. On 1 March, the feast of the Matronalia, the mothers of families would make their way up the Esquiline to the temple of Juno Lucina, whose anniversary it was. Together with their husbands they prayed "for the safeguarding of their union" and received presents. They themselves then prepared dinner for their slaves. Macrobius (*Saturnalia* 1.12.7), who mentions this custom, adds that on 17 December, the feast of the Saturnalia, it was the masters' turn to serve their slaves, unless they preferred to share dinner with them (*Saturnalia* 1.7.37).

At the end of life, the Feria Denecales (*denecales* or *deni-,* no doubt from *de nece,* "following death") were matched by the Feriae Natales. Their purpose was to purify the family in mourning. For the deceased was regarded as having defiled his family, which thus became *funesta* ("defiled by death"). To this end, a *novemdiale sacrum* was offered on the ninth day after burial. As for the deceased, his body, or a finger thereof kept aside *(os resectum)* in the case of cremation, was buried in a place that become inviolable *(religiosus).* The burial was indispensable in order to assure the repose of the deceased, who from then on was venerated among the *di parentes* (later the *di manes*). (If there were no burial, he risked becoming one of the mischievous spirits, the *lemures,* which the father of the family would expel at midnight on the Lemuria of 9, 11, and 13 May.)

During the Dies Parentales, from the thirteenth to the twenty-first of February, the family would go to the tomb of their dead in order to bring them gifts. [*See* Parentalia.] Since the period of time ended on 21 February with a public feast, the Feralia, the next day, 22 February, reverted to a private feast, the Caristia or Cara Cognatio; the members of the family gathered and comforted one another around a banquet. This explains the compelling need in an old family for legitimate offspring (either by bloodline or by adoption). In their turn, the duty of the descendants was to carry on the family worship and to calm the souls of their ancestors.

BIBLIOGRAPHY

Bayet, Jean. *Histoire politique et psychologique de la religion romaine.* 2d ed. Paris, 1969.

Castagnoli, Ferdinando. *Lavinium.* Vol. 1, *Topografia generale, fonti et storia delle richerche.* Rome, 1972.

Castagnoli, Ferdinando, et al., eds. *Lavinium.* Vol. 2, *Le tredici are.* Rome, 1975.

Catalano, Pierangelo. *Contributi allo studio del diritto augurale.* Vol. 1. Torino, 1960.

Connor, W. R. *Roman Augury and Etruscan Divination.* Salem, N.Y., 1976.

Conway, Robert S. *The Italic Dialects.* 2 vols. Cambridge, 1897. On the Tabula Agnonensis, see pages 191–193. On the Tabula Bantina, see pages 22–29.

Crawford, Michael. *The Roman Republic.* Cambridge, Mass., 1982.

Dumézil, Georges. *Rituels indo-européens à Rome.* Paris, 1954.

Dumézil, Georges. *Déesses latines et mythes védiques.* Brussels, 1956.

Dumézil, Georges. *Idées romaines.* Paris, 1969.

Dumézil, Georges. *La religion romaine archaïque.* 2d ed. Paris, 1974. Translated from the first edition by Philip Krapp as *Archaic Roman Religion,* 2 vols. (Chicago, 1970).

Dumézil, Georges. *Camillus: A Study of Indo-European Religion as Roman History.* Edited by Udo Strutynski and translated by Annette Aronowicz et al. Berkeley, 1980.

Fowler, W. Warde. *The Roman Festivals of the Period of the Republic* (1899). Port Washington, N.Y., 1969.

Fowler, W. Warde. *Religious Experience of the Roman People: From Earliest Times to the Age of Augustus* (1911). Totowa, N.J., 1971.

Latte, Kurt. *Römische Religionsgeschichte.* Munich, 1960.

Marquardt, Joachim. *Le culte chez les Romains.* 2 vols. Paris, 1889–1890.

Michels, Agnes K. *The Calendar of the Roman Republic.* Princeton, 1967.

Mommsen, Theodor. *Römisches Staatsrecht* (1871–1888). 3 vols. Basel, 1952.

Schilling, Robert. *Rites, cultes, dieux de Rome.* Paris, 1979.

Schilling, Robert. "Rome: Les dieux." In *Dictionnaire des mythologies et des religions,* vol. 2. Paris, 1981.

Schilling, Robert. *La religion romaine de Vénus, depuis les origines jusqu'au temps d'Auguste.* 2d ed. Paris, 1982.

Wikander, Stig. "Les '-ismes' dans la terminologie historico-religieuse." In *Les syncrétismes dans les religions grecque et romaine,* pp. 9–14. Paris, 1973.

Wissowa, Georg. *Religion und Kultus der Romer.* 2d ed. Munich, 1912.

12 ROMAN RELIGION OF THE IMPERIAL PERIOD

Arnaldo Momigliano

The Roman state's extraordinary and unexpected transformation from one that had hegemony over the greater part of Italy into a world state in the second and first centuries BCE had implications for Roman religion which are not easy to grasp. After all, Christianity, a religion wholly "foreign" in its origins, arose from this period of Roman ascendancy. To begin, then, to understand the religious system of imperial Rome, it is best to confine ourselves to three elementary and obviously related facts.

The first is that the old Roman practice of inviting the chief gods of their enemies to become gods of Rome *(evocatio)* played little or no part in the new stage of imperialism. *Evocatio* does not seem to have had any role in the wars in Spain, Gaul, and the East; it is mentioned only, and on dubious evidence (Servius, *Ad Aeneidem* 12.841), in relation to Rome's conquest of Carthage.

The second fact is that while it was conquering the Hellenistic world Rome was involved in a massive absorption of Greek language, literature, and religion, with the consequence that the Roman gods became victorious over Greece at precisely the time that they came to be identified with Greek gods. As the gods were expected to take sides and to favor their own worshipers, this must have created some problems.

The third fact is that the conquest of Africa, Spain, and, ultimately, Gaul produced the opposite phenomenon of a large, though by no means systematic, identification of Punic, Iberian, and Celtic gods with Roman gods. This, in turn, is connected with two opposite aspects of the Roman conquest of the West. On the one hand, the Romans had little sympathy and understanding for the religion of their Western subjects. Although occasionally guilty of human sacrifice, they found the various forms of human sacrifices which were practiced more frequently in Africa, Spain, and Gaul repugnant (hence their later efforts to eliminate the druids in Gaul and in Britain). On the other hand, northern Africa, outside Egypt, and western Europe were deeply latinized in language and romanized in institutions, thereby creating the conditions for the assimilation of native gods to Roman gods.

Yet the Mars, the Mercurius, and even the Jupiter and the Diana we meet so frequently in Gaul under the Romans are not exactly the same as in Rome. The individuality of the Celtic equivalent of Mercurius has already been neatly noted by

Caesar. Some Roman gods, such as Janus and Quirinus, do not seem to have penetrated Gaul. Similarly, in Africa, Saturnus preserved much of the Baal Hammon with whom he was identified. There, Juno Caelestis (or simply Caelestis, destined to considerable veneration outside Africa) is Tanit (Tinnit), the female companion of Baal Hammon. The assimilation of the native god is often revealed by an accompanying adjective (in Gaul, Mars Lenus, Mercurius Dumiatis, etc.,). An analogous phenomenon had occurred in the East under the Hellenistic monarchies: native, especially Semitic, gods were assimilated to Greek gods, especially to Zeus and Apollo. The Eastern assimilation went on under Roman rule (as seen, for example, with Zeus Panamaros in Caria).

Roman soldiers, becoming increasingly professional and living among natives for long periods of time, played a part in these syncretic tendencies. A further consequence of imperialism was the emphasis on Victory and on certain gods of Greek origin (such as Herakles and Apollo) as gods of victory. Victoria was already recognized as a goddess during the Samnite Wars; she was later associated with various leaders, from Scipio Africanus to Sulla and Pompey. Roman emperors used an elaborate religious language in their discussions of Victory. Among Christians, Augustine of Hippo depicted Victory as God's angel (*City of God* 4.17).

The Romans also turned certain gods of Greek origin into gods of victory. As early as 145 BCE L. Mummius dedicated a temple to Hercules Victor after his triumph over Greece. After a victory, generals often offered 10 percent of their booty to Hercules, and Hercules Invictus was a favorite god of Pompey. Apollo was connected with Victory as early as 212 BCE. Caesar boosted her ancestress Venus in the form of Venus Victrix. But it was Apollo who helped Octavian, the future Augustus, to win the Battle of Actium in September of 31 BCE.

IMPERIAL ATTITUDES TOWARD AND USES OF RELIGION

Augustus and his contemporaries thought, or perhaps in some cases wanted other people to think, that the preceding age (roughly the period from the Gracchi to Caesar) had seen a decline in the ancient Roman care for gods. Augustus himself stated in the autobiographical record known as the *Res gestae* that he and his friends had restored eighty-two temples. He revived cults and religious associations, such as the Arval Brothers and the fraternity of the Titii, and appointed a *flamen dialis,* a priestly office that had been left vacant since 87 BCE. This revivalist feeling was not entirely new: it was behind the enormous collection of evidence concerning ancient Roman cults, the "divine antiquities," which Varro had dedicated to Caesar about 47 BCE in his *Antiquitatum rerum humanarum et divinarum libri*; the rest of the work, the "human antiquities," was devoted to Roman political institutions and customs. Varro's work became as much a codification of Roman religion for succeeding generations as existed, and as such it was used for polemical purposes by Christian apologists; it was, however, never a guide for ordinary worshipers.

For us, inevitably, it is difficult to do justice at the same time to the mood of the Augustan restoration and to the unquestionable seriousness with which the political and military leaders of the previous century tried to support their unusual adventures by unusual religious attitudes. Marius, a devotee of the Magna Mater (Cybele), was accompanied in his campaigns by a Syrian prophetess. Sulla apparently brought from Cappadocia the goddess Ma, soon identified with Bellona, whose orgiastic and prophetic cult had wide appeal. Furthermore, he developed a personal devotion to Venus and Fortuna and set an example for Caesar, who claimed Venus as the ancestress of the *gens Julia*. As *pontifex maximus* for twenty years, Caesar reformed not only individual cults but also the calendar, which had great religious significance. He tried to support his claim to dictatorial powers by collecting religious honors which, though obscure in detail and debated by modern scholars, anticipate later imperial cult.

Unusual religious attitudes were not confined to leaders. A Roman senator, Nigidius Figulus, made religious combinations of his own both in his writings and in his practice: magic, astrology, and Pythagoreanism were some of the ingredients. Cicero, above all, epitomized the search of educated men of the first century BCE for the right balance between respect for the ancestral cults and the requirements of philosophy. Cicero could no longer believe in traditional divination. When his daughter died in 45 BCE he embarked briefly on a project for making her divine. This was no less typical of the age than the attempt by Clodius in 62 BCE to desecrate the festival of Bona Dea, reserved to women, in order to contact Caesar's wife; he escaped punishment.

The imperial age was inclined to distinctions and to compromises. The Roman *pontifex maximus* Q. Mucius Scaevola is credited with the popularization of the distinction, originally Greek, between the gods of the poets as represented in myths, the gods of ordinary people to be found in cults and sacred laws, and finally the gods of the philosophers, confined to books and private discussion. It was the distinction underlying the thought of Varro and Cicero. No wonder, therefore, that in that atmosphere of civil wars and personal hatreds, cultic rules and practices were exploited ruthlessly to embarrass enemies while no one could publicly challenge the ultimate validity of traditional practices.

The Augustan restoration discouraged philosophical speculation about the nature of the gods: Lucretius's *De rerum natura* remains characteristic of the age of Caesar. Augustan poets (Horace, Tibullus, Propertius, and Ovid) evoked obsolescent rites and emphasized piety. Vergil interpreted the Roman past in religious terms. Nevertheless, the combined effect of the initiatives of Caesar and Augustus amounted to a new religious situation.

For centuries the aristocracy in Rome had controlled what was called *ius sacrum* ("sacred law"), the religious aspect of Roman life, but the association of priesthood with political magistracy, though frequent and obviously convenient, had never been institutionalized. In 27 BCE the assumption by Octavian of the permanent title *augustus* implied, though not very clearly, permanent approval of the gods (*augustus* may connote a holder of permanent favorable auspices). In 12 BCE Augustus assumed the position of *pontifex maximus,* which became permanently associated with the figure of the emperor *(imperator),* the new head for life of the Roman state. Augustus's new role resulted in an identification of religious with political power, which had not existed in Rome since at least the end of the monarchy. Furthermore, the divinization of Caesar after his death had made Augustus, as his adoptive son, the son of a *divus.* In turn Augustus was officially divinized *(apotheosis)* after his death by the Roman Senate. Divinization after death did not become automatic for his successors (Tiberius, Gaius, and Nero were not divinized); nevertheless, Augustus's divinization created a presumption that there was a divine component in an ordinary emperor who had not misbehaved in his lifetime. [*See* Augustus.] It also reinforced the trend toward the cult of the living emperor, which had been most obvious during Augustus's life. With the Flavian dynasty and later with the Antonines, it was normal for the head of the Roman state to be both the head of the state religion and a potential, or even actual, god.

As the head of Roman religion, the Roman emperor was therefore in the paradoxical situation of being responsible not only for relations between the Roman state and the gods but also for a fair assessment of his own qualifications to be considered a god, if not after his life, at least while he was alive. This situation, however, must not be assumed to have applied universally. Much of the religious life in individual towns was in the hands of local authorities or simply left to private initiative. The financial support for public cults was in any case very complex, too complex to be discussed here. It will be enough to mention that the Roman state granted or confirmed to certain gods in certain sanctuaries the right to receive legacies (Ulpian, *Regulae* 22.6). In providing money for a local shrine an emperor implied no more than benevolence toward the city or group involved.

Within the city of Rome, however, the emperor was in virtual control of the public cults. As a Greek god, Apollo had been kept outside of the *pomerium* since his introduction into Rome: his temple was in the Campus Martius. Under Augustus, however, Apollo received a temple inside the *pomerium* on the Palatine in recognition of the special protection he had offered to Octavian. The Sibylline Books, an ancient collection of prophecies that had been previously preserved on the Capitol, were now transferred to the new temple. Later, Augustus demonstrated his preference for Mars as a family god, and a temple to Mars Ultor (the avenger of Caesar's murder) was built. It was no doubt on the direct initiative of Hadrian that the cult of Rome as a goddess (in association with Venus) was finally introduced into the city centuries after the cult had spread outside of Italy. A temple to the Sun (Sol), a cult popular in the empire at large, and not without some roots in the archaic religion of Rome, had to wait until the emperor Aurelian in 274 CE, if one discounts the cult of the Ba'al of Emesa, a sun god, which came and went with the emperor Elagabalus in 220–221. Another example of these changes inside Rome is the full romanization of the Etruscan haruspices performed by the emperor Claudius in 47 CE (Tacitus, *Annals* 11.15).

A further step in the admission of Oriental gods to the official religion of Rome was the building of a temple to Isis under Gaius. The cult of Isis had been contested and ultimately confined outside the *pomerium,* associated as it was with memories of Cleopatra, the Egyptian enemy of Augustus. Jupiter Dolichenus, an Oriental god popular among soldiers, was probably given a temple on the Aventine in the second century CE.

We have some evidence that the Roman priestly colleges intervened in the cults of *municipia* and *coloniae,* but on the whole we cannot expect the cults of Rome herself to remain exemplary for Roman citizens living elsewhere. For example, Vitruvius, who dedicated his work on architecture to Octavian before the latter became Augustus in 27, assumes that in an Italian city there should be a temple to Isis and Sarapis (*De architectura* 1.7.1); Isis, we know, was kept out of Rome in those years. Caracalla, however, presented his grant of Roman citizenship to the provincials in 212 CE in hope of contributing to religious unification (*Papyrus Giessen* 40). Although the cult of the Capitoline triad appears in Egypt, the results of this grant were modest in religious terms.

Coins and medals, insofar as they were issued under the control of the central government, provide some indication of imperial preferences in the matter of gods and cults. They allow us to say when and how certain Oriental cults (such as that of Isis, as reflected on coins of Vespasian) or certain attributes of a specific god were considered helpful to the empire and altogether suitable for the man in the street who used coins. But since as a rule it avoided references to cults of rulers, coinage can be misleading if taken alone. Imperial cult and Oriental cults are, in fact, two of the most important features of Roman religion in the imperial period. But we also have to take into consideration popular, not easily definable trends; the religious beliefs or disbeliefs of the intellectuals; the greater participation of women in religious and in intellectual life generally; and, finally, the peculiar problems presented by the persecution of Christianity.

THE IMPERIAL CULT

Imperial cult was many things to many people. The emperor never became a complete god, even if he was considered a god, because he was not requested to produce miracles, even for supposed deliverance from peril. Vespasian performed miracles in Alexandria soon after his proclamation as emperor, but these had no precise connection to his potential divine status; he remained an exception in any case. Hadrian never performed miracles, but his young lover Antinoüs, who was divinized after death, is known to have performed some (F. K. Dörner, *Denkschriften der Wiener Akademie* 75, 1952, p. 40, no. 78).

Apotheosis, decided by the Senate, was the only official form of deification valid for everyone in the empire and was occasionally extended to members of the imperial family (Drusilla, the sister of Gaius, received apotheosis in 38 CE.) It had its precedent, of course, in the apotheosis of Romulus. [*See also* Apotheosis.] Ultimately, the cult of the living emperor mattered more. [*See* Emperor's Cult.] It was the result of a mixture of spontaneous initiative by provincial and local councils (and even by private individuals) and promptings from provincial governors and the emperor himself. It had precedents not only in the Hellenistic ruler cult but also in the more or less spontaneous worship of Roman generals and governors, especially in the hellenized East. Cicero, for example, had to decline such worship when he was a provincial governor (*Ad Atticum* 5.21.7).

The cult of Roman provincial governors disappeared with Augustus, to the exclusive benefit of the emperor and his family. When he did not directly encourage the ruler cult, the emperor still had to approve, limit, and occasionally to refuse it. Although he had to be worshiped, he also had to remain a man in order to live on social terms with the Roman aristocracy, of which he was supposed to be the *princeps*. It was a delicate balancing act. It is probably fair to say that during his lifetime the emperor was a god more in proportion to his remoteness, rather than his proximity, and that the success (for success it was) of the imperial cult in the provinces was due to the presence it endowed to an absent and alien sovereign. His statues, his temples, and his priests, as well as the games, sacrifices, and other ceremonial acts, helped make the emperor present; they also helped people to express their interest in the preservation of the world in which they lived.

The imperial cult was not universally accepted and liked. Seneca ridiculed the cult of Claudius, and Tacitus spoke of the cult in general as Greek adulation. In the third century the historian Dio Cassius attributed to Augustus's friend Maecenas a total condemnation of the imperial cult. Jews and Christians objected to it on principle, and the acts of the Christian martyrs remind us that there was an element of brutal imposition in the imperial cult. [*See* Persecution, *article on* Christian Experience.] But its controversial nature in certain circles may well have been another factor of the cult's success: conflicts help any cause. There is even some vague evidence (Pleket, 1965, p. 331) that some groups treated the imperial cult as a mystery religion in which priests revealed some secrets about the emperors.

Schematically it can be said that in Rome and Italy Augustus favored the association of the cult of his life spirit *(genius)* with the old cult of the public *lares* of the crossroads *(lares compitales):* such a combined cult was in the hands of humble people. Similar associations (Augustales) developed along various lines in Italy and gave respectability to the freedmen who ran them. Augustus's birthday was considered a public holiday. His *genius* was included in public oaths between Jupiter Optimus Maximus and the *penates.* In Augustus's last years Tiberius dedicated an altar to the *numen Augusti* in Rome; the four great priestly colleges had to make yearly sacrifices at it. *Numen,* in an obscure way, implied divine will.

In the West, central initiative created the altar of Roma and Augustus in Lyons, to be administered by the Council of the Gauls (12 BCE). A similar altar was built at Oppidum Ubiorum (Cologne). Later temples to Augustus (by then officially divinized) were erected in Western provinces. In the East, temples to Roma and Divus Julius and to Roma and Augustus were erected as early as 29 BCE. There, as in the West, provincial assemblies took a leading part in the establishment of the cult. Individual cities were also active: priests of Augustus are found in thirty-four different cities of Asia Minor. The organization of the cult varied locally. There was no collective provincial cult of the emperor in Egypt, though there was a cult in Alexandria. And any poet, indeed any man, could have his own idea about the divine nature of the emperor. Horace, for example, suggested that Augustus might be Mercurius.

Augustus's successors tended to be worshiped either individually, without the addition of Roma, or collectively with past emperors. In Asia Minor the last individual emperor known to have received a personal priesthood or temple is Caracalla. In this province—though not necessarily elsewhere—the imperial cult petered out at the end of the third century. Nevertheless, Constantine, in the fourth century, authorized the building of a temple for the *gens Flavia* (his own family) in Italy at Hispellum, but without "contagion of superstition"—whatever he may have meant by this (*Corpus inscriptionum Latinarum,* Berlin, 1863, vol. 11, no. 5265).

It is difficult to say how much the ceremonial of the imperial court reflected divinization of the emperors. We hear, however, that Domitian wanted to be called "dominus et deus" (Suetonius, *Domitian* 13.2). In the third century a specific identification of the living emperor with a known god seems to be more frequent (for instance, Septimius Severus and his wife, Julia Domna, with Jupiter and Juno). When the imperial cult died out, the emperor had to be justified as the choice of god; he became emperor by the grace of god. Thus Diocletian and Maximian, the persecutors of Christianity, present themselves not as Jupiter and Hercules but as Jovius and Herculius, that is, the protégés of Jupiter and Hercules. It must be added that during the first centuries of the empire the divinization of the emperor was accompanied by a multiplication of divinizations of private individuals, in the West often of humble origin. Such divinization took the form of identifying the dead, and occasionally the living, with a known hero or god. Sometimes the divinization was nothing more than an expression of affection by relatives or friends. But it indicated a tendency to reduce the distance between men and gods, which helped the fortunes of the imperial cult. We need to know more about private divinizations (but see Henning Wrede, *Consecratio in formam deorum,* Mainz, 1981).

ORIENTAL INFLUENCES

Oriental cults penetrated the Roman empire at various dates, in different circumstances, and with varying appeal, although on the whole they seem to have supplemented religious needs in the Latin West more than in the hellenized East. They tended, though not in equal measure, to present themselves as mystery cults: they often required initiation and, perhaps more often, some religious instruction.

Cybele, the first Oriental divinity to be found acceptable in Rome since the end of the third century BCE, was long an oddity in the city. As the Magna Mater ("great mother"), she had been imported by governmental decision, she had a temple within the *pomerium,* and she was under the protection of members of the highest Roman aristocracy. Yet her professional priests, singing in Greek and living by their temple, were considered alien fanatics even in imperial times. What is worse, the goddess also had servants, the Galli, who had castrated themselves to express their devotion to her. [*See also* Cybele.]

Under the emperor Claudius, Roman citizens were probably allowed some priestly functions, though the matter is very obscure. Even more obscure is the way in which Attis, who is practically absent from the republican written evidence concerning Cybele, became Cybele's major partner. A new festival, from 15 to 27 March, apparently put special emphasis on the resurrection of Attis. Concurrently, the cult of Cybele became associated with the ritual of the slaying of the sacred bull *(taurobolium),* which Prudentius (*Peristephanon* 10. 1006–1050) interpreted as a baptism of blood. The ritual was performed for the prosperity of the emperor or of the empire and, more frequently, for the benefit of private individuals. Normally it was considered valid for twenty years, which makes it questionable whether it was meant to confer immortality on the baptized.

Although Isis appealed to men as well as to women— and indeed her priests were male—it seems clear that her prestige as a goddess was due to the unusual powers she was supposed to have as a woman. The so-called aretalogies (description of the powers) of Isis insist on this. Thus the earliest aretalogy, found at Maroneia in Macedonia, tells of Isis as legislator and as protector of the respect of children for their parents (Merkelbach, 1976, p. 234). The Kyme text declares that she compelled husbands to love their wives (H. Engelmann, ed., *Kyme* 1.97), and the Oxyrhynchus hymn in her honor explicitly states that she made the power of women equal to that of men (*Oxyrhynchus Papyri* 11.1380). No god or goddess of Greece and Rome had achievements comparable with those of Isis. The girlfriends of the Augustan poets Tibullus and Propertius were captivated by her. In association with Osiris or Sarapis, Isis seems to have become the object of a mystery cult in the first century CE; as such she appears in Apuleius's *Metamorphoses.* [*See also* Isis.]

Late in the first century CE, Mithraism began to spread throughout the Roman empire, especially in the Danubian countries and in Italy (in particular, as far as we know, in Ostia and Rome). A developed mystery cult, it had ranks of initiation and leadership and was, to the best of our present knowledge, reserved to men—a clear difference from the cult of Isis. It was practiced in subterranean chapels rather than in temples, although his identification with the sun god gave Mithra some temples. The environment of the Mithraic cult, as revealed in numerous extant chapels, was one of darkness, secrecy, dramatic lighting effects, and magic.

What promise Mithra held for his devotees we do not know for certain. The cult seems to have encouraged soldierly qualities, including sexual abstinence. It certainly presented some correspondence between the degrees of initiation and the levels of the celestial spheres, which may or may not imply an ascent of the soul to these spheres. The killing of the bull (in itself different from the *taurobolium* and perhaps without any implication of baptism) was apparently felt to be a sacrifice performed not for the god but by the god. The initiates reenacted this sacrifice and shared sacred meals in a sort of communal life. Tertullian considered Mithraism a devilish imitation of Christianity, but the Neoplatonist Porphyry found in it allegorical depths. [*See also* Mithra; Mithraism; *and* Mystery Religions.]

The cult of Sabazios may have been originally Phrygian. Sabazios appears in Athens in the fifth century BCE as an orgiastic god. He was known to Aristophanes, and later the orator Aeschines became his priest. There is evidence of mysteries of Sabazios in Lydia dating from the fourth century BCE. In Rome the cult was already known in 139 BCE. It may at that time have been confused with Judaism, but Sabazios was often identified with Jupiter or Zeus, and there seems to be no clear evidence of syncretism between Sabazios and Yahveh. Sabazios was most popular in the second century CE, especially in the Danubian region. [*See* Sabazios.] In Rome his cult left a particularly curious document in the tomb of Vincentius, located in the catacomb of Praetextatus; it includes scenes of banquets and of judgment after death. Whether this is evidence of mystery ceremonies or of Christian influence remains uncertain. (See Erwin R. Goodenough, *Jewish Symbols in the Greco-Roman Period*, vol. 2, 1953, p. 45, for a description.) The tomb of Vincentius appears to belong to the third century, when, judging by the epigraphic evidence, there seems to have been a decline of the cult of Sabazios and, indeed, of all mystery cults. Although a shortage of inscriptions does not necessarily imply a shortage of adepts, one has the impression that by then Christianity was seriously interfering with the popularity of Oriental cults.

Another popular Oriental god occupies a place by himself. This is Jupiter Dolichenus, who emerged from Doliche in Commagene in the first century CE and for whom we have about six hundred monuments. Of the Oriental gods, he seems to have been the least sophisticated and to have disappeared earliest (in the third century). He was ignored by Christian polemicists. While he circulated in the empire, he preserved his native attributes: he is depicted as a warrior with Phrygian cap, double ax, and lightning bolt, standing erect over a bull. He was often accompanied by a goddess, called Juno Regina in the Roman interpretation. Twins, identified with the Castores, followed him; their lower parts were unshaped, and they were probably demons. Soldiers seem to have loved the cult of Jupiter Dolichenus. Its priests were not professional, and the adepts called each other brother. Admission to the cult presupposed instruction, if not initiation.

EXTENT OF SYNCRETISM

We are in constant danger of either overrating or underrating the influence of these Oriental cults on the fabric of the Roman empire. If, for instance, Mithraists knew of the Zoroastrian deity Angra Mainyu, what did he mean to them? How did this knowledge affect the larger society? At a superficial level we can take these cults as an antidote to the imperial cult, an attempt to retreat from the public sphere of political allegiance to the private sphere of small, free associations. The need for small loyalties was widely felt during the imperial peace. Distinctions between social, charitable, and religious purposes in these multiform associations are impossible. Tavern keepers devoted to their wine god and poor people meeting regularly in burial clubs are examples of such associations *(collegia)*. Ritualization of ordinary life emerged from their activities. Nor is it surprising that what to one was religion was superstition to another (to use two Latin terms which ordinary Latin speakers would have been hard-pressed to define). Although allegiance to the local gods (and respect for them, if one happened to be a visitor) was deeply rooted, people were experimenting with new private gods and finding satisfaction in them. Concern with magic and astrology, with dreams and demons, seems ubiquitous. Conviviality was part of religion. Aelius Aristides has good things to say about Sarapis as patron of the *symposium*. Pilgrimages to sanctuaries were made easier by relative social stability. Several gods, not only Asclepius (Gr., Asklepios), offered healing to the sick. (Here again we have Aelius Aristides as chief witness for the second century.) Hence miracles, duly registered in inscriptions; hence also single individuals, perhaps cranks, attaching themselves to temples and living in their precincts.

The real difficulties in understanding the atmosphere of paganism in the Roman empire perhaps lie elsewhere. It remains a puzzle how, and how much, ordinary people were supposed to know about official Roman religion. The same problem exists concerning the Greeks in relation to the religions of individual Greek cities. But in Greek cities the collective education of adolescents, as *epheboi,* implied participation in religious activities (for instance, singing hymns in festivals) which were a form of religious education. In the Latin-speaking world, however, there is no indication of generalized practices of this kind. People who tell us something about their own education, for example, Cicero, Horace, and Ovid, do not imply that it included a religious side. The situation does not seem to have changed in later times, as illustrated, for instance, in Tacitus's life of Agricola. Children at school no doubt absorbed a great deal from classical authors, but whether they read Homer or Vergil, they did not absorb the religion of their own city. Temples carried inscriptions explaining what was expected from worshipers as well as the qualities of the relevant god. Cultic performances, often in a theater adjoining the temple, helped to explain what the god was capable of. We cannot, however, draw a distinguishing line between cultic performances, perhaps with an element of initiation, and simple entertainment.

Another element difficult to evaluate is the continuous, and perhaps increased, appeal of impersonal gods within Roman religion. There is no indication that Faith (Fides) and Hope (Spes) increased their appeal. (They came to play a different part in Christianity by combining with Jewish and Greek ideas.) At best, Fides gained prestige as a symbol of return to loyalty and good faith during the reign of Augustus. But Fortuna, Tutela, and Virtus were popular; the typology of Virtus on coins seems to be identical with that of Roma. Genius was generalized to indicate the spirit of a place or of a corporation. Strangely, an old Latin god of the woods, Silvanus, whose name does not appear in the Roman calendar, became important, partly because of his identification with the Greek Pan and with a Pannonian god but above all because of his equation with Genius: we find the god protector of Roman barracks called Genius Castrorum or Silvanus Castrorum or Fortuna Castrorum. Victoria, too, was often connected with individual emperors and individual victories (Victoria Augusti, Ludi Victoriae Claudi, etc.).

A third element of complication is what is called syncretism, by which we really mean two different things. One is the positive identification of two or more gods; the other is the tendency to mix different cults by using symbols of other gods in the sanctuary of one god, with the result that the presence of Sarapis, Juno, and even Isis was implied in the shrine of Jupiter Dolichenus on the Aventine in Rome. In either form, syncretism may have encouraged the idea that all gods are aspects, or manifestations, of one god. [*See* Syncretism.]

Vaguely monotheistic attitudes were in any case encouraged by philosophical reflection, quite apart from suggestions coming from Judaism, Christianity, and Zoroastrianism. It is therefore legitimate to consider the cult of Sol Invictus, patronized by Aurelian, as a monotheistic or henotheistic predecessor of Christianity. But believers had to visualize the relation between the one and the many. This relation was complicated by the admission of intermediate demons, either occupying zones between god or gods and men or going about the earth and perhaps more capable of evil than of good. Even those who could think through, in some depth, the idea of one god (such as Plutarch) were still interested in Zeus or Isis or Dionysos, whatever their relation to the god beyond the gods. Those educated people who in late antiquity liked to collect priesthoods and initiations to several gods, in pointed contrast with Christianity, evidently did so because they did not look upon the gods concerned as one god only. The classic example of such a person is given by the inscription concerning Vettius Agorius Praetextatus dated 385 CE (*Corpus inscriptionum Latinarum*, Berlin, 1863, vol. 6, no. 1779).

This is not to deny the convergence of certain beliefs and experiences. To quote only an extreme case, a mystical experience like ascension to heaven was shared by Paul, Jewish rabbis, gnostics such as the author of the *Gospel of Truth*, and Plotinus.

ROLE OF WOMEN

Women seem to have taken a more active, and perhaps a more creative, part in the religious life of the imperial period. This was connected with the considerable freedom of movement and of administration of one's own estate which women, and especially wealthy women, had in the Roman empire. Roman empresses of Oriental origin (Julia Domna, wife of Septimius Severus, and Julia Mamaea, mother of Severus Alexander) contributed to the diffusion outside Africa of the cult of Caelestis, who received a temple on the Capitol in Rome. The wife of a Roman consul, Pompeia Agrippinilla, managed to put together a private association of about four hundred devotees of Liber-Dionysos in the Roman Campagna in the middle of the second century CE. (See the inscription published by Achille Vogliano in the *American Journal of Archaeology* 37, 1933, p. 215.) Women could be asked to act as *theologoi*, that is, to preach about gods in ceremonies even of a mystery nature. We have seen that Isis appealed to, and was supported by, women. It is revealing that Marcus Aurelius declared himself grateful to his mother for teaching him veneration of the gods.

The intellectual and religious achievements of women become more conspicuous in the fourth century. Women such as Sosipatra, described in Eunapius's account of the lives of the Sophists, and Hypatia of Alexandria are the counterparts (though apparently more broadly educated and more independent in their social actions) of Christian women such as Macrina, sister of Gregory of Nyssa (who wrote her biography), and the followers of Jerome. We are not surprised to find in the city of Thasos during the late Roman empire a woman with a resounding Latin name, Flavia Vibia Sabina, honored by the local Senate "as a most noteworthy high priestess . . . the only woman, first in all times to have honours equal to those of the senators" (H. W. Pleket, *Texts on the Social History of the Greek World,* 1969, no. 29).

Dedications of religious and philosophical books by men to women appear in the imperial period. Plutarch dedicated his treatise on Isis and Osiris to Clea, a priestess of Delphi; Diogenes Laertius dedicated his book on Greek philosophers (which has anti-Christian implications) to a female Platonist. Philostratus claims that Julia Domna encouraged him to write the life of Apollonius of Tyana. What is more, Bishop Hippolytos apparently wrote a book on resurrection dedicated to the pagan Julia Mamaea. We know from Eusebius that this same woman invited Origen to visit her in Antioch, obviously to discuss Christianity.

LITERARY EVIDENCE

Epigraphy and archaeology have taught us much, but the religion of the Roman empire survives mainly through writings in Latin, Greek, Syriac, and Coptic (not to speak of other languages): biographies, philosophical disputations, epic poems, antiquarian books, exchanges of letters, novels, and specific religious books. Most of the authors speak only for themselves. But taken together, they convey an atmosphere of sophisticated cross-questioning which would have prevented minds from shutting out alternatives or concentrating solely on ritual. We can only give examples. The Stoic Lucan in his *Pharsalia,* a poem on the civil wars, excludes the gods but admits fate and fortune, magic and divination. Two generations later, Silius Italicus wrote an optimistic poem, turning on Scipio as a Roman Herakles supported by his father, Jupiter. More or less at the same time, Plutarch was reflecting on new and old cults, on the delays in divine justice, and (if the work in question is indeed his) on superstition.

In the second part of the second century Lucian passed from the caricature of an assembly of gods and from attacks against oracles to a sympathetic description of the cult of Dea Syria; he abused such religious fanatics as Peregrinus, as well as Alexander of Abonuteichos, the author of a cult, whom he considered to be an impostor. Perhaps what Lucian wanted to give is, in fact, what we get from him— the impression of a mind that refuses to be imposed upon. Fronto's correspondence with Marcus Aurelius confirms what we deduce from other texts (such as Aelius Aristides' speeches): preoccupation with one's own health was a source of intense religious experience in the second century CE. Apuleius, in *De magia,* gives a glimpse of a small African community in which suspicion of magic practices can upset the town (as well as the author). In *Metamorphoses*, also known as *The Golden Ass*, Apuleius offers an account of the mysteries of Isis which may be based on personal experiences. But Apuleius's *Golden Ass* is only one of the many novels which were fashionable in the Roman empire. The appeal of such novels probably resided in their ability to offer readers vicarious experiences of love, magic, and mystery ritual.

The variety of moods and experiences conveyed by these texts, from the skeptical to the mystical, from the egotistic to the political in the old Greek sense, gives us an approximate notion of the thoughts of educated people on religious subjects. These books provide the background for an understanding of the Christian apologists who wrote for the pagan upper class. Conversely, we are compelled to ask how much of pagan religious thinking was conditioned by the presence of Jews and, even more, of Christians in the neighborhood. The anti-Jewish attitudes of a Tacitus or of a Juvenal offer no special problem: they are explicit. The same can be said about the anti-Christian polemics of Celsus; here the problem, if any, is that the text is lost and we are compelled to make inferences from the reply given in changed circumstances by the Christian Origen. But there are far more writers who seldom or never refer to Christianity yet can hardly have formulated their thoughts without implicit reference to it.

How much Lucian or Philostratus (in his life of Apollonius of Tyana) was trying to put across pagan points of view in answer to the Christian message is an old question. The biography of Philostratus was translated into Latin by a pagan leader, Nicomachus Flavianus, in the late fourth century. Another author who may be suspected of knowing more about Christianity than his silence about it would indicate is Diogenes Laertius. In his lives of philosophers, he pointedly refuses to admit non-Greek wisdom and enumerates all the Greek schools, from Plato to Epicurus, as worthy of study and admiration. With the renascence of Neoplatonic thought in the third and fourth centuries and the combination of Platonism with mystical and magical practices (the so-called theurgy) in the circles to which Julian the Apostate belonged, the attempt to erect a barrier to Christianity is patent but, even then, not necessarily explicit.

The most problematic texts are perhaps those which try to formulate explicit religious beliefs. Even a simple military religious calendar (such as the third-century Feriale Duranum, copied for the benefit of the garrison of Dura-Europos) raises the question of its purpose and validity: how many of these old-fashioned Roman festivals were still respected? When we come to such books as the *Chaldean Oracles* (late second century?) or the Hermetic texts, composed in Greek at various dates in Egypt (and clearly showing the influence of Jewish ideas), it is difficult to decide who believed in them and to what extent. Such texts present themselves as revealed: they speak of man's soul imprisoned in the body, of fate, and of demonic power with only a minimum of coherence. They are distantly related to what modern scholars call gnosticism, a creed with many variants which was supposed to be a deviation from Christianity and, as such, was fought by early Christian apologists. We now know much more about gnostics, thanks to the discovery of the Nag Hammadi library, which supplemented, indeed dwarfed, previous discoveries of Coptic gnostic texts. Assembled in the fourth century from books mainly translated from Greek, the Nag Hammadi library represents an isolated survival. It points to a previous, more central movement thriving in the exchange of ideas. Can we assess the impact of the gnostic sects when they placed themselves between pagans and Christians (and Jews) in the first centuries of the empire? [SeeGnosticism *and* Hermetism.]

STATE REPRESSION AND PERSECUTION

The Roman state had always interfered with the freedom to teach and worship. In republican times astrologers, magicians, philosophers, and even rhetoricians, not to speak of adepts of certain religious groups, had been victims of such intrusion. Under which precise legal category this interference was exercised remains a question, except perhaps in cases of sacrilege. From Tacitus we know that Augustus considered adultery in his own family a crime of *laesa religio* (*Annals* 3.24). Whatever the legal details, there was persecution of druidic cults and circles in Gaul and Britain in the first century. Augustus prohibited Roman citizens from participating in druidic cults, and Claudius prohibited the cult of the druids altogether. Details are not clear, and consequences not obvious, though one hears little of the druids from this time on. Abhorrence of druidic human sacrifices no doubt counted for much. But Augustus also did not like the practice of foretelling the future, for which the druids were conspicuous, and he is credited with the destruction of two thousand *fatidici libri* (Suetonius, *Augustus* 31). The druids were also known to be magicians, and Claudius condemned to death a Roman knight who had brought to court a druidic magic egg (Pliny, *Natural History* 29.54). [*See also* Druids.]

This being said, we must emphasize how unusual it was for the Roman government to come to such decisions. Existing cults might or might not be encouraged, but they were seldom persecuted. Even Jews and Egyptians were ordinarily protected in their cults, although there were exceptions. The long-standing conflict between the Christians and the Roman state—even taking into account that persecution was desultory—remains unique for several reasons which depended more on Christian than on imperial behavior. First, the Christians obviously did not yield or retreat, as did the druids. Second, the Christians hardly ever became outright enemies of, or rebels against, the Roman state. The providential character of the Roman state was a basic assumption of Christianity. The workings of providence were shown, for Christians, by the fact that Jesus was born under Roman rule, while the Roman state had destroyed the Temple of Jerusalem and dispersed the Jews, thus making the church the heiress to the Temple. Third, the Christians were interested in what we may call classical culture. Their debate with the pagans became, increasingly, a debate within the terms of reference of classical culture; the Jews, however, soon lost their contact with classical thought and even with such men as Philo, who had represented them in the dialogue with classical culture. Fourth, Christianity and its ecclesiastical organization provided what could alternatively be either a rival or a subsidiary structure to the imperial government; the choice was left to the Roman government, which under Constantine chose the church as a subsidiary institution (without quite knowing on what conditions). [*See* Constantinianism.].

The novelty of the conflict explains the novelty of the solution—not tolerance but conversion. The emperor had to become Christian and to accept the implications of his conversion. It took about eighty years to turn the pagan state into a Christian state. The process took the form of a series of decisions about public non-Christian acts of worship. The first prohibition of pagan sacrifices seems to have been enacted in 341 (*Codex Theodosianus* 16.10.2). Closing of the pagan temples and prohibition of sacrifices in public places under penalty of death was stated or restated at an uncertain date between 346 and 354 (ibid., 16.10.4).

Even leaving aside the reaction of Julian, these measures cannot have been effective. The emperor remained *pontifex maximus* until Gratian gave up the position in 379 (Zosimus, 4.36.5). Gratian was the emperor who removed the altar of Victoria from the Roman Senate and provoked the controversy between Symmachus and Bishop Ambrose, the most important controversy about the relative merits of tolerance and conversion in late antiquity. Then, in 391, Theodosius forbade even the private pagan cult (*Codex Theodosianus* 16.10.12). In the same year, following riots provoked by a special law against pagan cults in Egypt, the Serapeum of Alexandria was destroyed, an act whose significance was felt worldwide. The brief pagan revival of 393, initiated by the usurper Eugenius, a nominal Christian who sympathized with the pagans, was soon followed by other antipagan laws. Pagan priests were deprived of their privileges in 396 (ibid., 16.10.4). Pagan temples in the country (not in towns) were ordered to be destroyed in 399 (ibid., 16.10.16). But in the same year festivals which appear pagan to us were allowed (ibid., 16.10.17).

No doubt the Christians knew how and where they could proceed to direct action. The economic independence and traditional prestige of local pagan aristocrats, especially in Rome, allowed them to survive for a time and to go on elaborating pagan thought, as we can see from Macrobius's *Saturnalia* and even from Boethius's *The Consolation of Philosophy,* although Boethius was technically a Christian who knew his Christian texts. The Neoplatonists of Athens had to be expelled by Justinian in 529. But in Africa Synesius became the first Neoplatonist to be baptized in the early fifth century (c. 403–410).

Hopes that the pagan gods would come back excited the Eastern provinces during the rebellion against the emperor Zeno in about 483, in which the pagan rhetorician and poet Pampremius had a prominent part (Zacharias of Mitylene, *Vita Severi,* in *Patrologia Orient.* 2.1.40; M. A. Kugener, ed., Paris, 1903). The peasants *(rustici),* about whom Bishop Martin of Bracara in Spain had so many complaints, gave more trouble to the ecclesiastical authorities than did the philosophers and the aristocrats of the cities. Sacrifices, just because they were generally recognized as efficient ways of persuading the gods to act, were at the center of Christian suspicion. According to a widespread opinion shared by the apostle Paul (but not by all the church fathers) pagan gods existed—as demons.

BIBLIOGRAPHY

Georg Wissowa's *Religion und Kultus der Römer,* 2d ed. (Munich, 1912), and Kurt Latte's *Römische Religionsgeschichte* (Munich, 1960) are basic reading on the topic. They are supplemented by Martin P. Nilsson's *Geschichte der griechischen Religion,* vol. 2, 3d ed. (Munich, 1974), for the eastern side of the Roman empire. Jean Bayet's *Histoire politique et psychologique de la religion romaine* (Paris, 1957) proposes an alternative approach and is improved in the Italian translation, *La religione romana: Storia politica e psicologica* (Turin, 1959). All the publications by Franz Cumont and Arthur Darby Nock remain enormously valuable and influential. See, for instance, Cumont's *Astrology and Religion among the Greeks and Romans* (New York, 1912), *After Life in Roman Paganism* (New Haven, 1922), *Les religions orientales dans le paganisme romain,* 4th ed. (Paris, 1929), *Recherches sur le symbolisme funéraire des Romains* (Paris, 1942), and *Lux Perpetua* (Paris, 1949); see also Nock's *Conversion: The Old*

and the New in Religion from Alexander the Great to Augustine of Hippo (Oxford, 1933) and
his essays in *The Cambridge Ancient History,* vol. 10 (Cambridge, 1934) and vol. 12 (Cam-
bridge, 1939), and in *Essays on Religion and the Ancient World,* 2 vols., edited by Zeph Stewart
(Cambridge, Mass., 1972). The scattered contributions by Louis Robert on epigraphic evidence
are also indispensable; see, for instance, his *Hellenica,* 13 vols. (Limoges and Paris, 1940–1965).
Among more recent general books are J. H. W. G. Liebeschuetz's *Continuity and Change in
Roman Religion* (Oxford, 1979), Ramsay MacMullen's *Paganism in the Roman Empire* (New
Haven, 1981), Alan Wardman's *Religion and Statecraft among the Romans* (London, 1982), and
John Scheid's *Religion et piété à Rome* (Paris, 1985). Volumes 2.16, 2.17, and 2.23 of *Aufstieg
und Niedergang der römischen Welt* (Berlin and New York, 1978–1984) are mostly devoted to
Roman imperial paganism and are of great importance. Ramsay MacMullen's *Christianizing the
Roman Empire, A.D. 100–400* (New Haven, 1984) supplements his previous book from the
Christian side.

Numerous monographs have been published on various topics. Here I can indicate only a
few.

On the basic changes in Roman religion: Arthur Bernard Cook, *Zeus: A Study in Ancient
Religion,* 3 vols. (Cambridge, 1914–1940); Johannes Geffcken, *Der Ausgang des griechisch-rö-
mischen Heidentums* (Heidelberg, 1920); Bernhard Kötting, *Peregrinatio religiosa: Wallfahrten
in der Antike und das Pilgerwesen in der alten Kirche* (Münster, 1950); Frederick H. Cramer,
Astrology in Roman Law and Politics (Philadelphia, 1954); Arnaldo Momigliano, ed., *The Conflict between Paganism and Christianity in the Fourth Century* (Oxford, 1963); E. R. Dodds,
Pagan and Christian in an Age of Anxiety (Cambridge, 1965); Clara Gallini, *Protesta e integra-
zione nella Roma antica* (Bari, 1970); Peter Brown, *Religion and Society in the Age of Saint
Augustine* (London, 1972); Javier Teixidor, *The Pagan God: Popular Religion in the Greco-
Roman Near East* (Princeton, 1977); Sabine G. MacCormack, *Art and Ceremony in Late Antiq-
uity* (Berkeley, 1981); Peter Brown, *Society and the Holy in Late Antiquity* (Berkeley, 1982).
See also Morton Smith's article "Prolegomena to a Discussion of Aretalogies, Divine Men, the
Gospels and Jesus," *Journal of Biblical Literature* 90 (June 1971): 174–199.

On the imperial cult: Christian Habicht, *Gottmenschentum und griechische Städte,* 2d ed.
(Munich, 1970); Stefan Weinstock, *Divus Julius* (Oxford, 1971); Elias J. Bickerman et al., eds.,
Le culte des souverains dans l'empire romain (Geneva, 1973); J. Rufus Fears, *Princeps a diis
electus: The Divine Election of the Emperor as a Political Concept at Rome* (Rome, 1977); S. R.
F. Price, *Rituals and Power: The Roman Imperial Cult in Asia Minor* (Cambridge, 1984). Price's
book should be supplemented by his article "Gods and Emperors: The Greek Language of the
Roman Imperial Cult," *Journal of Hellenic Studies* 94 (1984): 79–95. See also H. W. Pleket's
"An Aspect of the Emperor Cult: Imperial Mysteries," *Harvard Theological Review* 58 (October
1965): 331–347; Lellia Cracco Ruggini's "Apoteosi e politica senatoria nel IV sec. d.C.," *Rivista
storica italiana* (1977): 425–489; and Keith Hopkins's *Conquerors and Slaves* (Cambridge,
1978), pp. 197–242.

On specific periods or individual gods: Jean Beaujeu, *La religion romaine à l'apogée de
l'empire,* vol. 1, *La politique religieuse des Antonins, 96–192* (Paris, 1955); Marcel Leglay, *Sat-
urne africaine* (Paris, 1966); R. E. Witt, *Isis in the Graeco-Roman World* (London, 1971); Robert
Turcan, *Mithras Platonicus: Recherches sur l'hellénisation philosophique de Mithra* (Leiden,
1975); Maarten J. Vermaseren, *Cybele and Attis* (London, 1977); Friedrich Solmsen, *Isis among
the Greeks and Romans* (Cambridge, Mass., 1979); Reinhold Merkelbach, *Mithras* (Königstein,
West Germany, 1984). See also Merkelbach's article "Zum neuen Isistext aus Maroneia," *Zeitschrift für Papyrologie und Epigraphik* 23 (1976): 234–235.

On Roman sacrifice (not yet studied so thoroughly as Greek practices), see *Le sacrifice dans l'antiquité,* "Entretiens Fondation Hardt," no. 27 (Geneva, 1981), and for a theory of the mystery cult in the novels, see Reinhold Merkelbach's *Roman und Mysterium in der Antike* (Munich, 1962). Kurt Rudolph's *Gnosis: The Nature and History of Gnosticism* (San Francisco, 1983) and Giovanni Filoramo's *L'attesa della fine: Storia della gnosi* (Bari, 1983) are the best introductions to the subject, while *Gnosis und Gnostizismus,* edited by Rudolph (Darmstadt, 1975), provides a retrospective anthology of opinions. The collective volumes *Die orientalischen Religionen im Römerreich,* edited by Maarten J. Vermaseren (Leiden, 1981), and *La soteriologia dei culti orientali,* edited by Ugo Bianchi and Vermaseren (Leiden, 1982), provide further guidance in current research on various topics. Noteworthy also are the seminal essays in *Jewish and Christian Self-definition,* vol. 3, *Self-definition in the Graeco-Roman World,* edited by B. F. Meyer and E. P. Sanders (London, 1982).

For the transition from paganism to Christianity, the work of Lellia Cracco Ruggini is essential. See, for example, her "Simboli di battaglia ideologica nel tardo ellenismo," in *Studi storici in onore di Ottorino Bertolini* (Pisa, 1972), pp. 117–300; *Il paganesimo romano tra religione e politica, 384–394 d.C.,* "Memorie della classe di scienze morali, Accademia Nazionale dei Lincei," 8.23.1 (Rome, 1979); and "Pagani, ebrei e cristiani: Odio sociologico e odio teologico nel mondo antico," *Gli ebrei nell'Alto Medioevo* (Spoleto) 26 (1980): 13–101.

THREE

RELIGIONS OF LATE ANTIQUITY

13 HELLENISTIC RELIGIONS

J. Gwyn Griffiths

Whereas religion is never a mere reflex of political, economic, and social conditions, there are periods in history when these factors exert a palpably strong influence on religious thinking. The Hellenistic age was certainly such a period. Its early phase, which began with the conquests of Alexander the Great in 334 BCE and continued with the rule of his successors, brought military and political upheaval to many peoples. When Roman imperialism later became the dominating power, there was greater apparent political stability, and the consciousness of a unified world, which Alexander's victories had furthered, was enhanced. The thought of one world does not necessarily lead to the idea of one God, but it does raise questions about a possible spiritual unity behind the manifold manifestations of religious experience.

Culturally this was a world that gave primacy to the Greek language, and Alexander himself, although a Macedonian, was a fervent disseminator of Greek culture. Within his empire other languages continued to flourish, including Aramaic, Hebrew, Egyptian, Babylonian, and Latin, but it was Greek that bore the official stamp of the ruling powers. Alexandria largely replaced Athens as the world's cultural capital, with Pergamum in northwestern Asia Minor as a splendid rival. Alexandria gave a Greek form to its glittering artistic and intellectual achievement, although it harbored several other cultural and religious groups, not the least of which were the Alexandrian Jews. In philosophy, however, Athens retained some of its pristine vigor since it was there that the new schools of Epicureanism and Stoicism first found a footing. In different ways both Epicurus and Zeno, the founders of these schools, were reacting to the broadened horizons created by Alexander's achievements. Even before this the Greek world was no narrow enclave, for Greek colonies had long since spread to Asia Minor and the Black Sea area, to Egypt and North Africa, and to southern Italy, Sicily, Spain, and Gaul. What was new in the Greek dimension of Alexander's conquests was the thrust in an easterly direction to Syria and Palestine, to Persia and Babylon, and through Central Asia to parts of northern India. In the wake of the military thrust, Greek settlements and cities were established in many non-Greek areas. Eventually the force of the population impact weakened, although Alexander's successors continued to hold sway for several centuries. An encounter with very diverse cultures ensued, and the traditional division between Greeks and barbarians underwent radical revision. In terms of religion the resulting counter-thrust of Eastern traditions meant that the Greeks received more than they gave.

It was not the brute power of military aggression that brought about the change in outlook. In his *Alexander the Great* (Cambridge, 1948), Sir William Tarn argues that Alexander himself had a dream of the unity and reconciliation of all peoples, but the sources are more faithfully interpreted as recording a prayer by him for the cooperation of Greeks and Persians as ruling imperial partners. Yet the aftermath of his victories brought a realization of the unity of East and West.

NEW TRENDS IN STATE-SUPPORTED RELIGION

In spite of the great change in worldview thus effected, the old order was not swept away quickly. In Greece itself the city-states continued to function after the Macedonian conquests, and this meant that the official religious cults espoused by these states were still maintained. Politically, however, the citizens were aware that they were carrying on under the shadow of Macedonian imperialism and that the substance of their political power, particularly in foreign policy, had much diminished. This sense of insignificance must have demeaned the quality of their religious worship. The Athenians continued to honor their patron goddess Athena, especially as Athena Promachos ("defender"), but they knew very well that they were subject now to whatever Macedonian dynast was in power in the area. Such a situation threw the citizens back on their own spiritual resources so that their concerns as individuals counted correspondingly more. In later ages the emphasis on the individual might often seem to be at the very heart of religion, as in A. N. Whitehead's well-known definition of it: "Religion is what the individual does with his own solitariness." The ancient world, in contrast, viewed religion as something essentially communal that was realized, above all, in public activities arranged by the state. In the Hellenistic age these activities continued to some extent, but in other ways there was a marked focus on the concerns of the individual.

Not that the social urges suffered atrophy: a popular feature of the religious life of this age was the great vitality of the associations or clubs formed by adherents of the various cults, with or without the sanction of the state. While these associations were often allowed the use of sacred premises, their main activities were usually convivial and charitable. They provided good cheer in the way of wine, beer, and banquets and also a good deal of help to needy members. Naturally the religious element was not ignored, and the name of the patron deity normally appears in records of their proceedings. The evidence concerning them derives from a great part of the Greek world. Prominent in this evidence are towns that were centers of trade and therefore rather cosmopolitan in character, such as Rhodes, Delos, and Piraeus (the harbor town of Athens). Abundant testimony has also been forthcoming from centers of the native cults in Egypt, and at that time these cults, especially those connected with Isis, were spreading to other countries. Thus at the end of the first century CE there was a club of this kind attached to a temple of Isis in London.

Emphasis on the importance of the individual came from a quarter that at first sight might seem surprising: the belief in astrology, which was then so fashionable. [*See* Astrology.] Its origins were in Babylon, where astronomy had also been pioneered. The Babylonians had shown that the heavenly bodies moved in a fixed order that could be scientifically forecast. Then their astrologers, who were also astronomers (the two fields had not yet diverged), introduced the belief that events in the world were somehow linked to events among the stars. It followed that worldly events could also be prophesied since they too had been ordained beforehand. Under the Roman emperors astrologers were several times banned and expelled; yet many of the emperors themselves had recourse to them. When applied to the individual, astrology meant that everything depended on the personal horoscope, which was based on the exact date and hour of birth and on the planet then in the ascendant and on its relation to the zodiac. The effect of the prognosis could be depressing, even terrifying. In a Greek magical papyrus (found in the corpus of Preisendanz, 13.708ff), the astrologer thus advises his anxious client:

> *You must enquire, "Lord, what is fated for me?" And he will tell you of your star and the nature of your Daemon [guiding spirit] and your horoscope and where you shall live and where you shall die. But if you hear something bad, do not break into screams and tears. Ask him, rather, to cancel it himself or to change its course. For this god has power to do everything.*

Here the astrologer is invoking the aid of religion with his allusion to a god who can change the prognosis. But a fatalistic acceptance is more often indicated. What is clear, in any case, is that the personal horoscope is the basis of the procedure. The fate of the individual is the center of attention.

A new development that imparted fresh vitality, albeit of dubious sincerity, to the official state worship was the gradual establishment of the cult of the ruler, whether king or emperor. The first clear instance of it in this period was the worship of Alexander the Great as a divine person. In his case it was conspicuously an upshot of religious practices long prevalent in the Eastern countries that he had conquered. In the nations of Mesopotamia the king had regularly been associated with the gods. He had not been defined theologically as a god, but there was an aura of divinity about him. [*See* Kingship.] A victory stela of Naram-Sin of Akkad shows him towering above his followers, with a clear suggestion of his superhuman standing. In Egypt, on the other hand, the pharaoh was given an official status of divinity. When alive he was equated with the god Horus, and in death he became the god Osiris, father of Horus. He was also called "the son of Re" (the sun god). The distinctions are well delineated by Henri Frankfort in his *Kingship and the Gods* (Chicago, 1948).

It is significant that the inital divinization of Alexander was associated with Egypt. According to ancient historians he visited the oracle of Amun at Siwa in the Libyan desert some four hundred miles southwest of what was later Alexandria. There, in 331 BCE, an Egyptian priest accosted him as the "son of Amun" in a way that corresponded to traditional Egyptian practice. To be regarded as the son of a god must have appealed to Alexander, and from that moment on he seems to have pressed the idea purposively, demanding obeisance and worship in many countries. Greeks and Macedonians did not take easily to the idea, yet there was a strand within the Greek tradition that allowed the divinization of dead heroes and eventually of living rulers. This contributed to the cult of the dead Alexander in Egypt and, in the time of his successors there, led to the worship of the living king and his queen, a practice started by Ptolemy II and his wife Arsinoë, who assumed the title *theoi adelphoi,* "the brother-sister gods." (The Ptolemaic kings regularly married their sisters.) Less thoroughgoing modes of the ruler cult prevailed in the other regions of Alexander's empire. By gradual steps the Seleucids of Syria and the Attalids of Pergamum eventually followed the practice, although the Attalids were accorded full divinity only after death. The Macedonians were slower still in coming to it, perhaps because of skeptical resistance.

To assess the depth or sincerity of the worship produced by the ruler cult is difficult since it soon came to be a test of political loyalty. In 307 BCE the Athenians paid divine honors to Demetrius Poliorcetes, the ambitious Macedonian soldier-king. Their hymn of praise to him couples him with the goddess Demeter and describes him as the son of Poseidon, god of the sea, and of Aphrodite, goddess of love. Then it contrasts his nearness with the distance of the traditional gods: "Other gods are far removed or do not listen; or they do not really exist or do not heed us at all. But thou are here with us; we can behold thee, not shaped in wood or stone, but here in person. And thus we pray to thee." In spite of some military successes, Demetrius was a rake and a scoundrel. We can therefore safely assume that the fulsome language of the hymn disguised a degree of disgust.

When the Romans took up the ruler cult, Egypt was again influential in the early stages, and there was a measure of continued tradition; yet in Rome itself there had been antecedents in relation to "the divine Julius" (Julius Caesar.) [See Emperor's Cult.] The full-scale cult was at first enacted in the provinces only, but eventually it was insisted on as a test of loyalty. To adherents of the many polytheistic religions there was no problem in this claim, since it merely meant that the divinized emperor was to be added to the variegated pantheon already in existence. Even followers of the mystery religions were not embarrassed by the claim, for the demands of these religions were by no means exclusive. Those in serious trouble were the adherents of Judaism and Christianity, two religions of uncompromising monotheism. "Thou shalt have no other gods before me" may not imply strict monotheism, since the commandment does not necessarily deny the existence of other gods, but rather demands the exclusive worship of Yahveh. By the Hellenistic era, however, Judaism had become unequivocally monotheistic, and Christianity inherited its unbending stance. To upholders of the polytheistic tradition it seemed a form of fanatical intolerance, and it sometimes provoked very harsh reactions.

An aspect of the ruler cult that affected the minds of men more seriously than the superficial matter of expressing political allegiance was the whole question of divine incarnation. Was it possible to conceive of the divine taking human form? [See Incarnation.] In early Greek thought it is sometimes suggested that the gulf between man and god is not wide and that an affinity exists between them. In the early fifth century BCE Pindar expresses it thus: "Of one stock are men and gods, and from one mother do we draw our breath" (*Nemean Odes* 6.1). Some of the heroes of Greek mythology were deemed to be offspring of mixed unions, the father being divine and the mother moral. Herakles is in this category, for his father was said to be Zeus and his mother the mortal Alkmene, daughter of a king of Mycenae. Zeus was not able to achieve union with her until he disguised himself as a victorious warrior.

Rather different is the process by which historical heroes came to be worshiped after death. Their historicity cannot always be demonstrated, but the likely evolution followed from a lively memory of their deeds. One might rephrase Shakespeare to explain the distinctions enacted: "Some men are born divine, some achieve divinity, and some have divinity thrust upon them." The hero worship that developed among the Greeks outside mythology is akin to the second category; it involved outstanding individuals who by their own merit and fame came to be especially honored after death. [*See* Heroes.] The triumphant commander who "liberated" or "saved" a city naturally qualified for special honors akin to those paid to divinity. An early and successful candidate was the Spartan commander Lysander, whose deeds secured for him this type of apotheosis even during his lifetime. [*See* Apotheosis.] But Alexander decisively outshone heroes of such caliber since his deeds encompassed not only the Greek world but much else as well. Quite apart, therefore, from his experience at Siwa, which gave him an Egyptian passport to divinity, he qualified splendidly according to the criterion of Greek hero worship. When his cult was established in Egypt, followed by that of the Ptolemies, several of the new royal divinities were inevitably ill qualified to attract real worship. They might be said to have had divinity thrust upon them automatically.

Behind the developments in Egypt stood the long-standing dogma of the god-man, and its influence in the Hellenistic world went beyond the particular instances of divine dynasty. This dogma became prominent in the New Kingdom (1551–1070 BCE) when the claim was made that the pharaoh had a mortal mother but a divine father. His procreation was explicitly, albeit tastefully, described as a visit by the god Amun to the queen. In so doing the god was said to take on the guise of the living pharaoh, so that what was ostensibly a natural process was given a supernatural interpretation.

A story told about Nectanebo, the last pharaonic king of Egypt, gives prominence to this doctrine. The Greek work called the *Alexander Romance* relates how Nectanebo, in spite of his vaunted magical power, was defeated by the Persians and fled to Pella in Macedonia after suitably changing his appearance. A prophecy from Memphis announced that he would return to Egypt as a young man who would overthrow his enemies and conquer the world (a reference, of course, to Alexander). Furthermore Alexander's mother, Queen Olympias, is said to have welcomed Nectanebo in Macedonia because of his fame as a magician, and he at once fell in love with her. When the queen informed him that her husband, Philip, being then away at war, was said to be beguiled by another woman, Nectanebo confirmed the rumor and told her that a god would visit her in a dream and have intercourse with her and that from this union would come a son who would avenge her on Philip. The god was to be the Libyan Amun, with golden hair and ram's horns. Olympias duly experienced the divine visit in a dream but then declared that she wanted not merely a dream but the real thing, whereupon Nectanebo impersonated the god and had intercourse with her himself. The son who was born of the union was naturally deemed to be Alexander, thus marked out as of divine origin. Although Alexander was said to have caused the death of Nectanebo, he was also said to have recognized him as his father and to have buried him with honor. The Greek writer of this story has told it with a sense of skeptical irony, yet it points to the fact that the people of the age were engrossed with the idea of the god-man and with the possibility that the divine could break into the sphere of human life through incarnation.

MAGIC, MYTH, AND MIRACLE

According to the Pauline saying, it was the Jews who demanded signs (that is, wonders or miracles) while the Greeks sought wisdom. In fact, it was not only the Jews who demanded miracles; the majority of the Greeks did also, and so did the majority of other peoples. From time immemorial religion had been mingled with magic, and the power to produce miraculous events was regarded as the mark of godhead acting either in a direct intervention or through chosen intermediaries.

In considering ancient magic, one must avoid any notion of conjuring tricks made possible by sleight of hand or by various illusionary processes. Some charlatans did resort to such stratagems, but the true medium of divine power did not approach his task thus. In the oldest myths of many nations, the creation of the world itself is the result of miraculous divine actions, and the teasing thought of what lay beyond the beginning of things often produced the image of one creator god, who was unbegotten and who had to initiate a process of creation without the help of a spouse. The early Greeks who followed the Orphic teaching believed that a cosmic egg was the source of everything. This idea might appear to derive from a natural symbol, but probably it came to the Greeks from Egypt, although the Egyptians had several other theories of creation. By the Hellenistic age some Greeks had become familiar with a similar doctrine that had spread from Iran.

Strangely enough, the Greeks did not regard their supreme god, Zeus, as a creator god. Yet their myths about him are replete with miracles, especially when his many dealings with mortal women are portrayed. For instance, having fallen in love with Io, a priestess at Argos, Zeus changed her into a heifer in order to hide her from his wife Hera. Metamorphosis became a frequent medium of miraculous intervention by gods. [See Shape Shifting.] Early in the first century CE, the Roman poet Ovid devoted a whole cycle of poems to this theme, and in the next century it was the central motif of the *Metamorphoses* of Apuleius, an entertaining and often ribald novel that nevertheless conveys a deeply religious vision.

It tells the story of Lucius of Corinth, a Greek who was changed into a donkey through a mistake made in the employment of magic. After many strange adventures in asinine form, he is restored to human form by the goddess Isis at Cenchreae, the harbor of Corinth, during the spring ritual of the Ship of Isis. The last part of the novel movingly portrays his devotion to this new religion.

Unlike the immortal gods, however, heroes are not usually invested with miraculous powers, in spite of their divine associations. Herakles achieves his great deeds with might and main, and Prometheus, while he sometimes deploys a kind of low cunning, is a culture hero intent on benefiting mankind.

Removed from the category of gods and heroes was the human purveyor of magic and miracle. At his best he had to be a knowledgeable person. Astrology was often within his professed prowess, and the secrets of astrology were not available to any ignoramus. His attitude to the gods seems to have varied. Respect and devout loyalty characterized him in the role of their chosen instrument. Yet sometimes the magician was expected to compel the gods to act in a certain way, and a number of magical spells are extant in which the gods are fiercely threatened unless they comply. But it was important to use the correct formula and to know the functions and mythology of the deity concerned. In the Hellenistic era magic was especially used for treating disease.

Here the doctrine of demons was often basic. Regarded as intermediate between man and god, demons (spirits) were divided into good and evil categories, with the possibility that good demons could be promoted to the rank of gods. Under the influence of Iran this sytem was sometimes developed into a thoroughgoing dualism connoting a hierarchy of both angels and devils but with devils headed by a supreme figure of evil. This view regarded all disease as the creation of evil demons. To conquer the disease therefore demanded the defeat and expulsion of the baleful spirit that had taken possession of the victim. A person's good demon, on the other hand, acted as his guardian angel. Yet the good demon was not normally regarded as potent enough to deal with an evil demon who had entered a person. A spiritual power from outside was needed, and the first task was one of diagnosis, which meant the correct identification of the occupying demon. The magician was expected to announce the name of the hostile power and to order its expulsion in the name of a superior and beneficent power; there are familiar examples in the New Testament. Treatment of disease in both the Jewish and the pagan world was often colored by these concepts.

This was not, however, the only technique practiced by magicians and priests. Instead of a frontal attack on the demon, a mollifying approach was sometimes adopted, as when insanity was treated by the playing of soft music. A multitude of medical charms have come down to us, and they combine popular medicine with magical rites. Central to these, very often, is the power of the spoken word of the magician himself, whose incantations are recorded, for purposes of reading and imitation, in Greek and Egyptian magical papyri. Moreover, the direct interventions of the gods of healing, particularly of Asklepios, Isis, and Sarapis, are often lauded.

In origin Asklepios was perhaps a hero; later he was raised to the rank of a divinity and became the foremost god of healing in the Hellenistic world, with temples at Epidaurus in the Peloponnese and at Athens, Rome, and Pergamum; the most celebrated of his temples was on the island of Kos, northwest of Rhodes, the home of a famous Greek medical school. Numerous inscriptions set up in the temples of Asklepios record the gratitude of worshipers for the cures obtained, which were frequently regarded as completely miraculous. Yet some of the techniques used partook of current orthodox medical practice, for example, prescribed dietetic rules, hot and cold baths, and various types of exercise. Special use was also made of incubation, whereby the worshiper slept in the temple of the god in order to experience a visitation from him through a dream or vision; such a visitation could bring both a cure for the disease (or advice as to how a cure might be obtained) and a revelation of a spiritual nature. The grateful records do not refer often to medical prescriptions or details of diet, so one may infer that psychological processes were involved: autosuggestion, experiences of spiritual illumination, and a sense of serenity deriving from a loving relationship. The term *faith healing* could well be applied to such felicitous procedures. What is particularly impressive, as well as eminently consonant with the temper of the Hellenistic age, is the fervent personal relationship with the god that ensued and the worshiper's sense of trust and devotion. We are fortunate to possess one intimate record of these experiences in the *Hieroi Logoi* (Sacred Stories) of Publius Aelius Aristides, a rhetorician of the second century CE.

Magic is customarily divided into the categories of "black" and "white," a division that can certainly be applied to the practice of it by the Greeks. In early prototypes, such as Circe and Medea, the two aspects appear. The Homeric Circe, semidivine in origin, is a powerful magician who uses potions and salves and also teaches Odysseus to summon the spirits of the dead. Medea was the outstanding enchantress of the myths used in Greek tragedy. She enabled the Argonauts to get the golden fleece by putting the dragon of Colchis to sleep; moreover, she possessed the evil eye and could make warriors invulnerable. Orpheus was another master of magic. Son of the muse Calliope, he rendered wild beasts spellbound with his music.

The two words most often used for "miracle" were *thauma* ("wonder") and *sē-meion* ("sign"). Obviously the two aspects could be embraced by either word. A miraculous event that astonishes people can be pleasing or punishing in intent and can be a sign, or omen, from the gods as an expression of their power but with a similar possible duality of purpose. Religion in ancient times had a bias toward beneficent magic, its prayers normally being expressions of devotion and appeals for help. But the appeal might concern the destruction of an enemy, which could involve harsh miraculous intervention by the gods. At the same time divine intervention could inflict moral retribution on individuals. Even the kindly Isis, whose magic was mainly beneficent, sometimes inflicted blindness on sinners.

When a beneficent miracle was enacted in public, it was regularly followed by an expression of blessing or felicitation, the macarism. Thus when Isis restores Lucius from asinine to human form in the *Metamorphoses* of Apuleius (also called *The Golden Ass* and written about 170 CE), the people who see the event declare:

> *This is the man who has been today restored to human shape through the splendid divinity of the all-powerful goddess. Happy is he, by heaven, and thrice blessed, to have clearly deserved, by the purity of his former life and his pious loyalty, such a wondrous favor from heaven that he is, as it were, born again and has at once pledged himself to service in the sacred rites.*
>
> *(11.16)*

Although the priests of Isis have taken part in the miracle, as for instance in providing the garland of roses to be eaten by the ass-man, it is the goddess herself who naturally receives the acclaim.

Sometimes, nevertheless, the human agents were not averse to claiming a measure of glory. Among the rhetorical practitioners of the second sophistic movement, which flourished in the first and second centuries CE, especially at Athens, Smyrna, and Ephesus, were a few literati who combined their philosophical and oratorical gifts, which they displayed as peripatetic lecturers, with a keen interest in magic. One was Apuleius, whose interest in magic is evident in much of his work, especially the *Metamorphoses*. Early in his career, however, he was accused of using magic to gain the hand of a rich widow in marriage. Although acquitted, thereafter he was reluctant to practice any form of the art.

In the context of magic and miracle the most remarkable person in the second sophistic movement was undoubtedly Apollonius of Tyana, who lived in the first century CE and came from Cappadocia in Asia Minor. An account of his life, written about 217 CE by another Sophist, Philostratus, presents him as a wandering scholar whose travels embraced Babylon, India, Egypt, and Ethiopia. In spite of his fame, his life was ascetic and disciplined and modeled on Pythagorean ideals. In addition, however, he frequently performed miracles that included acts of healing, magical disappearances, and even raising the dead, deeds that recall the claims made for Jesus of Nazareth.

The trustworthiness of Philostratus, however, has been much impugned. He cast his life of Appollonius in the form of a Greek travel romance, which suggests a fictitious element. Further, he wrote the book at the request of Julia Domna, the second wife of the emperor Septimius Severus, so that the possibility of anti-Christian animus and parody cannot be excluded. It is likely, then, that some more modest deeds by Apollonius provided a basis for the heightened account presented. The simple asceticism of his mode of life must also have impressed people, although Philostratus exaggerates even here, as when he says that Apollonius was "a more inspired student of wisdom than Pythagoras" (1.2).

One of the faculties ascribed to Apollonius was clairvoyance. At Ephesus in 96 CE, he is said to have had a miraculous vision of the emperor Domitian being murdered in distant Rome, a vision whose validity was afterward confirmed. The event is related by both Philo stratus and the historian Dio Cassius, so that its truth need not be questioned. Even the less sophisticated typeof magician was expected to indulge in processes of divination that would let him foretell the future. This did not usually imply powers of prophecy in a general sense but, rather, the ability to judge and foretell the outcome of a particular problem or issue. Methods of divination included dreams, incubation (sleeping in a temple), auguries based on observation of birds, extispicy (especially the inspection of the entrails of animals killed specifically for this purpose), and the interpretation of weather signs, not to mention the whole area of astrology. Several of these methods had been developed originally in Babylon and Egypt. [See Divination.]

Another important divinatory method was by oracle. [See Oracles.] In the Greek tradition the personal mouthpiece of the god of the oracle was the *prophētēs,* who might be a man or a woman. He or she was thought to be possessed by a divine power, a process that Plato compared to poetic inspiration. The medium became *entheos* ("full of the god") and was in a state of *ekstasis* ("standing out of oneself"). In the oracles the power of prophecy was linked to special sites and to particular gods. Here a paradox emerges: the Greeks are famed for their rationalism and are regarded as the pioneers of intellectual enquiry and scientific thinking, yet their belief in oracles belies this approach. To some extent, the inconsistency can be explained through social division: the credulous majority trusted oracles while the educated elite evinced skepticism, the latter trend becoming more pronounced in the Hellenistic era, as Plutarch showed in the first and second centuries CE.

The paradox reveals itself to some degree in the figure of Apollo himself. He is the god of light and reason, yet he is the dominant god at Delphi, seat of the most celebrated oracle. In his *Birth of Tragedy,* the philosopher Nietzsche contrasts Apollo and Dionysos, the one representing the cool temper of rationalism, the other the passionate surrender to ecstasy. Certainly this antithesis is at the heart of Greek thinking.

One noted feature of Greek oracles was the ambiguity of their response. Statements that could be interpreted in more than one way were often forthcoming. Among the problems posed on behalf of states were political issues, and this meant that some oracles, particularly the one at Delphi, exerted considerable influence on the states' policies. But the Hellenistic age saw the decline of Delphi and the rising prestige of other oracles, such as those of Asklepios at Epidaurus and Rome and that of Trophonios in central Greece.

Oracles in other countries were also much frequented, such as that of Zeus Amun in Libyan Siwa, where Alexander had a significant personal experience. Sometimes the questions raised were those of individuals, reflecting the private problems of simple people: a man is anxious to know whether his wife will give him a child, a woman wants to be cured of a disease, someone asks a commercial question about the best use of property, or a man wonders whether the child his wife is carrying is his own.

In his work *On the Obsolescence of Oracles,* Plutarch (c. 46–125 CE) discusses why so many oracles in Greece have ceased to function. Various answers are supplied in a discussion presented in the form of a dialogue. The population had decreased, says Plutarch, and there is some atrophy of belief. There is also the theory, seemingly endorsed by Plutarch himself, that in the oracles it is not the gods but beneficent demons who are at work.

Another writer who provides a revealing picture of what goes on at an oracle is Pausanias, who flourished about 150 CE. In his *Description of Greece* (9.39) he gives many details of the procedures at the oracle of Tropho nios in Lebadea (modern Levadhia) in Boeotia. Regarded as relating to the hero cult, Trophonios may have been in origin a fertility god with chthonic associations; his sanctuary was built over an alleged entrance to the underworld. The person who wished to consult the oracle had to first wait quietly in the house of Agathos Daimon ("gracious divine being"), where various rites of purification and dietetic regimen were observed. Then came whippings, various offerings and sacrifices, an anointing with oil, bathing in a river, a special drink, and a prayer, after which the inquirer was dressed in a linen tunic and pulled through a narrow hole into a subterranean cave where he was terrified by snakes but able to calm them with honey cakes. Only then did he see or hear Trophonios and become enlightened concerning his future, after which priests explained his experiences. It was said that the inquirer always came out of the cave of Trophonios dejected and pale. Psychologically the treatment was rigorous and searching; modern parallels might be sought in regimes using drugs such as methedrine with stringent concomitants. In ancient times the initiations in the mystery religions provide the nearest parallel.

UNIVERSALISM AND SYNCRETISM

Although Alexander the Great did not establish a world state in the world as then known, his empire transcended the national states and induced a sense of cohesion and interdependence. It was in this era that the word *kosmopolitēs* ("citizen of the world") came into vogue. The idea had occasionally appeared before this. Democritus of Abdera had said in the fifth century BCE, "To the wise every land is open; the good soul looks on the whole world as his country." More pointed and forceful expression was given to the idea by Diogenes the Cynic (c. 400–325 BCE), founder of the Cynic sect. He came from Sinope on the southern shore of the Black Sea but spent much of his life in Athens. He was given the nickname of "theDog," while his followers were similarly called "Dog Philosophers" or Cynics, from the snarling way in which they and their master condemned accepted conventions and defied civilized life, embracing instead a style of extreme poverty, simplicity, and hardship. Among the conventions that Diogenes rejected was attachment to the polis, or city-state. His rejection was practical in that he wandered from one country to another without accredited citizenship or a settled home (in Athens he lived in a tub). In principle he was a kind of anarchist. He called himself a "citizen of the world," but this did not imply any politically defined belief. It was in effect a negative claim denying the value of the city-state.

It was the Stoics, however, who succeeded in giving to this approach a more positive and meaningful basis. Initially they were intellectually indebted to the Cynics, but Zeno of Citium in Cyprus (335–263 BCE) went far beyond them and included a religious interpretation in his cosmopolitanism. According to Zeno the whole universe is governed by divine reason, and men should therefore live in conformity with it and with the order of nature established by it. A saying of Zeno that Plutarch has recorded presents the view that men should not live in a state of division according to separate cities and peoples and differing rules of justice; rather, all men should be viewed as belonging to one state and community and sharing one life and order. Plutarch wryly adds that in writing thus in his much-admired book *The State,* Zeno was presenting a dream or ideal of a well-ordered philosophical world.

It was indeed an age when several "utopias" were written. Plato had set an example with his *Republic,* but later writers in this genre deployed a good deal more fantasy, as when Iambulus in the early second century BCE wrote of his voyage to the southern seas, where he stayed for seven years in the seven "Islands of the Sun." He painted an idyllic picture of the islands: their climate is perfect and their land ever fruitful; the inhabitants are all supermen and there is no distinction between slave and free; property is shared and women and children are held in common; there is no strife of any kind, and their deities are the powers of nature—the sun, the heavenly bodies, and the sky.

There were a few practical ventures, too, in utopianism. Alexarchus, brother of King Cassander of Macedonia, after being given some land on the Athos peninsula, built a big city that he called Ouranopolis ("city of heaven"), where the citizens were called Ouranidai ("children of heaven"), and the coinage was adorned with figures of the sun, moon, and stars. Rather similar was the concept implemented briefly by Aristonicus of Pergamum (in 133–130 BCE), who led a popular rising against Rome. He planned a state called Heliopolis ("city of the sun"), whose inhabitants he called Heliopolitai ("citizens of the sun"); but after some initial successes he was captured and killed by the Romans. The Greek satirist Lucian, who wrote in the second century CE, provided a witty parody of literary utopias in *A True Story,* a travel romance full of irony and burlesque, of which Swift's *Gulliver's Travels* is a modern descendant.

In the context of Stoic philosophy the doctrine of world citizenship was elaborated somewhat by Chrysippus (c. 280–207 BCE), who noted that the word *polis* was given two senses: the city in which one lived; the citizens and the state machinery. Similarly, he argued, the universe is a *polis* that embraces gods and men, the former wielding sovereignty while the latter obey; yet gods and men, for all their difference in status, have a means of contact and converse since they both use reason, which is "law by nature." In the last phrase he is overturning a contrast present in previous political thought. A later Stoic, Panaetius (c. 185–109 BCE), was more pragmatic in his approach. A world state seemed no longer within practical reach, but he continued to believe in the general unity of all mankind. At the same time he restored to the city-state a certain secondary role, admitting its usefulness in a realistic sense while denying its claim to decide in any final sense, matters of right and wrong; such decisions were to remain in the domain of reason and nature.

It thus appears that the idea of being a citizen of the world, vague and ill defined as it often was, came to include, under Stoic inspiration, the religious concept of a ruling divine reason. Although the reality of a world state was missing, the idea of mankind as one community had a powerful spiritual effect. Whereas we cannot assume that everyone, or even the majority, embraced the idea fully and fervently, there are many signs that thinking people accepted it. A sharp division had existed previously in attitudes toward other nations: pride and prejudice were clearly present in the categories of Greeks versus barbarians or Jews versus gentiles. Certain nations enjoyed more power than others since, in the empire bequeathed by Alexander, Macedonians, Greeks, and Persians were in the ascendancy until Rome took control. In religious matters, nonetheless, the great variety of national traditions was often regarded as a common heritage of humanity. This is the attitude taken by Plutarch when he argues, doubtless under the influence of Stoicism, that the gods of Egypt should be preserved as "our common heritage" and not made the peculiar property of the Egyptians. In chapter 67 of his treatise *Isis and Osiris* he states his belief that the gods of the various nations, in spite of their differing names, are essentially the same and that behind the divergent forms there is a universal reason and providence:

> *Nor do we regard the gods as different among different peoples nor as barbarian and Greek and as southern and northern. But just as the sun, moon, heaven, earth and sea are common to all, though they are given various names by the varying peoples, so it is with the one reason* [logos] *which orders these things and the one providence which has charge of them, and the assistant powers which are assigned to everything: they are given different honours and modes of address among different peoples according to custom, and they use hallowed symbols, some of which are obscure and others clearer, directing the thought towards the divine, though not without danger. For some, erring completely, have slipped into supersition, and others, shunning it like a marsh, have unwittingly fallen in turn over the precipice of atheism.*

At the same time, Plutarch is occasionally ready, within the same work, to accept the Iranian doctrine about the happy end of the world, when Areimanius (Angra Mainyu), the god of evil, will be utterly obliterated by the gods who follow Horomazes (Ahura Mazdā), lord of light and good. The happy final state will reflect the blessed unity of mankind: "The earth shall be flat and level, and one way of life and one government shall arise of all men, who shall be happy and speak the same language" (chap. 47). Here the universalism envisaged is somewhat colorless and depressing; it accords with Iranian sources, one of which (*Bundahishn* 30.33) declares that when the universe is renewed, "this earth becomes an iceless, shapeless plain." According to this teaching, mountains were created by the Spirit of Evil and will disappear with his overthrow; *Isaiah* 40:4 reflects the same viewpoint when the prophet announces, as part of a serene vision, that "every mountain and hill shall be made low" and "every valley shall be exalted," thus achieving the uniform flatness of Plutarch's Iranian dictum.

The union and solidarity of the human race are also a part of the Iranian teaching, for the *Dēnkard* (9–18), a Pahlavi book of the ninth or tenth century CE that probably preserves earlier ideas, prophesies a final outcome in these terms: "At the final

Rehabilitation the whole of mankind will be firmly and unchangeably linked in mutual love, and this will mean that the demons will utterly despair of ever being able to harm man again. . . . Then there will be a universal joy for the whole of creation for all eternity; and fear will be no more" (trans. R. C. Zaehner, in *The Dawn and Twilight of Zoroastrianism,* London, 1961, pp. 280f.)

Stoicism may well have influenced the idea of "one government of men," but Stoic sources apparently do not mention the use of one language as a requirement of the cosmopolis. The inherited traditions vary on the question of languages. In chapter 11 of *Genesis* the story of the tower of Babel points to an original state of bliss when all men spoke one common language, and a Babylonian legend sees the multiplication of tongues as a cause of discord. Egyptian tradition, on the other hand, praised Thoth as the creator of languages and viewed his act as contributing to the rich variety of creation in general, with its many races and kinds of living beings. The Christian tradition, as in *Revelation* 7:9 with its allusion to "a great multitude of all tribes and peoples and tongues," certainly envisages a universalism in which diversity is present in unity and humanity is a "community of communities."

Whatever the variety of the traditions so freely transmitted in the Hellenistic age, in religious matters there was usually a readiness to acknowledge and respect diverging ways of belief, worship, and ritual. A process that went even beyond this was that of syncretism, a term often hailed as the hallmark of the age. In origin a Greek word, it was not used by the Greeks with the exact meaning assigned to it today. [*See* Syncretism.] It derives from the verb *sugkrētizō,* which itself derives from *Krēs,* "a Cretan"; it was used politically of two parties combining against a common enemy, while the noun *sugkrētismos* was used of a federation or union of Cretan communities.

In English and other modern languages the noun denotes the attempted union or reconciliation of diverse or opposite tenets or practices, especially in the philosophy of religion. The usage is also often extended to include the equation or identification of diverse deities and the combination or fusion of their cults, the latter practice being a specifically Hellenistic development. Earlier experience was indeed fully conversant with the equation of deities.

In ancient religions the most thorough process of syncretism in this sense is found in the developed phase of Roman religion, when Roman deities were identified with Greek counterparts—Jupiter with Zeus, Juno with Hera, Venus with Aphrodite, Ceres with Demeter, Mars with Ares, and so on. In some cases this conscious process found no easy counterpart: Janus, the god of the door, was a distinctively Roman concept. In other cases a Greek deity was adopted without any attempted assimilation. Thus the Greek god Apollo was worshiped in Italy by the Etruscans and was afterward much revered by the Romans, becoming a favorite god of the emperor Augustus. A simple act of comparison could lead to syncretism of this kind: one community compares its own gods with those of another; when similar powers or functions are recognized, the comparison may lead to identification. Of course, this process is valid only with polytheistic communities since monotheism rejects comparisons. Nor does the process arise when there is no contact between communities and therefore no need to make comparisons, except in instances where a plurality of deities within communities of the same culture invites an equation of functions. This may lead to assimilation and the use of one divine name instead of several. Thus it appears that among the Greek communities there were several forms of the corn mother, but eventually the name of Demeter, best known, was applied to most of them. Even so, local varieties persisted in several of the cults. The "Black" Demeter of Phigalia, a town of Arcadia, for instance, was very different from the Demeter of Eleusis. In Phigalia the Black Demeter was said to be the consort of a horse-shaped Poseidon.

In the fifth century BCE the Greek historian Herodotus indulged freely in the kind of syncretism that meant identifying the gods of different nations. In his second book, which deals with Egypt, he consistently identifies the Egyptian Osiris with the Greek Dionysos and the Egyptian Isis with the Greek Demeter. Probably this was prompted only by recognition of their similar functions, although he does refer to festivals. Later, however, in Hellenistic times, the cults of these deities influenced one another. Isis, for example, was often depicted with ears of wheat on her headdress in a manner traditionally associated with Demeter, while ivy, the plant of Dionysos, figured in the rites of Osiris. Again, the phallus was sometimes carried now in processions of Osiris in Egypt, as it had been regularly in the rites of Dionysos among the Greeks; the Egyptian tradition had previously known nothing of this. Another good instance of active syncretism was the god Sarapis, worshiped in Egypt and elsewhere under the Ptolemies. He derived from the Egyptian god Osir-Api (Osiris-Apis) but was now represented in Greek style in a form rather like that of Zeus (but with the *modius,* a measuring vessel, on his head). He was identified with Zeus and with Helios. He was not, however, a new creation; his emergence points to amalgamation and adaptation.

Increasingly in Hellenistic times, the cults of Oriental deities were introduced to the cities of the Greek world and Italy. Such a procedure had been very difficult, and indeed dangerous, in previous ages, for the orgiastic nature of some of these cults was much feared, and all public cults were rigidly controlled by the state. But a radical change of attitude came in Hellenistic times. State control remained, but often it now actively supported foreign cults, as for instance the cult of Dionysos in Ptolemaic Egypt. When Stratonice, the wife of Seleucus Nicator in Syria, resettled the city of Bambyce as Hierapolis in about 300 BCE, one feature of the worship sanctioned there was the fusion of the great Syrian goddess Atargatis with the Hellenic goddesses Artemis, Hera, and Aphrodite. In Egypt this type of cult syncretism was furthered by the system of the *sunnaoi theoi* ("temple-sharing gods"). This was used principally to advance the claims of the Ptolemaic kings and queens as divine beings in temples throughout Egypt in the reign of Ptolemy Philadelphus and afterward; the names of the royal divinities were added as gods who shared the temple with the main deity worshiped there. The reigning Ptolemies and their wives were thus promoted to an honored position on a par with that of the traditionally accepted deities.

Usually the Greeks raised a temple in honor of one particular deity, as Athena was honored in the Parthenon at Athens, Zeus in the great temple at Olympia, and Apollo in his temples at Delphi and Delos. Yet it was very natural that associated deities, especially those connected in myth, legend, and cult, should be represented and worshiped in the same temple. Thus Artemis was honored with Apollo as his twin sister, just as Hadad was honored with the Syrian goddess Atargatis as her consort.

Hellenistic practice went a good deal further than this in the mingling of gods, which the Greeks termed *theokrasia.* One is at first surprised to read in Apuleius's *Metamorphoses,* when he describes the preparations for the initiation of Lucius into the cult of Isis, that the high priest in charge of the rites is called Mithra and that he is linked to the initiand "by a certain divine association of constellations." A close and friendly attitude toward Mithraism is clearly indicated, and astrological lore is also openly deployed. Furthermore, when the temple of Mithra was discovered in the Walbrook area of London by W. F. Grimes in 1954, the finest work of statuary to come to light was of the Egyptian god Sarapis. Nor does the evidence of inscriptions and literature suggest anything other than an attitude of sympathetic cooperation between these and other religions.

There was, of course, no claim of exclusiveness to prevent such an attitude, as was the case with Judaism and Christianity. Well-known instances indicate that even priesthoods of different religions could be held by the same person. Plutarch's friend Clea, to whom he dedicated his study of the Egyptian cults, was a priestess of Dionysos and also of Isis and Osiris. Similarly, in the fourth century CE one Vettius Agorius Praetextatus was initiated into the Dionysian, Eleusinian, and Mithraic mysteries.

Popular religious practice and belief are undoubtedly best reflected in inscriptions, whether in temples, on tombstones, or on amulets, and in magical incantations. Often the gods of different countries are named together in dedications and formulaic expressions of thanksgiving. This is also true of inscriptions that are official and public in character. Thus, in an inscription dated between 50 and 35 BCE, Antiochus I of Commagene, a small kingdom north of Syria, presents an exposition of his religion. He begins by calling himself "the God, the righteous God" and "friend of Romans and Greeks," and then declares that he has made his kingdom "the common dwelling place of all the gods." He alludes to the ancient doctrine of Persians and Greeks and refers with reverence to Zeus-Oromasdes, to Apollo-Mithra-Helios-Hermes, and to Artagnes-Herakles-Ares. This showpiece of syncretism contains an element of political expediency: the king is eager to pander to both Romans and Greeks (the Seleucid rulers); his religion is basically Iranian but with Greek embellishments.

In contrast, the easy and fluid permutations of popular magical texts indicate a general readiness to mix varying religious traditions very freely. Two frequent names are the Greek *Zeus* and the Jewish *Iao (Yahveh)*. In the case of *Zeus* one cannot always be sure whether the name conceals a Mesopotamian or Egyptian deity since these brief formulas rarely reveal the double personality expressed in Antiochus's *Zeus-Oromasdes,* where the second element is obviously more important than the first. Sometimes the Jewish Iao is identified with Zeus or Dionysos.

Nor does the resulting fusion always refrain from a conflation of myths. Thus a magical papyrus now in Oslo (Papyrus Oslo 1.105–109) addresses the god Seth-Typhon, whose name combines Egyptian and Greek deities. The papyrus goes on to say that the god's mother is a white sow, an allusion to an Egyptian myth about Seth and the goddess Nut. It then hails the god as "thou who dost hold in Heliopolis an iron staff with which thou didst barricade the sea and enable them to pass through." Heliopolis here is the city of the sun god in Egypt, but the "iron staff" is apparently that of *Psalms* 2:9, "Thou shalt break them with a rod of iron," while the words that follow allude to the passage of the Hebrews through the Red Sea. The god addressed is therefore a fusion of the deities of three nations, including the Jewish Yahveh, and it is Yahveh who dominates the last part of the invocation.

One of the results of syncretism in religion was a sense of tolerance and sympathy. People who are ready to borrow from other religions are clearly not about to con-

demn them. Judaism and Christianity are again the exceptions, and their fervid intolerance was a source of strength in the struggle for survival. Only very rarely does
a sense of conflict and hostility appear among the adherents of the pagan religions.
Plutarch sometimes inveighs against the primitive cruelties unveiled in facets of mythology; his method is fairly radical in that he is prepared to reject such elements as
unworthy of the gods.

In his novel about the ass-man rescued by Isis, Apuleius is appreciative and respectful in his allusions to most other religions. Here there was almost a logical
imperative operating since Isis, as he often stresses, combined the attributes of all
other goddesses. Yet there are two glaring exceptions to his tolerant attitude. One
is the portrait of the baker's wife (9.14), who is described as a retailer of all the
vices and as one who "scorned and spurned divine beings and instead of accepting
a definite faith . . . falsely and blasphemously professed belief in a god whom she
regarded as the one and only god." The description might apply to the Jewish or
Christian faith, but the list of vices corresponds rather closely to those named in *1
Corinthians* 5:11, so that a Christian allusion is a little more likely. Even more hostile
is Apuleius's withering depiction (8.24ff., 9.3ff.) of the priests of the Syrian goddess
Atargatis. They are said to be addicted to homosexual practices, to crude begging,
to flagrant pilfering (they steal even the golden cup from the temple of the mother
of the gods), and to unscrupulous manipulation of an oracle. Doubtless the praise
of Isis was heightened by this attack, and for once the age seems to be characterized
by competing and conflicting religions.

In general, syncretism tended to induce a belief in pantheism. The free mingling
of many varying divinities suggested to some minds that the world was full of God
in some form or another. Aratus of Soli (c. 315–240 BCE), in his astronomical poem
Phaenomena, said that "all the ways are full of God, and all the meeting-places of
men, the sea and the harbors; and at every turn we all need God, for we are related
to him" (the Greek has *Zeus* for *God*). The last clause was quoted by Paul in his
address at Athens (*Acts* 17:28): "As some of your own poets have said, 'We are also
his offspring.' At the same time syncretism furthered the quest for the unity of the
divine. Earlier Greek philosophers had been concerned with the idea that there was
one god behind the many names and forms. Now that the deities of divergent national traditions were being actively equated and fused, the idea of one divine reality
was becoming still more widespread.

THE REJECTION OF RELIGION

It may seem a paradox that, in spite of the religious tendencies delineated, the direct
or indirect rejection of religion was also a feature of Hellenistic thinking. Direct
rejection was restricted to a small minority of philosophers, but its intellectual vitality is manifest, although it was not a completely new development. Several of the
Sophists of the fifth century BCE had propagated a doctrine that questioned accepted
religious beliefs. Before the Sophists, Anaxagoras had done the same. While he may
not have plainly denied the existence of God or the gods, his belief that mechanistic
laws were behind the workings of the universe excluded a divine causation or operation, even in Mind (Nous) was seen by him as the initiator of cosmic motion.

Among the Sophists, Protagoras was broadly in the same category. He once said
concerning the gods: "I am unable to know whether they exist or do not exist, nor

what they are like in form; for the factors obstructing knowledge are many: the obscurity of the subject and the shortness of human life." The relativism of Protagoras also tended in this direction, for it was he who said, "The measure of all things is man." If Protagoras may thus be rightly classified as an agnostic, Diagoras of Melos, also of the fifth century BCE, was definitely an atheist; indeed, he was called *ho Atheos.* Like Protagoras, he was condemned for impiety, but trials and convictions for this are not always clear indications of a denial of the gods. Diagoras wrote a book in which he attacked the Eleusinian mysteries, and with these remarks he doubtless caused great offense. The main thesis of his book went a good deal further, declaring that the gods did not exist at all. What he saw as the obvious absence of divine punishment in human life was the ground for his denial. He is the first uncompromising atheist in the history of European thought.

In the Hellenistic age Euhemerus of Messene, who for a time (311–298 BCE) served Cassander, king of Macedon, can also be listed as an atheist, although his attacks on traditional religion were more of a rationalizing reductionism than a frontal assault. In his travel romance *Sacred History,* which idealized life on the island of Panchaea in the Indian Ocean, he tells of an inscribed record of the deeds of the gods Ouranos, Kronos, and Zeus. According to the record, these mighty deities had originally been human kings whom their appreciative subjects elevated to the rank of divinity. Clearly this approach could be interpreted as a defense of contemporary ruler cults, but when generalized in relation to gods everywhere, it meant that real divinity disappeared in the postulated human origins. The Greek hero cults also fitted the theory. It is easy to understand why "euhemerism" is still an influential force in the study of religions.

It is not surprising that the Cynics, who tended to oppose all established values, sometimes included religion in their abuse. Diogenes of Sinope expressed contempt for the Eleusinian mysteries. A man who could defend stealing from temples, cannibalism, and incest obviously took pleasure in destructive challenge. Yet his teacher Antisthenes, who attacked all religious conventions and the belief in a multitude of gods, maintained that there existed one God beyond all visible phenomena. The Hellenistic Cynics developed the popular and hard-hitting speech form called the *diatribē,* which combined comic effects with satire that was often abusive. Yet in spite of the Cynics, continued attacks on religious conventions, it is doubtful whether a full-fledged atheism should be ascribed to them.

Features of the Cynic tradition can be recognized in the works of Lucian (120–180 CE), who ridiculed both religion and philosophy; under the latter heading he especially attacked the Cynics, indebted though he was to them. His attacks on religion are well exemplified in his comic picture of Zeus struggling at a celestial reception desk to cope with the countless prayers of humanity. Nor does Christianity escape his lash. He says of Christians that "the poor beggars have persuaded themselves that they will be absolutely immortal and live everlastingly, and for this reason they scorn death and willingly surrender when arrested" (*Peregrinus* 13); they are "simple-minded people," he adds, who can be easily imposed upon by any charlatan or trickster.

A certain criticism of religion emerges also in the works of the philosophers called Skeptics. Their main emphasis was on the reservation or suspension of judgment, but this was applied in a general sense to the validity of sense perceptions and thus to the uncertain claim that knowledge of things can be attained. Specific problems concerning religion were discussed by Sextus Empiricus (c. 160–210 CE), who noted the vast amount of disagreement on the subject that prevailed. The very existence of the gods or of God, the propriety or otherwise of animal sacrifices and dietetic rules, the problem of how the dead should be treated, the right attitude toward death itself—all these matters produced debate and radically differing views. He argues that relativism is inherent in these areas: "All are matters of custom." Therefore, he concludes, judgment on questions of religious belief and practice must also be suspended. [*See* Skeptics and Skepticism.]

PHILOSOPHY AND RELIGION

The two most popular and influential philosophical schools of Hellenistic times were those of the Epicureans and the Stoics, both of which originated in the period immediately following Alexander's conquests. Both were also much affected, albeit in very different ways, by the radical political changes of the age as well as by the new international horizons. To some extent, both took up attitudes that were critical of traditional religious beliefs. Indeed, some would describe them, particularly the Epicureans, as rejecting religion, but this would be misleading.

Epicurus (341–270 BCE) was born in Samos but spent much of his life in Athens, where he bought a house with a garden (his school was eventually called "the Garden"). For him, the aim of philosophy is to secure a happy life; "pleasure is the beginning and end of living happily." Pleasure of the soul is valued above bodily pleasure, and the ideal is *ataraxia,* "freedom from disturbance."

Epicureans were often accused of profligacy, but they lived a modest and simple life of seclusion. Women and slaves were allowed into the Garden, and among the women were several courtesans *(hetairai),* who obviously became a pretext for some of the accusations made against the Epicureans of gross sexual immorality and of overindulgence in wine and food. Such charges came mainly from adherents who later abandoned the school.

In his moral doctrine and spiritual temper Epicurus paid great attention to the idea of friendship (*philia,* for which Lucretius, the Roman Epicurean, used the word *amicitia*); and there is every reason to believe that he strove to follow his noble ideal. He says of friendship:"Of all things which wisdom supplies to make life entirely happy, by far the greatest is the possession of friendship." Again: "Friendship must always be sought for its own sake, although it has its origins in the need for help." And yet again: "That is also very beautiful, the sight of those near and dear to us, when to the bonds of kinship is joined a union of hearts." In his book *The Faith of Epicurus* (London, 1967), Benjamin Farrington aptly compares the saying of William Blake, "The bird a nest, the spider a web, man friendship" (p. 23), and even more appositely since its context is not far removed in time, cites the dictum of Aristotle: "Moreover friendship [*philia*] seems to hold states together and lawgivers are more concerned about friendship than about justice. For concord seems to be akin to friendship . . . , and when men are friends there is no need of justice" (p. 29; *Nichomachean Ethics* 1155a). Friendship is seen, then, not only as a personal tie between individuals but also as the motivating force of a healthy society.

If these ideas indicate the quality of Epicurus's spirituality, his precise attitude to religion must be examined. This is well expressed in his *Letter of Menoeceus,* a letter to a disciple of his to whom he wished to explain the basic principles of his creed.

First of all, one must believe that "God is a being immortal and blessed"; then, a little later, he says that "gods certainly exist, since our perception of them is clear." The apparent contradiction here between "God" and "gods" is familiar in previous Greek writing, especially in the works of Plato, who combines a suggestion of monotheism with the traditional polytheism.

Epicurus goes on to say that many false ideas are current about the gods, in particular the popular concept of reward and punishment whereby the injuries suffered by the wicked and the blessings enjoyed by the good are directly conferred by the gods. He then passes on to discuss death, a subject he often broaches in connection with religion. He tells Menoeceus that it is important to realize that death means nothing to us since it deprives us of all sensation. To realize this makes mortal life more enjoyable in that the desire for immortality is removed. The fear of death and of what may follow it is groundless; the wise man will think reverently of the gods and will be entirely fearless of death. Indeed, he will preserve his peace of mind and "live like a god among men." The life of the gods, as other Epicurean writings make clear, is regarded as one of calm beatitude. They enjoy a blissful existence far away from the turmoil of the human world, free of pain and peril. They take no interest in human affairs and are content with the immortality and supreme blessedness that is theirs.

Perhaps it is Lucretius (94–55 BCE), the Roman exponent of Epicureanism, who has given the most attractive expression to these ideas, both in his depiction of the bliss enjoyed by the gods in their remote paradise and in his searing attacks on popular notions of punishments after death, which were associated with the divine control of Hades. Some of the attacks made by Lucretius on these popular misconceptions sound very much like a condemnation of religion *in toto*. After a breathlessly pathetic picture of Agamemnon sacrificing his own daughter Iphigenia to satisfy the claims of religion, the poet declares, "So many evils was religion able to instigate" (*De rerum natura* 101).

Epicurus himself, on the other hand, is careful to point out that he regularly follows traditional religious observances: "Let it be enough to state now that the divine is in need of no mark of honor, but that it is natural for us to honor it, especially by having pious conceptions of it and secondly, by presenting to all the gods in turn the traditional sacrifices" (Philodemus, *De musica* 4.6, quoting Epicurus). At first sight a palpable contradiction occurs here. If the gods are not concerned with human life, why should human beings bother to honor them with prayer and sacrifice? Do not these religious acts imply a constant concern on both sides? To resolve this dilemma, it seems, one should ascribe to Epicurus the highest form of worship, the utterly disinterested adoration of the divine which expects nothing in return but has the joy of sharing in the divine happiness. Prayer and sacrifice enable such a worshiper to take part in the blessedness of the gods. It was said of Epicurus, "He appeals to the Completely Happy so as to strengthen his own blessedness." It could be argued that he is, therefore, receiving something from the gods, even though the gift is purely spiritual in character, and that the gods are ready to bestow it, thus belying the concept that they are a remote community of beings who have no care or concern for humanity.

Epicurus also recommended prayer because it enabled one to participate in the religious life of one's own country; he viewed it as natural and proper. This contrasts sharply with his constant advice to withdraw completely from political and public activity. But if there is a measure of inconsistency in his sanction of traditional religious rites, his condemnation of the astral religion propagated by Plato in his later years is perfectly consonant with the lofty view of the divine that Epicurus always tried to maintain. His creed is well summed up in the saying of Diogenes of Oenoanda in Asia Minor, who lived in the second century CE: "Nothing to fear in God. Nothing to feel in death."

In one respect the Stoics differed firmly from the Epicureans: they urged active participation in public life, not a retreat from it. While favoring the idea of a world state, they did not shrink from service to their own. Their basic teachings also differed. For them it was virtue, not pleasure, that was the supreme value in life; knowledge was important in the quest for virtue, but the essential thing was to live in agreement with nature since nature leads to virtue. In modern parlance, to follow nature may often imply an uninhibited pursuit of the natural instincts and their pleasures, but the Stoics' interpretation is quite different. For them the formative and guiding principle in nature is reason *(logos)*, which is identified with God himself and is said to manifest itself as fate or necessity and as providence. Another special manifestation is human reason, whose guidance it is our duty to obey. For rational beings such as man virtue alone is the vital possession, and from virtue alone comes happiness. Pleasure, on the other hand, is regarded as only a by-product of virtuous living and not as a proper end in itself. Like the Epicureans, the Stoics valued "freedom from disturbance" *(ataraxia)* as a desirable state, as well as "freedom from emotion" *(apatheia)* and "inward independence" *(autarkeia)*. The founder of Stoicism, Zeno of Citium (335–263 BCE), was highly regarded for his integrity, and it was said of him that "he made his life a pattern to all, for he followed his own teaching." He was succeeded as leader of the school by Cleanthes (331–232 BCE), who was followd in turn by Chrysippus (280–207 BCE). These philosophers showed varied emphases in their teachings, much more so than did the followers of Epicurus, who adhered closely to the precepts of their founding father and gave him almost divine status.

Among the Stoics, Cleanthes was the most concerned with religion. He is renowned for his beautiful *Hymn to Zeus,* where the god is addressed as the creator of the world and the universe and as a ruling spirit who continues to dwell in the whole of his creation. When we compare this hymn with previous Greek praises of the god, we are struck by the absence of any specific allusions to the mythology or cult of Zeus, and we recall that some of the mythology was quite scandalous. Instead, Zeus has become to Cleanthes an abstract figure standing for divine creativity, reason, law, and providence. He does refer to the thunderbolt of Zeus, but he links it to the Stoic doctrine of the conflagration that will end the world: "Nature's own stroke brings all things to their end." He also gives it a moral force, urging Zeus to use it to dispel darkness from the souls of men.

Both Cleanthes and Chrysippus assembled arguments to prove the existence of God, giving prominence to the argument from design: the order and regularity of the heavenly bodies could not be produced by man, it is urged; they must have been produced by something better than man. "And what name other than God would one give to this?" (Cicero, *On the Nature of the Gods* 2.16, quoting Chrysippus). As we have seen, in its whole view of nature and man early Stoicism assigns a built-in importance to religion. A moral earnestness is also evident in the writings of Stoics in the Roman imperial era, especially those of Seneca (5 BCE–65 CE) and

Epictetus (55–135 CE), whose idea of God is practically monotheistic. In their attitude to the gods of tradition, the Stoics were often charged with a pallid reductionism. They tended to equate the gods with the functions associated with them. Plutarch, a middle Platonist not unfriendly to Stoicism, complains in the early second century CE of the facile way in which gods were labeled according to their physical associations; Osiris was thus related to natural fertility while Dionysos was explained as wine and Demeter as grain. Another kind of reductionism was employed by the Stoics to explain myths whose primitive crudities offended them, namely, a wholesale use of allegory. Plutarch himself was prepared to use this method liberally. The Platonist school that he favored continued to flourish, but it had abandoned orthodoxy in its espousal of an open eclecticism.

The philosophical creeds with their variety of religious ingredients appealed, of course, only to an educated elite. Their quiet colonnades were far removed from the rough-and-tumble of the marketplace, as was the Epicurean Garden. Many confusing cries accosted the common man in the marketplace, and he often found it most satisfying, as far as religion was concerned, to follow the emotional uplift and the offer of salvation presented by the mystery religions and by Christianity.

[*For further discussion of Hellenistic religions, see* Gnosticism; Hermetism; Manichaeism; Mystery Religions; Neoplatonism; *and* Roman Religions, *article on* The Imperial Period. *For discussion of other religious movements of this period, see* Rabbinic Judaism in Late Antiquity; Jesus; Paul; *and* Apostles.]

BIBLIOGRAPHY

Bell, H. Idris. *Cults and Creeds in Graeco-Roman Egypt* (1953). Reprint, Chicago, 1975. This book deals with religious developments in Egypt that were, in several instances, influential in the Greek world generally.

Borghouts, J. F., trans. *Ancient Egyptian Magical Texts.* Leiden, 1978. Several spells from the Hellenistic period are included.

Farrington, Benjamin. *The Faith of Epicurus.* New York, 1967. A well-written study that shows the debt of Epicurus to Aristotle.

Festugière, A.-J. *Personal Religion among the Greeks.* Berkeley, 1954. A sensitive analysis of the devotional aspects of the cults of Asklepios and Isis.

Festugière, A.-J. *Epicurus and His Gods.* Translated by C. W. Chilton. Cambridge, Mass., 1956. A detailed and warmly sympathetic study that explains the spirit of evangelism in the Epicurean creed and apologetic.

Fraser, P. M. *Ptolemaic Alexandria.* 3 vols. Oxford, 1972. An authoritative work that gives detailed attention to religious themes.

Grant, Frederick C., ed. *Hellenistic Religions: The Age of Syncretism.* New York, 1953. A valuable collection of translated texts.

Griffiths, J. Gwyn, trans. and ed. *Plutarch's De Iside et Osiride.* Cardiff, 1970. An edition with translation and commentary. A representative of Greek culture and religion in the early centuries of imperial Rome, Plutarch presents remarks on the religions of Iran and Greece in addition to his ambitious analysis of the Egyptian cults.

Jones, Christopher P., trans. *Life of Apollonius* (Philostratus). Harmondsworth, 1970. Important for the study of magic and miracle.

Long, A. A. *Hellenistic Philosophy: Stoics, Epicureans, Sceptics.* London, 1974. A learned and lucid study.

Nock, Arthur Darby. *Essays on Religion and the Ancient World.* 2 vols. Cambridge, Mass., 1972. Rigorously academic in style, these collected essays are the work of an outstanding scholar who devoted his attention mainly to the Hellenistic and Roman eras.

Sinclair, Thomas Alan. *A History of Greek Political Thought.* London, 1952. A sound survey with three chapters on Alexander's age and the sequel.

Vermaseren, Maarten J. *Cybele and Attis: The Myth and the Cult.* Translated by A. M. H. Lemmers. London, 1977. A distinguished Dutch scholar traces the impact of these cults of Asia Minor on the Greco-Roman world.

Walbank, F. W. *The Hellenistic World.* Atlantic Highlands, N.J., 1981. Scholarly and readable.

Witt, R. E. *Isis in the Graeco-Roman World.* London, 1971. A comprehensive and well-illustrated study.

14 GNOSTICISM

Gilles Quispel

Gnōsis ("knowledge") is a Greek word of Indo-European origin, related to the English *know* and the Sanskrit *jñāna*. The term has long been used in comparative religion to indicate a current of antiquity that stressed awareness of the divine mysteries. This was held to be obtained either by direct experience of a revelation or by initiation into the secret, esoteric tradition of such revelations.

PRE-CHRISTIAN GNOSIS

The experience of gnosis was highly esteemed at the beginning of our era in various religious and philosophical circles of Aramaic and Greco-Roman civilization. It is a key word in the scrolls of the Jews of the Essene sect found at Qumran. In the canonical *Gospel of John,* Jesus is quoted as having said at the Last Supper: "This is [not "will be"] eternal life, that they know [not "believe in"] Thee [here and now], and know Jesus Christ, whom thou hast sent" (*Jn.* 17:3). Not even the prevailing philosophy of the time, so-called Middle Platonism, was completely beyond the influence of this general movement. Middle Platonism was primarily religious and otherworldly; it distinguished between discursive reasoning and intuition and taught the affinity of the soul with the godhead, basing these teachings on an oral tradition of the Platonic schools. The writings of Hermes Trismegistos ("thrice-greatest Hermes," identified with the Egyptian god Thoth) reflect the same atmosphere. [*See* Hermes Trismegistos.] These eighteen treatises, of which *Poimandres* and *Asclepius* are the most important, originate in the proverbial wisdom of ancient Egypt. A saying in a recently discovered Armenian collection attributed to Hermes Trismegistos is "He who knows himself, knows the All." The author of *Poimandres* expresses the same insight: "Let spiritual man know himself, then he will know that he is immortal and that Eros is the origin of death, and he will know the All." And to illustrate this saying the author tells the story of a divine being, Anthropos (Man), who becomes enamored of the world of (lower) nature and so falls into a material body. Most Hermetic treatises take up a short saying and expound on it in this manner. They also preserve the impact of Egyptian mythology. The ancient Egyptians spoke freely about sexual intercourse and about the homosexual behavior of their gods. The explicit sexual imagery of Egyptian mythology was adopted in a Hermetic prayer that addresses the spouse of God in the following words: "We know thee, womb pregnant by the phallus of the Father."

The idea of emanation was also prominent in Egyptian religion. Egyptian myth depicts the Nile as tears of the sun god Re. This concept too is found in Hermetic literature. On the other hand, the same writings show the influence of Greek philosophy; indeed, there was a Platonic school of Eudorus in Alexandria. And the impact of the biblical book of *Genesis* and that of Jewish mysticism are only too obvious. Christian influences, though, are completely absent from the so-called *Corpus Hermeticum*. The treatises in this group of works were all written around the beginning of the Christian era in Alexandria. They appear to be the scriptures of a school of mystics, a sort of lodge that practiced spiritualized sacraments such as "the bath of rebirth," a holy meal, and the kiss of peace.

GNOSTICISM

Ever since the congress on the origins of gnosticism held at Messina, Italy, in 1966, scholars have made a distinction between gnosis and gnosticism. *Gnosticism* is a modern term, not attested in antiquity. Even the substantive *gnostic* (Gr., *gnōstikos,* "knower"), found in patristic writings, was never used to indicate a general spiritual movement but was applied only to a single, particular sect. Today gnosticism is defined as a religion in its own right, whose myths state that the Unknown God is not the creator (demiurge, YHVH); that the world is an error, the consequence of a fall and split within the deity; and that man, spiritual man, is alien to the natural world and related to the deity and becomes conscious of his deepest Self when he hears the word of revelation. Not sin or guilt, but unconsciousness, is the cause of evil.

Until recent times the gnostic religion was almost exclusively known by reports of its opponents, ecclesiastical heresiologists such as Irenaeus (c. 180 CE), Hippolytus (c. 200), and Epiphanius (c. 350). Not until the eighteenth century were two primary sources, the Codex Askewianus (named for the physician A. Askew) and the Codex Brucianus (named after the Scottish explorer James Bruce), discovered in Egypt. These contained several Coptic gnostic writings: (1) *Two Books of Jeû* from the beginning of the third century; (2) book 4 of *Pistis Sophia* from about 225; and (3) *Pistis Sophia,* books 1, 2, and 3, from the second half of the third century. To these can now be added the writings found near Nag Hammadi in Upper Egypt in 1945. The stories told about the discovery are untrustworthy. The only certain fact is that, to date, about thirteen of the codices (books, not scrolls) comprising some fifty-two texts are preserved at the Coptic Museum in Old Cairo. They have been translated into English by a team under James M. Robinson (1977). Not all these writings are gnostic: the *Gospel of Thomas* (114 sayings attributed to Jesus) is encratitic; the *Thunder, Whole Mind* is Jewish; the *Acts of Peter and the Twelve Apostles* is Jewish-Christian; the *Prayer of Thanksgiving* is Hermetic; and the *Authoritative Teaching* is early Catholic (characterized by a monarchic episcopacy, a canon of holy writings, and a confession of faith). But the *Epistle of Eugnostos* and the *Apocryphon of John* lead us back very far, close to the sources of gnosticism in Alexandria.

Origins. The hypothesis once supported by Richard Reitzenstein, Geo Widengren, and Rudolf Bultmann that gnosticism is of Iranian origin has been abandoned; the alleged Iranian mystery of the "saved saviour" has been disproved. At present, many scholars are inclined to believe that gnosticism is built upon Hellenistic-Jewish foundations and can be traced to centers like Alexandria, which had a large Jewish population, much as the city of New York does today. Polemics in the writings of the Jewish philosopher Philo, who himself was an opponent of local heresies, make it clear that he knew Jewish groups that had already formulated certain basic elements of gnosticism, although a consistent system did not yet exist in pre-Christian times.

The Divine Man. The prophet Ezekiel tells us in the first chapter of the biblical book that bears his name that in 593 BCE, dwelling in Babylonia, he beheld the personified Glory of the Lord, who would not abandon him even in exile. This figure, at once Light and Man, is described as having a form like the appearance of Adam, or "Man" (*Ez.* 1:26). This vision became a stock image of Jewish mysticism. As early as the second century BCE, the Jewish Alexandrian dramatist Ezekiel Tragicus alludes to the same figure in his Greek drama *Exodus,* fragmentarily preserved in the *Praeparatio evangelica* (9.29) of the Christian bishop Eusebius. In the play, Moses in a dream beholds a throne on top of Mount Sinai. Upon this throne sits Man (Gr., *ho phōs*) with a crown on his head and a scepter in his left hand. With his right hand he beckons Moses to the throne, presents him with a crown, and invites him to sit beside him on an adjacent throne. Thus is Moses enthroned at the right hand of God. A parallel passage is found in Palestinian Judaism: according to the founding father 'Aqiva' ben Yosef (early second century BCE), there are two thrones in heaven, one for God and one for David (B.T., *Hag.* 14a). This is the oldest extant reference to Adam Qadmon, who later became the central figure of qabbalistic literature. Somewhat later, in the *Book of Daniel,* written soon after 168 BCE, this same figure is called the Son of Man (i.e., "divine Man"). The same figure is found in the Gospels. In the Fourth Gospel, the Son of Man is referred to as the Glory of God, which comes from heaven, touches the earth for a moment, is incarnated in the man Jesus, and eventually returns to the heavenly realm. In the letters of Paul, the Glory is called the last Adam (comparable to Ezekiel's *kavod*), who is from heaven and should be distinguished from the first Adam of *Genesis* 1 and 2, who is from the earth. In the Hellenistic world this divine Man is identified with the Platonic idea of man.

Plato himself never says that there is such a thing as an "idea of man." In the dialogue *Parmenides* this philosopher ridicules the concept of an *eidos anthrōpou* (130c). Probably this passage reflects a debate of Platonists among themselves and with other schools. It would seem that the Skeptics denied the idea of man a separate existence because then empirical man and his idea would have something in common, and this would require a new idea, the "third man." In several Middle Platonic sources, however, the idea of man is supposed to exist. The translator of Ezekiel in the Septuagint identifies the figure of divine Man with the Platonic idea when he translates the phrase *demut ke-mar'eh adam* (*Ez.* 1:26) as *homoiōma hōs eidos anthrōpou,* a hellenizing quotation of Plato.

The same figure is to be found in the Hermetic *Poimandres,* clearly influenced by Alexandrian Jews. This writing relates how God generated a son to whom he delivered all creatures. The son is androgynous, equally Phos (Man, Adam, Light) and Zoe (Eve, Life). This being, who is still to be distinguished from the Logos, descends in order to create but falls in love with nature and assumes a material body. That is why human beings are both mortal and immortal. And yet the human body has the form of the original Man. This view is very Jewish and has parallels in rabbinical literature: not the soul but the human body was created after the image and likeness of God.

A next stage is reached in Philo's works. He never quotes *Ezekiel* 1:26 about the Glory of God resembling the form of a man, and yet he must have been familiar with mystical speculations about this divine figure. Philo calls *logos* "Man after his [God's] image" or "Man of God" and identifies the *logos* with the idea of man: incorporeal and neither male nor female. Yet he polemicizes against the concept that this heavenly Man was androgynous: "God made man," he says, "made him after the image of God. Male and female he made—now not 'him' but 'them' " (*Who Is the Heir* 164). Obviously, before Philo there must have been Jewish thinkers who claimed that the heavenly Man was androgynous. Such circles originated the Anthropos model of *gnōsis,* which is found in the doctrine of Saturninus (Antioch, c. 150). In his system, the female figure is completely absent. Our world is said to have been created by seven angels, the seven planets. Thereupon the Unknown God manifested his shining image, the Glory of the heavenly Man. The angels of creation tried to detain this Anthropos but were unable to do so; it returned to heaven at once. Thereupon the angels shaped a human body in the likeness of the heavenly Man. But this creature was unable to stand erect and slithered upon the earth like a worm. The heavenly Adam, having pity on the earthly Adam, sent to him the spark of life, the Spirit, which raised him up and made him live. It is this spark that at death hastens back to its spiritual home, whereas the body dissolves into its constituent elements.

Variations of the myth of Saturninus are found in quite a few of the writings from Nag Hammadi. Valentinus (c. 150) alludes to this myth when, in a preserved fragment, he states that the Adam of *Genesis* inspired awe in the angels who created him because he had been fashioned after the preexistent Anthropos. Mani (216–277) refers to the same story when he relates that in the beginning the Primal Man is sent out to combat the powers of darkness. This Archanthropos is overpowered and forced to leave "the Maiden who is his soul" embedded in matter. The entire world process is necessary to shape the Perfect Man so that the original state of androgyny (male and maiden at the same time) will be restored. All these speculations presuppose the god Man of *Ezekiel* 1:26. Moreover, it is possible that Paul was familiar with the same concept when he said that Christ was both the power *(dunamis)* and the wisdom *(sophia)* of God (*1 Cor.* 1:24).

Sophia. In the *Wisdom of Solomon,* part of the Greek and Roman Catholic Bible, written in Alexandria close to the beginning of the Christian era, personified wisdom, called Sophia, is said to be a holy spirit or the Holy Spirit, which penetrates the All. [*See* Sophia.] She is also referred to as the effluence of God's glory, an emanation of eternal light, and an immaculate mirror of God's activity. She is described as the beloved both of the wise man and of God, even more as the spouse of the Lord (*Wis.* 8:30).

In the *Thunder, Whole Mind,* from the same period and milieu, Sophia manifests herself as the wisdom of the Greeks and the *gnōsis* of the barbarians, the saint and the whore, the bridegroom and the bride. Over and over, she introduces these startling and paradoxical revelations with the formula "I am."

According to the eighth-century BCE inscriptions found near Hebron and in the Negev, the God of Israel had a foreign spouse, the Canaanite goddess Asherah. And in the fifth century BCE, Jewish soldiers garrisoned in Elephantine (near Aswān, Egypt) venerated another pagan fertility goddess called Anat Yahu, the wife of the Lord. Prophets and priests in Judaea did all they could to represent Yahveh as exclusively male and to delete all traces of the primeval matriarchy. But Wisdom survived as Hokhmah, especially in Alexandria. [*See* Hokhmah.]

This is the basis of the Sophia model of *gnōsis,* which finds expression in the teaching of the famous Samaritan Simon, who was attracted to and yet rejected by incipient Christianity (*Acts* 8). The Samaritans, the last survivors of the ten tribes of northern Israel, were and are heterodox Jews who keep the Law while rejecting the rest of the Bible. They transmit a certain tradition about Wisdom as the personal creator of the world. According to Simon, Wisdom, the spouse of the Lord, was also called Holy Spirit and God's first idea, the mother of all. She descended to the lower regions and gave birth to the angels by whom the world was created. She was overwhelmed and detained by these world powers that she might not return to her abode. She was even incarnated and reincarnated in human bodies, such as that of the Helen of Greek myth and poetry. Finally, she came to dwell as a whore in a brothel of Tyre in Phoenicia, where Simon, "the great power" of God, found and redeemed her. In the *Apocryphon of John* as well as in the school of Valentinus, this Sophia model has been combined with the Anthropos model. Both are pre-Christian in origin.

The Unknown God and the Demiurge. The rabbis of the first Christian centuries complain repeatedly of the heretics *(minim)* who taught the existence of two gods. Dissident Jewish teachers believed that God had a representative, bearing his name Jao (the abbreviation of YHVH), who was therefore called Jaoel. According to this view, Jaoel sat upon a throne next to God's throne and was therefore called Metatron (a Greek loanword). In reality, however, Jaoel is nothing but an angel, the most important angel, the one who is called the angel of the Lord in the Hebrew Bible. Some dissident Jews called Magharians said that all anthropomorphisms in the Old Testament applied not to God himself but to this angel, who is also said to have created the world. In a Samaritan (i.e., heterodox Jewish) source called *Malef,* which is late but transmits earlier traditions, it is stated that the angel of the Lord formed the body of Adam from dust of the earth and that God breathed the breath of life into him.

Such views must have been known already to Philo of Alexandria, who polemicizes against them yet at the same time calls the Logos, who is instrumental in creation, both "a second god" and "archangel" on the one hand and "Lord" (YHVH) and "Name" (i.e., YHVH) on the other. Jewish gnostics such as Simon and Cerinthus affirm that the demiurge (identified with YHVH) was in fact this angel of the Lord, who had not yet rebelled against God. [*See* Demiurge.] In the *Apocryphon of John* the angel is called Saklas (Aramaic for "fool") because he does not know that there is a God greater than he. Valentinus, Marcion, and Apelles, who were familiar with the myth contained in the *Apocryphon of John,* all held that the demiurge was an angel. This is a typically Jewish concept. A non-Jew, when suffering under the misery of the world, would simply have declared that the *Genesis* story was a myth without truth; he could not have cared less about the origin of Jewish law. Only those who had been brought up to believe every word of the Bible and to cling to the faith that God is one, and who yet found reason to rebel against their inheritance, would have inclined toward the gnostic solution: God is one and the Bible reveals the truth, but anthropomorphisms such as the handicraft of a creative workman and personal lawgiving are to be attributed to a subordinate angel.

The God Within. The biblical *Book of Genesis* relates that God blew the breath of life into the nose of Adam, transforming him into a living being (*Gn.* 2:7). Already in certain passages of the Old Testament (*Jb.* 34:13–15, *Ps.* 104:29–30), this breath is identified with the spirit of God. That is especially clear in the Dead Sea Scrolls: "I, the creature of dust, have known through the spirit, that Thou hast given me." The Alexandrian Jews have integrated and amplified this concept. They were familiar with Greek philosophy and knew that the Orphics, Plato, and the Stoics considered the human soul to be a part of the deity. They were influenced by the Stoic Posidonius (c. 100 BCE), according to whom "the daimon in us [the spirit] is akin to *and of the same nature* as the Daimon [God] who pervades the All." The oldest translators of the Septuagint rendered "breath" (Heb., *neshamah*) in *Genesis* 2:7 as "spirit" (Gr., *pneuma*). This variant is evidenced by the Old Latin Version *(spiritus)* translated from the Septuagint. Philo polemicizesagainst this particular translation because it deifies sinful man (*Allegorical Interpretation* 1; 13). And yet the Alexandrian *Wisdom of Solomon,* still included in every Roman Catholic Bible, declares explicitly that God's incorruptible *pneuma* is in all things (12:1). Most gnostics preserved this tendentious translation and made it the basis for their mythological speculations. It enabled them to tell how it came to pass that the Spirit sleeps in man and how it can be made conscious. So it is with Valentinus and Mani. Few people nowadays are aware that these mythologems presuppose a consensus of virtually all Greek philosophers and have a biblical foundation.

JEWISH GNOSTICISM

The themes discussed above are the basic elements that contributed to the rise of a Jewish gnosticism, whose myth is contained in the *Apocryphon of John* and other related writings found at Nag Hammadi. The church father Irenaeus attributed this doctrine to the *gnōstikoi*. With this name he indicates not all those whom modern scholars call "gnostics" but only the adherents of a specific sect. It is misleading to call them Sethians (descendants of Seth, the son of Adam), as some scholars do nowadays. Notwithstanding its name, the *Apocryphon of John* (a disciple of Jesus) contains no Christian elements apart from the foreword and some minor interpolations. It can be summarized as follows: from the Unknown God (who exists beyond thought and name) and his spouse (who is his counterpart and mirror) issued the spiritual world. The last of the spiritual entities, Sophia, became wanton and brought forth a monster, the demiurge. He organized the zodiac and the seven planets. He proclaimed: "I am a jealous god, apart from me there is no other." Then a voice was heard, teaching him that above him existed the Unknown God and his spouse. Next, the "first Man in the form of a man" manifested himself to the lower angels. He is the Glory of *Ezekiel* 1:26. His reflection appears in the waters of chaos (cf. the mirror of the Anthropos in *Poimandres*). Thereupon the lower angels created the body of Adam after the image that they had seen, an imitation of the Man, who clearly serves as an ideal archetype for the human body. For a long time the body of Adam lay unable to move, for the seven planetary angels were unable to raise it up. Then Sophia caused the demiurge to breathe the *pneuma* he had inherited from her into the face of his creature. So begins a long struggle between the redeeming Sophia and the malicious demiurge, the struggle for and against the awakening of human spiritual consciousness.

Written in Alexandria about the beginning of the Christian era, the myth of the *Apocryphon of John,* a pivotal and seminal writing, combines the Anthropos model and the Sophia model. It is very complicated and confusing but had enormous influence in the Near East, where so many remnants of great religions survive today. (In the 1980s, for example, there were 420 Samaritans and 30,000 Nestorians.) Even today some 15,000 Mandaeans (the Aramaic term for gnostics) live in Iraq and Iran. Their religion features ablutions in streaming water and a funerary mass. When a Mandaean has died, a priest performs a complicated rite in order to return the soul to its heavenly abode, where it will receive a spiritual body. In this way, it is believed, the deceased is integrated into the so-called Secret Adam, the Glory, the divine body of God. This name confirms that, along with the Anthropos of *Poimandres* and the Adam Qadmon of later Jewish mysticism, this divine and heavenly figure is ultimately derived from the vision of the prophet Ezekiel. In Mandaean lore Sophia appears in degraded form as a mean and lewd creature called the Holy Spirit. The creation of the world is attributed to a lower demiurge. Ptahil, a pseudonym for the angel Gabriel (who, according to both the Mandaeans and the Magharians, is the angel who created the world).

The apostle Paul (or one of his pupils) maintains that Christ, who is for him the second Adam, is "the head of his Church, which is his body" (*Eph.* 1:22–23). The Christian is integrated into this body through baptism. Mandaean speculations about the Secret Adam may elucidate what Paul meant. In defining his view of the church as the mystical body of Christ, the apostle may be reflecting a familiarity with comparable Jewish and Hellenistic speculations about the *kavod* as the body of God. As a matter of fact, it has become clear from the verses of Ezekiel Tragicus that such ideas circulated in Alexandria long before the beginning of our era. They surfaced in Palestine toward the end of the first century CE in strictly Pharisaic circles that transmitted secret, esoteric traditions about the mystical journey of the sage through the seven heavenly places to behold the god Man on the throne of God. The author of the writing *Shi'ur Qoma,* the "measurement of the Body" of God, reports the enormous dimensions of the members of the Glory. The Orphics had taught that the cosmos was actually a divine body. Already early in Hellenistic Egypt similar speculations arose; these were the origin of the remarkable speculations of Palestinian rabbis concerning the mystical body of God. (These speculations ultimately led to the *Zohar.*) It is no coincidence that the Glory is called Geradamas (Arch-Adam) in some Nag Hammadi writings, Adam Qadmaia in Mandaean sources, and Adam Qadmon in medieval Jewish gnosticism.

In the ninth century several groups of Islamic gnostics arose in southern Iraq, where several other gnostic sects had found refuge during late antiquity and where the Mandaeans continue to live today. [*See* Mandaean Religion.] The best-known Islamic gnostics are the Ismā-'īlīyah, of which the Aga Khan is the religious leader. [*See* Aga Khan.] Mythological themes central to their religion are (1) the cycles of the seven prophets; (2) the throne and the letters; (3) Kuni, the creative principle, who is feminine (a typical remythologizing of a monotheistic Father religion); (4) the higher Pentad; (5) the infatuation of the lower demiurge; (6) the seven planets and the twelve signs of the zodiac; (7) the divine Adam; and (8) the fall and ascent of the soul.

Since the discovery of the Nag Hammadi codices it has been established that these themes are best explained as transpositions into an Islamic terminology of the gnostic mythemes that are found in the *Apocryphon of John* and kindred documents of Jewish gnosticism.

CHRISTIAN GNOSIS

According to a reliable tradition, Barnabas, a missionary of the Jerusalem congregation, was the first to bring the gospel to Alexandria, a relatively easy journey. Egyptian Christianity is Judaic in origin, not gentile, and the great Egyptian gnostics seem all to have been of Jewish birth. The adherents of Basilides claimed: "We are no longer Jews and not yet Christians." The followers of Valentinus reported: "When we were Hebrews, we were orphans." Basilides and Valentinus both proclaimed a God beyond the Old Testament God, and both were familiar with the myth of the *Apocryphon of John,* which they christianized. The case of Marcion is similar: he was so well-informed about the Hebrew Bible and its flaws that his father, a bishop, may well be presumed to have been Jewish. Through a certain Cerdo, Marcion came to know an already existing gnostic system. Those who reject the god of the Old Testament obviously no longer hold to the Jewish faith, but nevertheless still belong ethnically to the Jewish people. Both Valentinus and Marcion went to Rome and were excommunicated there between 140 and 150. Basilides, who stayed in Alexandria, remained a respected schoolmaster there until his death. The Christians in Alexandria were divided among several synagogues and could afford to be tolerant, for a monarchic bishop did not yet exist and their faith was pluriform anyhow. Basilides, Valentinus, and Marcion were Christocentric and let themselves be influenced by the *Gospel of John* and the letters of Paul.

Marcion. When Marcion, a rich shipowner from Si-nope in Pontus (on the Black Sea), was excommunicated, he organized an enormous alternative church that persisted for a long time, especially in the East (e.g., in Armenia). [*See* Marcion.] Marcion was a violin with one string, a religious genius with one overpowering idea: God, the Father of Jesus, was not the Hebrew YHVH. Like the gnostics, he distinguished between the Unknown God (whom he felt to be the only genuine God) and a lower divinity, the demiurge, who is responsible for creation and interacts with man. Above all, Marcion was fascinated by Paul's *Letter to the Galatians.* Following Paul, he contrasted the Law of the Old Testament and Israelite religion with the "gospel of forgiveness," which revealed the goodness of God.

Like his hero Paul, Marcion was overwhelmed by the unconditional and unwarranted love of God for poor creatures. This led him to deny the gnostic idea that man's inmost Self is related to the Godhead. For Marcion, man is nothing more than the creation of a cruel demiurge; the loving God who has rescued him, without any ulterior motive but simply out of a freely bestowed loving kindness, is totally alien to man, his nature, and his fate.

Until Augustine, no one understood Paul as well as Marcion; yet Marcion, the one genuine pupil, misunderstood Paul as well. Notwithstanding his dialectics, Paul never rejected the created world, sexuality, or the people of Israel, as did Marcion.

Basilides. Basilides was active as the leader of a school in Alexandria in the time of the emperors Hadrian (r. 117–138) and Antoninus Pius (r. 138–161). He seems to have been one of those many liberal Jews who had left behind the concept of a personal lord for belief in the Unknown God. Yet he was never excommunicated and remained a respected member of the church of Alexandria until his death.

Basilides must have known the earlier Alexandrian, pre-Christian myth contained in the *Apocryphon of John.* He too begins his cosmogony with the Unknown God, "the not-being God, who made a not-yet-being world out of nothing" by bringing forth a single germ of the All. This germ was the primeval chaos. From it in due time one element after another arose on high, while below there remained only the so-called third sonship, or the Spirit in the spiritual man.

When the time was right, Jesus was enlightened at his baptism in the river Jordan (a typically Jewish-Christian notion). He is considered to be the prototype of all spiritual men, who through his revealing word become conscious of their innermost being, the Spirit, and rise up to the spiritual realm.

When the entire third sonship has redeemed itself, God will take pity on the world, and he will allow the descent of "the great unconsciousness" upon the rest of mankind. Thereafter no one will have even an inkling that there was ever anything like the Spirit. Basilides foresees a godless and classless society.

Valentinus. The greatest gnostic of all times was the poet Valentinus. Despite his Latin name, he was a Greek born in the Nile Delta around the year 100 and educated in Alexandria. He and his followers did not separate from the church of Alexandria but created an academy for free research, which in turn formed a loose network of local groups within the institutional religion. Even among his opponents Valentinus became renowned for his eloquence and genius.

According to his own words, his views originated in a visionary experience in which he saw a newborn child. This vision inspired a "tragic myth," expressed by Valentinus in a psalm that described how the All emanates from the ground of being, called Depth, and his spouse, called Womb or Silence. Together they bring forth the Christ, or Logos, upon whom all aeons (half ideas, half angels) depend and through whom the All is coherent and connected. Through the revelation of Christ, Valentinus experienced the wholeness of the All, the fullness of being, and the nonentity "I and Thou" (known in Hinduism as *advaita*). Not dualism but duality is the underlying principle of reality, according to Valentinus: God himself is the transcendental unity of Depth and Silence; the aeons of the pleroma (spiritual world) are a diametrical union of the masculine, or creative, and the feminine, or receptive, principles; Christ and Sophia (Wisdom) are a couple (separated for a while on account of the trespass and fall of Sophia but in the end happily reunited). Man and his guardian angel, or transcendental counterpart, celebrate the mystical marriage of bride and bridgegroom (the Ego and the Self). Polarity (Gr., *suzugia;* Lat., *coniunctio*) is characteristic of all things spiritual. On the basis of this metaphysical view, Valentinus and his followers valued both sex and marriage, at least for the pneumatics. A preserved fragment from the school of Valentinus gives the following interpretation of Jesus' statement in the *Gospel of John* that the Christian lives in the world but is not from it (*Jn.* 17:14–16): "Whosoever is *in* the world and has not loved a woman so as to become one with her, is not out of the Truth and will not attain the Truth; but he who is *from* the world and unites with a woman, will not attain the Truth, because he made sex out of concupiscence alone." The Valentinians permitted intercourse only between men and women who were able to experience it as a mystery and a sacrament, namely, those who were pneumatics. They forbade it between those whom they called "psychics" (Jews and Catholics) or "hylics" (materialists), because these two lower classes knew nothing but libido. As the only early Christian on record who spoke lovingly about sexual intercourse and womanhood, Valentinus must have been a great lover.

The Jung Codex. On 10 May 1952, at the behest of the Jung Institute in Zurich, I acquired one of the thirteen codices found at Nag Hammadi in 1945. In honor of the great psychiatrist who helped to put this manuscript at the disposal of competent scholars, it is called the Jung Codex. It contains five Valentinian writings:

1. The *Prayer of the Apostle Paul.*
2. The *Apocryphon of James* is a letter purporting to contain revelations of the risen Jesus, written by James, his brother. In reality, it contains Valentinian speculations grafted onto the root and fatness of the olive tree planted beside the waters of the Nile by Hebrew missionaries from Jerusalem (c. 160).
3. The *Gospel of Truth* is a meditation on the true eternal gospel proclaimed by Christ to awaken man's innermost being, the unconscious Spirit, probably written by Valentinus himself in about 150.
4. The *Epistle to Rheginos concerning the Resurrection* is adequate explanation of Paul's view on the subject: already, here and now, man anticipates eternal life, and after death he will receive an ethereal body.
5. The so-called *Tripartite Treatise* is a systematic and consistent exposition of the history of the All. It describes how the Spirit evolves through the inferno of a materialistic (pagan or "hylic") phase and the purgatory of a moral (Jewish and Catholic or "psychic") phase to the coming of Christ, who inaugurates the *paradiso* of final consummation, in which spiritual man becomes conscious of himself and of his identity with the Unknown God. The author, a leader of the Italic (Roman) school of Valentinianism, was most likely Heracleon (c. 170). It was against this shade of Valentinian gnosis that Plotinus, the Neoplatonic philosopher, wrote his pamphlet *Against the Gnostics* (c. 250).

LATER DEVELOPMENTS

Scholars have always admitted that Origen (c. 180–254), the greatest dogmatician of the Greek church, had much in common with the Valentinians: the spirits fall away from God and become souls before the creation of the world; the world purifies the soul; Jesus brings not only redemption to the faithful but also gnosis to the pneumatics. But whereas Valentinus was said to have taught predestination physics (the teaching that spiritual man was saved by nature), Origen on the contrary allegedly stressed free will. The *Tripartite Treatise* has undermined this apologetic position. There evil is no longer a tragic neurosis that befell Sophia but a free decision. Moreover, this writing is thoroughly optimistic: all is for the best in the best of all possible worlds, and providence educates mankind toward the realization of complete consciousness, as in Origen's soteriology. Some path led from the tragic view of Valentinus to the optimism of Heracleon, and from Heracleon to Origen was only one step more.

The Valentinians of Carthage spoke Latin, whereas the Christians in Rome spoke Greek. Translating their technical terms from Greek, the Valentinians coined Latin equivalents of *infinite, consubstantial, trinity, person,* and *substance.* These terms were eventually adopted by the Roman Catholic church. If ever there was a community that created a special language, it was the school of Valentinus at Carthage.

Mani. Gnosticism became a world religion when Mani (216–277) founded his alternative Christian church, which existed for more than a thousand years with adherents in lands from the Atlantic Ocean to the Pacific. [*See* Mani *and* Manichaeism.] From his fourth until his twenty-fifth year Mani was raised in a Jewish-Christian community of Baptists, followers of the prophet Elxai (c. 100). There he heard, first, that Jesus was "the true prophet," a manifestation of God's glory *(kavod)* who was first embodied in Adam, then revealed himself to the Old Testament patriarchs and was ultimately incarnated in the Messiah, Jesus. He also heard, second, that baptisms and ablutions were necessary for salvation and, third, that God was the origin of evil since Satan was the left hand of God. He modified the first belief, identifying himself as the seal of the prophets, who included the Buddha and Zarathushtra in the East and Jesus in the West. The second belief he rejected; in fact, he admitted no sacraments at all. Against the third belief he, being a cripple, rebelled with all his might. Evil, in Mani's view, did not originate in the world of light but had its source in a different principle, the world of darkness, matter, and concupiscence.

Influenced by encratitic asceticism of the Aramaic Christians of Asia, Mani rejected marriage and the consumption of alcohol and meat, and he designated among his followers an upper class of the elect who lived according to the Sermon on the Mount and a lower class of auditors who were allowed to have wives or concubines and to practice birth control. But very much in the spirit of Valentinus was Mani's primary religious experience. The basis of his entire myth, the encounter with his "twin" or transcendental Self, is gnostic, very much in the spirit of Valentinus: "I recognized him and understood that he was my Self from whom I had been separated." Mani encountered his spiritual Self at the age of twelve and encountered it a second time at the age of twenty-five. He felt constantly accompanied by his twin, and when he died a martyr in prison he was gazing at this familiar. The encounter with one's twin is central to the life of every Manichaean. The mystery of conjunction, the holy marriage of Ego and Self, is thereby democratized. To illustrate this process, Mani related a myth that is indebted to earlier gnostic movements. For Mani the world is in truth created by the Living Spirit, a manifestation of God, and not by a lower demiurge. But a split within the deity takes place when the archetypal Man loses in the battle against darkness, is thus overwhelmed, and abandons his soul as sparks of light dispersed throughout the material world and mankind. Man is contaminated in this way by concupiscence, an evil force from the world of darkness. The entire world system is devised to save these light elements and to restore man as Perfect Man in his original purity and integrity.

Augustine (354–430) was a Manichaean auditor for more than nine years before he became a Father of the Roman Catholic church. During that period he wrote a treatise (since lost), *On Beauty and Harmony,* in which he stated that the asexual mind was linked with a completely alien element of ire and concupiscence. As a heresy-hunter he later maintained that concupiscence was not created by God but was instead a consequence of the Fall. The assertion that the reproductive instinct is not a part of human nature does certainly have Manichaean overtones.

The Middle Ages. Manichaeism disappeared completely in the West and had no successors there: the term *medieval Manichee* is a misnomer. And yet Christianity during the Middle Ages both in Western and in Eastern Europe was not monolithically orthodox. Gnosticism flourished at that time. Such books as *Montaillou* by Emmanuel Le Roy Ladurie and *The Name of the Rose* by Umberto Eco have drawn the attention of a large public of interested outsiders to the existence of dualistic sects such as the Cathari in southern France and northern Italy and the Bogomils (or "friends of God") in Yugoslavia and Bulgaria, because their views resemble those of the ancient gnostics. Indeed, their affiliation with ancient gnosticism, if somewhat complicated, is well established. [*See* Cathari.]

The Paulicians were typically Armenian sectarians who, persisting into modern times, turned up in 1837 in the village of Arh'wela (in Russian Armenia) with their holy book, the *Key of Truth* (eighth century). Two versions of their doctrine exist. According to one, Jesus was adopted to be the son of God. According to the second version, there are two gods; one is the Father in heaven, while the other is the creator of this world. This can be explained in the following way: Christianity was introduced to Armenia from Edessa at an early date, and Edessa owed its (adoptionist) Christology to Addai, the Jewish-Christian missionary from Jerusalem. When Roman Catholicism was established as the state church in 302 by Gregory the Illuminator, the Christians of Armenia were branded as heretics. Marcionites and gnostics had taken refuge in these marginal and mountainous regions. They united with the adoptionists to become one sect, the Paulicians, soon a warlike group. The emperors of Byzantium deported quite a few of them to the Balkans, especially to Bulgaria. It was there that the sect of the Bogomils originated, characterized by the belief that the devil (Satanael) created and rules this world. Their influence spread to the West, and from the beginning of the eleventh century gave rise to the church of the Cathari, which was strong in southern France and northern Italy. Thus gnosticism was never completely suppressed but survived into the Middle Ages.

Modern Gnosis. The gnosis of modern times, launched by the shoemaker Jakob Boehme (c. 1600), was generated spontaneously as a result of direct experience. [*See* Theosophy.] It differs from ancient gnosticism in that it derives not only the light but also the darkness (not only good but also evil) from the ground of being. Inspired by Boehme is the influential gnosis of the English poet and artist William Blake (1757–1827), the only authentic gnostic of the entire Anglo-Saxon world. It is in the school of Boehme that the scholarly study of gnosticism has its roots, beginning with the *Impartial History of the Churches and Heresies* (1699) by Gottfried Arnold. In this extremely learned work all heretics, including all gnostics, are represented as the true Christians—innocent and slandered lambs.

Ever since, the study of gnosticism has been an accepted academic subject in Germany, but in Germany alone. In his youth Goethe read Arnold's book and conceived his own gnostic system, as reported in his autobiography. Toward the end of his life Goethe recalled the love of his youth when he wrote the finale to *Faust*, the hierophany of "the Eternally Feminine," a version of the gnostic Sophia, the exclusive manifestation of the deity. Johann Lorenz von Mosheim and other great historians also took gnosis quite seriously. The brilliant August Neander, who belonged to the conservative reaction to the Enlightenment called the Great Awakening Revivalism *(Erweckungsbewegung)*, wrote his *Genetic Evolution of the Most Important Gnostic Systems* in 1818. Ferdinand Christian Baur, a prominent Hegelian, published his monumental *Christian Gnosis* in 1835, in which he defends the thesis that gnosis was a religious philosophy whose modern counterpart is the idealism of Schelling, Schleiermacher, and Hegel, all based upon the vision of Boehme. According to Baur, even German idealism was a form of gnosis. Yet when "the people of poets and thinkers" became, under Bismarck, a people of merchants and industrial workers, this wonderful empathy, this fantastic feel of gnosis, was almost completely lost.

Adolf von Harnack (1851–1930), the ideologue of Wilhelm's empire, defined gnosticism as the acute, and orthodoxy as the chronic, hellenization (i.e., rationalization) and hence alienation of Christianity. At the time it was difficult to appreciate the experience behind the gnostic symbols. Wilhelm Bousset, in his *Main Problems of Gnosis* (1907), described this religion as a museum of hoary and lifeless Oriental (Indian, Iranian, Babylonian) fossils. The same unimaginative approach led Richard Reitzenstein, Geo Widengren, and Rudolf Bultmann to postulate an Iranian mystery of salvation that never existed but was supposed to explain gnosticism, Manichaeism, and Christianity.

Existentialism and depth psychology were needed to rediscover the abysmal feelings that inspired the movement of gnosis. Hans Jonas (*The Gnostic Religion*, 1958) has depicted these feelings as dread, alienation, and an aversion to all worldly existence, as if the gnostics were followers of Heidegger. In the same vein are the writings of Kurt Rudolph, the expert on Mandaeism.

Under the influence of Carl Gustav Jung, I and other scholars (e.g., Henri-Charles Puech and Károly Kerényi) have interpreted the gnostic symbols as a mythical expression (i.e., projection) of self-experience. As a lone wolf, the Roman Catholic convert Erik Peterson suggested that the origins of gnosticism were not Iranian or Greek but Jewish. The gnostic writings from Nag Hammadi have shown Jung and Peterson to be in the right. At last the origins, development, and goal of this perennial philosophy have come to light.

BIBLIOGRAPHY

Jonas, Hans. *The Gnostic Religion: The Message of the Alien God and the Beginnings of Christianity.* 2d ed., rev. & enl. Boston, 1963.

Pagels, Elaine H. *The Gnostic Gospels.* New York, 1979.

Quispel, Gilles. *Gnostic Studies.* 2 vols. Istanbul, 1974–1975.

Robinson, James M., et al. *The Nag Hammadi Library in English.* San Francisco, 1977.

Rudolph, Kurt. *Gnosis.* San Francisco, 1983.

15 MYSTERY RELIGIONS

KURT RUDOLPH
Translated from German by Matthew J. O'Connell

Like many other terms that represent concepts in the history of religions, *mysteries,* or *mystery religions,* serves as an umbrella term covering a wide variety of referents. Since the word had its own origin and history, its use needs to be analyzed carefully, especially in the context of comparative studies.

DEFINITION OF TERMS

The Greek word *mustēria* refers initially only to the "mysteries" of Eleusis and signifies a secret celebration or secret worship that is accessible only to initiates *(mustai),* who have had themselves initiated *(muein* or *telein)* into it. Other terms used for the celebration are *teletē* and *orgia;* Latin writers either use the Greek word or translate it as *initia.* Originally, then, *mysteries* denotes a specific religious manifestation that is essentially different in character from other, official cultic functions; the mysteries are not open to everyone but require a special initiation. But in Greek, *mustēria* is already applied to comparable rituals of initiation (see below) and thus acquires a general meaning. When taken over by philosophy (especially Neoplatonism and Neo-Pythagoreanism) and Christianity, the term increasingly loses its original concrete religious referent and acquires instead the sense of a revealed or mysterious divine wisdom ("mysteriosophy") that is only available to or attainable by adepts.

The term *mysteries* was familiar, of course, to classical philologists, who knew it from the ancient tradition, but it was not until the nineteenth century that it again became a technical term in the history of religions for secret cults or ceremonies of initiation (owing especially to James G. Frazer). In particular it was much used by the history of religions school, most often by Richard Reitzenstein and Wilhelm Bousset, in their attempt to render comprehensible the multiplicity that marked the history of religions in the Hellenistic period and late antiquity, as well as to demonstrate the connections between that world and early Christianity. In the view of the history of religions school, the mysteries were an expression of popular piety that drew sustenance especially from the so-called Oriental mystery religions of the Roman imperial age; in the long run, it was claimed, even the early church could not escape the influence of those religions. Discussion of the beginnings of Christianity was carried on for a long time under the sign of the mysteries, which were regarded as one of Christianity's roots; this approach can still be found today.

There can be no objection to a general use of the term *mysteries* provided that its original meaning continues to resonate even as its application is extended. The problem here is the same as with *gnosis* or *gnosticism*. These technical terms have been given a broader meaning, but scholars have not on that account ceased to use them in a restricted regional sense: *gnōsis* as a Greek word meaning "esoteric knowledge" and referring to religious groups of late antiquity. My own inclination is not to detach these terms from the historical context in which they exercised historical influence but to continue to use them primarily in their restricted sense, without, however, forgetting that the history of religions needs such umbrella terms—especially in comparative studies. The danger otherwise is that the terminology will become blurred and cease to be of help in describing original religious phenomena and will serve only for a religious typology that lacks historical depth.

Thus, for example, Buddhism has been explained by Paul Lévy (1957) as a "mystery religion," simply because of certain ritual factors that play a part in the consecration of Buddhist monks and resemble to some extent ritual elements in the Greek and Oriental mysteries. This demonstration I regard as an unsuccessful venture into dangerous territory. Certainly, Buddhism (especially Tibetan Mahāyāna or Vajrayāna Buddhism) has its "mysteries" in the sense of esoteric rituals, just as do most of the other great religions (especially Hinduism). But such instances occur during later historical stages that presuppose a developed hierarchy and represent a kind of ritualization of esoteric teachings that can in turn be traced back in part to older foundations. It is possible in the same way to give the name *mysteries* to various disputed early Mesopotamian and early Egyptian rituals.

We really have no choice but to understand the term *mysteries* as a historical category that registers a specific historico-religious content and that relates in particular to the Greco-Roman age. The general, typological use of the word must be measured against that standard. Mysteries, then, are special initiation ceremonies that are esoteric in character and often connected with the yearly agricultural cycle. Usually they involve the destiny of the divine powers being venerated and the communication of religious wisdom that enables the initiates to conquer death. The mysteries are part of the general religious life, but they are to a special degree separated from the public cult that is accessible to all, and on this account they are also called "secret cults."

THE "PHENOMENOLOGY" OF THE MYSTERIES

Mysteries, then, refers primarily to the content as found in the history of Greco-Roman and Near Eastern religions. At the cultic-ritual level, which is the dominant level, the discipline of the *arcanum* (the obligation of strict secrecy) means that we know very little more about the mysteries than the ancient sources—including ancient Roman literature—occasionally pass on as supposedly reliable information. Our historical knowledge is limited because Christian writers (such as Clement of Alexandria and Firmicus Maternus) who reported on the mysteries allowed their own polemical or apologetic interpretations to color their accounts.

We are relatively well informed about the general structure of the ceremonies (Eleusis, Samothrace, Isis, Mithras). Processions and public functions (sacrifices, dances, music) framed the actual celebration, which was held in closed rooms (*te-lestērion, spelunca,* temple) and usually comprised two or three acts: the dramatic action *(drōmenon)* with the "producing and showing" of certain symbols *(deiknu-mena)* and the interpretation (exegesis), through a communication of the myth *(le-gomena)* and its attendant formulas, of what had been experienced. The sacred action *(drōmenon)* and the sacred narrative *(legomenon, muthos, logos)* were closely connected. We are still rather ignorant regarding the central ceremony, that is, the initiation proper. Any interpretation of it can be hypothetical only, never certain. In my opinion, the heart of the celebration was the linking of the initiate with the destiny of the divinity or divinities, as expressed in performance and word, and the resultant bestowal of hope for some kind of survival after death. This inter-pretation is also suggested by burial gifts for the deceased (e.g., the "Orphic" gold plate from southern Italy). The ancient human problems of suffering, death, and guilt undoubtedly played an important part in the efficacy of the mysteries. The idea of rebirth can be documented only in later Hellenism. In any case, there is no evidence of a unitary theology of the mysteries that was common to all the mysteries; the origins and historical course of the several mysteries were too discrepant for that. Even the later philosophical explanation of the *logos* of the mysteries was not everywhere the same.

A word must be said here about the connection often made between the mysteries and the idea of "dying and rising divinities," who are linked to the vegetation cycle. James G. Frazer, who accepted the ideas of Wilhelm Mannhardt on nature myths and folk myths, was the leader and main influence in this area. In addition to an unin-hibited use of terminology (e.g., *resurrection* is usually understood in the biblical and Christian sense), the chief defect of this theory is its utter neglect of source criticism. Strictly speaking, the "vegetation theory" is a theory at two removes that, as Carsten Colpe has shown, simply takes a theory at one remove, namely, the an-cient *interpretatio Graeca,* and prolongs it in the spirit of nineteenth-century Ro-manticism. The nineteenth-century scholars did not further analyze the ancient use of symbols and metaphors in which the vegetative processes of withering and blooming (in the myth of Adonis) were already described (especially from the sec-ond century on) by such terms as *dying, declining, disappearing,* and *being re-newed, reappearing, rising.* I say nothing of the fact that these same scholars made no distinction between primary, cult-related myth and secondary, literary mythology. A whole series of so-called vegetation divinities, such as Adonis, Attis, and Osiris, or Tammuz, were interpreted according to the same pattern, namely, as dying and rising gods; their cults, with their "mystery" character, supposedly served to com-municate to the "initiates" the powers associated with the "fruitfulness" of nature. [*See* Dying and Rising Gods.]

As we know today, there is no evidence at all that any of these gods was thought of as "rising" in any proper sense of the term. In actual fact, there were great differ-ences in mythology and ritual; only secondarily (often as early as late antiquity) were the divinities assimilated to one another (e.g., Osiris to Adonis and Attis). The often only fragmentary mythology centering on these divinities told of the disappearance or stay of the god in the lower world, where he lived on (as lord of the lower world or, in the case of Osiris, as judge of the dead) or from which in one or another manner he returned to the light of day (on earth, in the air, or in heaven) and resumed his role as a god (which he had never abandoned). The connection with rituals was also quite diverse; there was by no means always a question of mysteries in the sense of secret cults (see below). We must also allow for the possibility that some of the so-called Oriental mysteries acquired their mystery character only secondarily, under the influence of Greek and especially the Eleusinian mysteries (this was certainly the case with Osiris in relation to Adonis). The interpretation of the mysteries as being, without distinction, ancient vegetation cults should therefore no longer be used as a magic hermeneutical key.

In view of this critique, the historical and phenomenological problem of the origin of the mysteries remains unresolved. Repeated attempts have been made to move beyond the now-outdated nature-myth theory. Ethnologists in particular have repeatedly focused on the mysteries and interpreted them as survivals of ancient "rites of passage" (Arnold van Gennep); in our day this theory has been maintained especially by Mircea Eliade. There is much that is correct in it. The ethnological contributions that play a role in it come in part from the morphology of culture school (Frobenius), in part from the history of culture school of Vienna. The latter, represented by Wilhelm Schmidt and Wilhelm Koppers, sees the initiation of young men or boys and the whole organization of adult male society as one of the important roots of the mysteries. In cultural and historical terminology the mysteries reflect the agrarian, matriarchal stage, in which for the first time the male sector of society, as distinct from the female sector, developed secret societies and initiation ceremonies (as a protest against matriarchal tyranny, according to Koppers). That stage would be located chronologically in the Mesolithic period. The Greek mysteries are not directly linked to that stage and its events, but they are pre-Indo-Germanic and ultimately have their roots in it.

The history of culture theory as developed by Wilhelm Schmidt has been largely abandoned today. It has left behind only the idea—itself not new—that the origin of the mysteries is to be sought in some stage of primitive agricultural development. Even this, however, does not apply to Osiris, who from the beginning was associated with pastoral symbols, thus reflecting a nomadic culture, and had close ties with the Egyptian ideology of kingship; the later Corn Osiris has been assimilated to Adonis, and the Hellenistic mysteries of Osiris, which focus primarily on Isis, have in turn been influenced by the Eleusinian mysteries of Demeter and Persephone (Kore). The role played by female divinities need not be linked to a hypothetical matriarchy; these goddesses are phenomena belonging to an agrarian culture (Mother Earth). Among modern philologists Walter Burkert is the chief proponent of the view that the root of the mysteries is to be looked for in agrarian culture and specifically in secret society ceremonies (with their tests of courage and their sexual, orgiastic traits) and that they originated in the Neolithic age; the dawning Greek individualism of the seventh and sixth centuries BCE took over these ancient cults and turned them into a deliberately adopted religion centered on the conquest of death.

Adolf E. Jensen has suggested a different ethnological approach. He sees behind the Greek mysteries (especially those of Eleusis) a conception of the world proper to the culture of early food growers; this conception centered on the death or possibly the sacrifice of a female prototypical being (or divinity) who was the source of the life-sustaining cultivated vegetation, and thus it thematized for the first time the mystery of death and life ("the slain god"). There has since been occasional criticism of the interpretation of the Melanesian starting point (the myth of Hainuwele; see Jonathan Z. Smith's "A Pearl of Great Price and a Cargo of Yams: A Study in Situational Incongruity" in *History of Religions* 16, 1976, pp. 1–19, and his *Imagining Religion*, Chicago, 1982, pp. 90–101); nonetheless it is a legitimate question whether earlier food-cultivation stages are to be glimpsed behind the mysteries. The answer can be found only through cooperative study by ethnologists, prehistorians, lologists, and historians of religion. In any case an answer is not directly required for understanding our historical and philological material, which comes to us primarily from Greek sources. All our ancient informants confirm the view that the mysteries in general took their character primarily from the Greek mysteries and became widespread only as a result of hellenization.

THE HISTORICAL MULTIPLICITY OF MYSTERIES
Within the confines of this article it is necessary to start with the ancient Greek mysteries and move on to related Oriental mysteries.

The Greek Mysteries. The Greek mysteries were from the outset cults of clan or tribe. They can in many cases be traced back to the pre-Greek Mycenaean period and were probably ancient rituals of initiation into a clan or an "association." The most important were the mysteries of Eleusis, which in fact provided the pattern for the idea of mysteries. [*See* Eleusinian Mysteries.] The independent town of Eleusis (there is evidence of a prehistoric settlement there in the third millennium BCE) became an Athenian dependency in the seventh century BCE and thereby acquired, especially from the sixth century on, a pan-Hellenic role that in the Roman imperial age attracted the attention of Rome. Augustus, Hadrian, Marcus Aurelius, Commodus, and Gallienus had themselves initiated into the Eleusinian mysteries. An attempt under Claudius (r. 41–54) to move the celebration to Rome failed. The destruction of the sanctuary came under Alaric's Christian Goths in 395 CE. The mythological background for the Eleusinian mysteries was provided by the story of the goddesses Demeter and Kore, preserved in the Homeric *Hymn to Demeter*. The pair were presented as mother and daughter. Their relationship developed in a gripping manner the theme of loss (death), grief, search, and (re)discovery (life). The interpretation of the story as purely a nature myth and specifically a vegetation myth is actually an old one and can appeal to ancient witnesses for support; nonetheless it is oversimplified precisely because it loses sight of the human and social content of the myth.

The public ceremonies of the annual Eleusinian ritual are well known to us and confirmed from archaeological findings. The director was the hierophant, who from time immemorial had been a member of the Eumolpides, a noble family that had held the kingship of old. The Kerukes family filled the other offices. All classes, including slaves, were admitted to the cult. According to degree of participation, a distinction was made between the *mustēs* ("initiate") and the *epoptēs* ("viewer"); only the latter was regarded as fully initiated. But this distinction was not original and came in when the Eleusinian mysteries were combined with the mysteries of Agrai on the Ilissos (near Athens) in the seventh century BCE. The Lesser Mysteries at Agrai took place annually in February (the month Anthesterion) and were regarded as a preliminary stage leading to the Greater Mysteries held at Eleusis in September (16–20 Boedromion). Sacrifices, libations, baths, ablutions, fasts, processions (especially bringing the "holy things," the cult symbols, to Eleusis), and torches all played an important role in both feasts. The center of all activity was the ceremony that was not open to the public. It was held in the "place of consecration" known as the *telestērion,* which is not to be confused with the temple of Demeter at the same location.

We know that at the ceremonies at Agrai the initiate knelt down with a ram's skin draped around him and held an unlit torch in his hand. The priestess shook a winnowing fan *(liknon)* over him, and he handled a serpent (sacred to Demeter and Kore). Finally water was poured over him. In the Eleusinian ceremony, of which we know less, the initiation took place at night. It included the handling of an object, not identified with certainty, which was taken from a "coffer" (perhaps the instrument—mortar and pestle—used in preparing the sacred potion; other interpretations see the coffer as an image of the womb). In addition, there was a "viewing" *(epopteia)* of the (rescued?) Kore, probably in dramatic form *(drōmenon).* The cry that the hierophant uttered at this point suggests as much: "The Lady bore a holy boy-child: Brimo bore Brimos" (Hippolytus, *Refutations* 5.8.40). The reference is probably to the birth of Ploutos, the personification of wealth, from Demeter; yet it is questionable whether this was intended as a symbol of the new birth of the initiate and not as a symbol of the limited power of the lower world or death. The latter meaning seems to be suggested by the concluding rite: the showing of an ear of grain by the priest (Hippolytus, ibid.). This must have signified that life is "Mother" Demeter's gift to human beings. A fragment of Pindar (Bowra 121) says of the initiates: "Happy they who see it and then descend beneath the earth. They know life's end but also a new beginning from the gods." To them alone is life given in the underworld; all others encounter evil (see Sophocles, frag. 837, Pearson).

In addition to the mysteries of Eleusis, there was a series of others about which there is unsatisfactory information. Almost all of them were very ancient. They include the mysteries at Phenas in Arcadia (also mysteries of Demeter); those at Andania in Messenia, in which Demeter and Hermes were venerated as great gods; those at Phyle, dedicated to "Earth, the great mother"; and those on Paros and Thasos, which were again mysteries of Demeter. More important were the mysteries of the great gods, or Kabeiroi, on the island of Samothrace, where there was an ancient place of worship until the fourth century CE that attracted many, especially in the second century BCE. The gods in question were probably a pair of Phrygian divinities, father and son *(kabeiros* is a Semitic word). The ceremonies had a pronounced orgiastic and burlesque character and were probably connected with what had originally been associations of smiths (iron rings played a role). Later, however, the Kabeiroi were regarded as helpers in distress at sea. Practically nothing is known of these mysteries; there are hints of links with Demeter and Orpheus.

More important were the Dionysian mysteries, information on which has come down to us from as early as the fifth century BCE (see Euripides, *The Bacchae).* As is well known, Dionysos was an unusual god who represented a side of Greek life long regarded as un-Greek—a view that has caused interpreters many difficulties. His *thiasos* ("company") was probably originally an association of women that spread throughout Greece, especially the islands, and carried on a real proselytizing activity by means of itinerant priestesses. There was no one central sanctuary, but there were centers in southern Italy (Cumae), Asia Minor, and Egypt. Ecstatic and orgiastic activity remained characteristic of this cult as late as the second century CE and only then assumed more strictly regulated, esoteric forms, as can be seen from the laws of the Iobacchant community at Athens, where the cult of Dionysos (Bacchus) had become a kind of club. The myth of Dionysos had for its focus the divine forces hidden in nature and human beings; these forces were thematized and applied chiefly by women. The ecstatic nocturnal celebrations showed traits of promiscuity (Maenads and satyrs) and took place in the open air. It is uncertain to what extent the paintings in the Villa Item at Pompeii and in the Casa Omerica reproduce the later ritual of the Dionysian mysteries. These paintings are more likely a mysteriosophic interpretation within the framework of a bridal mysticism in which the soul (the immortal element as part of the god Dionysos) presents the pattern of a cycle of purifications. The myth of Dionysos was at an early stage combined with the Orphic mysteries. The hope of another world that was promised and confirmed in the rites is well attested by burial gifts (gold plates) from Greece and southern Italy. Even after death, the initiate remained under the protection of the god. [*See* Dionysos.]

The Orphic mysteries are a difficult phenomenon to deal with. Often they are not easily distinguished from the Dionysian mysteries. Also, it is not certain whether they were actually mysteries and, if they were, where we should look for their origin. Testimonies do not go back beyond the sixth century BCE and vary widely. It is certain that at an early date Orpheus was turned into the founder of the Eleusinian, Dionysian, and Samothracian mysteries. [*See* Orpheus.] Orphism therefore had no central sanctuary. It seems to have been more of a missionary religion that, unlike the official cults, devoted itself to the theme of the immortal soul *(psuchē)* and its deliverance from the present world. It had an ethical view of the relation between initiation and behavior. A way of life that was shaped by certain rules served to liberate the soul or the divine in human beings. The anthropogonic and cosmogonic myth that provided an explanation of the hybrid human condition also showed the way to redemption; cosmology and soteriology were thus already closely connected. As a result, Orphism broke away from the religion of the *polis,* not only because it possessed holy books that contained its teachings, but also because the idea of the immortality of the soul made the official cult superfluous. Greek philosophy, beginning with Socrates and Plato, gave a theoretical justification for all this.

The Oriental Mysteries. Narrowly understood, the Oriental mysteries comprised only the mysteries of Isis and of Mithras. But since the ancient Alexandrian reporters applied the technical terms *mustēria* and *teletai* in their proper sense to any orgiastic cult or ritual, and especially to the numerous and often quite exotic Oriental cults of the imperial period, a whole series of these religions came to be classified as mysteries; this usage has prevailed down to our own time.

Mysteries of Cybele are attested on the Greek mainland and islands from the third century BCE. Oddly, no mention is made of Attis. Pausanias, in the second century CE, is the first witness to the connection; the mythological relation is attested by Catullus in his "Poem 63" (first century BCE). We know nothing about the structure and content of these mysteries; perhaps they were an imitation of the Eleusinian mysteries. In any case, the Roman cult of Cybele, who was worshiped on the Palatine from 204 BCE on, was not a mystery religion. Beginning in the second century CE and down to the fifth century, the literature speaks of the mysteries of Mater Magna (Mētēr Megalē) but tells us no more about them. On the supposition that we are not dealing simply with a misleading terminology, these mysteries may have focused on the ritual castration of novices (Galli) and its deeper meaning. With regard to

Attis, inscriptions in Asia Minor dating from the first century CE speak of the "initiates of Attis" (Attabokaoi). Some formulas, preserved by Clement of Alexandria and Firmicus Maternus, show that the reference is to a participation in the destiny of the divinity whereby the faithful are promised deliverance: "Be consoled, O initiates, for the god is delivered; therefore we too shall have deliverance from our troubles" (Firmicus Maternus, *De erroribus profanarum religionum* 22.1–3).

The initiation involved an anointing; there is also reference to a kind of sacred meal (eating from a tambourine, drinking from a cymbal). The meaning of an accompanying formula is uncertain in the version given by Clement of Alexandria (*Protrepticus* 15): "I have entered the *aduton* [bridal chamber?]." Firmicus Maternus has a simpler version: "I have become an initiate of Attis." At the end of the fourth century CE, the cult of Cybele and Attis also included baptism in bull's blood *(taurobolium)*. This ceremony had developed out of an older sacrifice of a bull, attested from the middle of the second century on. It was supposed to bring renewal to the initiates; only a single inscription interprets the renewal as a "new birth." The baptism was a onetime rite and perhaps was intended to compete with Christian baptism.

The Hellenistic cult of Isis in late antiquity undoubtedly involved secret initiatory celebrations. We learn something about them from Apuleius's famous novel, *Metamorphoses,* or *The Golden Ass* (second century CE). Greek influence is especially clear here: it was only through the identification of Isis with Demeter (attested in Herodotus, 2.59) and the hellenization of the cult of Isis that the latter came to include mysteries (first attested c. 220 BCE on Delos). In this form it spread, despite occasional opposition, throughout the whole civilized world of the time, reaching Rome in the first century BCE. It became one of the most widely disseminated Oriental religions of late antiquity, especially from the second century BCE on. Isis became the great thousand-named, universal goddess *(panthea)* who had conquered destiny and was invoked in numerous hymns and aretalogies that display a remarkable Greco-Egyptian atmosphere and tone.

This successful hellenization was probably due to the introduction of the cult of Sarapis under Ptolemy I, son of Lagus (305–283 BCE), when this novel Greco-Egyptian cult (*Sarapis* combines *Osiris* and *Apis*) was celebrated with both an Eleusinian priest (Timothy, a Eumolpid) and an Egyptian priest (Manetho) participating. Isis, Thoth, and Anubis were naturally linked with Sarapis (Osiris). The well-known story of Isis, Osiris, and Horus (Harpocrates) acquired its complete form only in Greek and in this version was probably a product of Hellenism (Osiris being assimilated to Adonis). The ancient Egyptian cult of Osiris was originally connected with the monarchy and displayed the character of a mystery religion only to the extent that the dead pharaoh was looked upon as Osiris and brought to Abydos not simply to be buried but also to be greeted by the people as one restored to life in the form of a new statue in the temple. The hope of survival *as* or *with* or *like* Osiris was the predominant form that the hope of another world took in ancient Egypt, and it continued uninterrupted in the Greco-Roman period; it provided a point of attachment for the mysteries of Isis. [*See* Isis.]

The cult of Isis had its official place in the Roman festal calendar (beginning in the second century CE) and comprised two principal feasts: the Iseia, which was celebrated from 26 October to 3 November and included the *drōmenon* of the myth, with the "finding" *(heurēsis, inventio)* of Osiris as its climax; and the sea-journey feast (Navigium Isidis, Ploiaphesia) on 5 March, the beginning of the season for seafaring, of which Isis had become the patron deity. According to Apuleius (*Metamorphoses* 11) the actual mysteries began with preliminary rites such as baptism (sprinkling), a ten-day fast, and being clothed in a linen robe. At sunset the initiates entered the *aduton* for further ceremonies to which only allusions are made: a journey through the lower world and the upper world (the twelve houses of the zodiac, which represented the power of destiny) and a vesting of the initiate as the sun god *(instar solis);* the initiate was *renatus* ("reborn") and became *sol* ("the sun"), or in other words experienced a deification *(theomorphōsis).* He thereby became a "servant" of Isis and "triumphed over his destiny *[fortuna]."* In addition to a consecration to Isis, there was evidently also a consecration to Osiris, but we know even less about this ceremony.

The cult of Mithras (Mithra) in the Roman imperial age, like that of Isis, was not originally Oriental but was a creation of Hellenistic syncretism. It is true that the name of the god Mithras is Indo-Iranian in origin and originally meant "contract" *(mithra, mitra)* and that some Iranian-Zoroastrian elements are recognizable in the iconographic and epigraphic sources; these facts, however, do not point to a Persian origin of the cult. No testimonies to the existence of Mithraea in Iran have as yet been discovered. On the other hand, the vast majority of these sanctuaries have been found in the Roman military provinces of central and eastern Europe, especially in Dalmatia and the Danube Valley. The Mithraeum at Dura-Europos on the Euphrates is the most eastern. It was built by Roman soldiers from Syria in 168 CE, rebuilt in 209 CE, and expanded in 240 CE. It was thus not the creation of a native community. The "Parthian" style is simply a matter of adaptation to local tradition and no proof of an Iranian origin of the mysteries. There is as yet no evidence of Mithraea in Babylonia (Mesopotamia); three Mithraea have been found in Asia Minor, one in Syria. The oldest Mithraea are from the middle of the second century CE; most are from the third and fourth centuries. Thus an Eastern origin for the Mithraic mysteries is most uncertain.

According to Plutarch (*Life of Pompey* 24) they were introduced into the West by Syrian pirates in the first century BCE. This report may have a historical basis because the veneration of Mithras in Syria, Pontus, and Commagene is well attested, though no reference is made to any mysteries of Mithras. It is likely that soldiers from this area, where Greeks and Orientals came in contact, brought the cult of Mithras to the West in the first century CE. In the second century CE, however, the cult was transformed into mysteries in the proper sense and widely disseminated as a soldiers' religion, until finally Mithras was elevated to the position of Sol Invictus, the god of the empire, under Diocletian (r. 284–305). As in the case of the cult of Isis, the Hellenistic worshipers of Mithras transformed the foreign god and his cult along lines inspired by the awakening individualism of the time with its rejection of the traditional official cult and its longing for liberation from death and fate—a longing especially understandable in soldiers. In addition, the exotic elements (Egyptian, Persian) are to be attributed to the contemporary tendency to emphasize and cultivate such traits as being especially efficacious.

We are, once again, poorly informed about the myth and rites of the Mithraic mysteries. We have no account by an Apuleius as we do for the mysteries of Isis. Instead we have a large mass of archaeological documents that are not always easy to interpret. The so-called *Mithraic Liturgy* is a magical text concerned only marginally with the mysteries of Mithras. What Porphyry has to say about these mysteries in his *Cave of the Nymph* is philosophical exegesis in the Neoplatonic vein.

The Mithraic mysteries took place in small cavelike rooms that were usually decorated with the characteristic relief or cult statue of Mithras Tauroctonus ("bull-slayer" or "bull-sacrificer"). In form, this representation and its accompanying astrological symbols is Greco-Roman; its content has some relation to cosmology and soteriology, that is, the sacrifice of a bull is thought of as life-giving. Other iconographic evidence indicates that the god was a model for the faithful and wanted them to share his destiny: birth from a rock, combats like those of Herakles, ascent to the sun, dominion over time and the cosmos. Acceptance into the community of initiates *(consecranei)* or brothers *(fratres)* was achieved through consecratory rites in which baptisms or ablutions, purifications (with honey), meals (bread, water, wine, meat), crownings with garlands, costumes, tests of valor, and blessings played a part. There were seven degrees of initiation (Corax, Nymphus, Miles, Leo, Perses, Heliodromus, Pater), which were connected with the planetary deities and certain symbols or insignia. Surviving inscriptions attest the profound seriousness of the mysteries. Mithras is addressed: "You have rescued us, too, by shedding the blood that makes us immortal." Since these groups accepted only men (mostly soldiers), they can be considered true religious associations of males. Also worth noting is the close link between Mithras and Saturn (Kronos) as god of the universe and of time (Aion, Saeculum, Aevum); Saturn is the father of Mithras and the one who commissions him, while Mithras is in turn connected with the sun god (Sol, Apollo). (There is still a good deal of obscurity in this area.) Christian apologists (Justin, Tertullian, Jerome, Firmicus Maternus) regarded the mysteries of Mithras as a serious rival of early Christianity; several Christian churches were built over Mithraea. [*For further discussion, see* Mithra *and* Mithraism.]

IMPACT OF THE MYSTERIES

Because the Greek mysteries, especially the Eleusinian and the Dionysian, exerted a growing attraction and influence, Hellenistic literature accepted and developed in varying ways the ideas and representations proper to the mysteries. An effort has been made (Kerényi, 1927; Merkelbach, 1984) to extend our knowledge of the mysteries, and especially of the ritual concealed from us by the discipline of the secret *(arcanum)*, by examining the novels of late antiquity. Such fictional themes as loss, search, and recovery, (apparent) death and return to life, the passing of tests, transformations (metamorphoses), hints of "mysteries," and so on may very well have been reflections of the mysteries. Ambiguity, allegory, and symbolism served as codes that could be broken only by initiates (and in our day by scholars). Reinhold Merkelbach speaks in this context of an "Isis novel" (in Apuleius, Xenophon of Ephesus, Achilles Tatius, the *Historia Apollonii Regis Tyri,* and parts of the pseudo-Clementine literature as reworked by Christian gnostics); a "Mithras novel" (Syrian Iamblichus, *Babylonica*); a Dionysos novel (Longus, *Daphne and Chloe*); and, in the *Aethiopiaca* of Heliodorus, a "syncretistic Helios novel" that combines the mysteries of Isis, Mithras, and Dionysos.

The philosophical and religious literature of the Hellenistic age was also affected by the mysteries. The *Corpus Hermeticum,* for example, is filled with reminiscences of the terminology of the mysteries, and we are quite justified in assuming that the circles responsible for the corpus had "mysteries" that were given ritual expression. The same holds for some of the gnostic writings, which not only frequently discuss the concept of *mustērion/mysterium* but also adopt in their rituals various aspects of the mysteries and especially the notion of a *disciplina arcani* (see below). Even Hellenistic Judaism, especially in the person of Philo Judaeus (first century CE), underwent the same influence. A work like *Joseph and Aseneth* is unintelligible without a knowledge of the mysteries. Even the Greek translation (the Septuagint) of the Hebrew Bible does not escape their influence, any more than the subsequent writings of the Christian community. The language of Christ's apostle Paul (especially in *1 Corinthians* and *2 Corinthians*) and of his disciples (in *Ephesians* and *Colossians*) betrays this environment, as does, no doubt, the *First Letter of Peter*.

The impact of the mysteries became more concrete beginning in the second century CE, as the Christian church found itself increasingly in competition with these forms of worship. The cultic area of the church's life, especially baptism and eucharist, underwent a profound transformation as the sacraments became "mysteries" to which not everyone had immediate access. Preparation (initiation) was now required in the form of fasts, instructions, purifications. The unbaptized and those on the way to baptism (catechumens) were not admitted to the sacred Christian cultic meal, which was regarded as the "remedy bringing immortality" and acquired its efficacy through the epiclesis (invocation) of the priest; in other words, the cultic meal was placed under a kind of discipline of secrecy. As the church became hierarchically organized (especially from the third century on) and as it became an established church under Constantine in the fourth century, it not only won greater publicity to the detriment of the old established religion but at the same time acquired an aspect of mystery whereby it sought to give a Christian direction to a new phenomenon, the religiosity of the masses. *Mystery* now became not only a cultic term but also, following a path blazed by ancient philosophy, made its way into Christian theology, where *mysticism* came to mean a kind of knowledge of God that is not available to everyone.

"MYSTERIOSOPHY"

A typically Hellenic spiritualization of the language of the mysteries had been going on in Greek philosophy since Plato; in the ensuing period, as the mysteries spread, *mysterium* and *sophia* became more and more closely associated, and in late antiquity the distinction between religion and philosophy became ever more tenuous. The parallelism of the two was due to the fact that, according to Greek philosophy, knowledge of God was attainable only by a path resembling the one followed in the mysteries at the ritual and religious level: that is, there was need of preparations, instructions, and even a kind of authorization *(katharsis)*. For Plato, knowledge of God is identical with the vision of supreme and utterly pure being; the vision brings a participation in that being and even bestows immortality. For this reason, terms taken from the mysteries were often used in philosophy: *epopteia, teletē, mustēria*. Platonic and Stoic philosophers began to impose their own meaning on the available myths connected with the mysteries; they began to "mythologize" them, that is, to link *muthos* and *logos*. Preliminary steps in this direction, or at least parallel manifestations, were already to be found in Orphism, which posited a "hidden" (mystic) link between the cosmos and human beings and made use in addition of the doctrine of the soul (a divine element located in the body). This paraphilosophical explanation has been called "mysteriosophy" (Bianchi, 1979); we met it earlier in the traditions concerned with Eleusis, where it already bore a strong Orphic impress.

Insofar as the philosophy of the Hellenistic age and late antiquity was interested in the mysteries, it took the often bizarre mythical traditions associated with them and sought to extract their rational (logical) nucleus by interpreting them as pieces of natural philosophy or as nature myths (this was especially the case with the Stoics). Unfortunately, we possess only fragmentary examples of such interpretations of the mysteries. Thus Cybele (Magna Mater) was interpreted as Mother Earth (Lucretius, Varro) and as the origin of being, and Attis as the instrument of creation (i.e., of becoming) or as Logos and Savior (Emperor Julian). Isis, understood as mother of the gods and universal goddess *(panthea),* was identified with Demeter (Plutarch). Mithras (the Sun) became principle ("Creator and Father") of the universe (Porphyry); his identification with Aion ("eternal time") probably also goes back to a philosophical interpretation.

The influence of this kind of philosophical interpretation on the later theology of the mysteries cannot simply be rejected out of hand. Traditions such as Hermetism, a Greco-Egyptian revelatory religion, show the path followed in this alignment of philosophy and religion, which the Neo-Phythagoreanism and late Platonism (Plotinus) led to philosophy being turned into religion, philosophical knowledge into the vision of God, and the life of the philosopher into a religious *bios* ("life"). At work in this process was the conviction that behind both religion (the mysteries) and philosophy was the "ineffable," the "mystery," or "being," as opposed to everything transient or to "becoming," and that this ultimate reality was to be approached not simply through thought *(theōria)* but also through one's way of life *(praxis);* only the two together could lead one to vision, enlightenment, and immortality (see especially Iamblichus, *De mysteriis).*

This current of thought provided the matrix for gnosticism, a movement that not only continued to some extent the ritual practices of the mysteries, such as cultic meals, baptisms, purifications, anointings, and *drōmena* and was organized as a mystery-association *(thiasos)* but also borrowed from the mysteries at the level of ideology (mythology). The so-called Naassene sermon "On Man" (Hippolytus, *Refutatious* 5.6, 4–10, 2) is an instructive example of this borrowing and, at the same time, one of the few sources that preserve authentic citations from the Eleusinian mysteries. Among other things, Attis is here interpreted as the gnostic Primal Man (Anthropos); his castration by Cybele becomes a deliverance from what is earthly. Osiris, Adonis, and Adam are likewise variants of the perfect human being or of the immortal soul. According to this gnostic sermon, the mysteries of Isis are the root of all nongnostic cults, and Persephone-Kore, in the form of Aphrodite, represents transient becoming. For this reason, all these mysteries are looked upon as the "lesser mysteries," while the mysteries of gnosticism become the "greater mysteries" or the "heavenly mysteries." This synoptic view of all mysteries in the service of a mysteriosophic and gnostic interpretation was a path by which the traditions embodied in the ancient mysteries made their way into late antiquity. Thus transformed and preserved, they became part of the heritage left by heathen and Christian antiquity and, to that extent, remained alive even after the cessation of the cultic practices that had once been their true reality.

BIBLIOGRAPHY

General Works

Bornkamm, Günther. "Mustērion." In *Theological Dictionary of the New Testament,* edited by Gerhard Kittel, vol. 4. Grand Rapids, Mich., 1967.

Campbell, Joseph, ed. *Papers from the Eranos Yearbooks,* vol. 2, *The Mysteries.* Princeton, 1955.

Lévy, Paul. *Buddhism: A "Mystery Religion"?* London, 1957.

Metzger, Bruce. "Bibliography of Mystery Religions." In *Aufstieg und Niedergang der römischen Welt,* vol. 2.17.3, pp. 1259–1423. Berlin and New York, 1984.

Greek Mysteries

Bianchi, Ugo. *The Greek Mysteries.* Leiden, 1976.

Burkert, Walter. *Griechische Religion der archaischen und klassischen Epoche.* Stuttgart, 1977. Translated as *Greek Religion* (Cambridge, Mass., 1985).

Casadio, G. "Per un'indagine storico-religioso sui culti di Dioniso in relazione alla fenomenologia dei misteri, I." *Studi storico-religiosi* 6 (1982): 210–234 and 7 (1983): 123–149.

Foucart, Paul-François. *Les mystères d'Eleusis* (1914). New York, 1975.

Guthrie, W. K. C. *Orpheus and Greek Religion: A Study of the Orphic Movement.* 2d ed., rev. London, 1952.

Hemberg, Bengt. *Die Kabiren.* Uppsala, 1950.

Kern, Otto. *Die griechischen Mysterien der klassischen Zeit.* Berlin, 1927. Amended in *Die Antike* 6 (1930): 302–323.

Nilsson, Martin P. *The Dionysiac Mysteries of the Hellenistic and Roman Age* (1957). New York, 1975.

Nilsson, Martin P. *Geschichte der griechischen Religion* (1941–1957). 2 vols. 3d rev. ed. Munich, 1967–1974.

Otto, Walter F. *Dionysos: Myth and Cult.* Bloomington, Ind., 1965.

Turchi, Nicola. *Fontes historiae mysteriorum aevi hellenistici.* Rome, 1923.

Oriental Mysteries

Bianchi, Ugo, ed. *Mysteria Mithrae.* Leiden, 1979.

Bianchi, Ugo, and Maarten J. Vermaseren, eds. *La soteriologia dei culti orientali nell'Impero Romano.* Leiden, 1982.

Colpe, Carsten. "Zur mythologischen Struktur der Adonis-, Attis- und Osiris-Überlieferungen." In *Lišān mitḫurti: Festschrift Wolfram Freiherr von Soden,* edited by Wolfgang Röllig, pp. 23–44. Neukirchen-Vluyn, 1969.

Cumont, Franz. *The Mysteries of Mithra* (1903). New York, 1956.

Cumont, Franz. *The Oriental Religions in Roman Paganism* (1911). New York, 1956.

Hepding, Hugo. *Attis: Seine Mythen und sein Kult* (1903). Berlin, 1967.

Hinnel, John R., ed *Mithraic Studies.* 2 vols. Totowa, N.J., 1975.

Kerényi, Károly. *Die griechisch-orientalische Romanliteratur in religionsgeschichtlicher Beleuchtung.* Tübingen, 1927.

Merkelbach, Reinhold. *Mithras.* Konigstein, 1984.

Reitzenstein, Richard. *Die hellenistischen Mysterienreligionen nach ihren Grundgedanken und Wirkungen.* Berlin, 1927. Translated as *The Hellenistic Mystery Religions* (Pittsburgh, 1978).

Vermaseren, Maarten J. *Die orientalischen Religionen im Römerreich.* Leiden, 1981.

Christianity and Gnosticism

Angus, S. *The Mystery-Religions and Christianity.* 2d ed. London, 1928. Reprinted as *The Mystery-Religions: A Study in the Religious Background of Early Christianity* (New York, 1975).

Frickel, J. *Hellenistische Erlösung in christlicher Deutung.* Leiden, 1984.

Loisy, Alfred. *Les mystères païens et le mystère chrétiens.* 2d ed. Paris, 1930.

Wagner, Günter. *Das religionsgeschichtliche Problem von Römer 6,1–11.* Zurich, 1962.

16 MANICHAEISM

GHERARDO GNOLI
Translated from Italian by Ughetta Fitzgerald Lubin

The doctrine professed by Mani and the path to salvation that he revealed constitute a form of gnosis. It originated during the first half of the third century in Mesopotamia, a region of the Parthian empire in which a number of different religious and philosophical schools were actively present, notably Christianity, Judaism, and Zoroastrianism. The sects and communities of the region reflected the influence of one or the other of these cults to varying degrees and were often characterized by an evident gnostic orientation. Hellenism was well rooted and widespread in Mesopotamia (as in neighboring Syria), especially in the urban centers of Seleucid origin. Open to commercial and cultural exchanges, Mesopotamia was the region within the vast Parthian empire that was most likely to absorb syncretic and eclectic cultural and spiritual trends. Manichaeism, however, was not only a gnosis in the narrow sense; it was primarily a universal gnostic religion—the only great universal religion to arise from the Near Eastern gnostic tradition. No other gnostic school was as successful as Manichaeism, and no other aimed, as it did, to establish itself as a truly universal religion, founded and nurtured by an enterprising missionary spirit.

As with all gnostic movements, Manichaeism holds that knowledge leads to salvation and that this is achieved through the victory of the good light over evil darkness. As with all gnosticism, Manichaeism is permeated by a deep and radical pessimism about the world, which is seen as dominated by evil powers, and by a strong desire to break the chains holding the divine and luminous principle inside the prison of matter and of the body. Knowledge leads to salvation through an anamnesis, in which the initiate recognizes that his soul is a particle of light, consubstantial with the transcendental God.

MANICHAEAN LITERATURE AND SOURCES

Very little remains of the rich and varied Manichaean literature. We know the canon of its scriptures mainly through the titles of individual works, of which seven were attributed to Mani himself, and through fragments preserved in quotations by authors who were hostile to Manichaeism. Sometimes we do have most of the text, as, for example, in the *Living Gospel,* which was translated from Syriac to Greek (Oxyrhynchus Codex). So too was the *Treasure of Life,* some passages of which were quoted by Augustine and by al-Bīrūnī; the *Mysteries,* of which we know the subtitles quoted by Ibn al-Nadīm and a few passages preserved by al-Bīrūnī; the *Treatise,* the *Book of Giants,* and the *Epistles,* of which Ibn al-Nadīm gives a list; and the *Psalms* and *Prayers.* All of these works were attributed to the founder of the faith, and rare and scattered fragments of them have been preserved in Manichaean texts from Central Asia (Turfan) and Egypt (Fayum). Two more works were attributed to Mani but are outside of the canon: the *Image* and the *Shābuhragān,* the book dedicated to the Sasanid king Shāpūr I. The purpose of the *Image* was to illustrate the main themes of the doctrine in a way that would be clear even to those not able to read. The *Shābuhragān,* the only work written in Middle Persian—Mani usually wrote in Syriac or Eastern Aramaic—discussed cosmology, anthropogony, and eschatology and is known to us through fragments preserved in the Turfan manuscripts and through an essential quotation by al-Bīrūnī concerning the Seal of the Prophecy.

Manichaean patrology is relatively better known to us than Mani's writings, mainly through the texts discovered at Turfan around the beginning of this century and those found at Fayum in 1930. Among the hagiographic works, we should mention the Manichaean Codex of Cologne, a Greek translation of a Syriac original, from Oxyrhynchus (?) and dating from the fifth century, and the Coptic *Homilies;* among the doctrinal ones, the Coptic *Kephalaia* and the *Chinese Treatise* of Tun-huang; among the hymns, the Coptic *Psaltery* and the Iranian hymn books, in Middle Persian and in Parthian, found in Turfan, as well as those in Chinese from Tun-huang; among the practical and liturgical writings, the *Compendium of Doctrines and Rules of the Buddha of Light, Mani,* a treatise dating from 731, found in Tun-huang, that was translated from Parthian into Chinese for use in the administration of the cult. To the last category also belonged the *Khwāstwānēft,* a handbook of formulas for the confession of sins, which has come down to us in a Uighur text from Central Asia.

Thus the discoveries of the twentieth century have brought to light, albeit only partially and in a fragmented fashion, a literature that in many cases, especially in the psalms and hymns, is distinguished by its considerable litarary value and by its strong and delicate poetic sensibility. These writings substantially modified the picture of Manichaeism that had been reconstructed through indirect sources before the end of the nineteenth century.

These sources, however, are still valuable, and they contribute now in a more balanced way to a reconstruction of Manichaean doctrine and history. They are numerous, and all by hostile authors, Neoplatonic, Christian, Zoroastrian, Muslim. There are Greek sources, from Alexander of Nicopolis to the *Acta Archelai;* Latin sources, from the Pseudo-Marius Victorinus to Augustine; Syrian sources, from Aphraates and Ephraem of Syria in the fourth century to Theodoros bar Kōnaī in the eighth; Middle Persian and Pahlavi sources, from passages in the *Dēnkard* (The Acts of Religion) to a chapter of the *Shkand-gumānīg Wizār* (The Definitive Solution to Doubts), a Zoroastrian apologetic work (ninth and tenth centuries); Arabic and Persian Muslim sources, from al-Yaʿqūbī (ninth century), al-Ṭabarī, al-Masʿūdī, and Ibn al-Nadīm (tenth century) to al-Bīrūnī, Taʿālibī (eleventh century), al-Sharastānī (twelfth century), Abūal-Fidā, and Mirkhwānd (fourteenth and fifteenth centuries).

Until Manichaean literature was rediscovered, the works of Augustine, al-Bīrūnī, Ibn al-Nadīm, and the *Acta Archelai* were the cornerstones of Manichaean studies. Although the situation has undoubtedly changed considerably thanks to the more recent discoveries, the accounts of some anti-Manichaean authors remain extremely important, especially when viewed alongside those passages in Manichaean literature that discuss similar or identical subjects. It is now easier to distinguish between that which was written in polemic and apologetic ardor and that which resulted from accurate and intelligent information concerning Manichaean doctrines. Some of the sources are particularly relevant since they provide likely and precious data: for example, the *Letter of Foundation* by Augustine, the Manichaean cosmogony of Theodoros bar Kōnaī, and a few quotations and excerpts by al-Bīrūnī and Ibn al-Nadīm.

THE FUNDAMENTAL DOCTRINES

Manichaean doctrine places great importance on the concept of dualism, which is deeply rooted in Iranian religious thought.

Dualism. Like Zoroastrian cosmology, which we know through relatively late texts (ninth century CE), Manichaean dualism is based on the doctrine of the two roots, or principles, of light and darkness and the three stages of cosmic history: the golden age before the two principles mixed together; the middle, or mixed, period, Gumēzishn (MPers.); the present age, in which the powers of light and darkness battle for ultimate control of the cosmos; and the last age, when the separation of that which had become mixed, and between followers of good and evil, occurs. According to the Zoroastrian doctrine, this is the time of *frashgird* (MPers., "rehabilitation"; Av., *frashōkereti*) in which the two poles of good and evil will once again be distinguished. [*See* Frashōkereti.] The holy books that he himself has revealed are those of the two principles and three stages. The two principles are light and darkness; the three stages are the past, the present, and the future; this information comes to us from a fragment of a Chinese text. This is the doctrine to which Augustine makes reference—*initium, medium, et finis*—in his anti-Manichaean treatises *Against Felix* and *Against Faustus*. It is more fully expressed in another Chinese text:

> First of all, we must distinguish between the two principles. He who wishes to join this religion must know that the two principles of light and darkness have absolutely distinct natures; if he cannot distinguish this, how can he practice the doctrine? Also, it is necessary to understand the three stages, that is, the prior stage, the middle stage, the posterior stage. In the prior stage, heaven and earth do not yet exist: there are only light and darkness, and they are separate from each other. The nature of light is wisdom, the nature of darkness is ignorance. In all motion and in all repose, these two are opposed to each other. At the middle stage, darkness has invaded light. The latter lunges forward to drive it back and thus itself enters the darkness and attempts at all costs to drive it out. Through the great calamity we acquire disgust, which, in turn, drives us to separate our selves from our bodies; in the burning abode the vow is made to attempt an escape.
>
> (Chavannes and Pelliot, 1913)

The "great calamity" is a metaphor for the body, and the "burning abode" stands for the world, seen as a burning house from which one is saved by escaping. The text continues: "At the later stage, instruction and conversion are accomplished, truth and falsehood have returned each to its roots: light has returned to the great light, and darkness has returned to the mass of darkness. The two principles are reconstituted" (Chavannes and Pelliot, 1913).

The two roots are not generated and have nothing in common: they are irreducible opposites in every way. Light is good, equated with God; darkness is evil, equated with matter. Because good and evil are coeval, the problem of the origin of evil (a central dilemma of Christian doctrine) is resolved, in the most radical and extreme way. Its existence cannot be denied; it is everywhere, it is eternal and can only be defeated by knowledge (gnosis), which leads to salvation through the separation of light and darkness.

The way in which the two principles are represented is reminiscent of the two spirits, or *mainyus*, in the original Zoroastrian concept. Spenta Mainyu and Angra Mainyu are opposites in all things (*Yasna* 30.3–6), and their choice between good and evil, between *asha* ("truth") and *druj* ("falsehood"), is also prototypical of the choice that must be made by man. The ethical value of Manichaean dualism is no less strong, although its answer to the problem of evil is, of course, more typically gnostic. The Manichaeans refused to consider Ōhrmazd and Ahriman, the Pahlavi equivalents of the two *mainyus*, as two brothers who are opposed one to the other. The Uighur text *Khwāstwānēft* states: "If we once asserted that Khormuzta [Ōhrmazd] and Shīmnu [Ahriman] are brothers, one the cadet, one the firstborn . . . I repent of it . . . and I beg to be forgiven for that sin" (1c.3–4). Thus they were not so much addressing the dualism of the *Gāthās,* as opposing the later dualism of Zurvanism, which had demoted Ahura Mazdā to the role of a symmetrical opposite of Angra Mainyu andplaced Zurwān, who personified infinite time, above the dualistic formula. In fact, it is interesting to observe how the Manichaeans restored Ōhrmazd to a central role in the drama of salvation and in the very gnostic approach to the *prōtos anthrōpos,* while considering *Zurwān* as one of the names. The other Iranian name was *Srōshaw*—for the Father of Greatness, "sovereign god of the heaven of light," "god of truth," that is, one of the two terms of the dualistic formula. Terms for the opposite pole are *Devil, Satan, Ahriman, Shīmnu, Hulē, Matter, Evil,* the *Great Archon,* and the *Prince of Darkness.*

Rather than metaphysical speculation, we find at the root of Manichaean dualism a merciless analysis of the human condition, a pessimism largely common to all forms of gnosis and to Buddhism. By the mere fact of being incarnate, man suffers; he is prey to evil, forgetful of his luminous nature as long as he remains asleep and dimmed by ignorance in the prison of matter. While the two principles remain mixed, all is waste, torture, death, darkness: "Liberate me from this deep nothingness, from this dark abyss of waste, which is naught but torture, wounds unto death, and where there is no rescuer, no friend. There can be no salvation here, ever! All is darkness . . . all is prisons, and there is no exit" (Parthian fragment T2d.178).

This pessimistic attitude toward the world and toward life, which perpetuates itself in the snares of matter, accompanied Manichaeism throughout its history, increasingly strengthened by the bitter and often violent confrontations between its followers and the other established religions of the eastern and western empires. It was probably also at the root of an antinomic tendency of these "subversives," who could see nothing good in a world full of horror, evil, and injustice. This was probably also an important reason for the fierce persecutions they suffered—as is evident from the testimony of Zoroastrian sources (*Dēnkard,* Madan edition, pp. 216–218)— as well as for their refusal to conform to traditional customs and practices. It also helped to bring about that *damnatio memoriae* to which Mani and Manichaeism were universally subjected.

Knowledge as the Path to Salvation. An essential and specific characteristic of Manichaeism is its gnosticism, that is, its mixture of religion and science in a sort of theosophy. Manichaeism was attempting to give a universal explanation of the world, and it did not believe that mere faith and dogma were effective instruments in the search for redemption. On the contrary, Manichaean soteriology was based on knowledge. So it is understandable that Augustine should confess that he had most been attracted by precisely this aspect of Manichaeism during the years of his adherence to it (377–382), that is, to the promise that man could be freed of the authority of faith and tradition and led back to God simply by the strength of reason.

Manichaeans did not accept tradition, be it that of the New Testament or that of the Zoroastrian scriptures (*Kephalaia* 7), without first making a distinction between what they recognized as true and authentic in them and what, in their view, was simply the result of deceitful manipulations and interpolations by ignorant or insincere disciples. Only Mani's authority was worthy of trust, as it was based on reason and drawn from revelation. It was also set down in writing by him with extreme care and with the precise intent of not letting his teachings be misrepresented. Manichaeans, therefore, prided themselves on not asserting any truth without a logical and rational demonstration thereof, and without first opening the doors of knowledge.

Such knowledge was, ultimately, an anamnesis, an awakening; that is, gnosis was an *epignosis*, a recognition, a memory of self, knowledge of one's true ego and, at the same time, knowledge of God, the former being consubstantial with the latter, a particle of light fallen into matter's obfuscating mix. Thus God is a "savior saved," or one to be saved: a transcendental, luminous principle, spirit, or intelligence *(nous)*. It is the superior portion of man's ego, exiled in the body, and is the subject of the act of knowledge, thanks to which we will know where we are, where we come from, and where we are going. Man has forgotten his nature, a blend of light and darkness, spirit and matter. The enlightening power of knowledge makes him understand his own nature, that of the universe, and their destiny. It is, therefore, a universal science, blending theology, cosmology, anthropology, and eschatology. It includes everything: physical nature as well as history. Reason can penetrate anything: "Man must not believe until he has seen the object with his own eyes" (*Kephalaia* 142).

The Cosmogonic and Anthropogonic Myths. It may appear paradoxical to find that the doctrine of Manichaeism, founded in reason, whose ability and dignity it praised, was expressed in a language of myth, one that was crowded with figures and images and painted in strong, often dark colors. In fact, its mythology, which was invented by Mani himself, is intellectualistic and reflexive, almost metaphorical in character: Manichaean myths serve the purpose of illustrating the truth about the drama of existence, both macrocosmic and microcosmic. They achieve their objective with the aid of powerful images, most of which are derived from the mythological heritage of previous traditions—a fact that lent them greater weight and authority—and by the use of divine figures, both angelic and demoniacal, familiar, at least in part, to the popular imagination. Because Mani's teachings were directed to all the world's peoples, the actors in the great play could, to be more easily understood, adopt different names in different countries, drawing from local pantheons. Thus, Manichaean mythology is like a great album of pictures arranged in a sequence aimed at awakening in the adept reminiscences and intuitions that will lead him to knowledge. Small wonder, then, that Mani, who was famous for his paintings, should also use a book of illustrations, the *Image* (Gr., *Eikon;* MPers., and Pth., *Ārdahang*), to convey his doctrine, or that his disciples later continued to do the same in their missionary activities.

Such a mythology must, of necessity, have keys to its interpretation. The first of these is the omnipresent dominant theme: that of the soul which has fallen into matter and is freed by its *nous.* Next, in order to understand what are often described as the aberrations of Manichaean myths—those repugnant acts of cannibalism and sexual practices with which they are studded, as well as the self-destructiveness and autophagia of matter—one must keep in mind two basic concepts: the Indo-Iranian idea of the equivalence of spirit, light, and seed (Eliade, 1971, pp. 1–30) and that of the distillation of light through the "gastric machine" of the chosen, an act that corresponds to the great purification of the luminous elements (Syr., *zīwānē*), which was carried out by the demiurge and his children at the beginning of time (Tardieu, 1981). The premise of the first concept isthat light resides in the seed and through procreation is decanted from one body into another, undergoing the painful cycles of births and deaths (Skt., *saṃsāra*). This follows the related doctrine of metempsychosis (Syr., *tashpīkā;* Lat., *revolutio;* Gr., *metangismos*), an idea that originally came from India and that Mani adopted as pivotal to his system. The premise of the second is that just as the universe is the place in which all luminous bodies are healed, so the stomach is like a great alchemist's alembic, in which the chosen, thanks to the high degree of purification he has attained, is able to separate the light present in food from all impurities, through a double cycle of filtering and return. This cycle is a microcosm, whose corresponding macrocosm is the distillation of the *zīwānē* into the moon and the sun (Tardieu, 1981).

The Manichaean origin myth is based on the doctrine of two principles (light and darkness) and three stages of creation. During the first stage of existence, the two principles, personified as the Father of Greatness and the Prince of Darkness, are separate, residing, respectively, in the north and in the south, kept apart by a border between their two kingdoms. The Prince of Darkness—that is, agitated and disorderly matter—wishes to penetrate the kingdom of the Father of Greatness. Thus begins the second stage, in which the Father of Greatness, not wishing to compromise his five "dwellings" (Intelligence, Science, Thought, Reflection, and Conscience), decides to battle the Prince of Darkness and engenders an avatar, the Mother of the Living, who, in turn, produces Primordial Man. But the Prince of Darkness defeats Primordial Man and devours his five children. The avidity and greed of the Prince of Darkness, however, bring about his downfall; the five children of Primordial Man are like a poison within his stomach.

The Father of Greatness responds by creating a second being: the Living Spirit (who corresponds to the Persian god Mithra). The Living Spirit, who is also the father of five children, and Primordial Man confront the demons of the powers of darkness, and so the demiurgic action begins: from the bodies of the demons arise the skies, the mountains, the soil, and, finally, from a first bit of liberated light, the sun, moon, and stars. The Father of Greatness then creates a third being, called the

Messenger, who incarnates *nous;* he is also called the Great Wahman, the Good Thought (Av., Vohu Manah). The Messenger calls forth twelve Virgins of Light, and they show themselves nude to the demons, both male and female, so that they will all ejaculate at the sight of such beauty and thus free the elements of light that they had ingested and imprisoned. The seed spilled on the dry earth gives life to five trees: thus is accomplished the creation of the world.

The creation of the human race then occurs as follows. The she-demons, thus impregnated, thanks to the Messenger's ruse, give birth to monsters, who swallow plants in order to absorb the light contained within them. Then Matter (darkness), in the guise of Az, the personification of concupiscence, in order to imprison the elements of light in a more secure fashion, causes the demons Ashaqlun and Nam-rael, male and female, to devour all the monsters, and then to mate. They then generate the first human couple, Adam and Eve. At this point, the work of salvation begins: Adam, kept wild and ignorant by the snares of darkness, is awakened from this state by the savior, the son of God, sent by the powers above. The savior is identified with Primordial Man, Ōhrmizd, or, later, with the transcendental Jesus, or the god of *nous*. The savior awakens Adam from his slumber, opens his eyes, shows him his soul, which is suffering in the material world, and reveals to him the infernal origins of his body and the heavenly origins of his spirit. Thus Adam acquires knowledge of himself, and his soul, thanks to gnosis, is resuscitated.

The third stage is the Great War between the forces of good and evil, characterized on the one hand by the desperate attempt of the Prince of Darkness to spread evil throughout the world by means of procreation—that is, by the creation of more and more corporeal prisons to entrap the elements of light—and on the other hand by the the efforts of the Father of Greatness to spread good. Through the practice of the laws of the religion and, in particular, by interrupting the cycle of reincarnation, light is liberated; that is, the soul is freed by knowledge. When the church of justice triumphs, the souls will be judged, and those of the chosen will rise to Heaven. The world will then be purified and destroyed by a fire lasting 1,468 years. All, or most, of the light particles, will be saved; Matter, in all its manifestations, and with its victims (the damned), will be forever imprisoned in a globe inside a gigantic pit covered with a stone. The separation of the two principles will thus be accomplished for all eternity.

ORIGINS

We now know something more about the origins of the Manichaean religion, by comparing the Manichaean Codex of Cologne to other available sources, mainly the Arabic ones. Mani was raised in the environment of a Judeo-Christian gnostic and baptist sect, which had been founded by a figure, almost more mythical than historical, by the name of Elkesai (Gr., Alkhasaios; Arab., al-Khasayh). Elkesaism was a particularly widespread movement during the third and fourth centuries in Syria, Palestine, Mesopotamia, Transjordan, and northern Arabia. It survived for many centuries and is mentioned by the Arabic encyclopedist Ibn al-Nadīm as still existing during the fourth century AH in what is today southeastern Iraq.

It would, however, be a mistake to view the origins of Manichaeism only, or even mainly, in the light of such information, for one might erroneously conclude that the principal inspiration for the Manichaean doctrine was Judeo-Christian gnosticism. The origins of Manichaeism are still open to question (as are, in fact, those of gnosticism). The most likely interpretation would recognize the dominating imprint of Iranian dualism since without a doubt the dualistic doctrine is central and pivotal to Mani's thought and to the teachings and practices of his church. We must, however, consider the presence of three different forms of religious doctrine: the Iranian, which is basically Zoroastrian; the Christian or Judeo-Christian; and the Mahāyāna Buddhist. Of these, the Iranian form held the key to the Manichaean system and provided the essence of the new universalistic religious concept that developed from the main themes and aspirations of gnosticism. If we were to separate the Manichaean system from its Christian and Buddhist elements, it would not suffer irreparably.

Manichaeism was long thought of as a Christian heresy, but this interpretation was already being abandoned during the last century and has now been entirely rejected. We must also reject the approach that perceives the Judeo-Christian components, more or less affected by Hellenism, as dominant (Burkitt, 1925; Schaeder, 1927). There is a widespread tendency today to give equal emphasis to what we have called the three forms of Manichaeism and to consider it a great and independent universal religion, although such an approach is sometimes still weighted in favor of the relationship between Manicheaism and Christianity (Tardieu, 1981). Nevertheless, if we discount certain obvious differences, we can assert that Manichaeism has its roots in the Iranian religious tradition and that its relationship to Mazdaism, or Zoroastrianism, is more or less like that of Christianity to Judaism (Bausani, 1959, p. 103).

HISTORY

We can trace the beginnings of the religion to the second revelation received by the prophet at the age of twenty-four, that is, on the first of Nisan of 551 of the Seleucid era, which corresponds to 12 April 240 CE (his first occurred at the age of twelve while he was living in the baptist community). It was then that there appeared to him an angel, his "twin" (Gr., *suzugos;* Arab., *al-Tawm*), described as the "beautiful and sublime mirror" of his being, and it was then that Mani began his prophetic and apostolic ministry, breaking off from Elkesaism and its strict legalistic ritualism. He presented himself as the Seal of the Prophets and preached a new doctrine aimed at all peoples—Buddhists, Zoroastrians, and Christians.

A number of factors lead us to believe that, at the beginning of his ministry, Mani saw the universalistic religion he was founding as one that could be adapted to the new political reality of the Persian empire of the Sasanids, founded by Ardashīr I. To the emperor Shāpūr he dedicated a work, written in Middle Persian, that opened with a declaration of the universalistic idea of the Seal of the Prophecy. Any ambitions that great Sasanid ruler might have harbored for a universal empire would have found congenial a religious doctrine that presented itself as the sum and perfection of all the great prior religious traditions.

A missionary spirit moved Manichaeism from its very inception. Mani traveled first in the direction of the "country of the Indians" (perhaps in the footsteps of the apostle Thomas), with the hope of converting the small Christian communities scattered along the coast of Fārs and Baluchistan (Tardieu, 1981) and perhaps, also, in order to penetrate lands in which Buddhism was already widespread. Manichaean tradition remembers this first apostolic mission by its conversion of Tūrān-shāh, that is, the Buddhist ruler of Tūrān, a kingdom in southeastern Iran. That mission was a relatively brief one owing to the turn of events in the Sasanid empire. The death of Ardashīr and the accession to the throne of Shāpūr, the "king of kings of Ērānshahr," recalled Mani to Persia. Manichaeism began at that time to spread to Iran, where it acquired a prominent position, thanks also to the conversion of high court officials and even members of the royal family, and encouraged, to a certain degree, by the king's support. In fact, the image of Shāpūr in Manichaean tradition is a positive one: Manichaeism almost became the official religion of the Persian empire. Mani himself, after obtaining a successful audience with Shāpūr, joined the ruler's court and obtained his permission to preach the new creed throughout the empire, under the protection of local authorities. During this fortunate period for Manichaean propaganda in Iran, in the 250s, Mani wrote the *Shābuhragān*, a work he dedicated to his royal protector and which has reached us only in a fragmented form.

Once the work of its founder had established it as a real church, Manichaeism soon spread beyond the borders of Persia, both in the Roman empire and in the east, southeast, and south. Mani wrote: "My hope [that is, the Manichaean church] has reached the east of the world and all inhabited regions of the earth, both to the north and to the south. . . . None of the [previous] apostles has ever done anything like this" (*Kephalaia* 1).

The political good fortune of Manichaeism in the Persian empire lasted only a few years. The official state religion, Zoroastrianism, grew increasingly hostile as the Magian clergy, guided by influential figures such as the high priest Kerdēr, organized it into a real national church, with its own strict orthodoxy and a strong nationalistic spirit. The reasons for the conflict between the Zoroastrianism of the Magi and Manichaeism during the third century are numerous: a hereditary clerical caste within a hierarchical social structure based on caste tended to be conservative and traditionalist; the eastern empire's cultural and spiritual horizons were narrow, typical of an agrarian and aristocratic society such as that of the Iranian plateau and very different from the ethnically and culturally diverse and composite one in the westernmost regions of the empire, where there had arisen a flourishing and cosmopolitan urban civilization. The alliance between the throne and the Magi, which remained strong despite some internal contrasts for the entire duration of the Sasanid empire, did not allow Manichaeism to take over and, by subjecting it to periodical and fierce persecutions, finally weakened its drive and confined it to a minority position.

On the one hand, Manichaeism accurately reflected the most widespread anxieties and aspirations of that period's religious preoccupations, through its soteriology, the idea of knowledge as freedom, and the value it placed on personal experience of the divine; on the other hand, the restored Zoroastrianism of the Magi reflected a tendency, widespread during the third century in both the Persian and Roman empires, toward the formation of a national culture. From this standpoint, we can view Manichaeism more as heir to Parthian eclecticism and syncretism—"one of the last manifestations of Arsacid thought" (Bivar, 1983, p. 97)—than as an interpreter of the vast cultural and political changes witnessed in Iran upon the ascent to power of the Sasanid dynasty.

The first anti-Manichaean persecution in the Iranian state began, after the death of Shāpūr and of his successor, Hormīzd I, with the killing of Mani himself, ordered by Bahrām I, probably around the beginning of the year 277. Many other episodes followed, affecting Manichaean communities in all regions of the empire, from Khorasan to Mesopotamian Seleucia (Ctesiphon), the seat of the Manichaean papacy. Manichaeism, however, was not completely eradicated from the Iranian world; in fact, it survived for centuries. Under the caliphate of the Umayyads it remained alive in those territories that had been Sasanid, despite internal schisms and disciplinary controversy.

During the third and fourth centuries Manichaeism moved west, into the Roman empire. It spread through Egypt, North Africa, Palestine, Syria, Asia Minor, Dalmatia, and Rome and as far north as southern Gaul and Spain. Its adherents were the subjects of persecution by both central and peripheral imperial authorities, meeting everywhere with the strong hostility of the political and religious establishment. The Manichaeans were seen by Rome as a dangerous subversive element and were often thought to be agents of the rival Persian power. Despite persecutions and imperial edicts, such as that of Diocletian in 297, the faith for the most part persisted, except in some western areas of the Roman empire. Manichaeism was perceived as a threat well into the Christian era. Repressive measures were repeatedly taken by Roman imperial and church authorities (notably Pope Leo the Great, in 445); nevertheless, in 527 the emperors Justin and Justinian still felt the need to promulgate a law inflicting capital punishment on the followers of Mani's teachings.

Like Zoroastrianism and Christianity, Islam had at first been tolerant of Manichaeism but in the end acted with equal violence against it. The advent of the Abbasid caliphate marked a renewal of bloody repressive measures, which succeeded in pushing the Manichaeans east, in the direction of Transoxiana, during the tenth century. It was in Khorasan, Chorasmia, and Sogdiana that the Manichaean faith expanded and gained strength, and there it became an outpost for the dissemination of Mani's gospel to China and Central Asia. In the last decades of the sixth century, the religion suffered a schism with the so-called Dēnāwars ("observers of *dēn*," i.e., of the true religion), a rigorist and puritan sect. Samarkand became the new see of the Manicaean papacy.

Toward the end of the seventh century, Manichaeism reached the Far East. As the great caravan route from Kashgar to Kucha to Karashahr was reopened following the Chinese conquest of eastern Turkistan, Manichaeism made its appearance in China, mainly through Sogdian missionaries. In 732, an imperial edict allowed Manichaeans the freedom to practice their cult there. The religion also spread to Central Asia and Mongolia, to the vast empire of the Uighurs, who adopted Manichaeism as their official religion in 763. But political and military events following the fall, in 840, of the Uighur empire caused Manichaeism's supremacy in Central Asia to be short lived, although it probably survived there until the thirteenth century. In China, where the Manichaeans were persecuted during the ninth century and banned by edict in 843, just after the collapse of the Uighurs, Manichaeism nonetheless survived until the fourteenth century, protected by secret societies, alongside Taoism and Buddhism.

THE MANICHAEAN CHURCH

At the core of the ecclesiastical structure was a marked distinction among classes of clergy, which were subdivided into four. The first included teachers or apostles, never more than 12; the second, minister deacons, never more than 72; the third, stewards, never more than 360; and the fourth were the chosen (that is, the chosen in general). The laity made up a fifth class. Only men could belong to the first three classes, that is, the true clergy, and above these stood the leader of the faithful, the Manichaean pope. The clergy lived in monasteries in the cities and supported itself through the gifts and foundations of the laity, according to a system clearly derived from Buddhist, rather than Christian, monasticism (Baur, 1831; Widengren, 1965).

Different moral codes governed the clergy and the lay population. The former was required to observe the five commandments: truth, nonviolence, sexual abstinence, abstinence from meat and from food and drink that were considered impure, poverty. The laity was required (1) to observe the ten laws of good behavior, which, among other things, prescribed a strictly monogamous marriage and abstinence from all forms of violence, both against men and against animals; (2) to pray four times a day (at dawn, midday, sunset, and night), after observing particular rituals of purification; (3) to contribute the tenth, or the seventh, part of their worldly goods to support the clergy; (4) to fast weekly (on Sundays) and yearly for the thirty days preceding the celebration of the festival of the Bēma; and (5) to confess their sins weekly (on Mondays), as well as during a great yearly collective confession at the end of the fasting period.

The liturgy was simple: it recalled episodes of the life of Mani, his martyrdom, and that of the first apostles. The principal festivity was the Bēma (Gr.; MPers., *gāh;* "pulpit, throne, tribunal"), which, on the vernal equinox, celebrated Mani's passion through gospel worship; the collective confession of sins; the recitation of three hymns to Mani; the reading of the apostle's spiritual testament, the *Letter of the Seal;* chants glorifying the triumphant church; and a sacred banquet offered to the elect by the listeners. In Manichaean holy places the *bēma,* a throne on five steps, was left empty in memory of the one who, having left the world, nonetheless remained as an invisible guide and judge of his church. The empty throne was probably originally a Buddhist symbol.

HERITAGE AND SURVIVING ELEMENTS

The survival of Manichaeism as a source of inspiration for a number of medieval heresies in the West poses complex questions. Manichaean dualism has been adduced as an explanation for the origin of those heretical movements that were based on dualism, on moral asceticism, and on a more or less pronounced antinomism. Accusations of Manichaeism—the most widely despised of Christian heresies—were pronounced by adversaries against heretics to show their relation to the doctrines of Mani, although such a connection has been generally hard to prove beyond doubt.

Priscillianism, which arose in Spain at the end of the fourth century, was probably not related to Manichaeism, although Paulicianism, in seventh-century Armenia, probably was, as was Bogomilism. The latter arose in Bulgaria during the tenth century and spread along the Balkan Peninsula to the coastline of Asia Minor, along with the Cathari in southern France and northern Italy during the twelfth and thirteenth centuries; together they were considered links in the same chain, which might be called "medieval Manichaeism" or "Neo-Manichaeism." A connection among these movements is probable, and in fact such a link is certain between the Bogomils and the Cathari. However, it is not possible to prove their derivation from Manichaeism. Their popular character, the social environment in which they developed, and the typically gnostic nature of Manichaeism all suggest a generalized influence rather than a direct derivation, that is, a background inspiration from the great dualistic religion of late antiquity. It now appears certain that in some instances Manichaeism itself did survive in the West in clandestine groups and secret forms, especially in Roman Africa, despite the proscriptions and persecutions of the sixth century.

The problem is analogous in the East, except in China, where we know that Manichaeism did survive, camouflaged in Taoist or Buddhist guise, until the fourteenth century. A Manichaean origin has been ascribed to Mazdakism, a religious and social movement of Sasanid Iran between the fifth and sixth centuries (Christensen, 1925), and some degree of Manichaean influence upon it is undeniable, although a more accurate perception would probably see the movement as a heretical form of Zoroastrianism. There has been an occasional attempt to consider Manichaean any Muslim *zindīq* (Arab., "heretic, free thinker"). The word derives from the Middle Persian *zandīg*, used by Zoroastrians to describe those who used the *Zand,* the Middle Persian translation of and commentary on the Avesta, in a heterodox manner. Although it is true that *zindīq* is often used to mean "Manichaean," its sense is actually broader; *zandaqah* cannot, therefore, be strictly identified with Manichaeism.

In any case, Manichaeism survived in the Islamic world, even through the persecutions of the Abbasid caliphate, and exercised some degree of influence on gnostic currents in this world. Finally, there is a great likelihood of a direct connection between Manichaeism and some Tibetan cosmological concepts, presumably transmitted through the Hindu Kush (Tucci, 1970).

[*For further discussion of Manichaeism, see* Mazdakism. *See also the biography of Mani.*]

BIBLIOGRAPHY

A work that by now belongs to the prehistory of Manichaean studies is Isaac de Beausobre's *Histoire critique de Manichée et du manichéisme,* 2 vols. (Amsterdam, 1735–1739), which presented Manichaeism as a reformed Christianity. A hundred years later, Manichaean studies reached a turning point with F. C. Baur's *Das manichäische Religionssystem nach den Quellen neu untersucht und entwickelt* (Tübingen, 1831), which gave particular consideration to the Indo-Iranian, Zoroastrian, and Buddhist backgrounds.

In the years following, a number of general studies were published that still remain important—G. Flügel's *Mani, seine Lehre und seine Schriften* (Leipzig, 1862); K. Kessler's *Mani: Forschungen über die manichäische Religion,* vol. 1 (Berlin, 1889); F. C. Burkitt's *The Religion of the Manichees* (Cambridge, 1925); and H. H. Schaeder's *Urform und Fortbildungen des manichäischen Systems* (Leipzig, 1927)—even though more recent studies and discoveries have, by now, gone beyond them. Also useful are A. V. W. Jackson's *Researches on Manichaeism, with Special Reference to the Turfan Fragments* (New York, 1932) and H.-J. Polotsky's *Abriss des manichäischen Systems* (Stuttgart, 1934).

A quarter of a century apart, two important status reports concerning the question of Manichaean studies were published: H. S. Nyberg's "Forschungen über den Manichäismus," *Zeitschrift für die neutestamentliche Wissenschaft und die Kunde der älteren Kirche* 34 (1935): 70–91, and Julien Ries's "Introduction aux études manichéennes," *Ephemerides Theologicae Lovanienses* 33 (1957): 453–482 and 35 (1959): 362–409.

General works that remain valuable, although they give a partially different picture of Manichaeism, are Henri-Charles Puech's *Le manichéisme: Son fondateur, sa doctrine* (Paris, 1949) and Geo Widengren's *Mani and Manichaeism* (London, 1965). We are also indebted to Puech for a very useful collection of essays, *Sur le manichéisme et autres essais* (Paris, 1979), and to Widengren for another, with an important introduction, *Der Manichäismus* (Darmstadt, 1977), pp. ix–xxxii, as well as for a more recent essay, "Manichaeism and Its Iranian Background," in *The Cambridge History of Iran,* vol. 3, edited by Ehsan Yarshater (Cambridge, 1983), pp. 965–990.

The volume *Der Manichäismus* contains some of the most important contributions to Manichaean studies, reprinted entirely or partially (all in German), by H. S. Nyberg, F. C. Burkitt, H. H. Schaeder, Richard Reitzenstein, H.-J. Polotsky, Henri-Charles Puech, V. Stegemann, Alexander Böhlig, Mark Lidzbarski, Franz Rosenthal, W. Bang-Kaup, A. Baumstark, Charles R. C. Allberry, Prosper Alfaric, W. Seston, J. A. L. Vergote, W. B. Henning, Georges Vajda, Carsten Colpe, and A. V. W. Jackson. Two noteworthy syntheses of Manichaeism in French are François Decret's *Mani et la tradition manichéenne* (Paris, 1974) and M. Tardieu's *Le manichéisme* (Paris, 1981); the latter is particularly full of original suggestions.

Two works from the 1960s are dedicated more to Mani himself than to Manichaeism, one concerning mainly the social and cultural background from which Manichaeism emerged and the other mainly dedicated to the religious personality of the founder: Otakar Klíma's *Manis Zeit und Leben* (Prague, 1962) and L. J. R. Ort's *Mani: A Religio-Historical Description of His Personality* (Leiden, 1967).

Although the once-classic work on Manichaean literature, Prosper Alfaric's *Les écritures manichéennes,* 2 vols. (Paris, 1918), is now quite dated, there is a wealth of more recent works to which we can turn. A whole inventory of Iranian documents from Central Asia can be found in Mary Boyce's *A Catalogue of the Iranian Manuscripts in Manichaean Script in the German Turfan Collection* (Berlin, 1960). Excellent editions of Iranian and Turkic texts are due to F. W. K. Müller, A. von Le Coq, Ernst Waldschmidt and Wolfgang Lentz, W. Bang, and Annemarie von Gabain, F. C. Andreas, and W. B. Henning, published in the *Abhandlungen* and in the *Sitzungsberichte* of the Prussian Academy of Sciences between 1904 and 1936. W. B. Henning's pupil, Mary Boyce, has also published, in addition to the above-mentioned catalog, two other important contributions to Manichaean studies, *The Manichaean Hymn Cycles in Parthian* (Oxford, 1954) and *A Reader in Manichaean Middle-Persian and Parthian,* "Acta Iranica," no. 9 (Tehran and Liège, 1975). Editions of Iranian texts, as well as a number of extremely careful philological studies, can be found in W. B. Henning's *Selected Papers,* 2 vols., "Acta Iranica," nos. 14–15 (Tehran and Liège, 1977), where are reprinted also Henning's fundamental *Mittel-iranische Manichaica aus Chinesisch-Turkestan,* written in collaboration with F. C. Andreas between 1932 and 1934.

W. Sundermann and P. Zieme, two scholars from the Academy of Sciences of the German Democratic Republic, are currently responsible for continuing research in the Iranian and Turkish texts from Turfan, which are preserved in Berlin. We owe to them, among other things, Sundermann's *Mittelpersische und parthische kosmogonische und Parabeltexte der Manichäer* (Berlin, 1973) and Zieme's *Manichäisch-türkische Texte* (Berlin, 1975). On the state of research into Iranian texts, see also Sundermann's "Lo studio dei testi iranici di Turfan," in *Iranian Studies,* edited by me (Rome, 1983), pp. 119–134. Recent research on Sogdian Manichaean texts has been done by N. Sims-Williams (London) and E. Morano (Turin), following the lead of Ilya Gershevitch (Cambridge). Again in the context of Central Asian texts, the handbook for the confession of sins has been carefully edited, after the work of W. Bang and W. B. Henning, and with an ample commentary, by Jes P. Asmussen in *X̌āstvānīft: Studies in Manichaeism*

(Copenhagen, 1965); the *Shābuhragān* is the subject of an extremely useful work by D. N. MacKenzie, "Mani's *Šābuhragān,*" *Bulletin of the School of Oriental and African Studies* 42 (1979): 500–534 and 43 (1980): 288–310.

Concerning the Chinese texts, the following are useful works. On the *Treatise,* see Édouard Chavannes and Paul Pelliot's "Un traité manichéen retrouvé en Chine," *Journal asiatique* (1911): 499–617 and (1913): 99–392. On the *Compendium,* see Chavannes and Pelliot's "Compendium de la religion du Buddha de Lumière, Mani," *Journal asiatique* (1913): 105–116 (Pelliot fragment), and Gustav Haloun and W. B. Henning's "The Compendium of the Doctrines and Styles of the Teaching of Mani, the Buddha of Light," *Asia Major,* n.s. 3 (1952): 184–212 (Stein fragment). On the London Chinese hymn book, see, in addition to the work of Ernst Waldschmidt and Wolfgang Lentz, Tsui Chi's "Mo-ni-chiao hsia-pu tsan," *Bulletin of the School of Oriental and African Studies* 11 (1943): 174–219.

On the Coptic texts of Fayum, a survey of the state of research can be found in Alexander Böhlig's "Die Arbeit an den koptischen Manichaica," in *Mysterion und Wahrheit* (Leiden, 1968), pp. 177–187. Among editions of the texts are *Manichäische Homilien,* by H.-J. Polotsky (Stuttgart, 1934), *Kephalaia,* by C. Schmidt, H.-J. Polotsky, and Alexander Böhlig (Stuttgart, 1935–1940; Berlin, 1966), and Charles R. C. Allberry's *A Manichaean Psalm-Book,* vol. 2 (Stuttgart, 1938). On the Manichaean Codex of Cologne, see Albert Henrichs and Ludwig Koenen's "Ein griechischer Mani-Codex," *Zeitschrift für Papyrologie und Epigraphik* 5 (1970): 97–216, 19 (1975): 1–85, and 32 (1979): 87–200.

Of indirect sources, I shall mention here only the following few. On Augustine, see R. Jolivet and M. Jourion's *Six traités anti-manichéens,* in *Oeuvres de Saint Augustin,* vol. 17 (Paris, 1961); on Theodoros bar Kōnaī, see Franz Cumont's *Recherches sur le manichéisme,* vol. 1 (Brussels, 1908); on Zoroastrian sources, see J.-P. de Menasce's *Une apologétique mazdéenne du neuvième siècle 'Škand-gumānīk vicār'* (Fribourg, 1945); and on Islamic sources, see Carsten Colpe's "Der Manichäismus in der arabischen Überlieferung" (Ph.D. diss., University of Göttingen, 1954).

Three valuable anthologies of Manichaean texts are A. Adams's *Texte zum Manichäismus,* 2d ed. (Berlin, 1962), Jes P. Asmussen's *Manichaean Literature* (Delmar, N.Y., 1975), and Alexander Böhlig and Jes P. Asmussen's *Die gnosis,* vol. 3 (Zurich, 1980).

Concerning the spread of Manichaeism in Asia, in North Africa, and in the Roman empire, there are numerous works. The old text by E. de Stoop, *Essai sur la diffusion du manichéisme dans l'Empire romain* (Ghent, 1909), heads the list, followed by Paul Pelliot's "Les traditions manichéennes au Fou-kien," *T'oung pao* 22 (1923): 193–208; M. Guidi's *La lotta tra l'Islam e il manicheismo* (Rome, 1927); Uberto Pestalozza's "Il manicheismo presso i Turchi occidentali ed orientali," *Rendiconti del Reale Istituto Lombardo di Scienze e Lettere,* 2d series, 67 (1934): 417–497; Georges Vajda's "Les Zindiqs en pays d'Islam au debout de la période abbaside," *Revista degli Studi Orientali* 17 (1937): 173–229; Giuseppe Messina's *Cristianesimo, buddhismo, manicheismo nell'Asia antica* (Rome, 1947); H. H. Schaeder's "Der Manichäismus und sein Weg nach Osten," in *Glaube und Geschichte: Festschrift für Friedrich Gogarten* (Giessen, 1948), pp. 236–254; O. Maenchen-Helfen's "Manichaeans in Siberia," in *Semitic and Oriental Studies Presented to William Popper* (Berkeley, 1951), pp. 161–165; Francesco Gabrieli's "La *zandaqa* au premier siècle abbasside," in *L'élaboration de l'Islam* (Paris, 1961), pp. 23–28; Peter Brown's "The Diffusion of Manichaeism in the Roman Empire," *Journal of Roman Studies* 59 (1969): 92–103; François Decret's *Aspects du manichéisme dans l'Afrique romaine* (Paris, 1970); and S. N. C. Lieu's *The Religion of Light: An Introduction to the History of Manichaeism in China* (Hong Kong, 1979) and *Manichaeism in the Later Roman Empire and Medieval China* (Manchester, 1985).

Among studies devoted to special topics, note should be taken of Charles R. C. Allberry's "Das manichäische Bema-Fest," *Zeitschrift für die neutestamentliche Wissenschaft und die Kunde der älteren Kirche* 37 (1938): 2–10; Geo Widengren's *The Great Vohu Manah and the Apostle of God* (Uppsala, 1945) and *Mesopotamian Elements in Manichaeism* (Uppsala, 1946); Henri-Charles Puech's "Musique et hymnologie manichéennes," in *Encyclopédie des musiques sacrées,* vol. 1 (Paris, 1968), pp. 353–386; and Mircea Eliade's "Spirit, Light, and Seed," *History of Religions* 11 (1971): 1–30. Of my own works, I may mention "Un particolare aspetta del simbolismo della luce nel Mazdeismo e nel Manicheismo," *Annali dell'Istituto Universitario Orientale di Napoli* n.s. 12 (1962): 95–128, and "Universalismo e nazionalismo nell'Iran del III secolo," in *Incontro di religioni in Asia tra il III e il X secolo,* edited by L. Lanciotti (Florence, 1984), pp. 31–54.

In the most exhaustive treatment of Manichaeism to have appeared in an encyclopedic work, Henri-Charles Puech's "Le manichéisme," in *Histoire des religions,* vol. 2, edited by Puech (Paris, 1972), pp. 523–645, we also find a full exposition of the problem concerning the heritage and survival of Manichaeism, with a bibliography to which one should add Raoul Manselli's *L'eresia del male* (Naples, 1963).

Despite the length of the present bibliography, there are some works cited in the text of my article that have not yet been mentioned here. On the relationship between Manichaeism and Zoroastrianism, see Alessandro Bausani's *Persia religiosa* (Milan, 1959); on the Parthian heritage in Manichaeism, see A. D. H. Bivar's "The Political History of Iran under the Arsacids," in *The Cambridge History of Iran,* vol. 3, edited by Ehsan Yarshater (Cambridge, 1983), pp. 21–97; and on the influence of Manichaeism in Tibet, see Giuseppe Tucci's *Die Religionen Tibets* (Stuttgart, 1970), translated as *The Religions of Tibet* (Berkeley, 1980).

17 MITHRAISM

GHERARDO GNOLI

Translated from Italian by Roger DeGaris

A "mystical" religion with a structure akin to that of other mystery religions, Mithraism was founded on the notion of a god who remains unconquered throughout a complex series of events. Although it had Iranian roots, as we can see by the fact that Mithra was always known as a Persian god, the religion took shape and developed outside Iran, spreading throughout the Roman empire. The cult appealed to the Roman world because of its mysteriosophic views, which centered on the concept of the life of the soul and its ascension through the seven planetary spheres. The ascension was symbolized by seven grades of initiation, culminating in the transcendent level of the fixed stars, or *aeternitas*.

SOURCES

The background and sources of Mithraism are most likely to be found in Asia Minor, where Persian communities and their priests, the Magi, were established toward the end of the Achaemenid period (sixth to fourth centuries BCE). These communities favored a syncretic approach to the local religions, and Mithraism may have arisen from some hybrid of the Magi. It cannot, however, be explained without mention of the encounter of the Iranian and Mesopotamian religious worlds. The spread of astrological motifs, today more thoroughly understood, suggests that the astral religion of Babylonia, particularly developed in the first millennium BCE, had an important role in the formation of Mithraism. It is also correct to suppose that at an earlier time the Iranian god Mithra was identified with the Mesopotamian solar deity, Shamash. Many factors indicate that in the second half of the first millennium BCE there was significant diffusion of the cult of Mithra throughout the more westerly regions of the Achaemenid domain, from Asia Minor to Babylonia and Armenia. In this case, however, we cannot speak of Mithraism but only of a cult of Mithra different from that found in Zoroastrian Iran. In any event, the Greek version of the Iranian god during the end of the first century BCE is clear, as shown in the monuments of Mithradates Kallinikos and Anthiochus I, the rulers of Commagene, in which Mithra is identified with Helios, Apollo, and Hermes.

The testimony of Plutarch in his *Life of Pompey* is important in understanding the religion's development in the Roman empire. It concerns a cult of Mithra as practiced among the pirates of Cilicia, the district in southern Asia Minor from which the mysteries celebrated during the lifetime of Plutarch were supposed to have come. Plutarch's source is more ancient (perhaps Posidonius), so we can perhaps trace the Roman cult back to 100 BCE. The incubation period of the new religion was rather long. Statius in the *Thebais* (about 80 CE) describes an image of Mithra Tauroctonus ("bull-slayer") and attests to the arrival of the cult in Rome itself. This was the beginning of the wide diffusion of Mithraism that occurred under the Flavian emperors in the last quarter of the first century CE.

We cannot identify the specific stages of the Iranian god's transformation into the mystery god of the Romans. We can deduce, however, that at the basis of the transformation were two essential characteristics of the Iranian divinity: Mithra is the divinity of light, closely linked to the sun, and he is a divinity of salvation.

The solar characteristics of the Iranian Mithra are documented in the sources, but in Iran Mithra was not a personification of the sun, though his name, *Mihr,* is one of the names of the sun. In the Avesta, the god seems to have a connection with Hvar Khshaēta ("resplendent sun"), analogous to the connection of the Roman Mithra with Sol. The nature of the Iranian god as a god of salvation can be inferred from myriad indications. In the Parthian epoch, for example, there existed a great syncretic myth of the Cosmocrator Redemptor, of which Mithra, born of a rock or out of a cave, was the protagonist. His birth, which would later be celebrated on 25 December, was accompanied by special signs and by luminous epiphanies and taken as a symbol of a kind of royal initiation (Widengren, 1965).

HISTORY

The Mithraic mysteries spread between the end of the first century and the fourth century CE, gradually dying out toward the end of that period. Their maximum expansion occurred toward the middle of the third century. They spread throughout a great part of the Roman empire. Rome and Ostia, Latium, southern Etruria, the Campania, and Cisalpine Gaul are, in Italy, the places and provinces that offer the most evidence of this diffusion, but a number of other sites must also be kept in mind: Aquileia and the main ports of Sicily, Syracuse, Catania, and Palermo; Austria and Germany along the Rhine frontier; the Danubian provinces Pannonia, Mesia, Dacia; the Tracia; Dalmatia; the valley of the Rhone and Aquitania in France; Belgium; and England, in the London region and to the north along Hadrian's wall. The mysteries were diffused to a lesser extent in the Iberian Peninsula and Macedonia, while there was almost no trace of them in Greece. Evidence shows that they were present along the Asian and African coasts of the Mediterranean, although their presence was limited (especially in the Asian provinces) to the major maritime ports.

For the most part the evidence is archaeological, iconographic, and epigraphic. The greatest scholar of Mithraism, Franz Cumont, has attempted to reconstruct the religion's mythology, theology, cosmology, eschatology, and rites, basing his work primarily on the numerous sculptural reliefs that have been preserved.

The Mithraeum, a kind of temple, served as a meeting place for followers of the religion. Partly underground, it was a replica of the cave *(spelaeu.n)* in which Mithra caught the mystic bull and killed it. Built in a long rectangle, it had lateral brick benches on which the participants in the ceremonies could sit and gaze at the imageof Mithra Tauroctonus placed in a special niche at the end of the nave. An altar was often placed in front of the image of the Tauroctonus. On the ceiling the starry firmament was generally depicted. Because the grotto was supposed to be a representation of the world, it contained reproductions of the signs of the zodiac and of the planets. Water played a purificatory role in Mithraism, and a natural or artificial spring had to be near every Mithraeum. Very often other rooms surrounded the spelaeum proper, designed, perhaps, for initiation rites or as chapels. As a rule these were entered through a pronaos. These places of worship, so unusual and different from the high temples dedicated to the divinities of the public cults, had the additional characteristic of being of modest size. The worship service, which culminated in a common banquet, was officiated over by a small community, usually consisting of a few dozen people.

Esoteric and initiatory in nature, Mithraism was, in fact, a private cult, intended for only the few. Though it professed universalism, the cult excluded women. It had emerged in a predominantly military environment and was practiced and spread primarily by the Roman army, which elevated loyalty and compliance with agreements and promises to the status of a supreme value. It was not only a soldiers' religion, however; it also appealed to other social and professional groups, including, for example, public officials and persons who worked in commercial enterprises. It has often been pointed out, quite rightly, that Mithraism promoted camaraderie on the battlefield and in the barracks, as well as in offices and enterprises (Will, 1955, pp. 125ff., pp. 356ff), among individuals who rarely had a permanent residence and who were called upon to carry out their work, because of duty or interest, in the most varied parts of the empire.

DOCTRINES

In the Roman cult, initiates progressed through seven levels: Corax ("raven"), Nymphus ("bride"), Miles ("soldier"), Leo ("lion"), Perses ("Persian"), Heliodromus ("courier of the sun"), and Pater ("father"). Each grade was protected by a particular celestial body: respectively, Mercury, Venus, Mars, Jupiter, the moon, the sun, and Saturn.

The doctrines of the Mithraic mysteries have been much discussed, both in terms of their origin and content and in terms of their uniqueness and orientation. Several views opposed to the Iranian origin of the titulary god of the mysteries notwithstanding (Wikander, 1950), there is a broad consensus on the religion's Iranian background. Some scholars, however, do not believe that Mithraism's Iranian roots have much significance for an accurate understanding of the religion, which they feel should be considered only in terms of what occurred in the empire and in Roman society (Gordon, 1972). This position is no less exaggerated than that which wishes to explain the entire religion, or most of it, by its Iranian heritage.

From the total body of evidence we can infer that Mithra's central act of killing the bull—in Zoroastrianism the work of Ahriman, if it is a question of the primordial bull, and of the Saoshyant if it is a question of the bull of the Frashōkereti—has a regenerative function: death produces a new life, richer and more fecund. Mithra, the god of light who has saved creation from the threat of darkness, clasps the right hand of the Sun, who kneels before the Tauroctonus. Mithraists consecrated the alliance between Mithra and the Sun through a banquet, which prefigured the ritual. Mithra reaches the heavens in the Sun's chariot. It is certainly this image of Mithra that most moved and exalted the initiate, for it renewed hope in the ascension of the soul beyond the planetary spheres all the way to *aeternitas*.

Mithraism is thought to have developed in the Hellenistic period through one of two processes: by a slow and complex evolution of fertility cults or, as seems more likely, through the survival of initiatory models characteristic of archaic societies—specifically, warrior initiations, or *Männerbünde* (Widengren, 1965). In any case, it showed a great ability to adapt and to expand while remaining a religion of initiates. It had to give way, however, to a triumphant Christianity, and the intolerance and politics of such emperors as Constantine and Theodosius did the rest. At the end of the fourth century, the religion was attacked by Christians because of certain liturgical and doctrinal resemblances between Christianity and Mithraism: Christians saw Mithraism's "baptism" as inspired by Satan, and its "eucharist" as a diabolical parody of the Christian sacrament. As a result the religion was in its death throes. Numerous Mithraea were abandoned, destroyed, or transformed and incorporated into Christian churches.

[*For further discussion of Mithraism, see* Mithra; Mystery Religions; Roman Religion, *article on* The Imperial Period; *and* Sun.]

BIBLIOGRAPHY

Bianchi, Ugo, ed. *Mysteria Mithrae: Proceedings of the International Seminar on the Religio-Historical Character of Roman Mithraism, with Particular Reference to Roman and Ostian Sources.* Leiden, 1979.

Colpe, Carsten. "Development of Religious Thought." In *The Cambridge History of Iran,* vol. 3, edited by Ehsan Yarshater, pp. 819–866. Cambridge, 1983.

Cumont, Franz. *Textes et monuments figurés relatifs aux mystères de Mithra.* 2 vols. Brussels, 1896–1899.

Cumont, Franz. *Les mystères de Mithra.* Brussels, 1913. Translated as *The Mysteries of Mithra,* 2d rev. ed. (New York, 1956).

Duchesne-Guillemin, Jacques, ed. *Études mithriaques: Actes du Deuxième Congrès International.* Acta Iranica, no. 17. Tehran and Liège, 1978.

Gordon, R. L. "Mithraism and Roman Society: Social Factors in the Explanation of Religious Change in the Roman Empire." *Religion* 2 (1972): 92–121.

Hinnells, John R., ed. *Mithraic Studies: Proceedings of the First International Congress of Mithraic Studies.* 2 vols. Manchester and Totowa, N.J., 1975.

Nock, Arthur Darby. "The Genius of Mithraism." *Journal of Roman Studies* 27 (1937): 108–113.

Pettazzoni, Raffaele. *I misteri: Saggio di una teoria storico-religiosa.* Bologna, 1924.

Saxl, Fritz. *Mithras: Typengeschichtliche Untersuchungen.* Berlin, 1931.

Turcan, Robert A. *Mithra et le mithriacisme.* Paris, 1981.

Vermaseren, Maarten J. *Corpus inscriptionum et monumentorum religionis Mithriacae.* 2 vols. The Hague, 1956–1960.

Vermaseren, Maarten J. *Mithras, de geheimzinnige God.* Amsterdam, 1959. Translated as *Mithras, the Secret God* (London, 1963).

Widengren, Geo. "The Mithraic Mysteries in the Graeco-Roman World with Special Regard to Their Iranian Background." In *La Persia e il mondo greco-roman,* issued by the Accademia Nazionale dei Lincei, pp. 433–456. Rome, 1965.

Wikander, Stig. *Études sur les mystères de Mithra.* Lund, 1950.

Will, Ernest. *Le relief culturel gréco-romain.* Paris, 1955.

CONTRIBUTORS

ALAN M. COOPER, Hebrew Union College—Jewish Institute of Religion, Cincinnati

GHERARDO GNOLI, Istituto Italiano per il Medio ed Estremo Oriente, Rome

J. GWYN GRIFFITHS, University College of Swansea

HARRY A. HOFFNER, JR., University of Chicago

THORKILD JACOBSEN, Harvard University (emeritus)

LEONARD H. LESKO, Brown University

ARNALDO MOMIGLIANO (deceased)

OLIVIER PELON, Université Lyon II

GILLES QUISPEL, Rijksuniversiteit te Utrecht

KURT RUDOLPH, Philipps-Universität Marburg

ROBERT SCHILLING, École Française des Hautes Études, Collège de France, and Université de Strasbourg II

MERLIN STONE, New York, New York

JEAN-PIERRE VERNANT, Collège de France

MOSHE WEINFELD, Hebrew University of Jerusalem

ROBERT M. SELTZER is professor of History at Hunter College and the Graduate School, City University of New York

FINDING LIST OF
ARTICLE TITLES

The following table lists the article titles (in parentheses) as they originally appeared in *The Encyclopedia of Religion*. Titles not listed below are unchanged.

Mesopotamian Religions (Mesopotamian Religions: An Overview)
Egyptian Religion (Egyptian Religion: An Overview)
Goddess Worship in the Ancient Near East (Goddess Worship: Goddess Worship in the Ancient Near East)
Canaanite Religion (Canaanite Religion: An Overview)
Roman Religion to 100 BCE (Roman Religion: The Early Period)
Roman Religion of the Imperial Period (Roman Religion: The Imperial Period)
Gnosticism (Gnosticism: Gnosticism from Its Origins to the Middle Ages)
Manichaeism (Manichaeism: An Overview)